FAIRY TAIL 100 YEARS QUEST

8

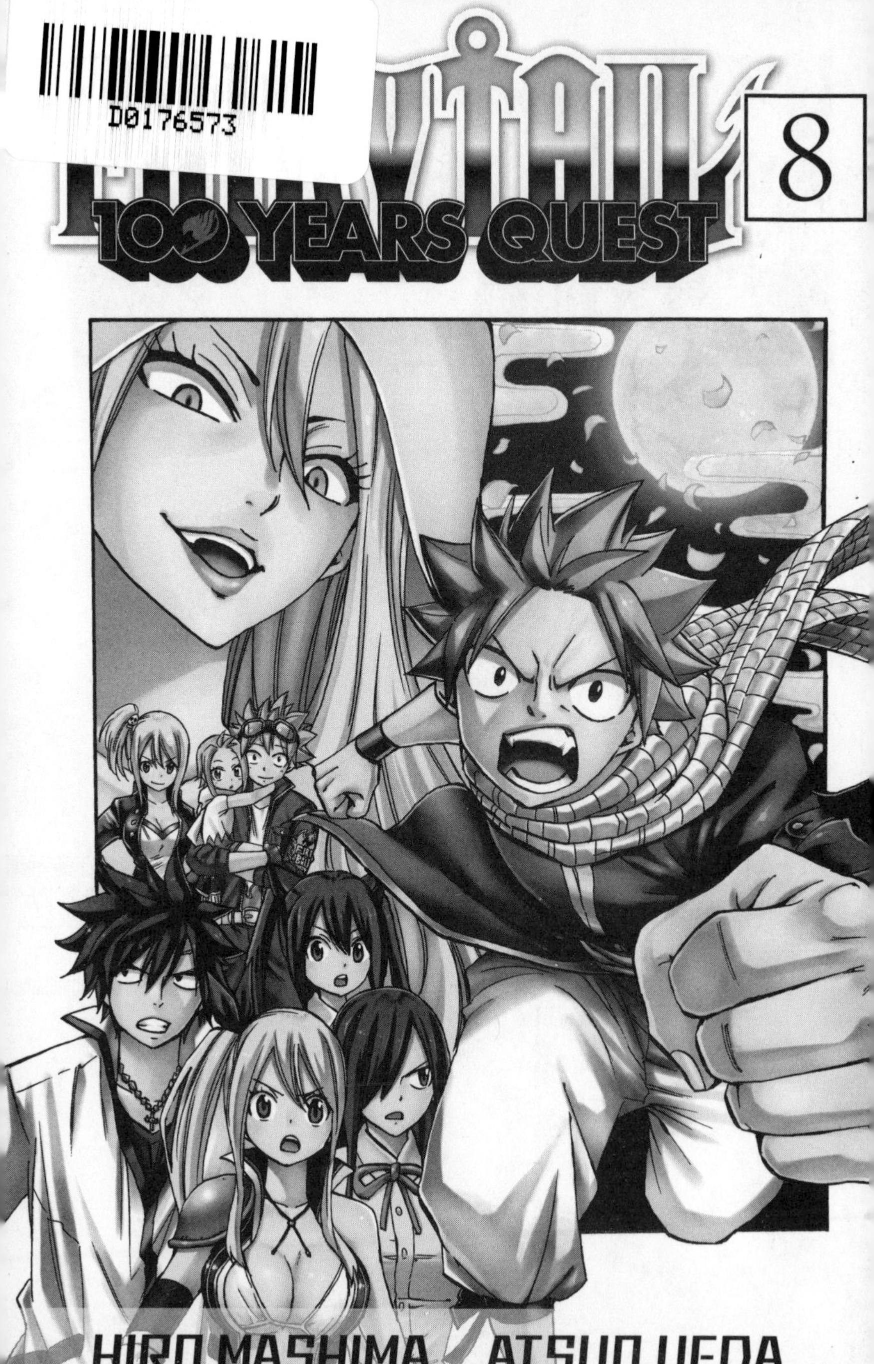

HIRO MASHIMA ATSUO UEDA

FAIRY TAIL
100 YEARS
QUEST
8 ♡ CONTENTS

FAIRY TAIL 100 YEARS QUEST

Chapter 64: Aldo-no-Yu

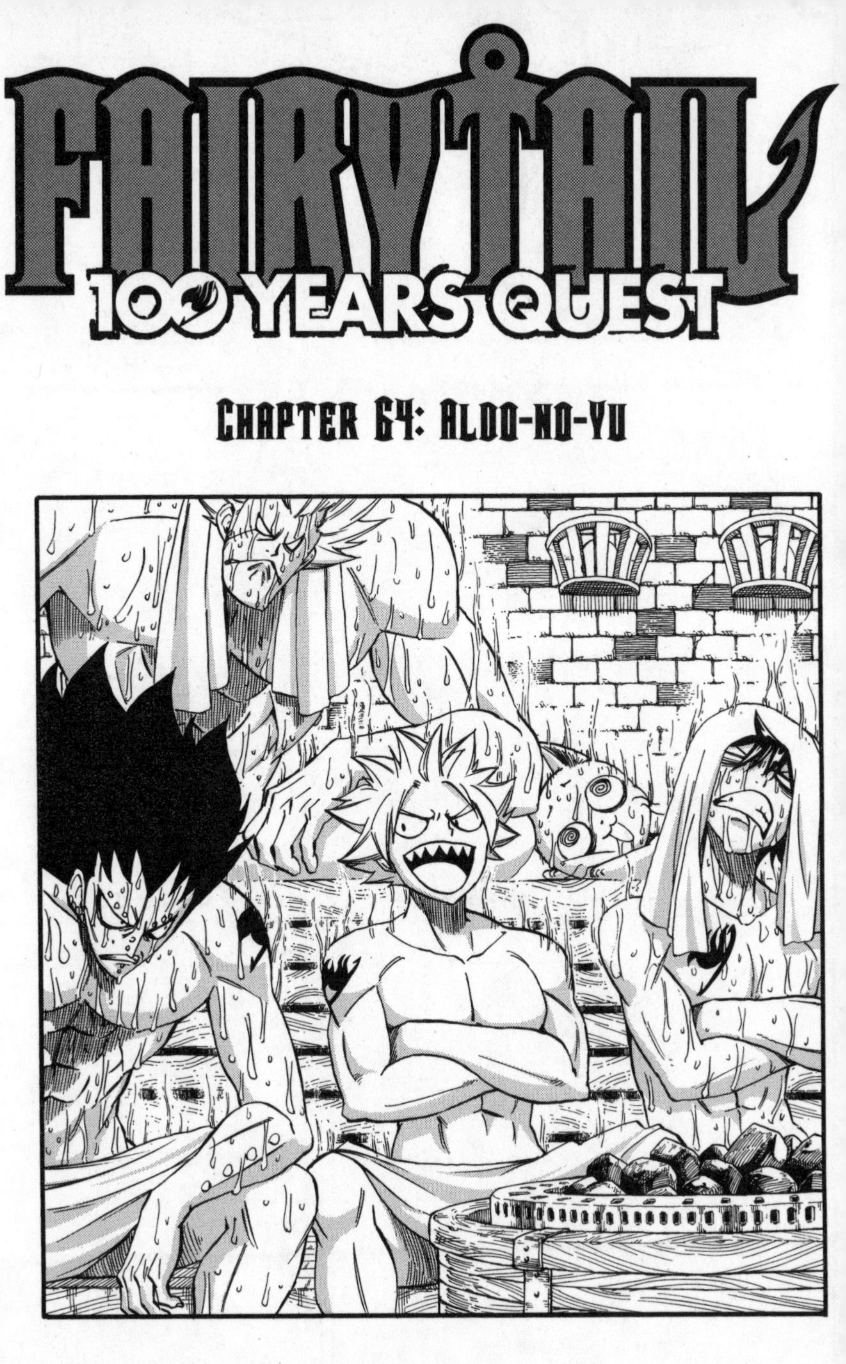

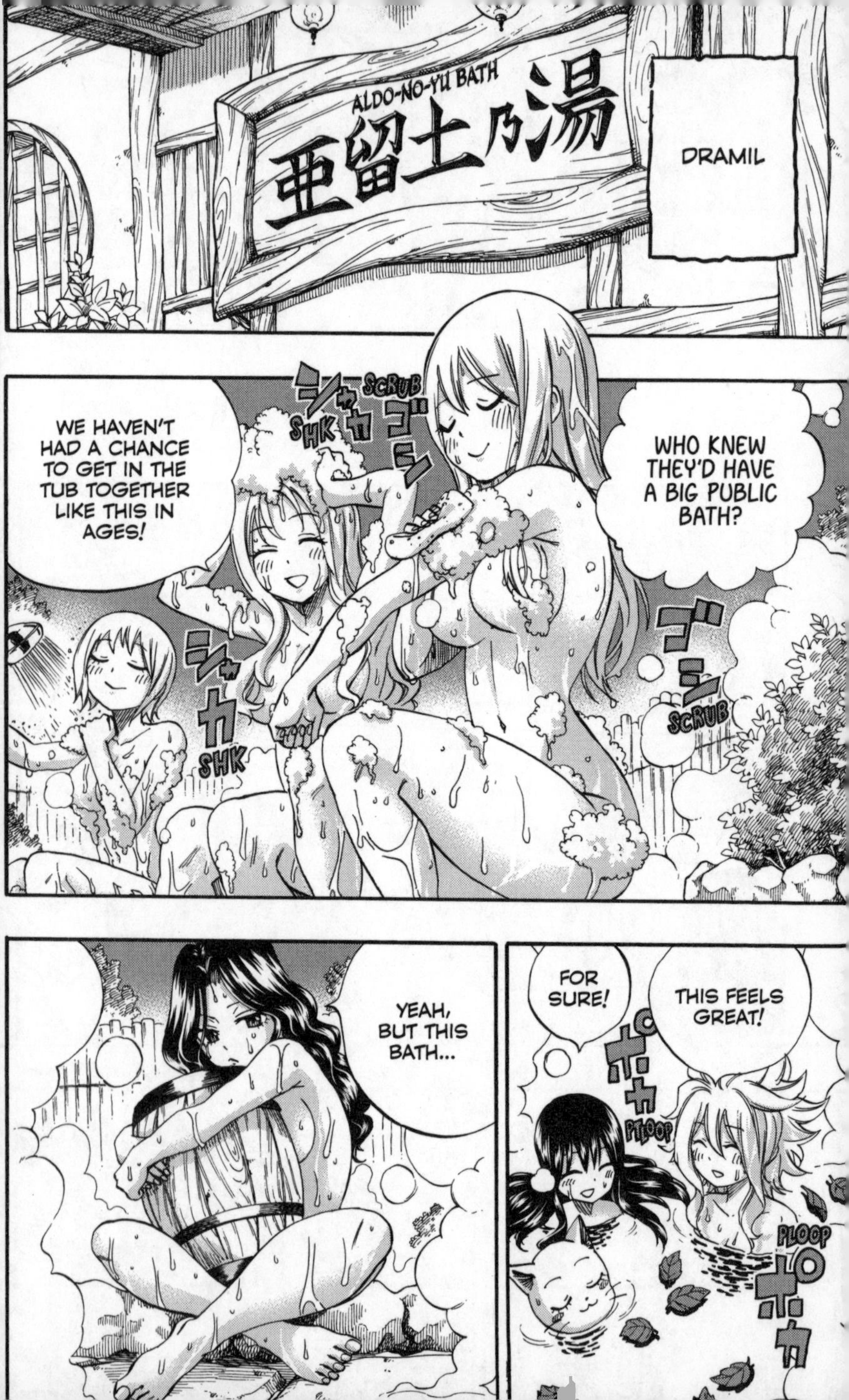
DRAMIL
ALDO-NO-YU BATH
亜留土乃湯
WHO KNEW THEY'D HAVE A BIG PUBLIC BATH?
SCRUB
WE HAVEN'T HAD A CHANCE TO GET IN THE TUB TOGETHER LIKE THIS IN AGES!
SCRUB
SHK
SHK
THIS FEELS GREAT!
FOR SURE!
PLOOP
PLOOP
YEAH, BUT THIS BATH...

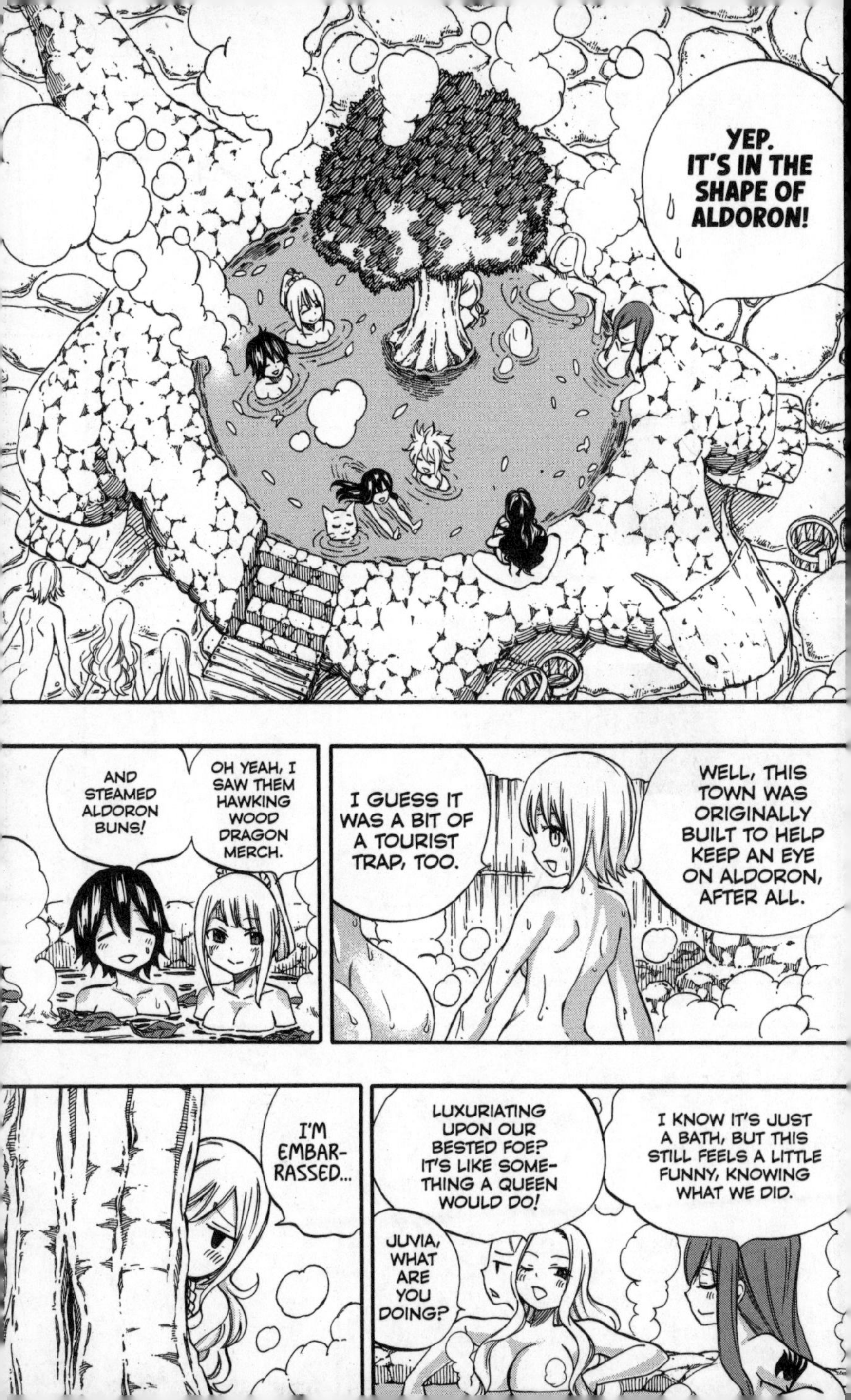
YEP. IT'S IN THE SHAPE OF ALDORON!
WELL, THIS TOWN WAS ORIGINALLY BUILT TO HELP KEEP AN EYE ON ALDORON, AFTER ALL.
I GUESS IT WAS A BIT OF A TOURIST TRAP, TOO.
OH YEAH, I SAW THEM HAWKING WOOD DRAGON MERCH.
AND STEAMED ALDORON BUNS!
I KNOW IT'S JUST A BATH, BUT THIS STILL FEELS A LITTLE FUNNY, KNOWING WHAT WE DID.
LUXURIATING UPON OUR BESTED FOE? IT'S LIKE SOME-THING A QUEEN WOULD DO!
JUVIA, WHAT ARE YOU DOING?
I'M EMBAR-RASSED...

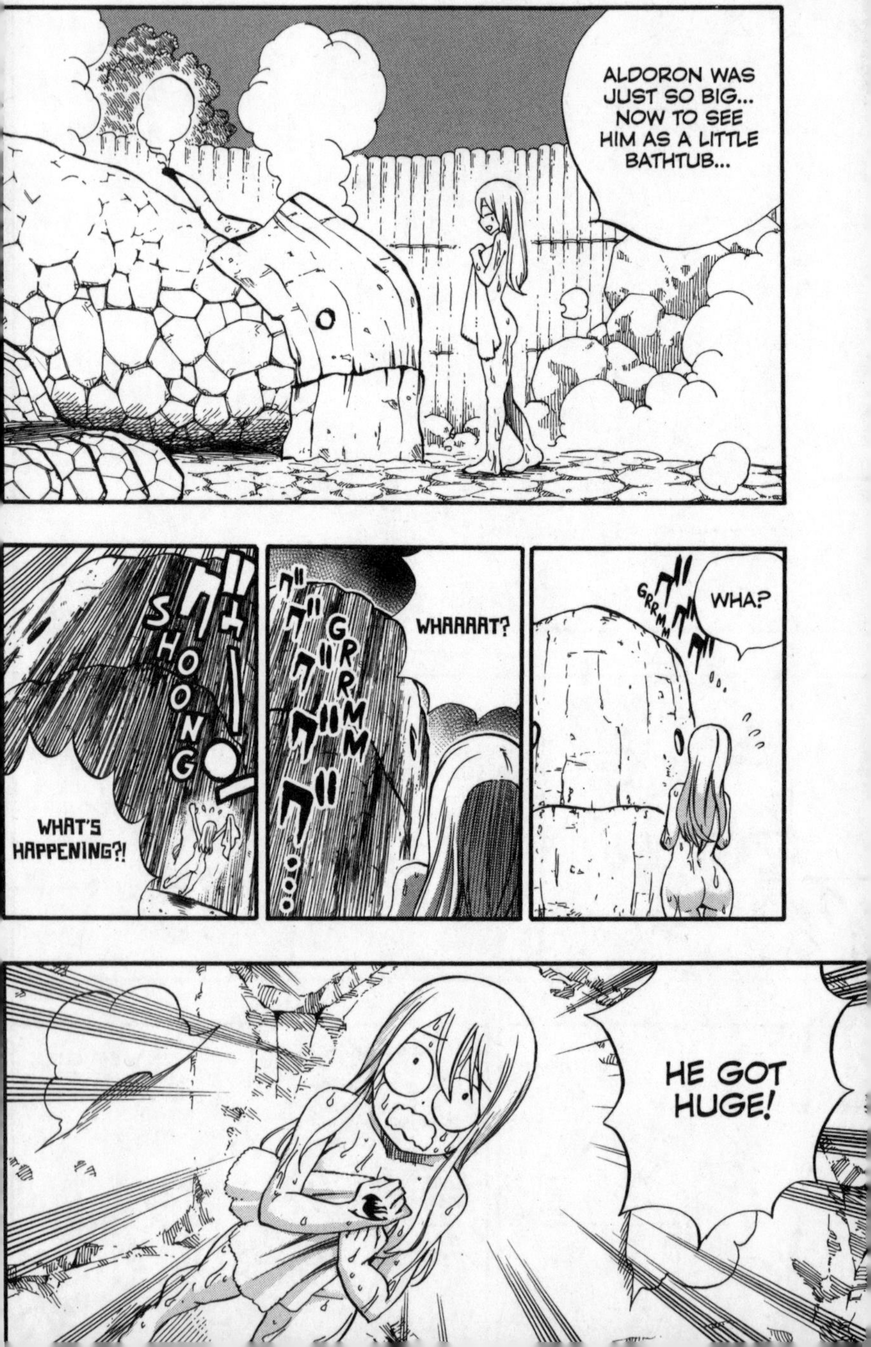
ALDORON WAS JUST SO BIG... NOW TO SEE HIM AS A LITTLE BATHTUB...
GRRMM
WHA?
GRRMM
WHAAAAT?
SHOONG
WHAT'S HAPPENING?!
HE GOT HUGE!

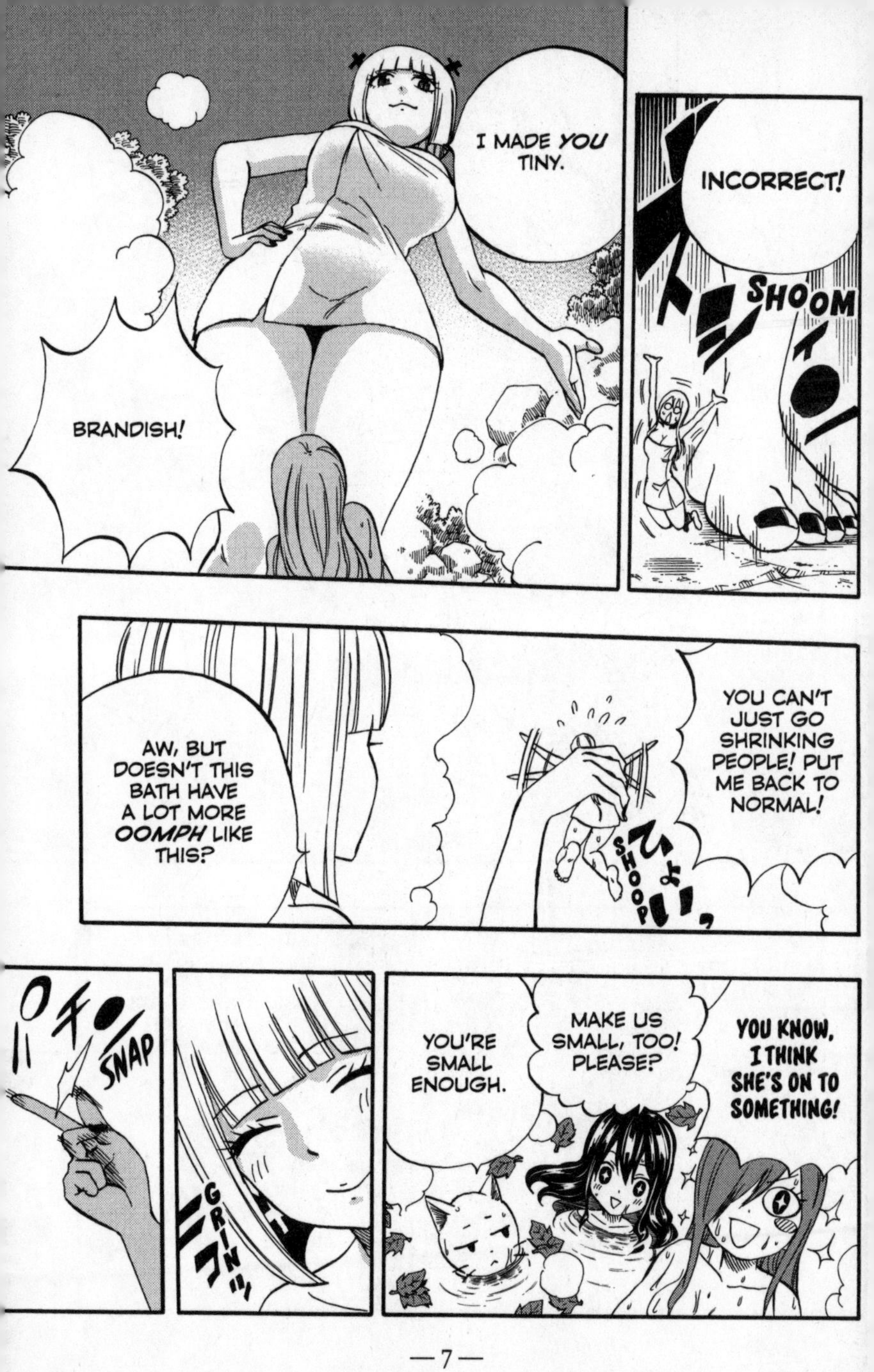
INCORRECT!
SHOOM
I MADE YOU TINY.
BRANDISH!
YOU CAN'T JUST GO SHRINKING PEOPLE! PUT ME BACK TO NORMAL!
SHOOP
AW, BUT DOESN'T THIS BATH HAVE A LOT MORE OOMPH LIKE THIS?
YOU KNOW, I THINK SHE'S ON TO SOMETHING!
MAKE US SMALL, TOO! PLEASE?
YOU'RE SMALL ENOUGH.
GRIN
SNAP

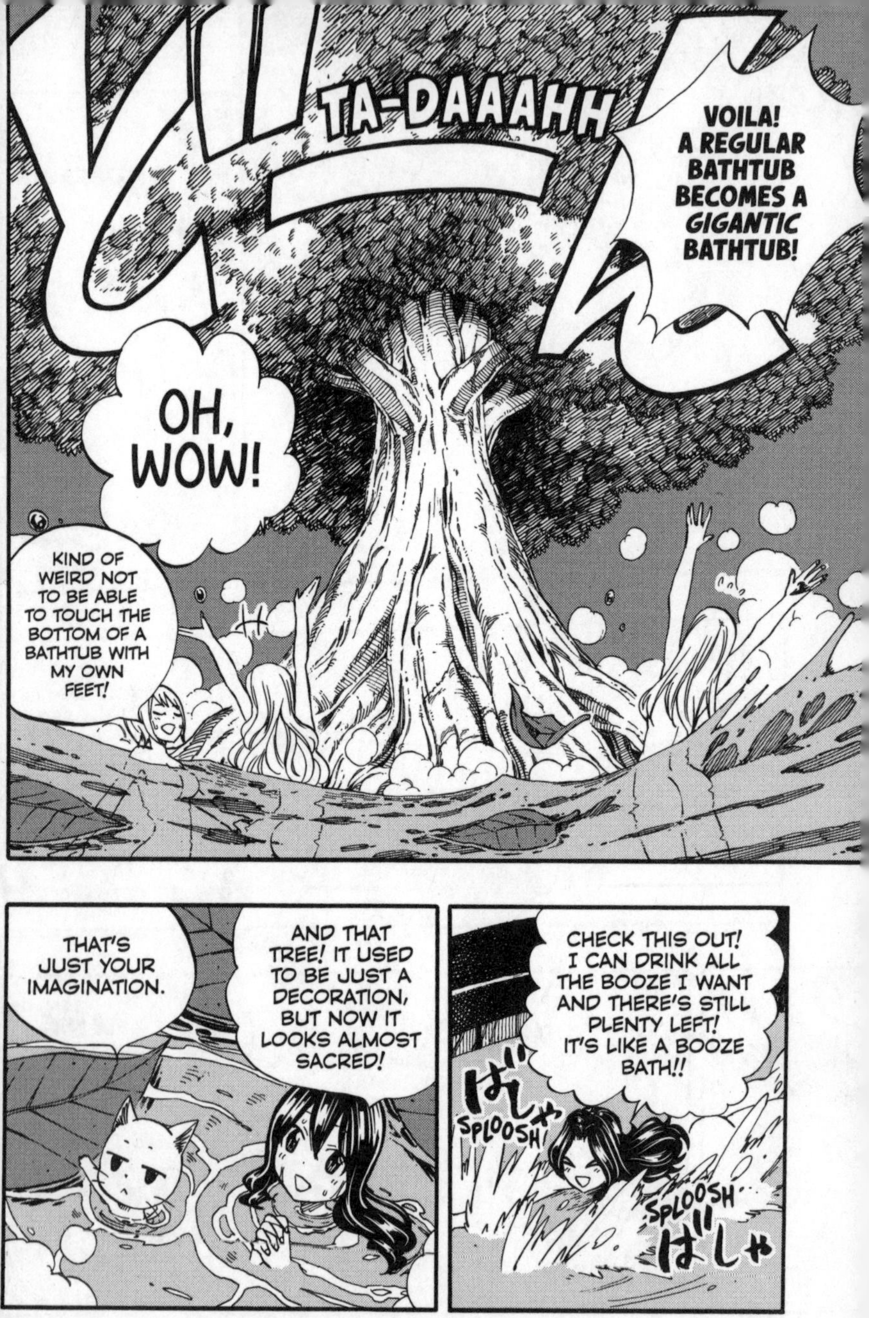
TA-DAAAHH
VOILA! A REGULAR BATHTUB BECOMES A *GIGANTIC* BATHTUB!
OH, WOW!
KIND OF WEIRD NOT TO BE ABLE TO TOUCH THE BOTTOM OF A BATHTUB WITH MY OWN FEET!
CHECK THIS OUT! I CAN DRINK ALL THE BOOZE I WANT AND THERE'S STILL PLENTY LEFT! IT'S LIKE A BOOZE BATH!!
ばしゃ
SPLOOSH
SPLOOSH
ばしゃ
AND THAT TREE! IT USED TO BE JUST A DECORATION, BUT NOW IT LOOKS ALMOST SACRED!
THAT'S JUST YOUR IMAGINATION.

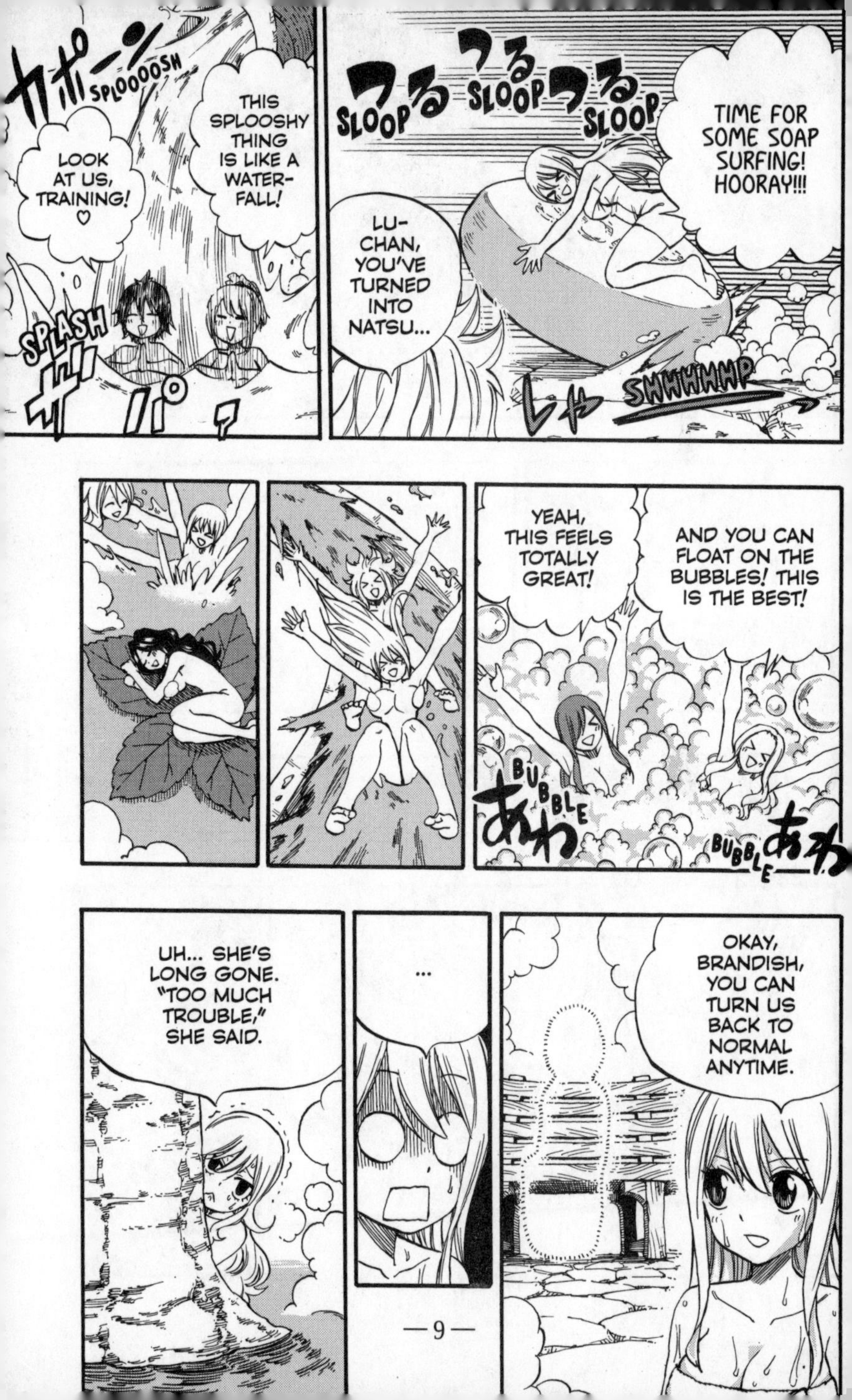
SLOOP
SLOOP
SLOOP
TIME FOR SOME SOAP SURFING! HOORAY!!!
LU-CHAN, YOU'VE TURNED INTO NATSU...
SHWHHHP
THIS SPLOOSHY THING IS LIKE A WATER-FALL!
SPLOOOOSH
LOOK AT US, TRAINING! ♡
SPLASH
AND YOU CAN FLOAT ON THE BUBBLES! THIS IS THE BEST!
YEAH, THIS FEELS TOTALLY GREAT!
BUBBLE
BUBBLE
OKAY, BRANDISH, YOU CAN TURN US BACK TO NORMAL ANYTIME.
...
UH... SHE'S LONG GONE. "TOO MUCH TROUBLE," SHE SAID.

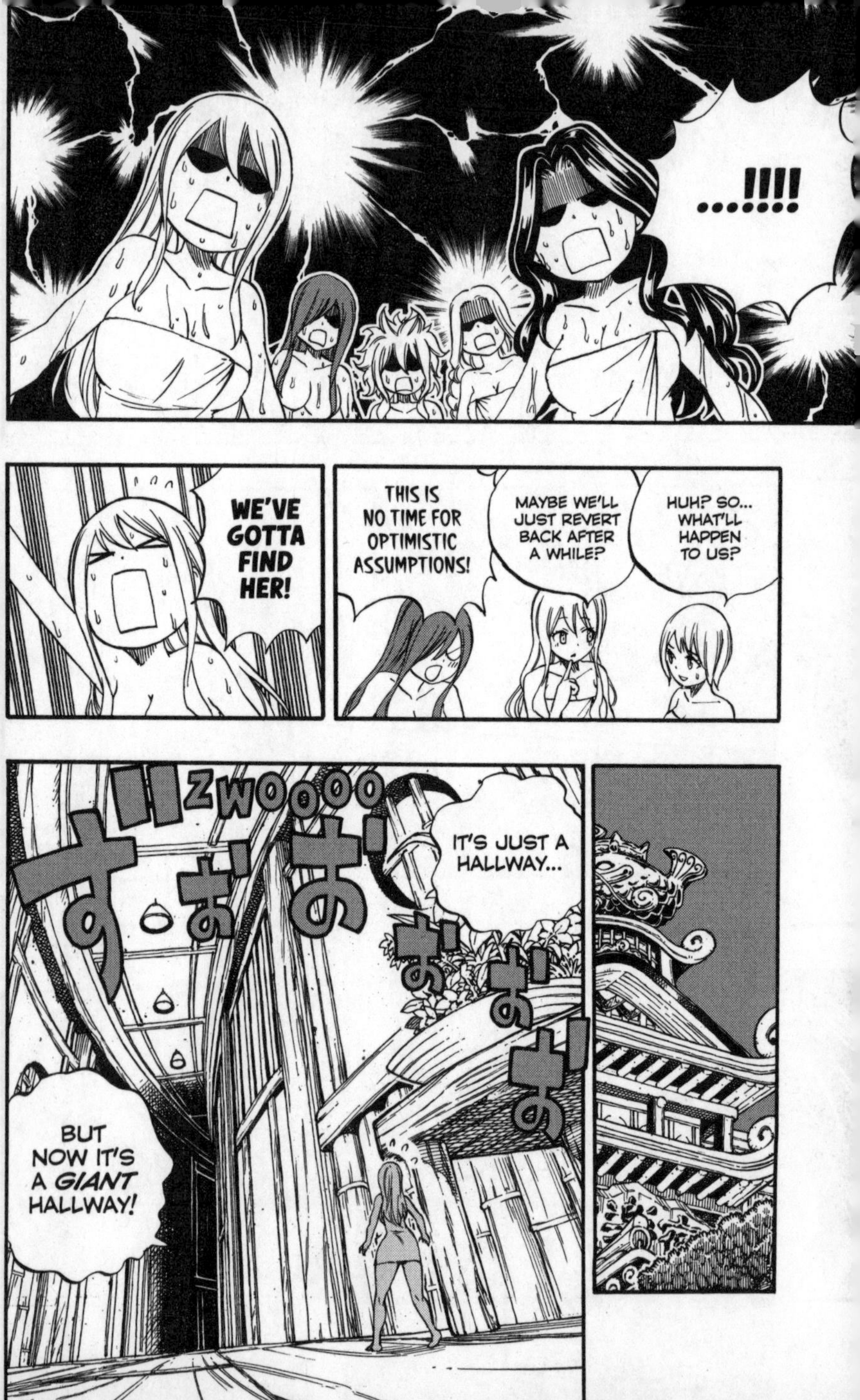

...!!!!
HUH? SO... WHAT'LL HAPPEN TO US?
MAYBE WE'LL JUST REVERT BACK AFTER A WHILE?
THIS IS NO TIME FOR OPTIMISTIC ASSUMPTIONS!
WE'VE GOTTA FIND HER!
ZWOOOOO
すぉ゛お゛ぉ゛ぉ゛お
IT'S JUST A HALLWAY...
BUT NOW IT'S A *GIANT* HALLWAY!

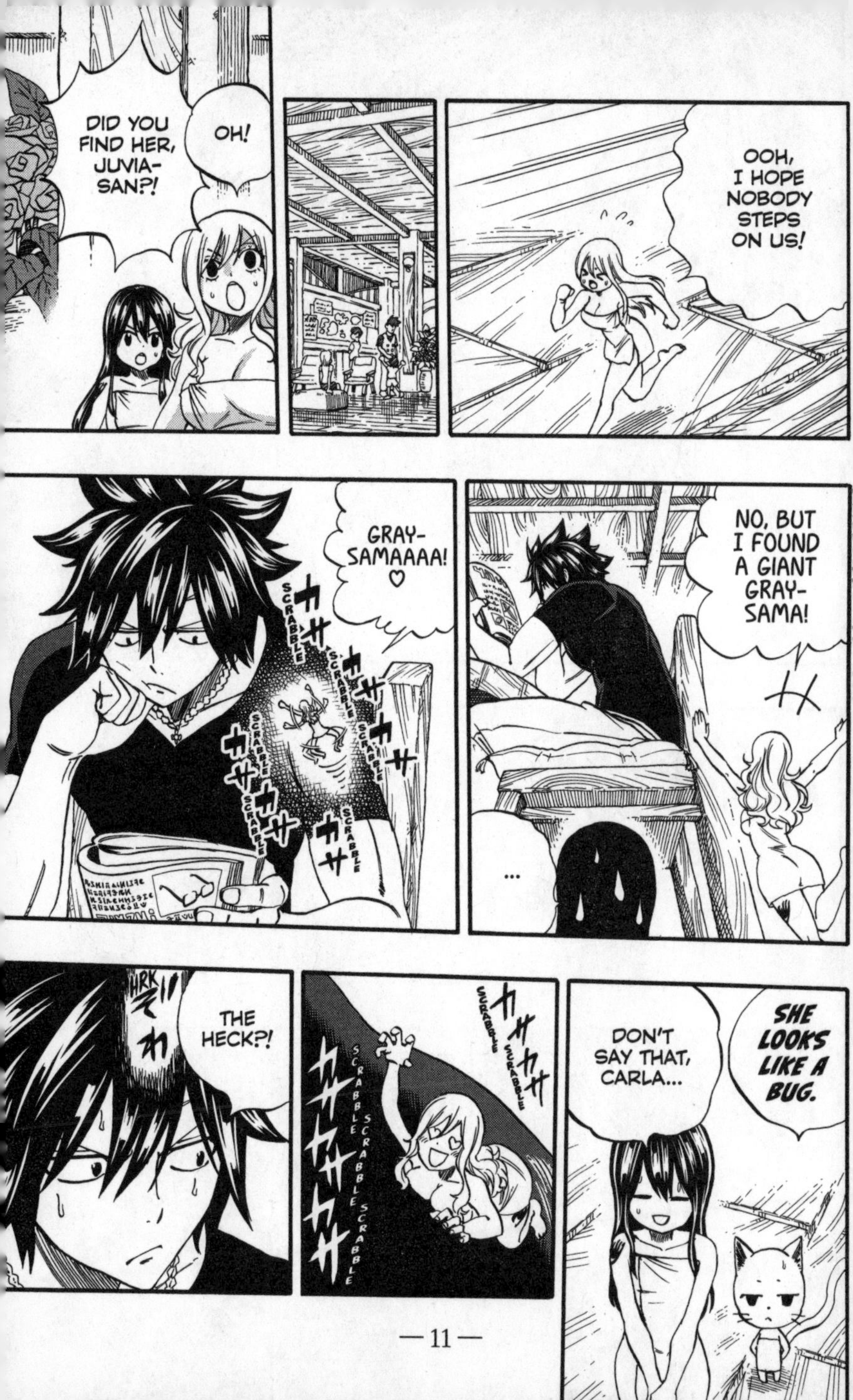
OOH, I HOPE NOBODY STEPS ON US!
OH!
DID YOU FIND HER, JUVIA-SAN?!
NO, BUT I FOUND A GIANT GRAY-SAMA!
...
GRAY-SAMAAAA! ♡
SCRABBLE SCRABBLE SCRABBLE SCRABBLE SCRABBLE SCRABBLE
SHE LOOKS LIKE A BUG.
DON'T SAY THAT, CARLA...
SCRABBLE SCRABBLE SCRABBLE SCRABBLE SCRABBLE
HRK
THE HECK?!

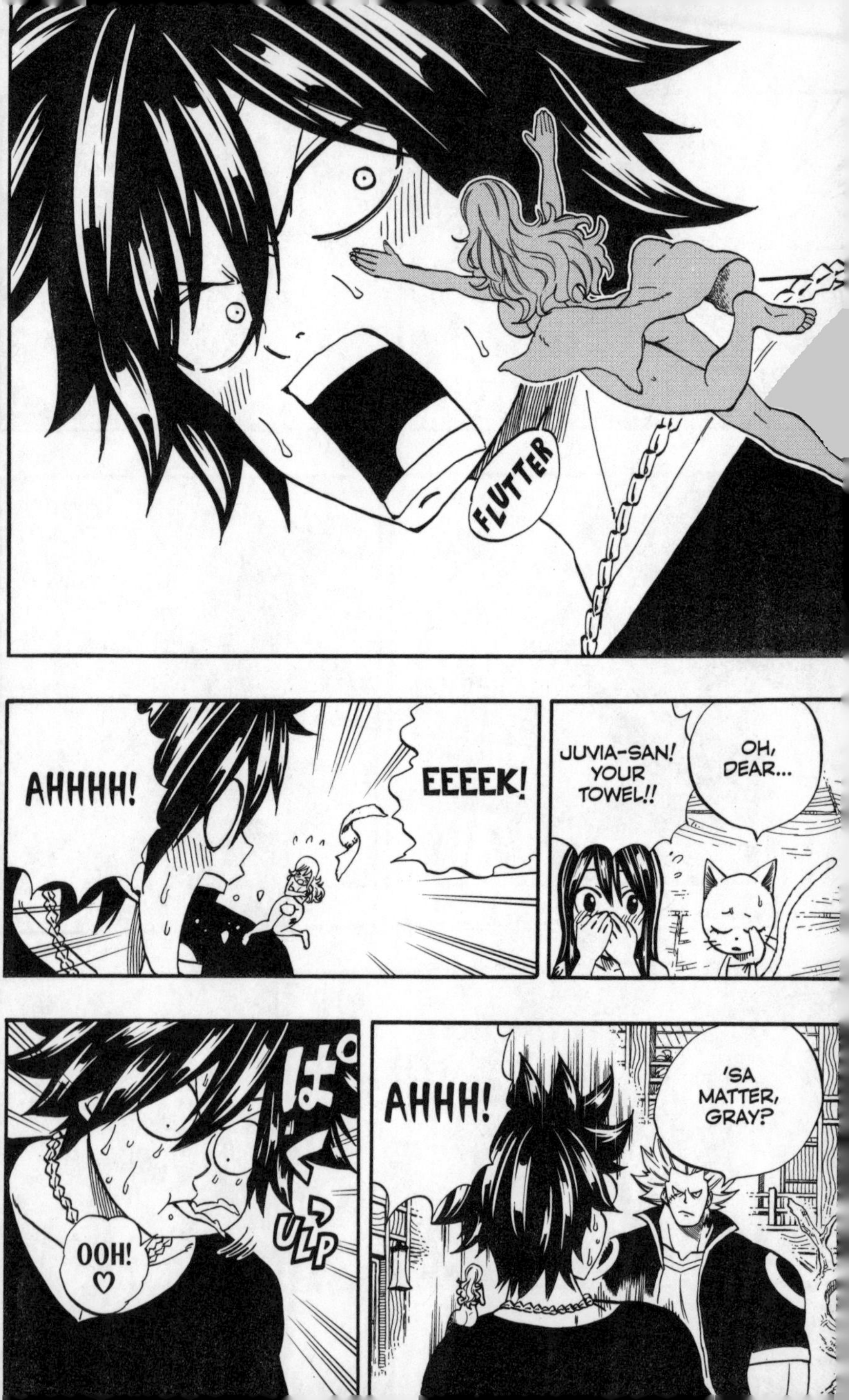
FLUTTER
OH, DEAR...
JUVIA-SAN! YOUR TOWEL!!
EEEEK!
AHHHH!
'SA MATTER, GRAY?
AHHH!
ぱ
ULP
OOH! ♡

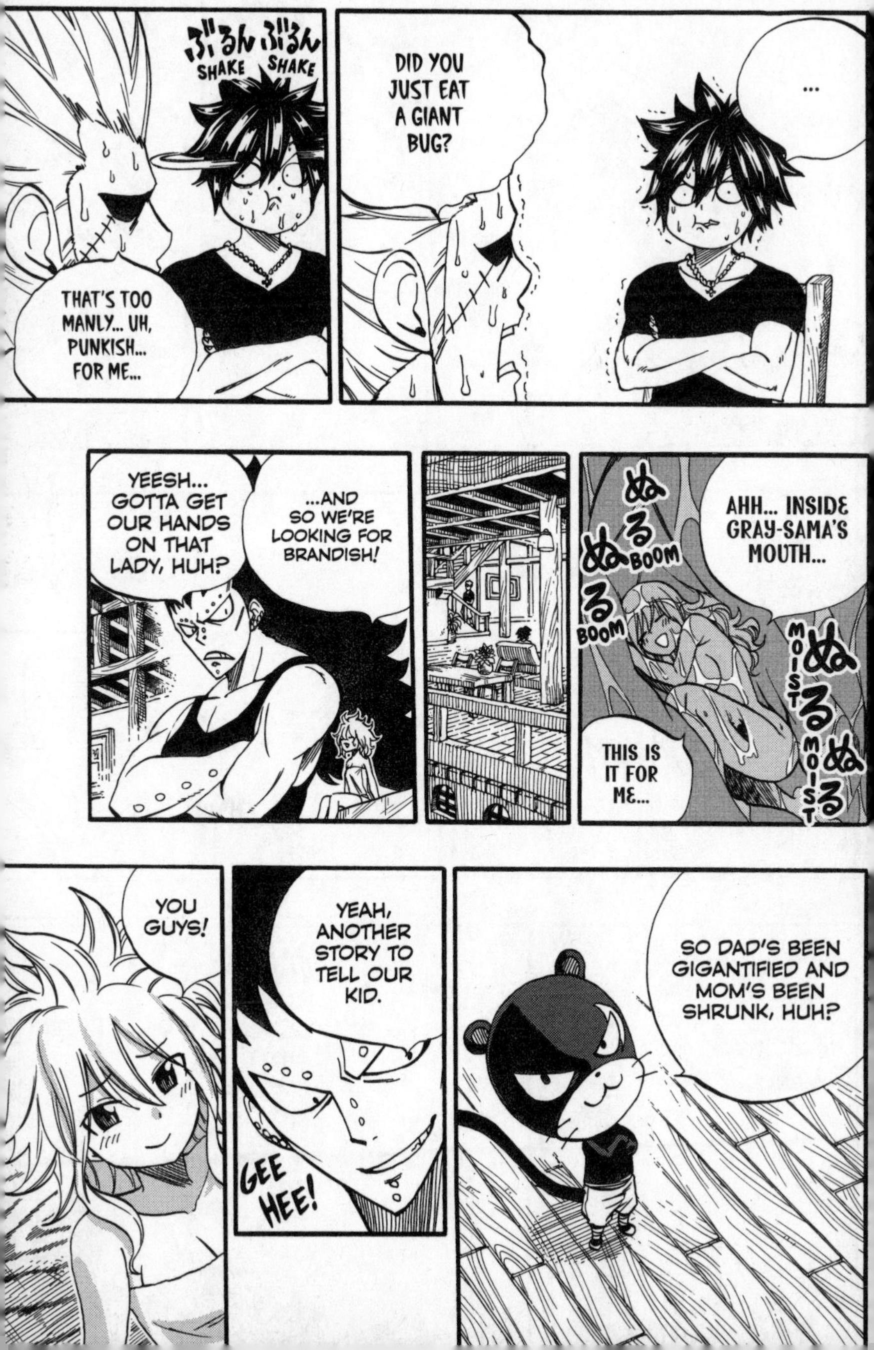
...
DID YOU JUST EAT A GIANT BUG?
ぶるん ぶるん
SHAKE SHAKE
THAT'S TOO MANLY... UH, PUNKISH... FOR ME...
AHH... INSIDE GRAY-SAMA'S MOUTH...
ぬるぬる
BOOM BOOM
ぬるぬる
MOIST MOIST
THIS IS IT FOR ME...
...AND SO WE'RE LOOKING FOR BRANDISH!
YEESH... GOTTA GET OUR HANDS ON THAT LADY, HUH?
SO DAD'S BEEN GIGANTIFIED AND MOM'S BEEN SHRUNK, HUH?
YEAH, ANOTHER STORY TO TELL OUR KID.
GEE HEE!
YOU GUYS!

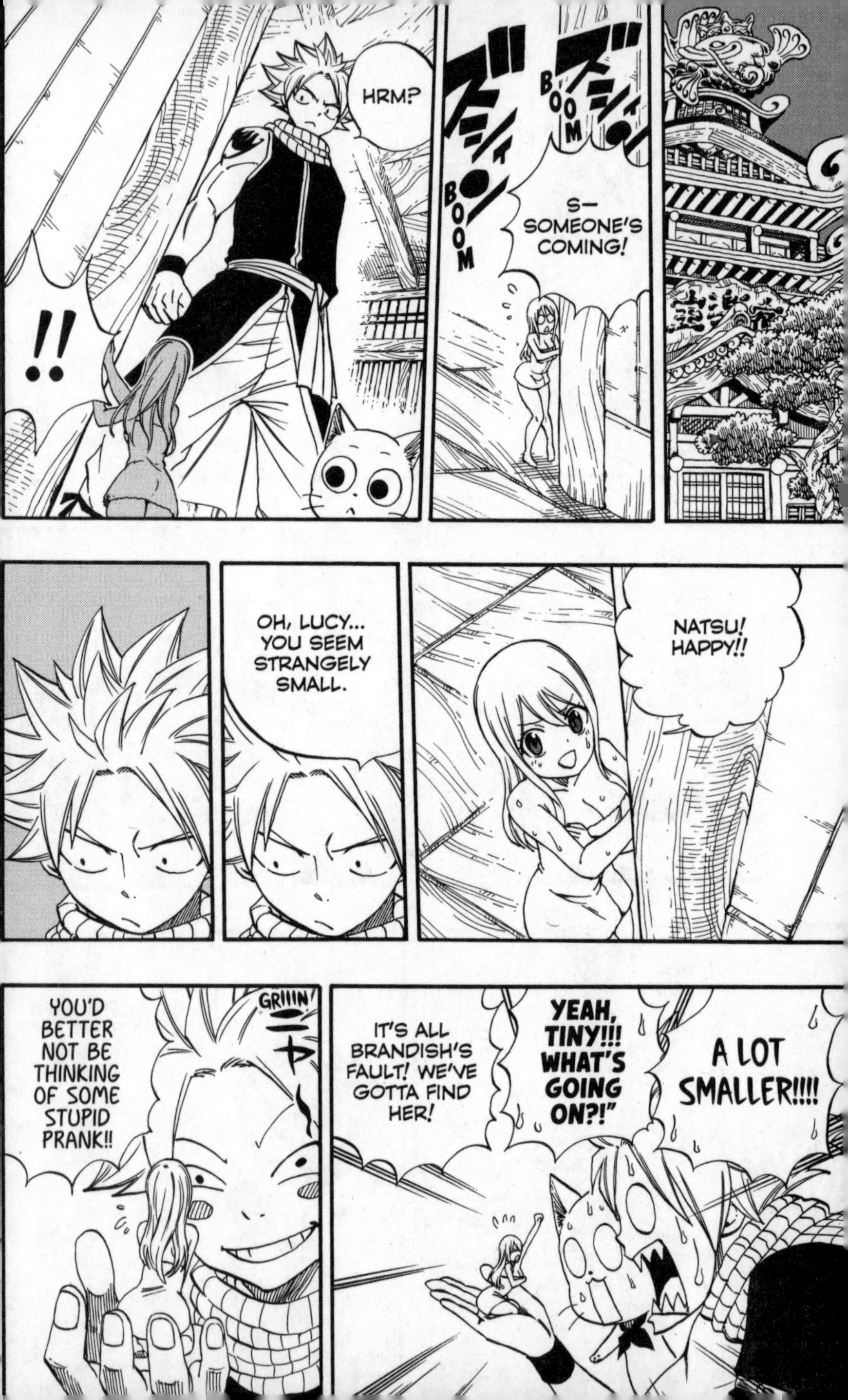
BOOM BOOM
BOOM BOOM
S— SOMEONE'S COMING!
HRM?
!!
NATSU! HAPPY!!
OH, LUCY... YOU SEEM STRANGELY SMALL.
A LOT SMALLER!!!!
YEAH, TINY!!! WHAT'S GOING ON?!"
IT'S ALL BRANDISH'S FAULT! WE'VE GOTTA FIND HER!
GRIIIN
YOU'D BETTER NOT BE THINKING OF SOME STUPID PRANK!!

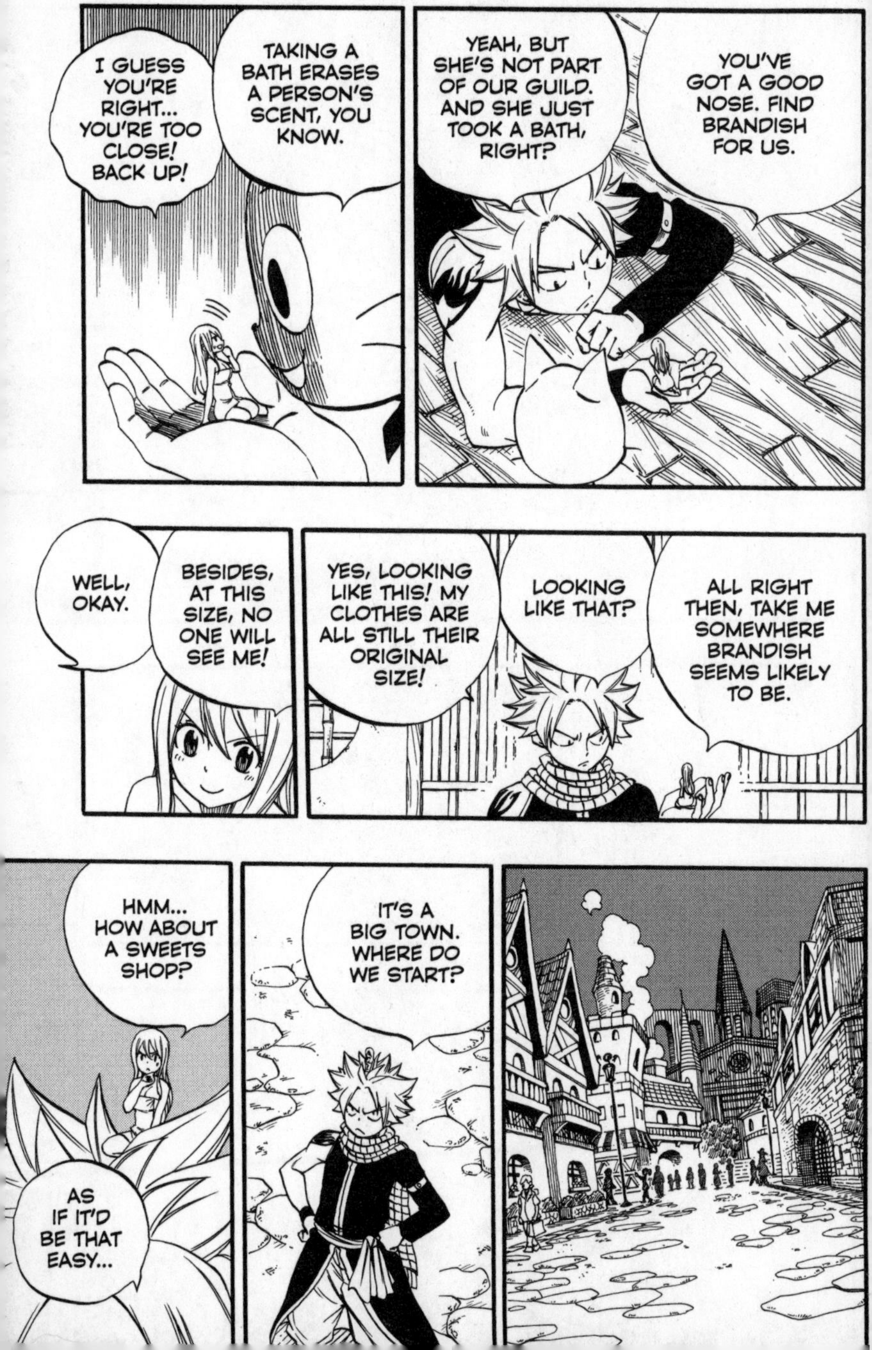
YOU'VE GOT A GOOD NOSE. FIND BRANDISH FOR US.
YEAH, BUT SHE'S NOT PART OF OUR GUILD. AND SHE JUST TOOK A BATH, RIGHT?
TAKING A BATH ERASES A PERSON'S SCENT, YOU KNOW.
I GUESS YOU'RE RIGHT... YOU'RE TOO CLOSE! BACK UP!
ALL RIGHT THEN, TAKE ME SOMEWHERE BRANDISH SEEMS LIKELY TO BE.
LOOKING LIKE THAT?
YES, LOOKING LIKE THIS! MY CLOTHES ARE ALL STILL THEIR ORIGINAL SIZE!
BESIDES, AT THIS SIZE, NO ONE WILL SEE ME!
WELL, OKAY.
IT'S A BIG TOWN. WHERE DO WE START?
HMM... HOW ABOUT A SWEETS SHOP?
AS IF IT'D BE THAT EASY...

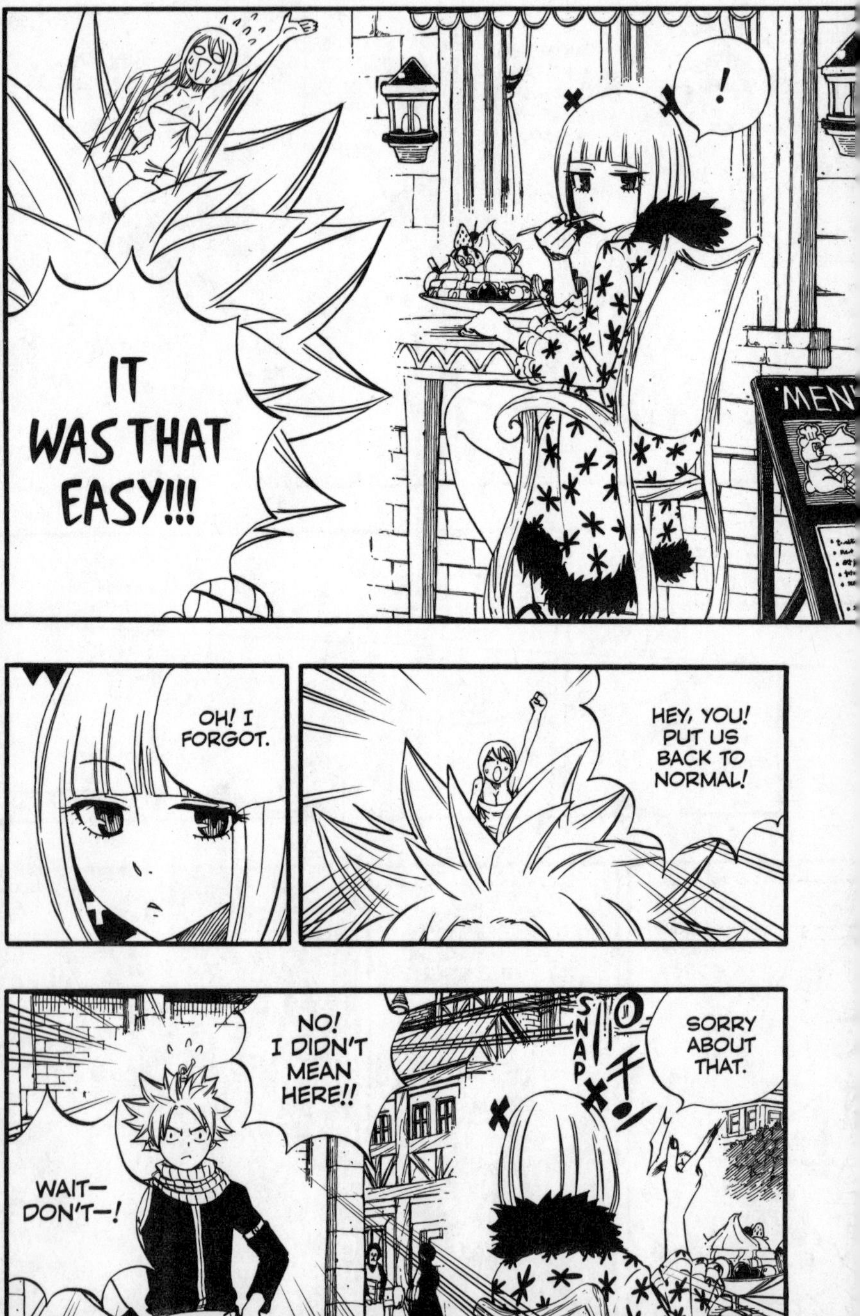
!
IT WAS THAT EASY!!!
HEY, YOU! PUT US BACK TO NORMAL!
OH! I FORGOT.
SORRY ABOUT THAT.
SNAP
NO! I DIDN'T MEAN HERE!!
WAIT— DON'T—!

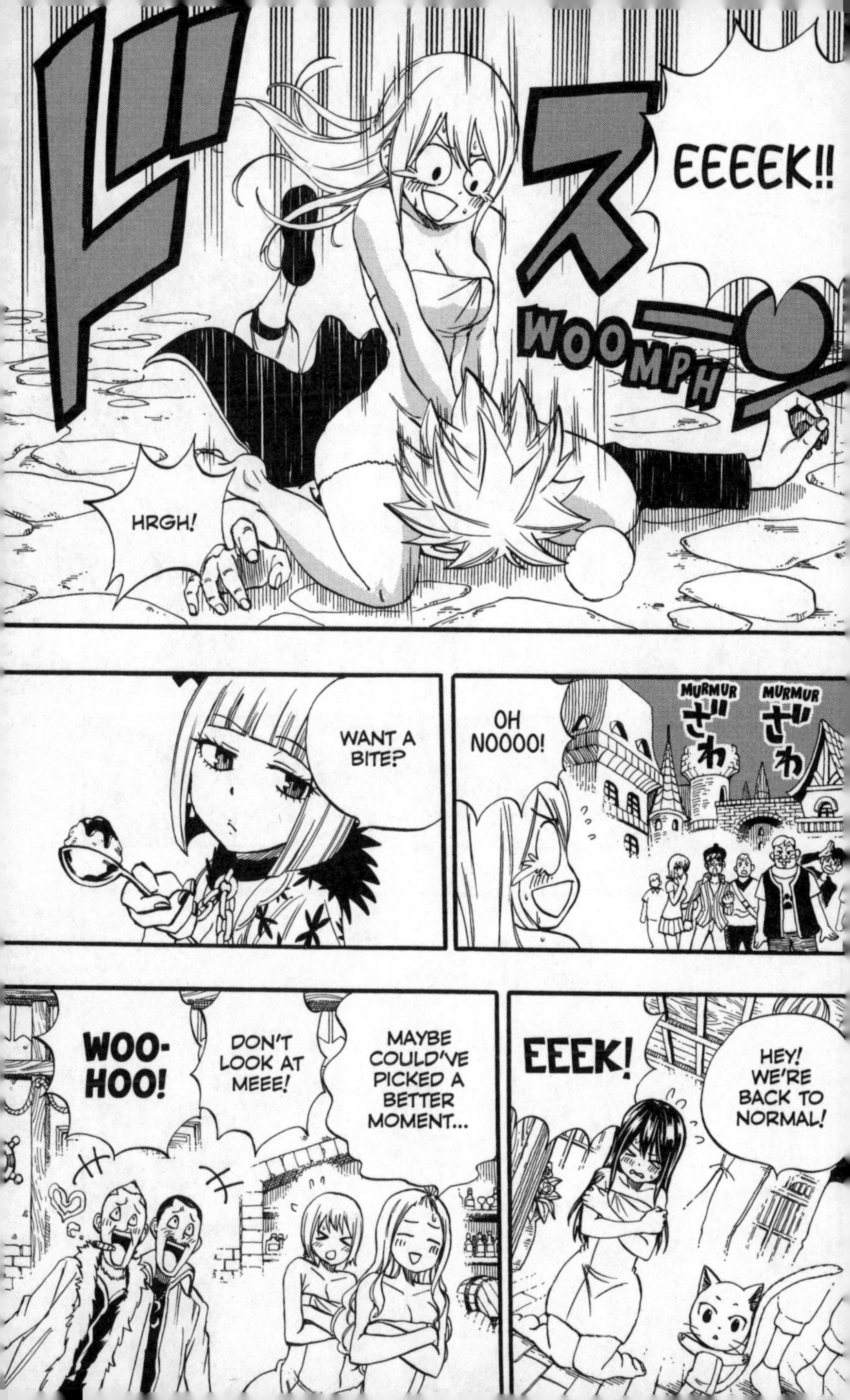
EEEEK!!
ドス
WOOMPH
HRGH!
MURMUR ざわ
MURMUR ざわ
OH NOOOO!
WANT A BITE?
HEY! WE'RE BACK TO NORMAL!
EEEK!
MAYBE COULD'VE PICKED A BETTER MOMENT...
DON'T LOOK AT MEEE!
WOO-HOO!

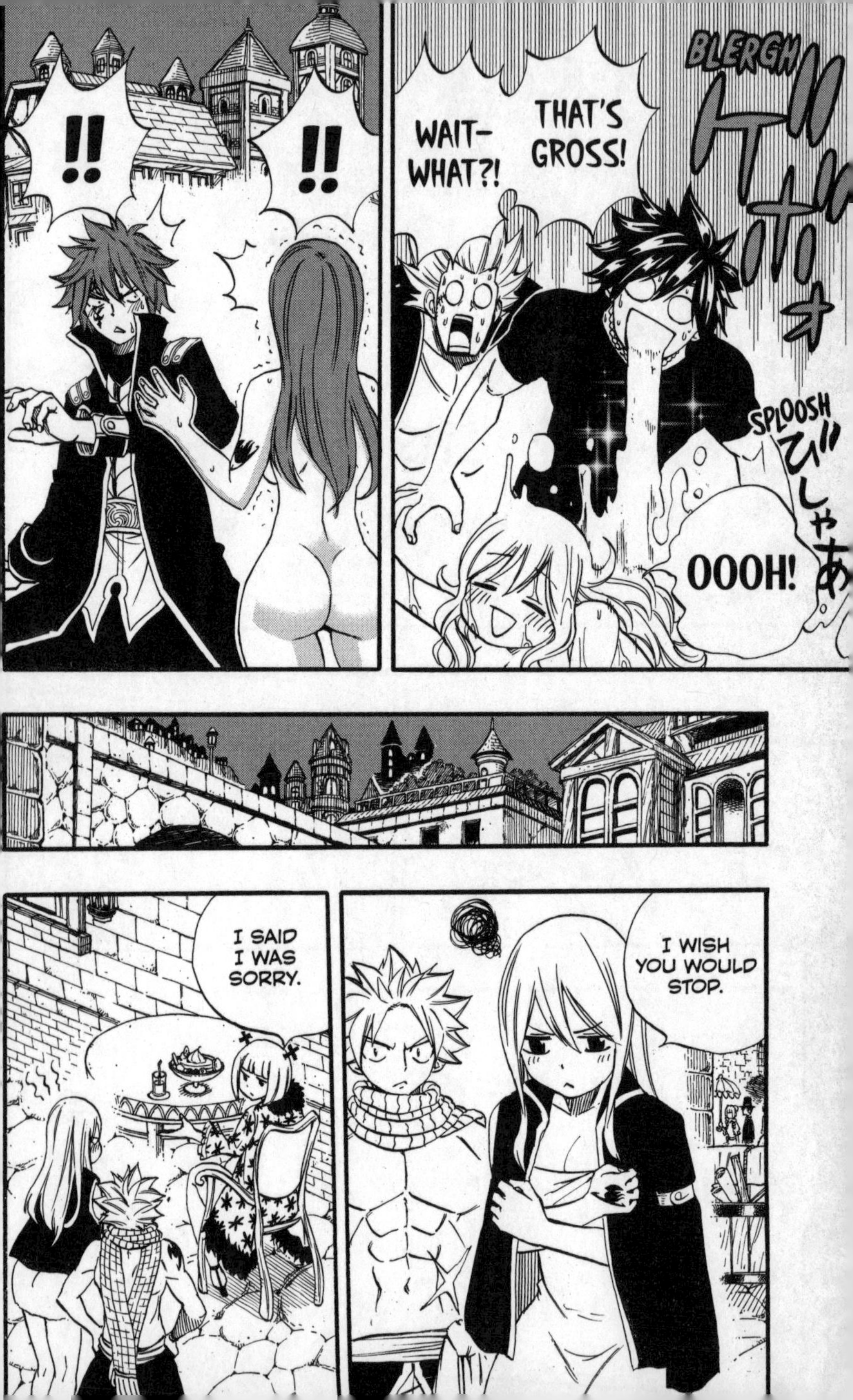
BLERGH
THAT'S GROSS!
WAIT-WHAT?!
SPLOOSH
びしゃあ
OOOH!
!!
!!
I WISH YOU WOULD STOP.
I SAID I WAS SORRY.

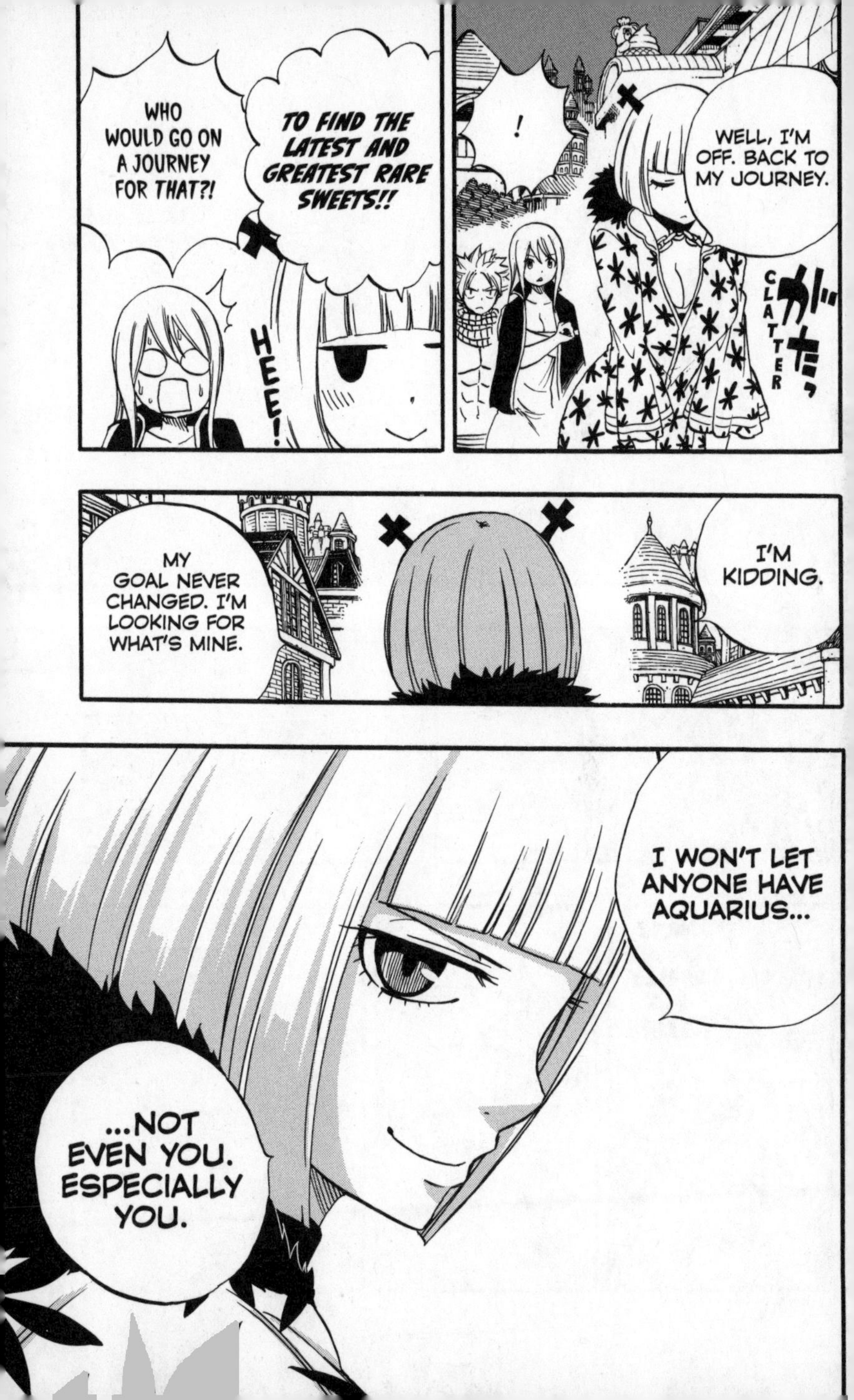
!
WELL, I'M OFF. BACK TO MY JOURNEY.
CLATTER
TO FIND THE LATEST AND GREATEST RARE SWEETS!!
WHO WOULD GO ON A JOURNEY FOR THAT?!
HEE!
I'M KIDDING.
MY GOAL NEVER CHANGED. I'M LOOKING FOR WHAT'S MINE.
I WON'T LET ANYONE HAVE AQUARIUS...
...NOT EVEN YOU. ESPECIALLY YOU.

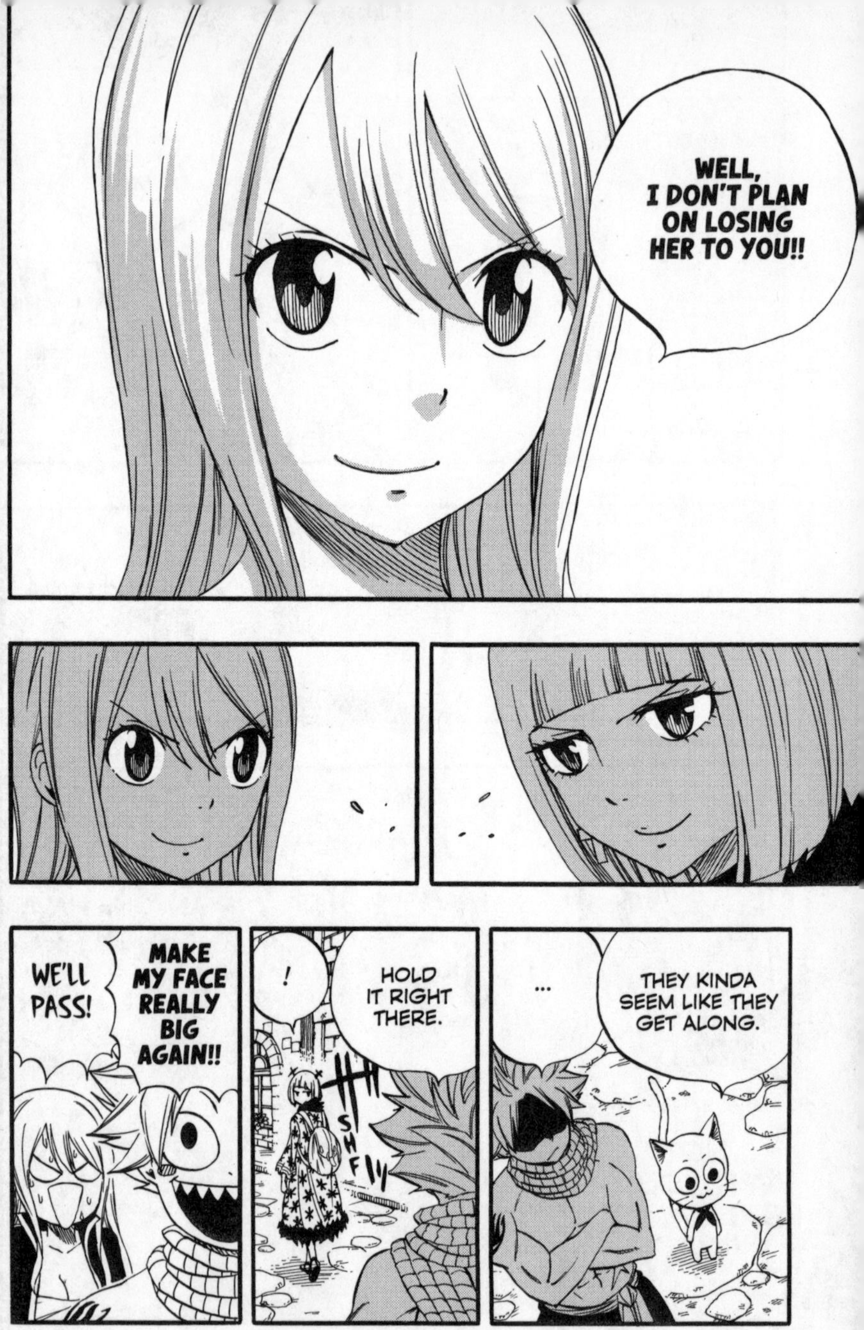
WELL, I DON'T PLAN ON LOSING HER TO YOU!!
THEY KINDA SEEM LIKE THEY GET ALONG.
...
HOLD IT RIGHT THERE.
!
SHF
MAKE MY FACE REALLY BIG AGAIN!!
WE'LL PASS!

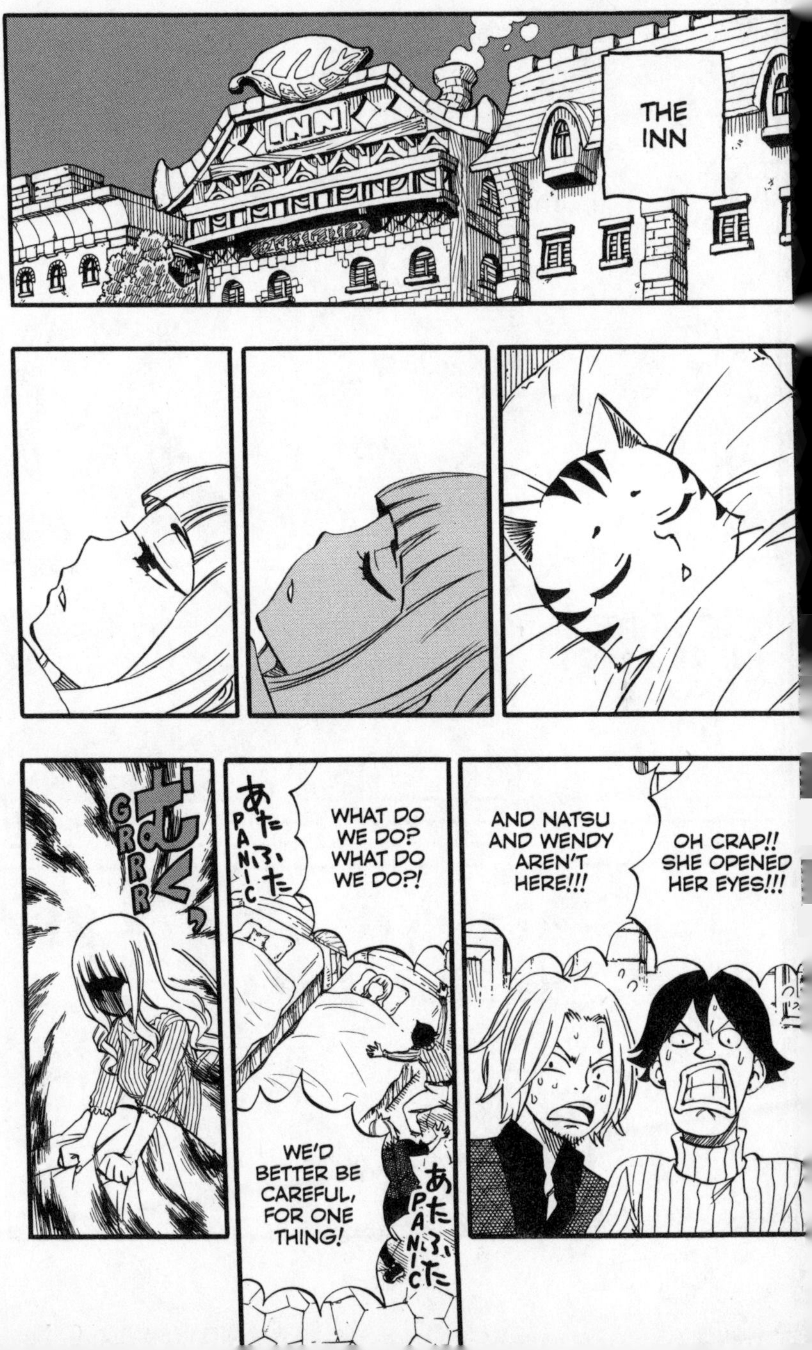
INN
THE INN
OH CRAP!! SHE OPENED HER EYES!!!
AND NATSU AND WENDY AREN'T HERE!!!
あたふた
PANIC
WHAT DO WE DO? WHAT DO WE DO?!
WE'D BETTER BE CAREFUL, FOR ONE THING!
あたふた
PANIC
むくっ
GRRR

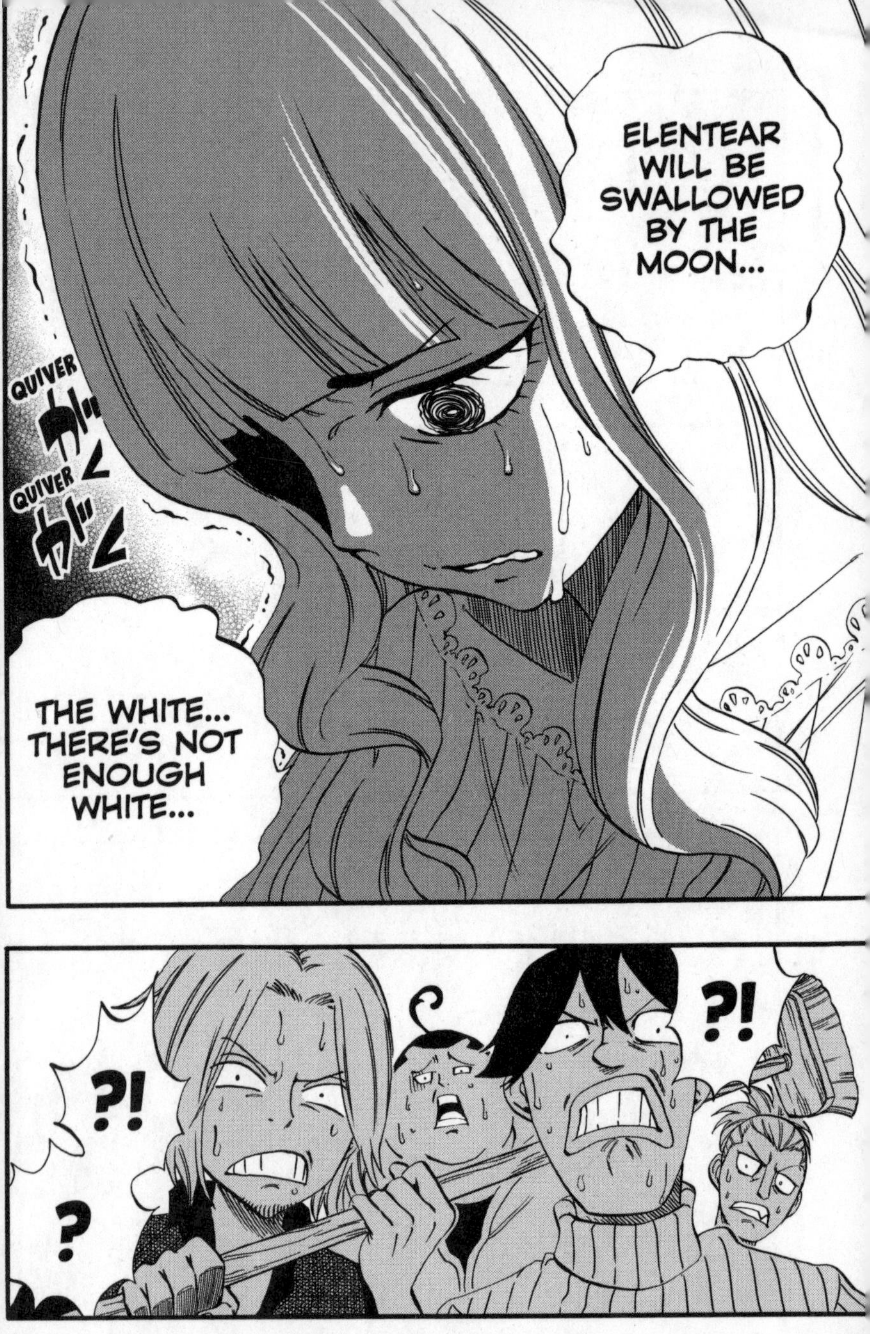
ELENTEAR WILL BE SWALLOWED BY THE MOON...
QUIVER
QUIVER
THE WHITE... THERE'S NOT ENOUGH WHITE...
?!
?!
?

FAIRY TAIL 100 YEARS QUEST

Chapter 65: Elentear

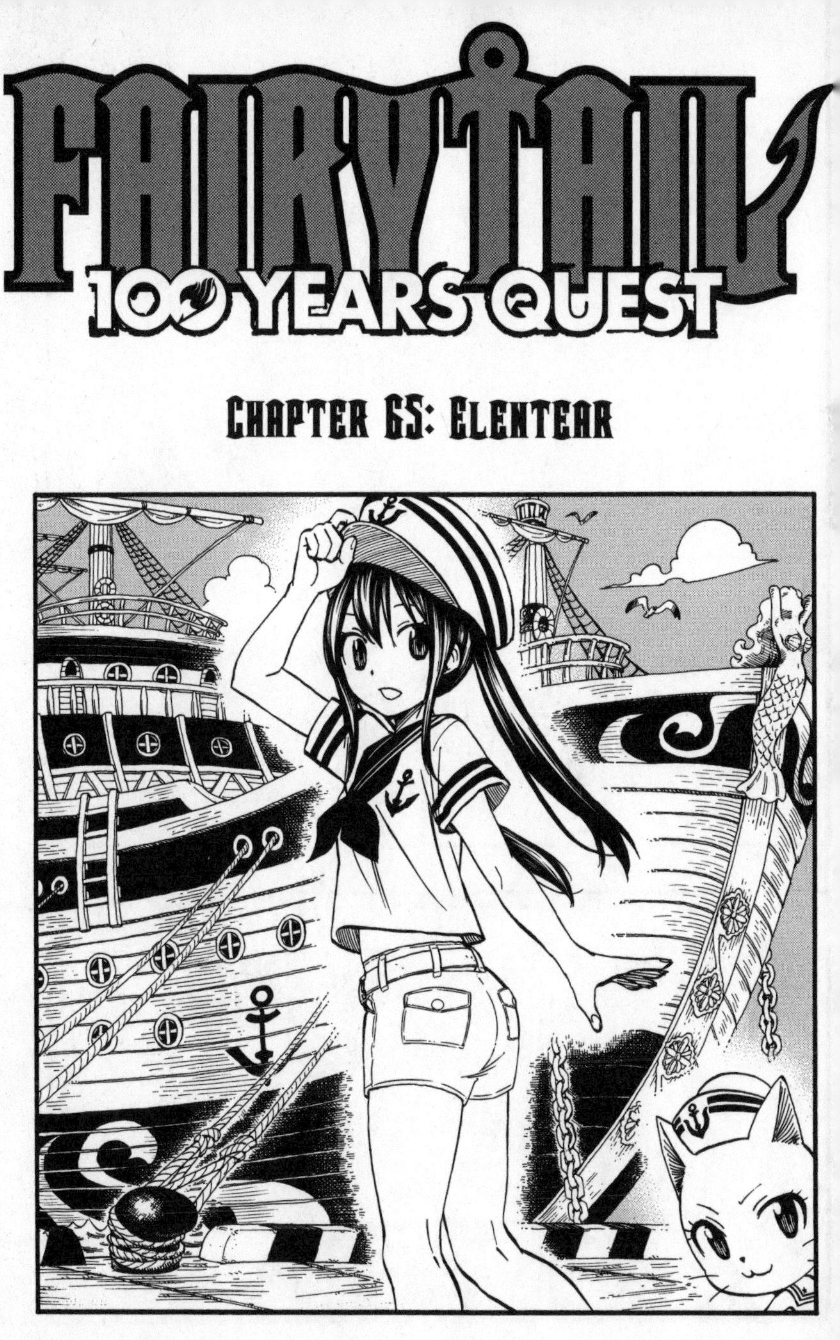

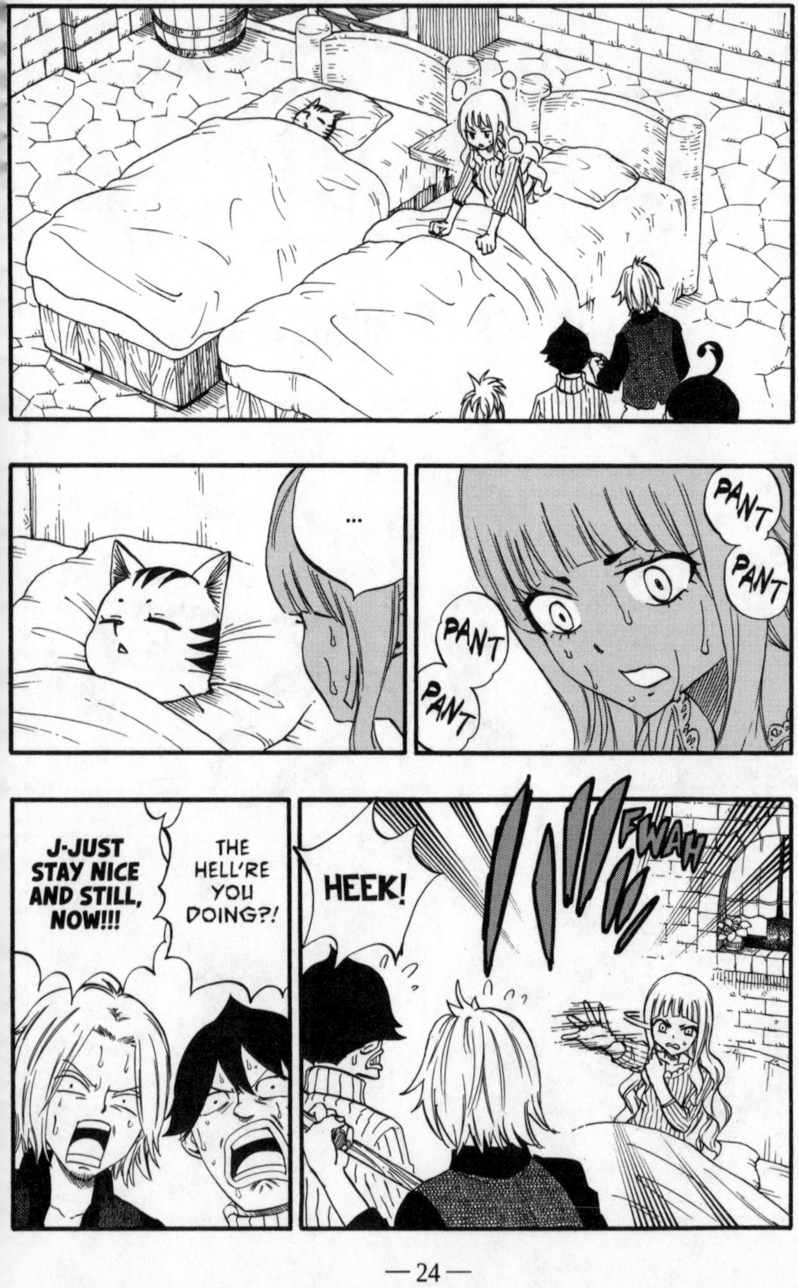
PANT
PANT
PANT
PANT
...
HEEK!
FWAH
THE HELL'RE YOU DOING?!
J-JUST STAY NICE AND STILL, NOW!!!

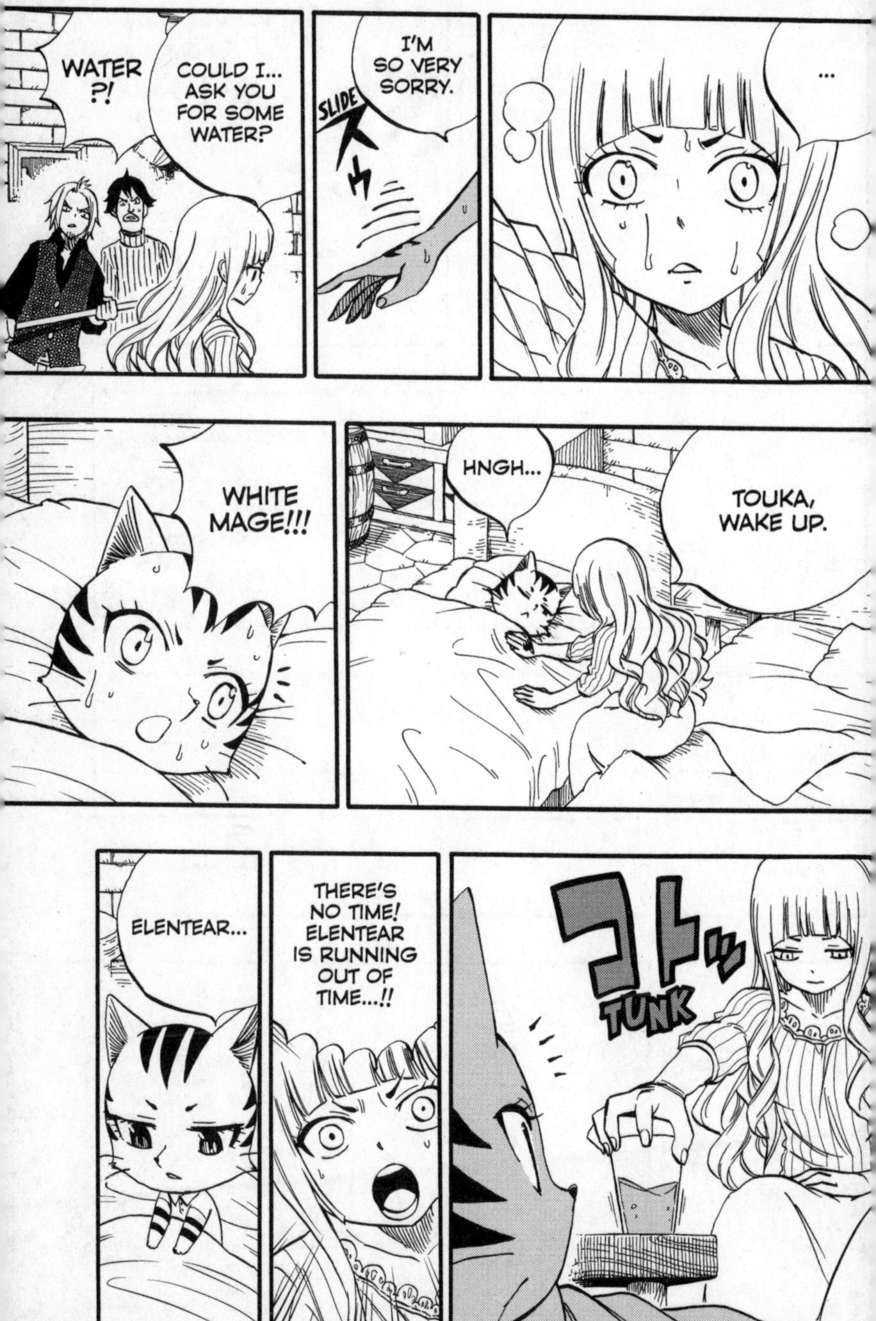
...
I'M SO VERY SORRY.
SLIDE
COULD I... ASK YOU FOR SOME WATER?
WATER ?!
TOUKA, WAKE UP.
HNGH...
WHITE MAGE!!!
コトッ
TUNK
THERE'S NO TIME! ELENTEAR IS RUNNING OUT OF TIME...!!
ELENTEAR...

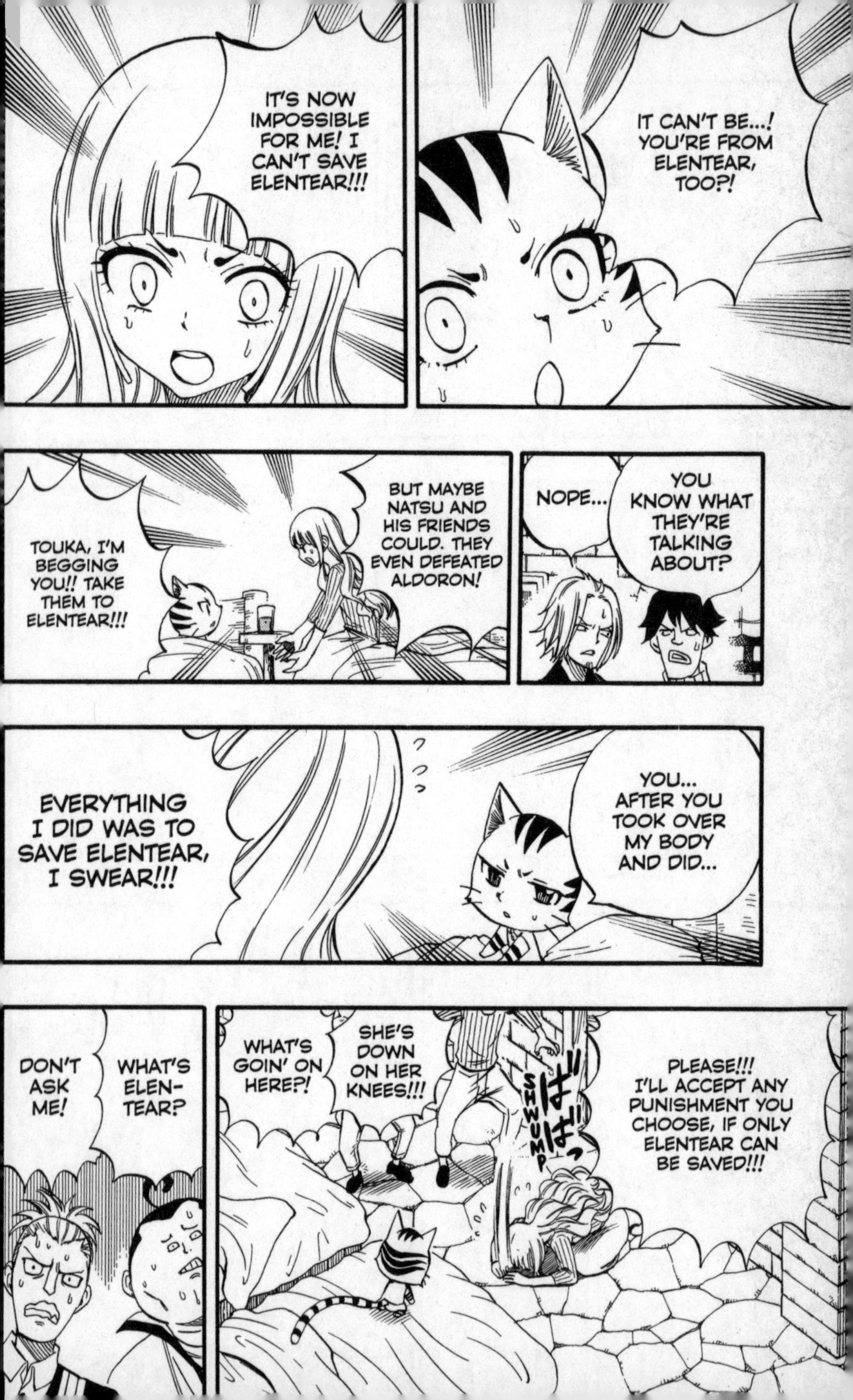
IT CAN'T BE...! YOU'RE FROM ELENTEAR, TOO?!
IT'S NOW IMPOSSIBLE FOR ME! I CAN'T SAVE ELENTEAR!!!
YOU KNOW WHAT THEY'RE TALKING ABOUT?
NOPE...
BUT MAYBE NATSU AND HIS FRIENDS COULD. THEY EVEN DEFEATED ALDORON!
TOUKA, I'M BEGGING YOU!! TAKE THEM TO ELENTEAR!!!
YOU... AFTER YOU TOOK OVER MY BODY AND DID...
EVERYTHING I DID WAS TO SAVE ELENTEAR, I SWEAR!!!
PLEASE!!! I'LL ACCEPT ANY PUNISHMENT YOU CHOOSE, IF ONLY ELENTEAR CAN BE SAVED!!!
SHWUMP
SHE'S DOWN ON HER KNEES!!!
WHAT'S GOIN' ON HERE?!
WHAT'S ELEN-TEAR?
DON'T ASK ME!

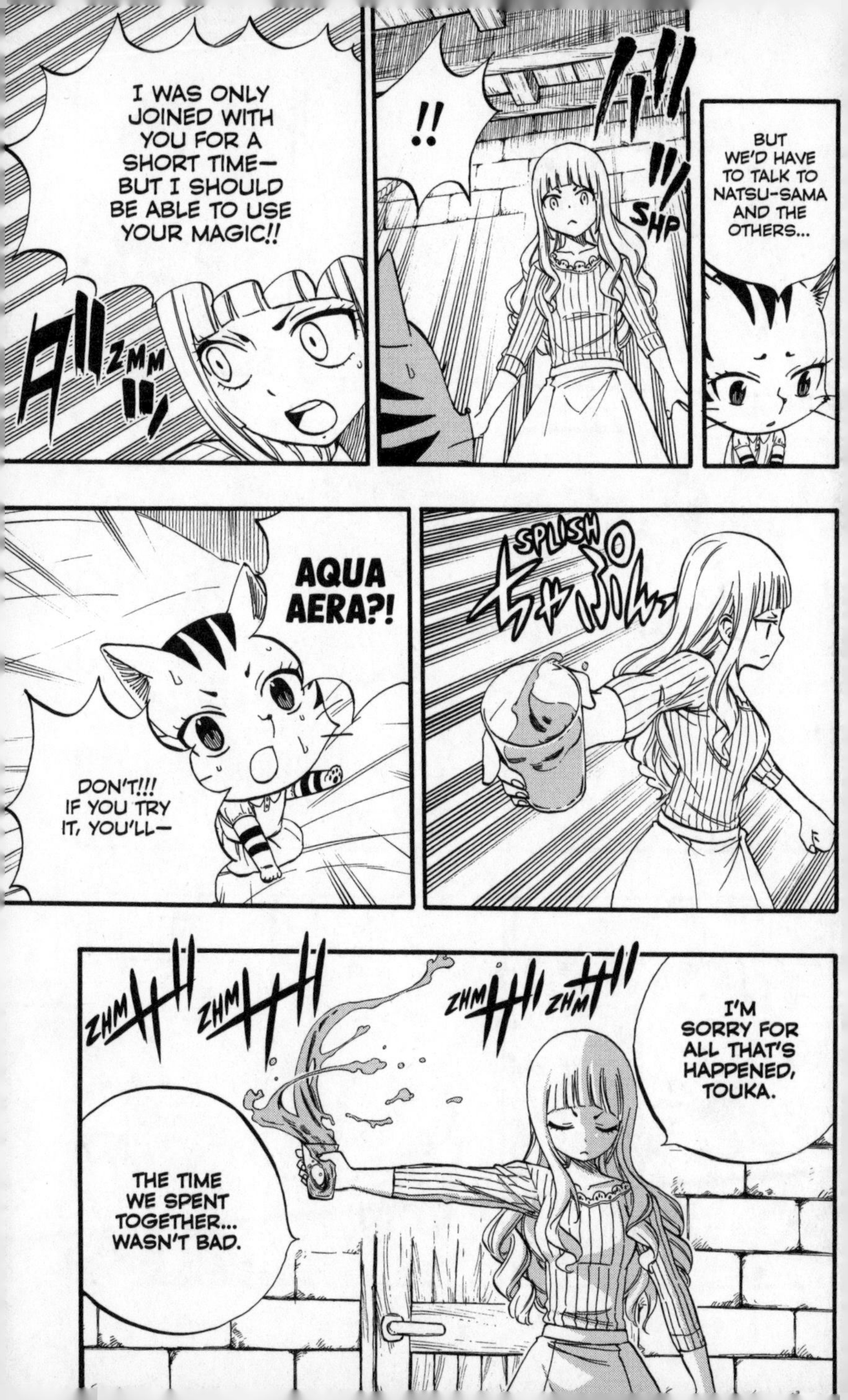
BUT WE'D HAVE TO TALK TO NATSU-SAMA AND THE OTHERS...
SHP
!!
I WAS ONLY JOINED WITH YOU FOR A SHORT TIME—BUT I SHOULD BE ABLE TO USE YOUR MAGIC!!
ZMM
SPLISH
AQUA AERA?!
DON'T!!! IF YOU TRY IT, YOU'LL—
I'M SORRY FOR ALL THAT'S HAPPENED, TOUKA.
ZHM
ZHM
ZHM
ZHM
THE TIME WE SPENT TOGETHER... WASN'T BAD.

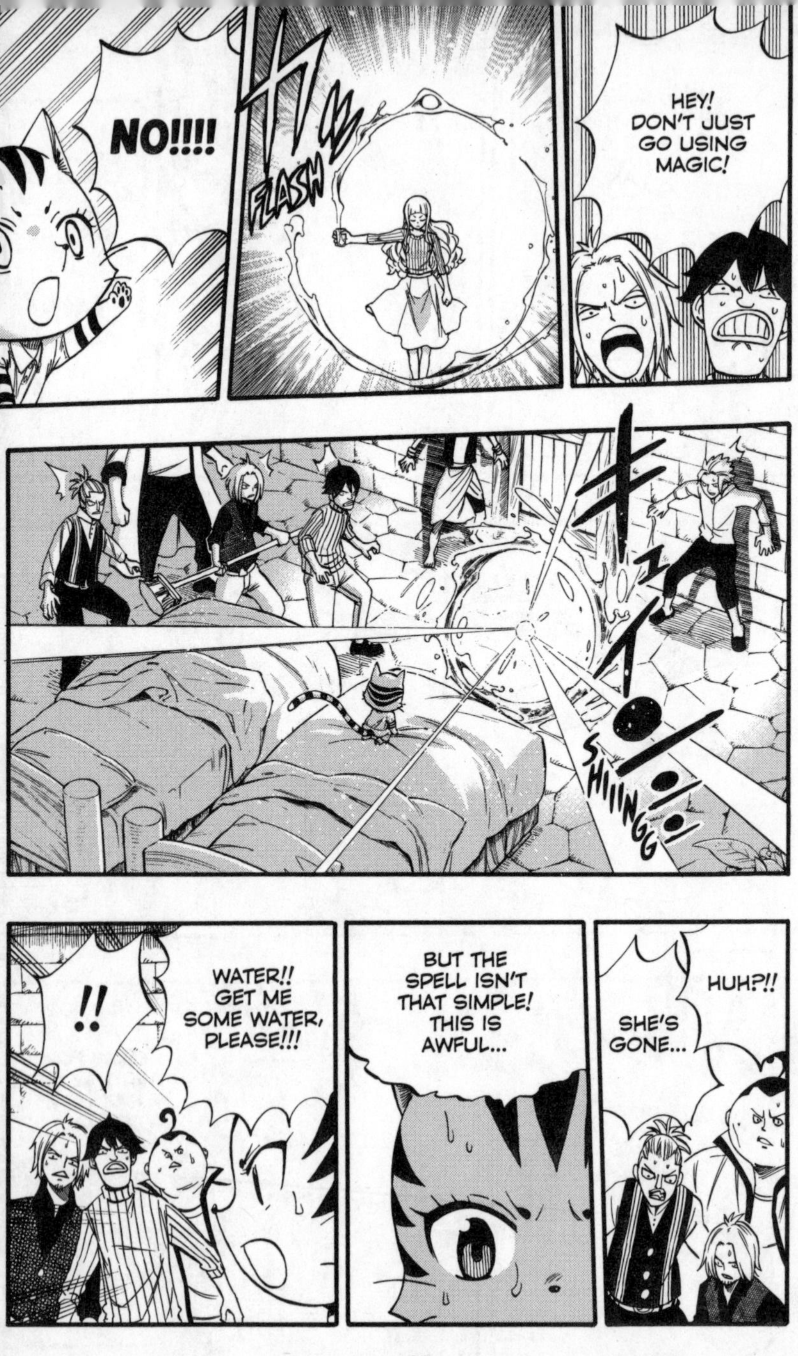
HEY! DON'T JUST GO USING MAGIC!
FLASH
NO!!!!
SHIIINGG
HUH?!!
SHE'S GONE...
BUT THE SPELL ISN'T THAT SIMPLE! THIS IS AWFUL...
WATER!! GET ME SOME WATER, PLEASE!!!
!!

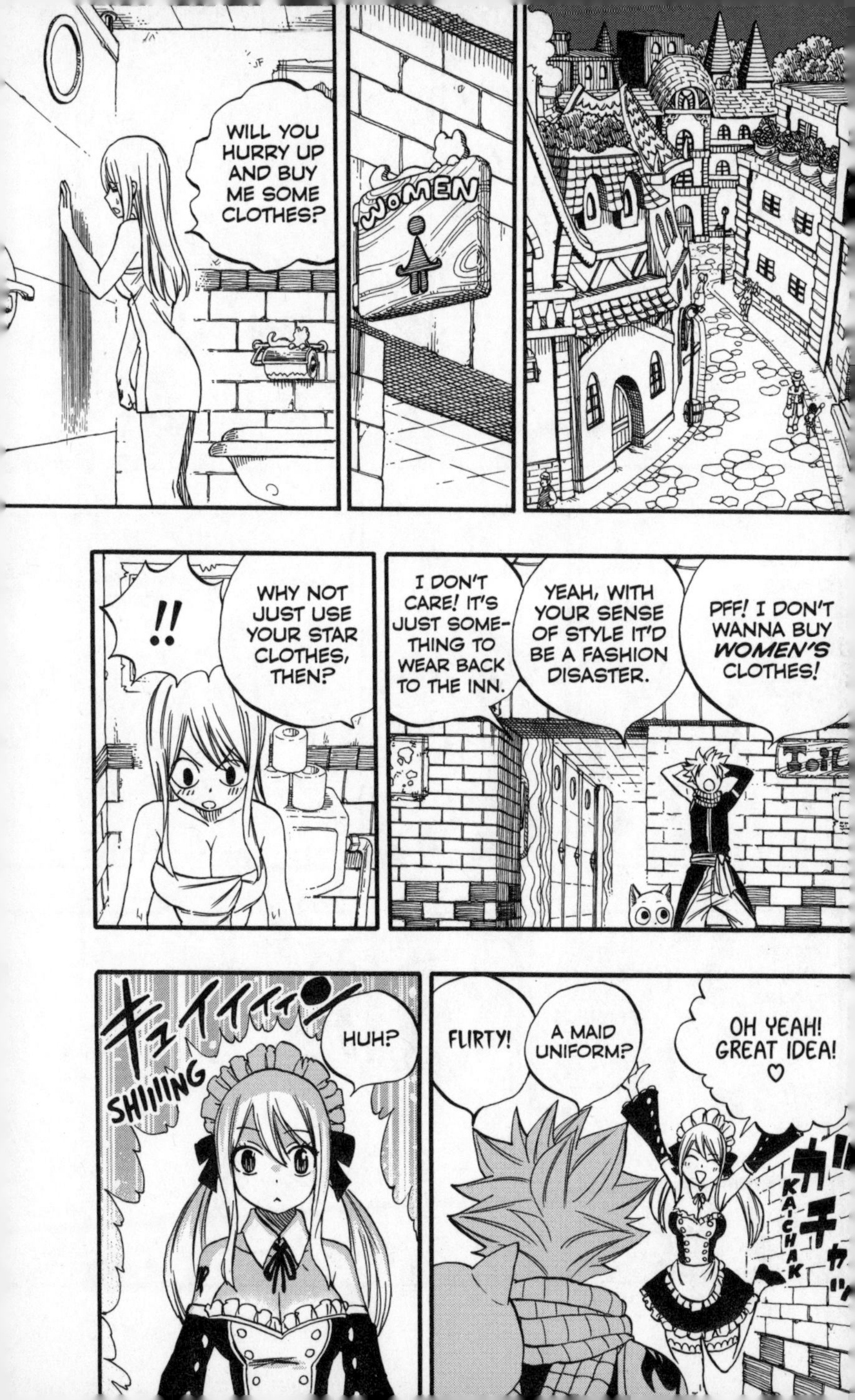
WOMEN
WILL YOU HURRY UP AND BUY ME SOME CLOTHES?
PFF! I DON'T WANNA BUY *WOMEN'S* CLOTHES!
YEAH, WITH YOUR SENSE OF STYLE IT'D BE A FASHION DISASTER.
I DON'T CARE! IT'S JUST SOMETHING TO WEAR BACK TO THE INN.
WHY NOT JUST USE YOUR STAR CLOTHES, THEN?
!!
OH YEAH! GREAT IDEA! ♡
ガチャッ
KAICHAK
A MAID UNIFORM?
FLIRTY!
キュイイイン
SHIIIING
HUH?

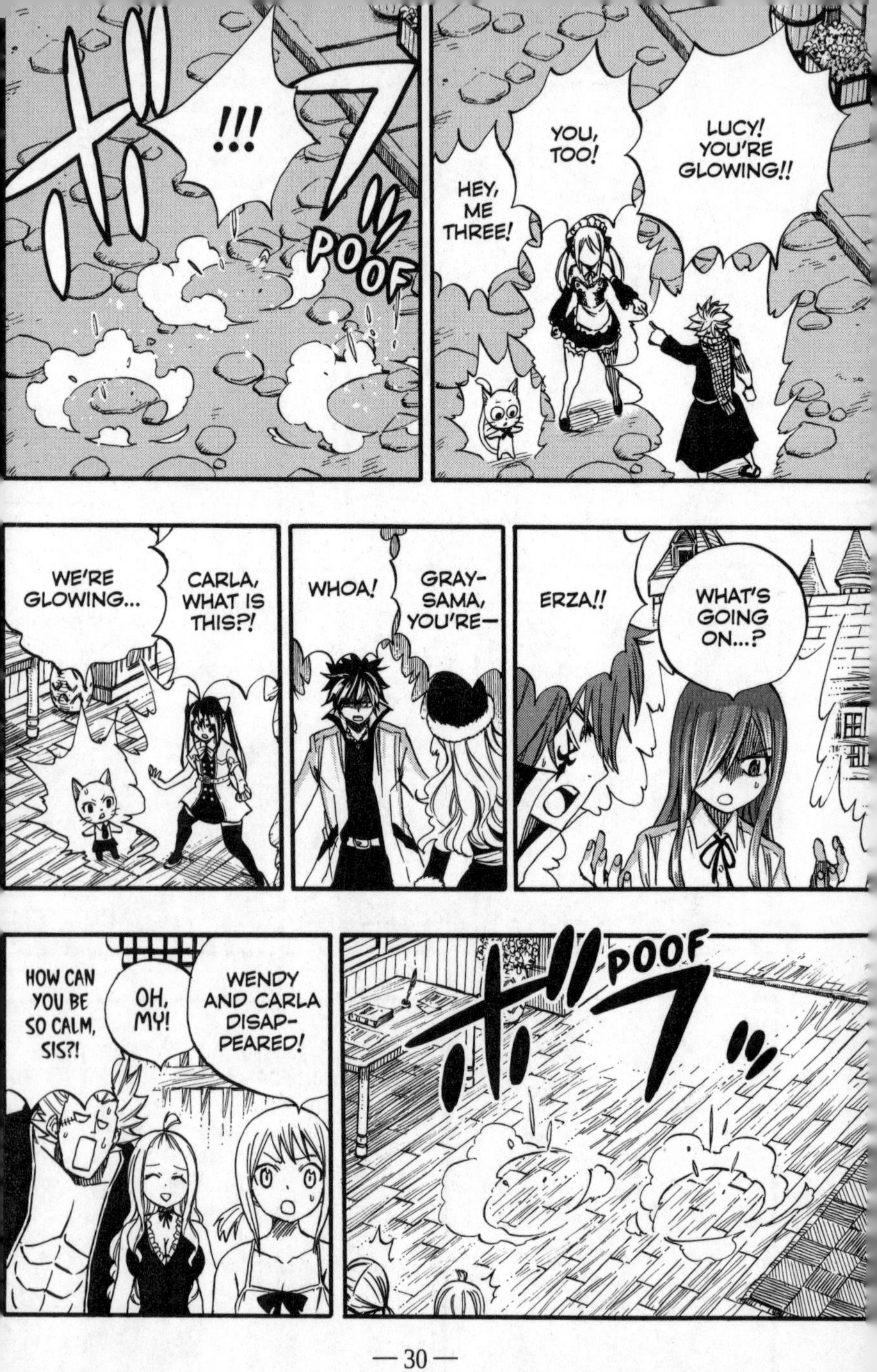
LUCY! YOU'RE GLOWING!!
YOU, TOO!
HEY, ME THREE!
!!!
POOF
WHAT'S GOING ON...?
ERZA!!
GRAY-SAMA, YOU'RE—
WHOA!
CARLA, WHAT IS THIS?!
WE'RE GLOWING...
POOF
WENDY AND CARLA DISAP-PEARED!
OH, MY!
HOW CAN YOU BE SO CALM, SIS?!

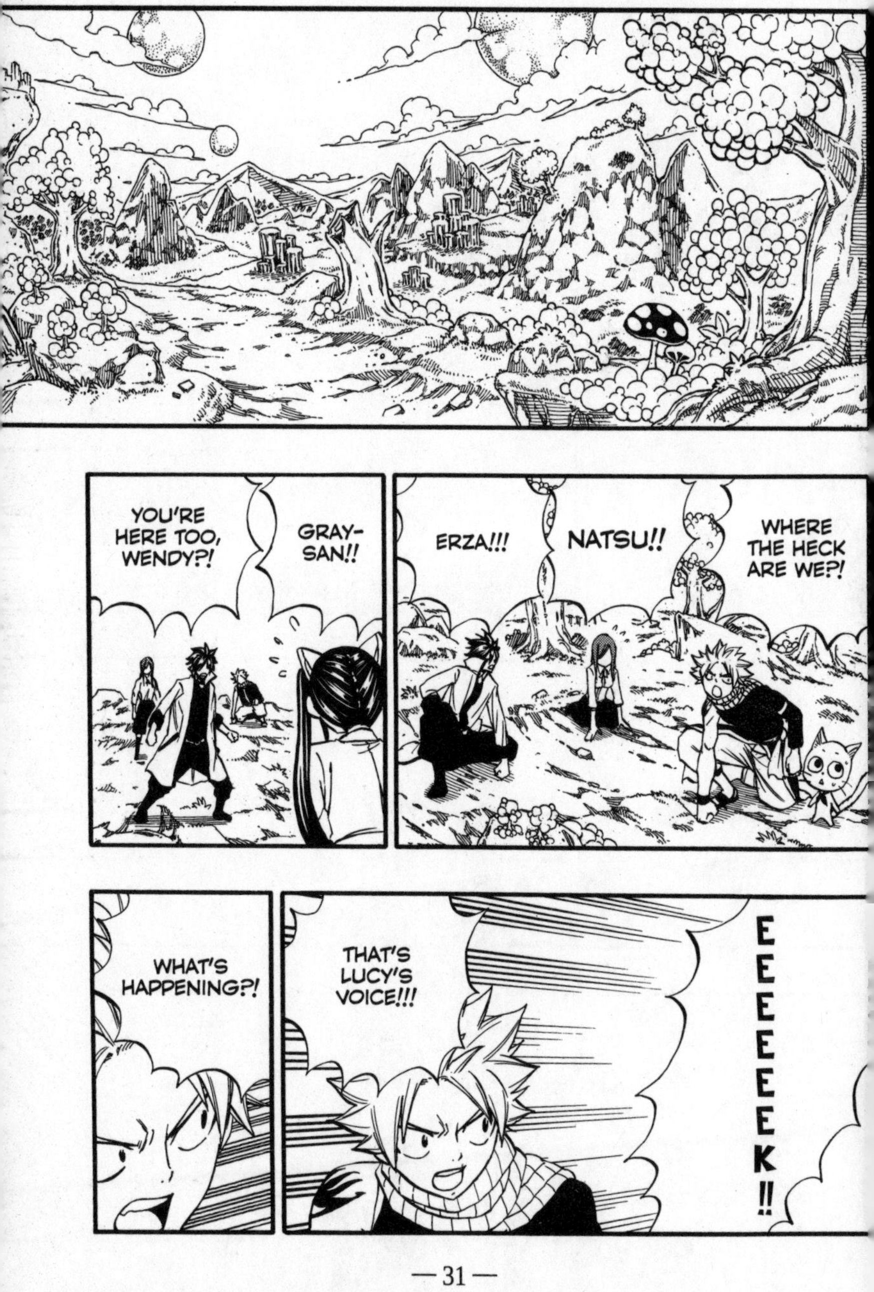
WHERE THE HECK ARE WE?!
NATSU!!
ERZA!!!
GRAY-SAN!!
YOU'RE HERE TOO, WENDY?!
EEEEEEEK!!
THAT'S LUCY'S VOICE!!!
WHAT'S HAPPENING?!

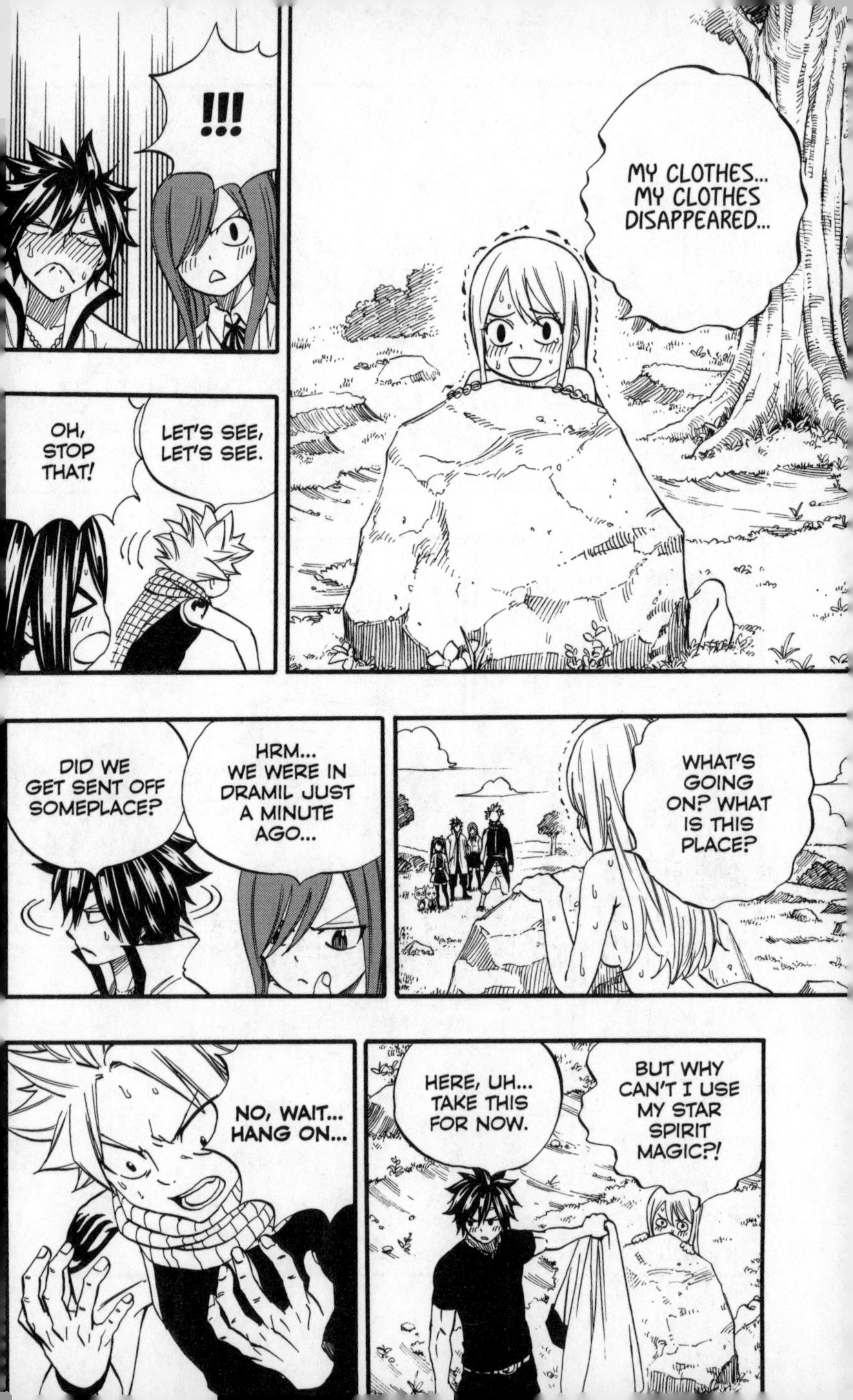
MY CLOTHES... MY CLOTHES DISAPPEARED...
!!!
LET'S SEE, LET'S SEE.
OH, STOP THAT!
WHAT'S GOING ON? WHAT IS THIS PLACE?
HRM... WE WERE IN DRAMIL JUST A MINUTE AGO...
DID WE GET SENT OFF SOMEPLACE?
BUT WHY CAN'T I USE MY STAR SPIRIT MAGIC?!
HERE, UH... TAKE THIS FOR NOW.
NO, WAIT... HANG ON...

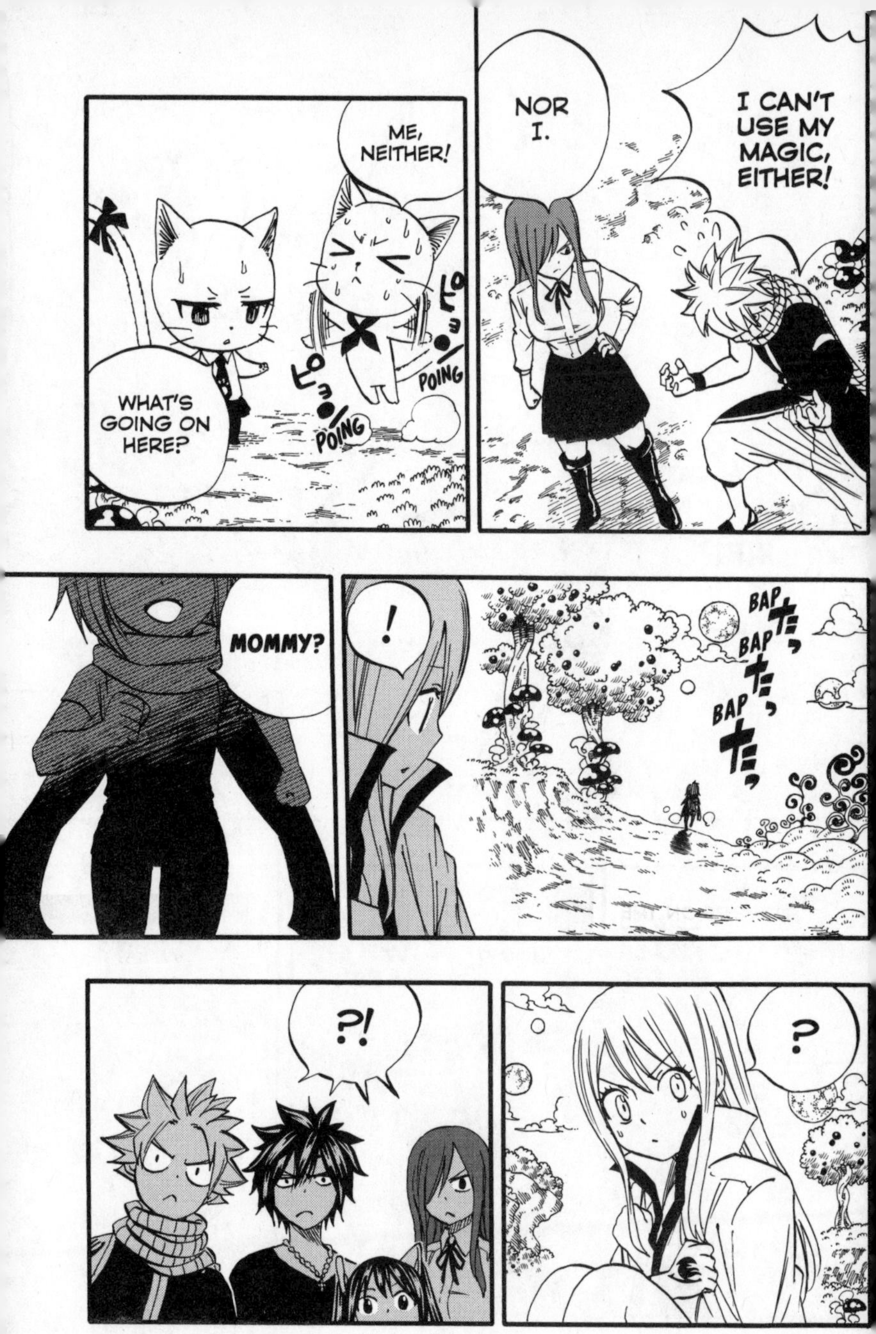
I CAN'T USE MY MAGIC, EITHER!
NOR I.
ME, NEITHER!
POING
POING
WHAT'S GOING ON HERE?
BAP
BAP
BAP
!
MOMMY?
?
?!

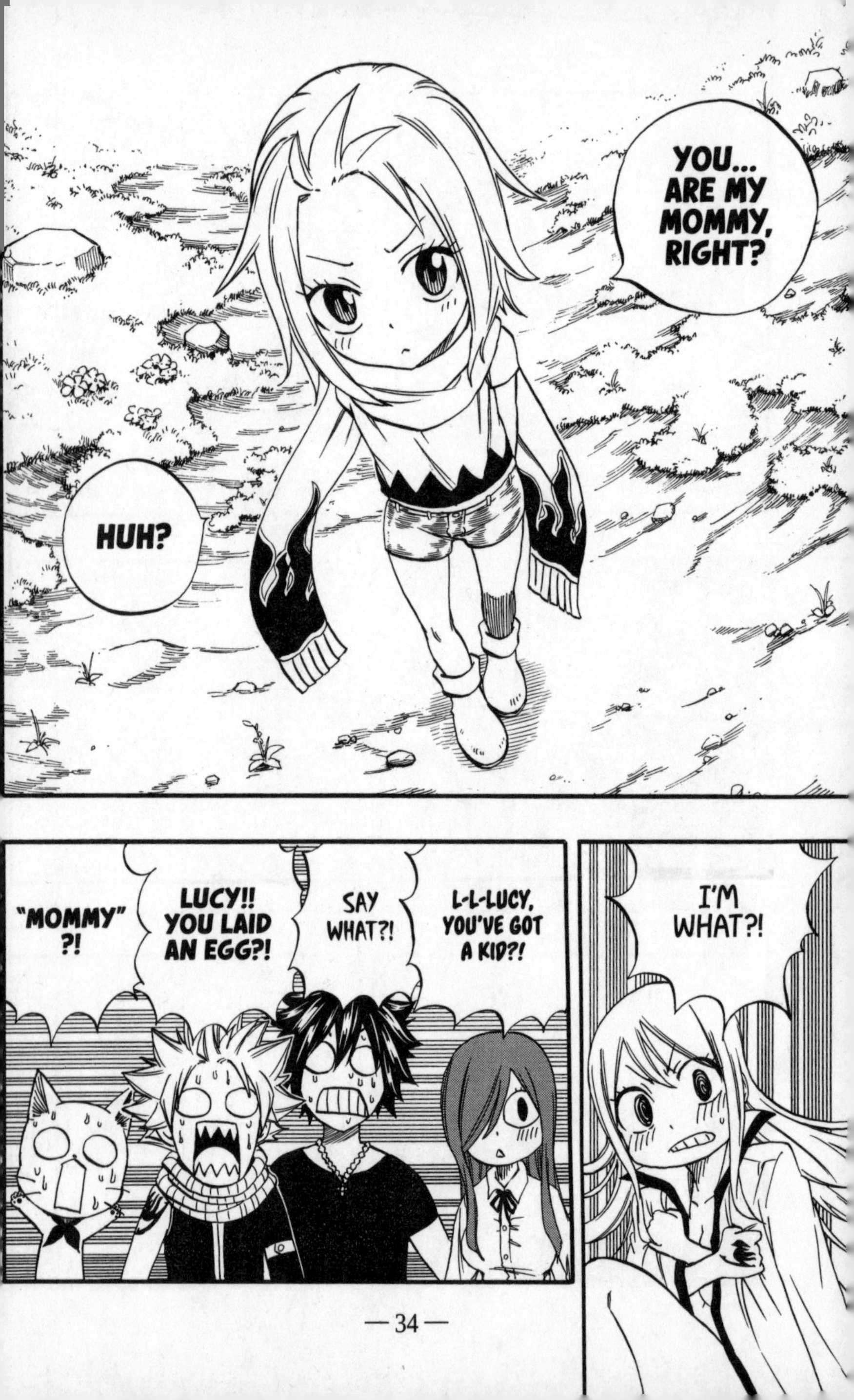
YOU... ARE MY MOMMY, RIGHT?
HUH?
I'M WHAT?!
L-L-LUCY, YOU'VE GOT A KID?!
SAY WHAT?!
LUCY!! YOU LAID AN EGG?!
"MOMMY" ?!

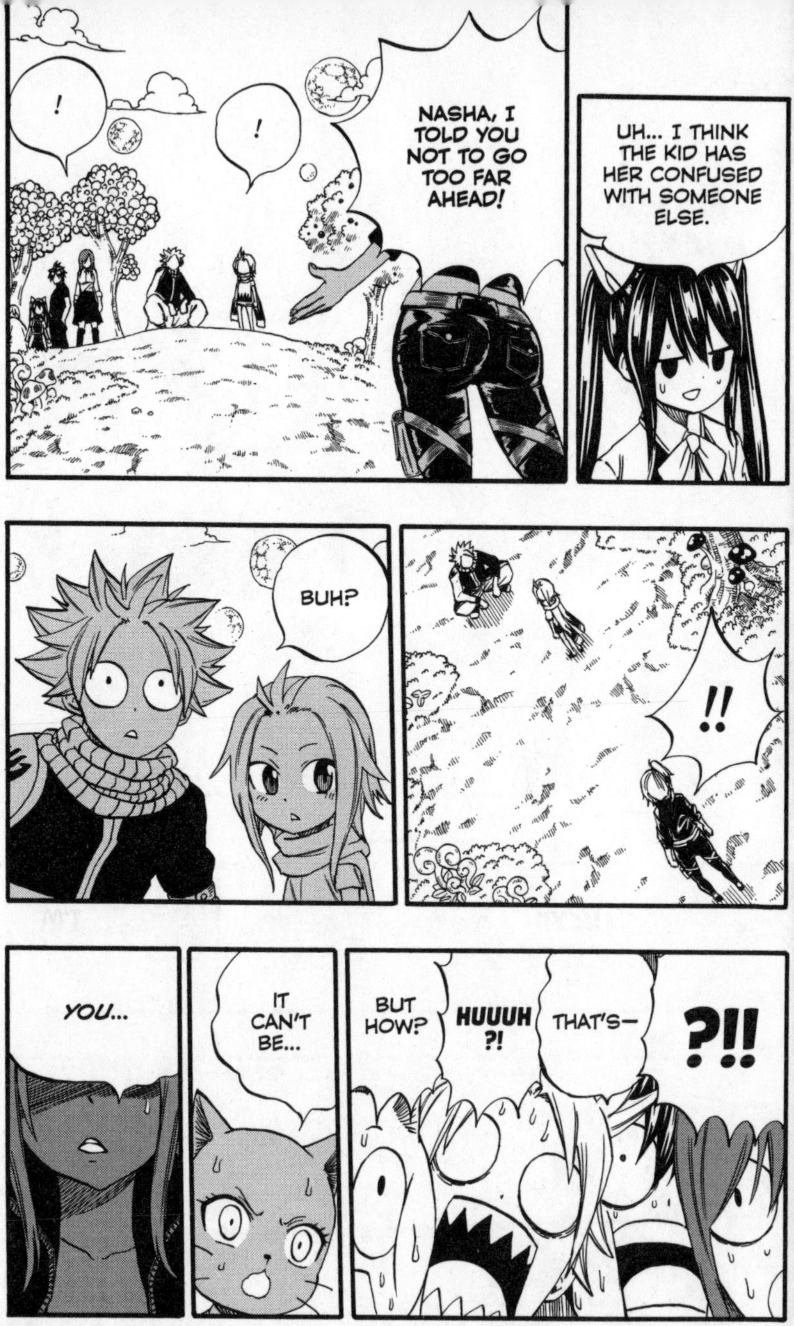
UH... I THINK THE KID HAS HER CONFUSED WITH SOMEONE ELSE.
NASHA, I TOLD YOU NOT TO GO TOO FAR AHEAD!
!
!
!!
BUH?
?!!
THAT'S—
HUUUH ?!
BUT HOW?
IT CAN'T BE...
YOU...

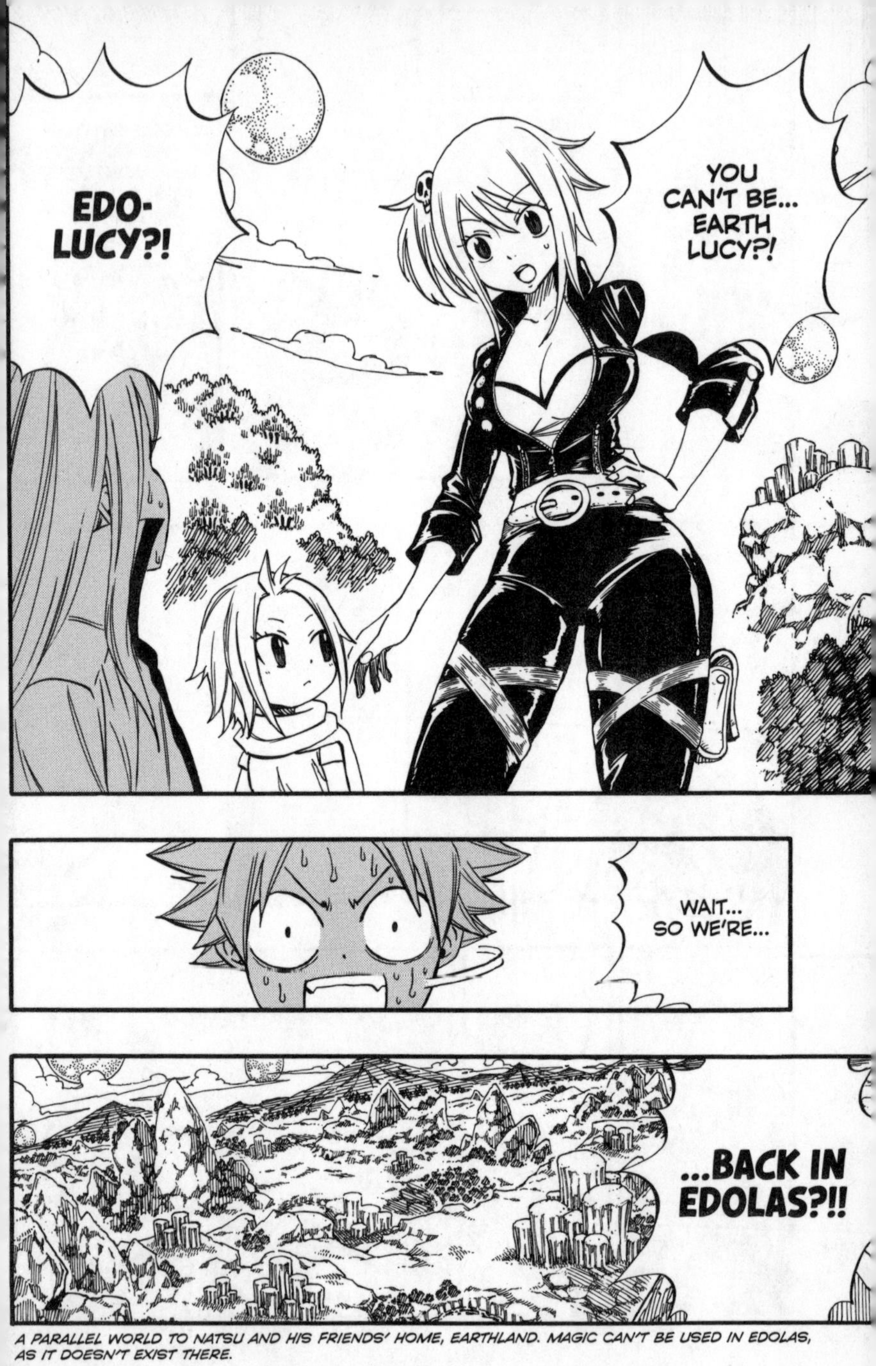
YOU CAN'T BE... EARTH LUCY?!
EDO-LUCY?!
WAIT... SO WE'RE...
...BACK IN EDOLAS?!!

A PARALLEL WORLD TO NATSU AND HIS FRIENDS' HOME, EARTHLAND. MAGIC CAN'T BE USED IN EDOLAS, AS IT DOESN'T EXIST THERE.

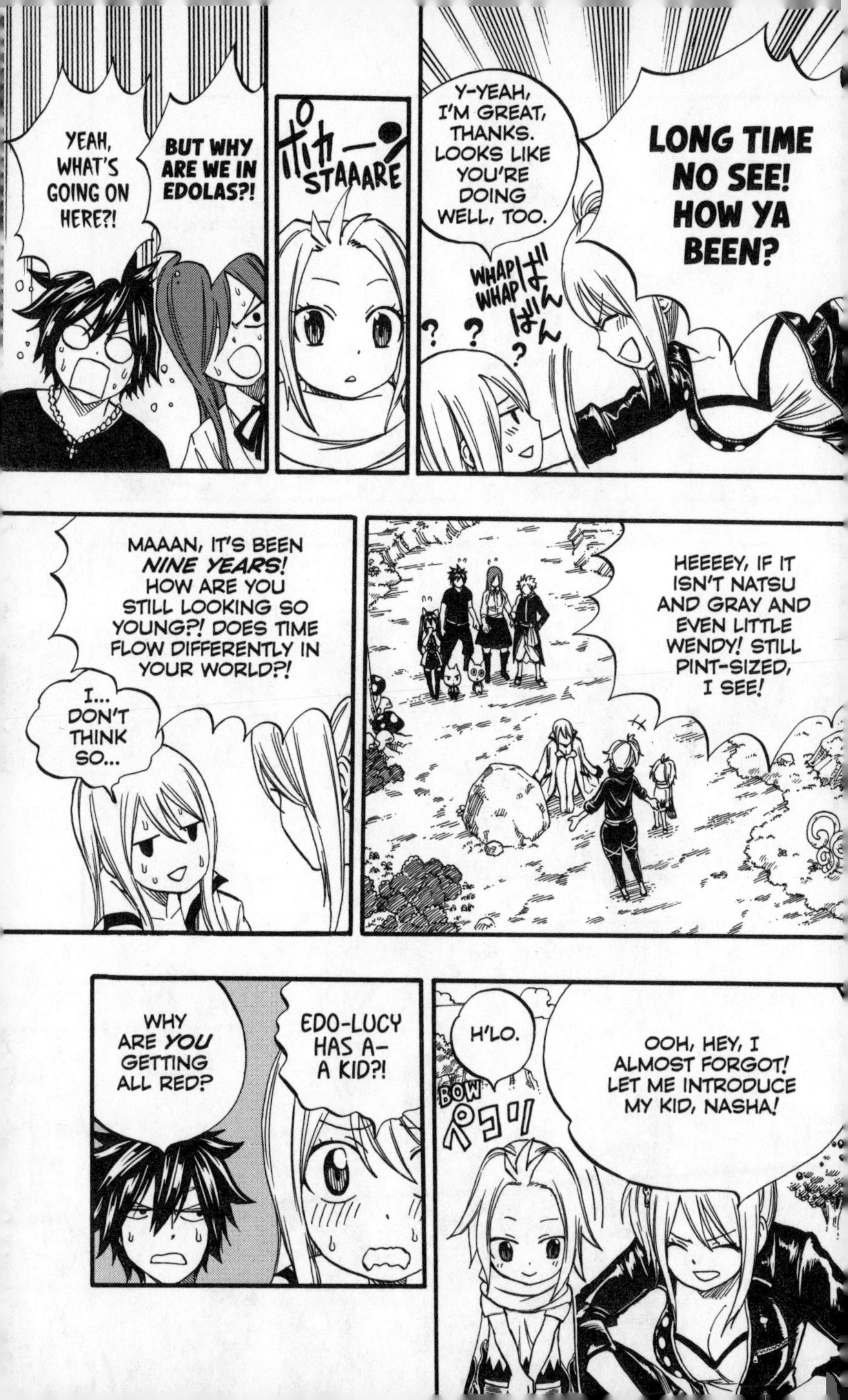
LONG TIME NO SEE! HOW YA BEEN?
Y-YEAH, I'M GREAT, THANKS. LOOKS LIKE YOU'RE DOING WELL, TOO.
WHAP WHAP ばんばん
ポカーン STAAARE
BUT WHY ARE WE IN EDOLAS?!
YEAH, WHAT'S GOING ON HERE?!
HEEEEY, IF IT ISN'T NATSU AND GRAY AND EVEN LITTLE WENDY! STILL PINT-SIZED, I SEE!
MAAAN, IT'S BEEN *NINE YEARS*! HOW ARE YOU STILL LOOKING SO YOUNG?! DOES TIME FLOW DIFFERENTLY IN YOUR WORLD?!
I... DON'T THINK SO...
OOH, HEY, I ALMOST FORGOT! LET ME INTRODUCE MY KID, NASHA!
H'LO.
BOW ペコリ
EDO-LUCY HAS A- A KID?!
WHY ARE *YOU* GETTING ALL RED?

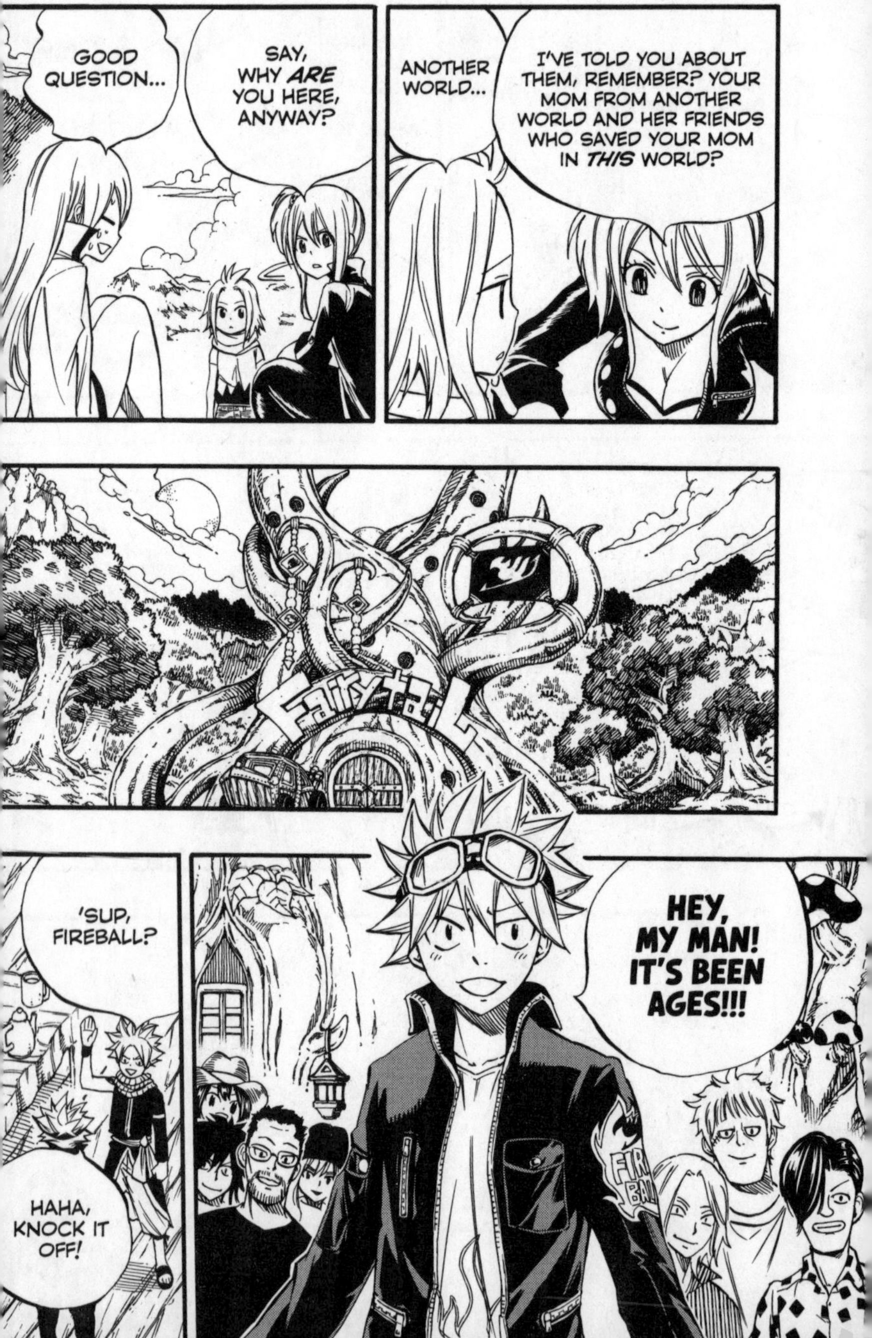
I'VE TOLD YOU ABOUT THEM, REMEMBER? YOUR MOM FROM ANOTHER WORLD AND HER FRIENDS WHO SAVED YOUR MOM IN *THIS* WORLD?
ANOTHER WORLD...
SAY, WHY *ARE* YOU HERE, ANYWAY?
GOOD QUESTION...
HEY, MY MAN! IT'S BEEN AGES!!!
'SUP, FIREBALL?
HAHA, KNOCK IT OFF!

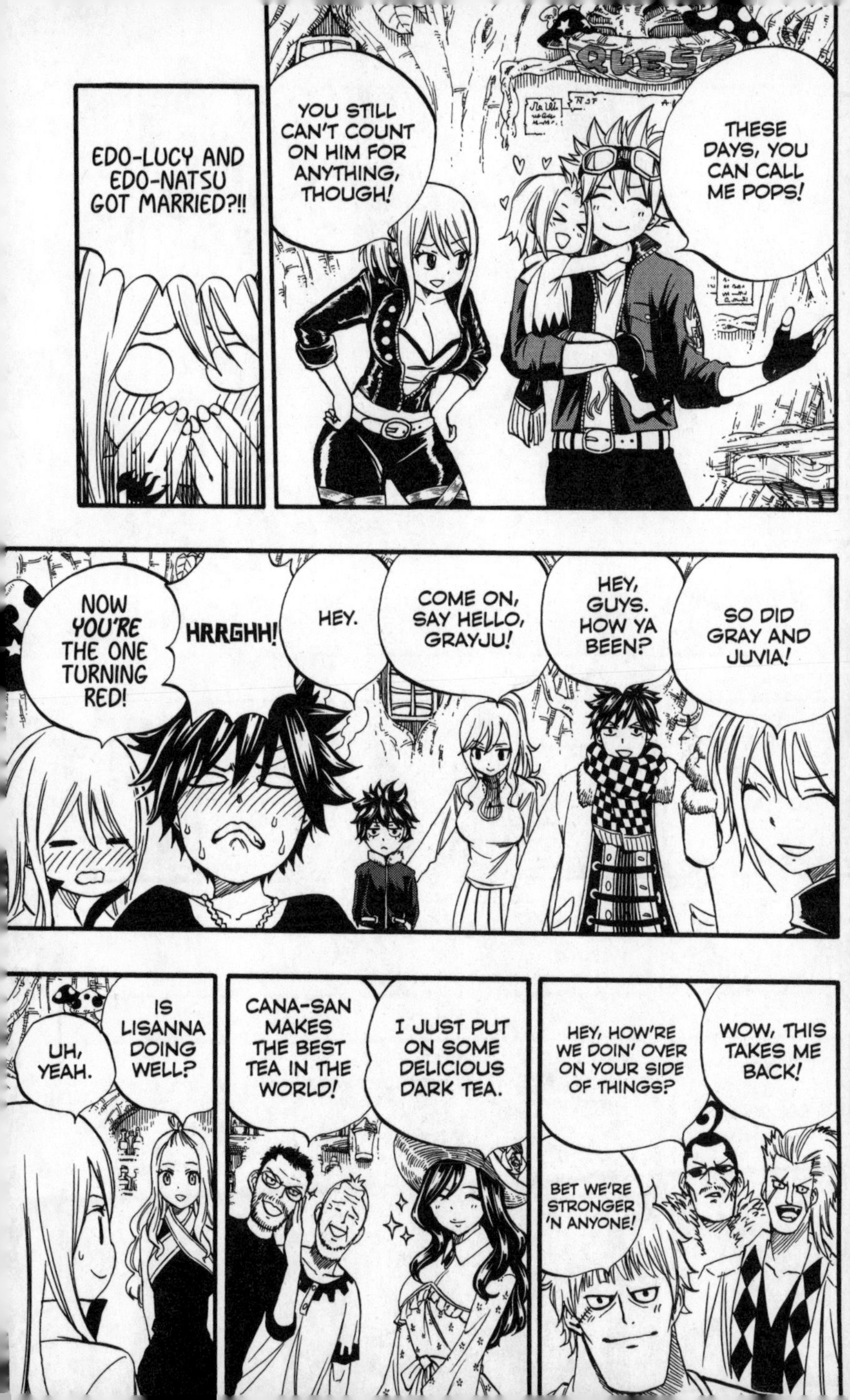
THESE DAYS, YOU CAN CALL ME POPS!
YOU STILL CAN'T COUNT ON HIM FOR ANYTHING, THOUGH!
EDO-LUCY AND EDO-NATSU GOT MARRIED?!!
SO DID GRAY AND JUVIA!
HEY, GUYS. HOW YA BEEN?
COME ON, SAY HELLO, GRAYJU!
HEY.
HRRGHH!
NOW *YOU'RE* THE ONE TURNING RED!
WOW, THIS TAKES ME BACK!
HEY, HOW'RE WE DOIN' OVER ON YOUR SIDE OF THINGS?
BET WE'RE STRONGER 'N ANYONE!
I JUST PUT ON SOME DELICIOUS DARK TEA.
CANA-SAN MAKES THE BEST TEA IN THE WORLD!
IS LISANNA DOING WELL?
UH, YEAH.

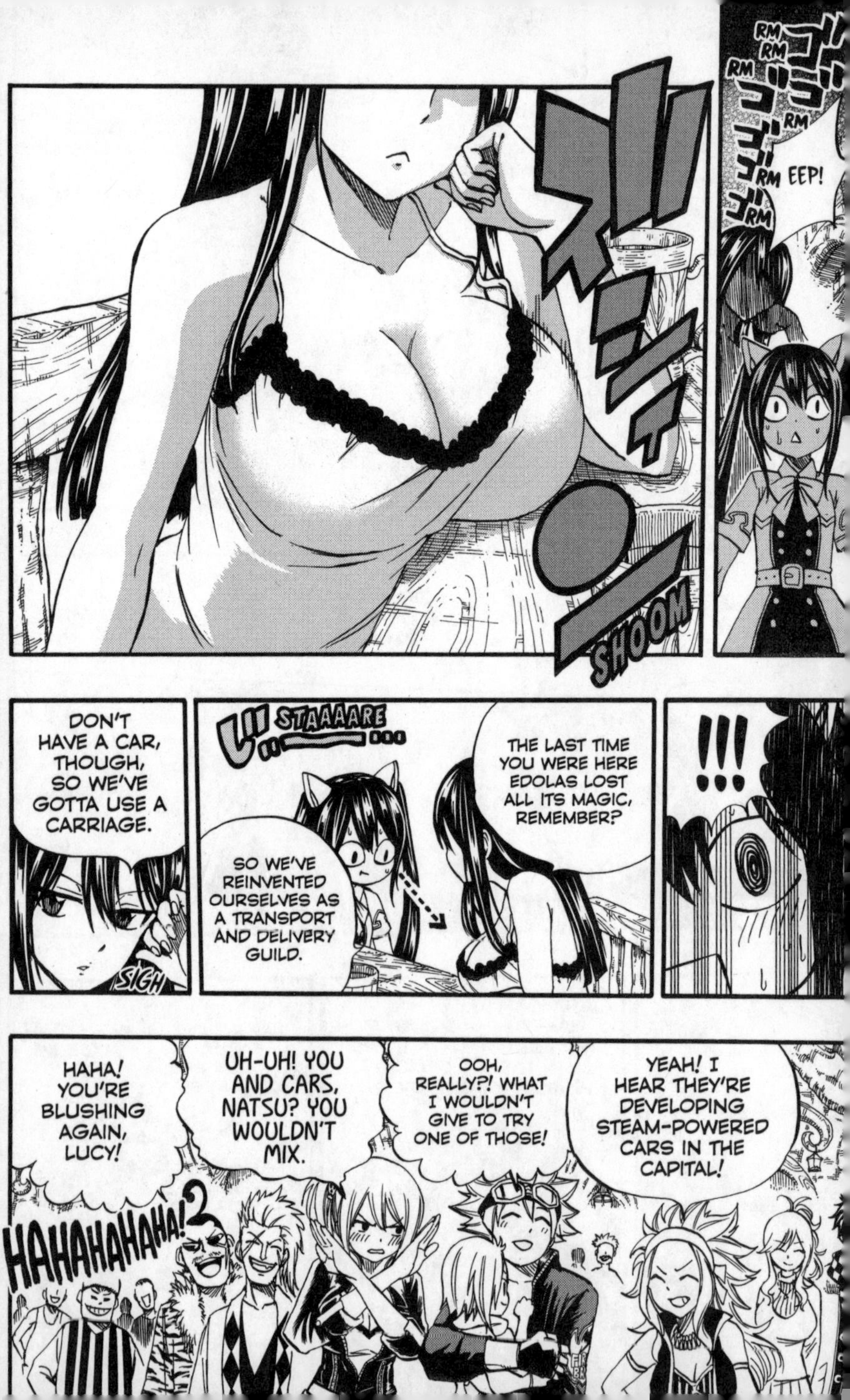
RM RM RM RM RM RM
EEP!
SHOOM
!!!
STAAAARE
THE LAST TIME YOU WERE HERE EDOLAS LOST ALL ITS MAGIC, REMEMBER?
SO WE'VE REINVENTED OURSELVES AS A TRANSPORT AND DELIVERY GUILD.
DON'T HAVE A CAR, THOUGH, SO WE'VE GOTTA USE A CARRIAGE.
SIGH
YEAH! I HEAR THEY'RE DEVELOPING STEAM-POWERED CARS IN THE CAPITAL!
OOH, REALLY?! WHAT I WOULDN'T GIVE TO TRY ONE OF THOSE!
UH-UH! YOU AND CARS, NATSU? YOU WOULDN'T MIX.
HAHA! YOU'RE BLUSHING AGAIN, LUCY!
HAHAHAHAHA!

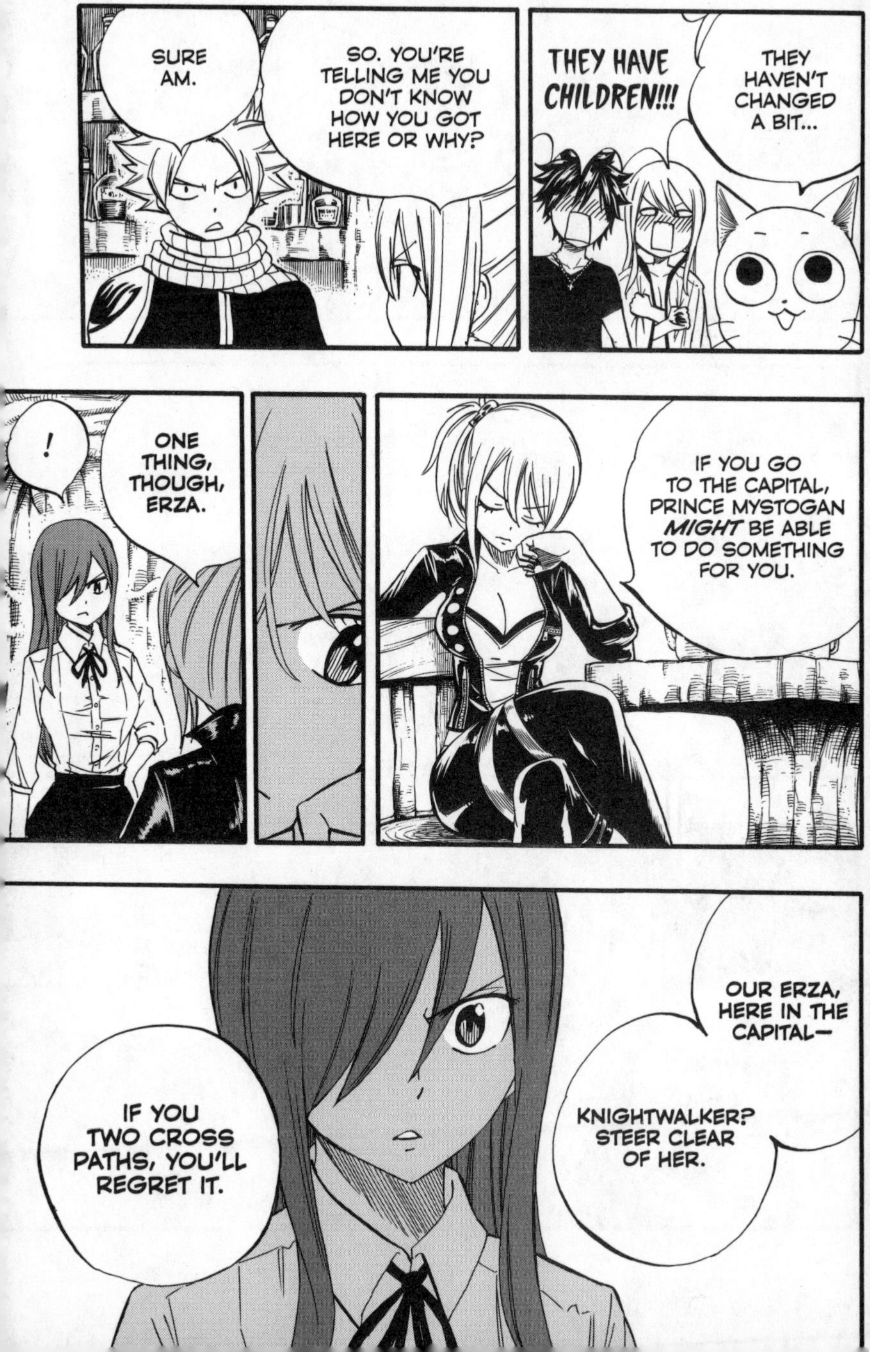
THEY HAVEN'T CHANGED A BIT...
THEY HAVE CHILDREN!!!
SO. YOU'RE TELLING ME YOU DON'T KNOW HOW YOU GOT HERE OR WHY?
SURE AM.
IF YOU GO TO THE CAPITAL, PRINCE MYSTOGAN *MIGHT* BE ABLE TO DO SOMETHING FOR YOU.
ONE THING, THOUGH, ERZA.
!
OUR ERZA, HERE IN THE CAPITAL—
KNIGHTWALKER? STEER CLEAR OF HER.
IF YOU TWO CROSS PATHS, YOU'LL REGRET IT.

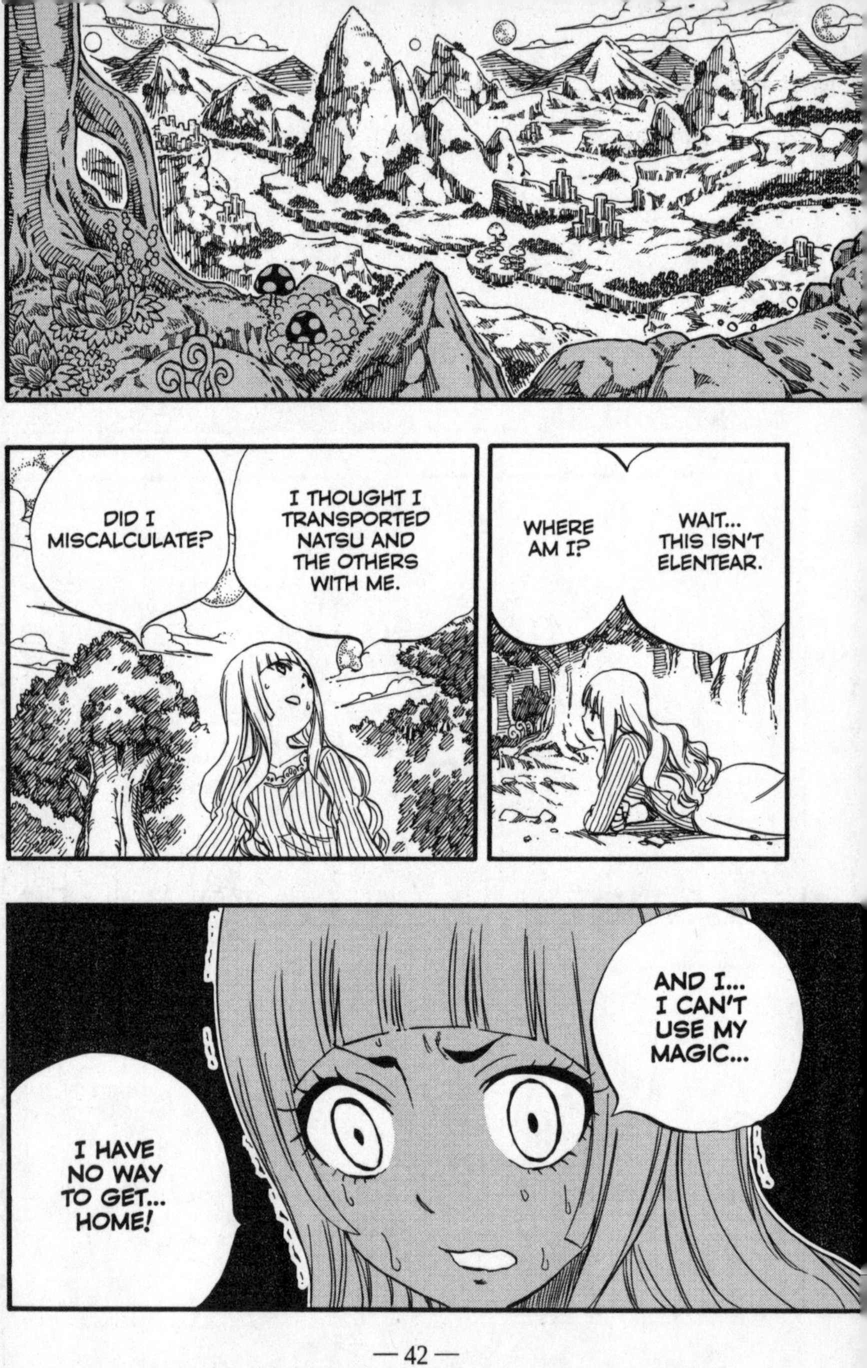
WAIT... THIS ISN'T ELENTEAR.
WHERE AM I?
I THOUGHT I TRANSPORTED NATSU AND THE OTHERS WITH ME.
DID I MISCALCULATE?
AND I... I CAN'T USE MY MAGIC...
I HAVE NO WAY TO GET... HOME!

FAIRY TAIL 100 YEARS QUEST

Chapter 66: In Edolas

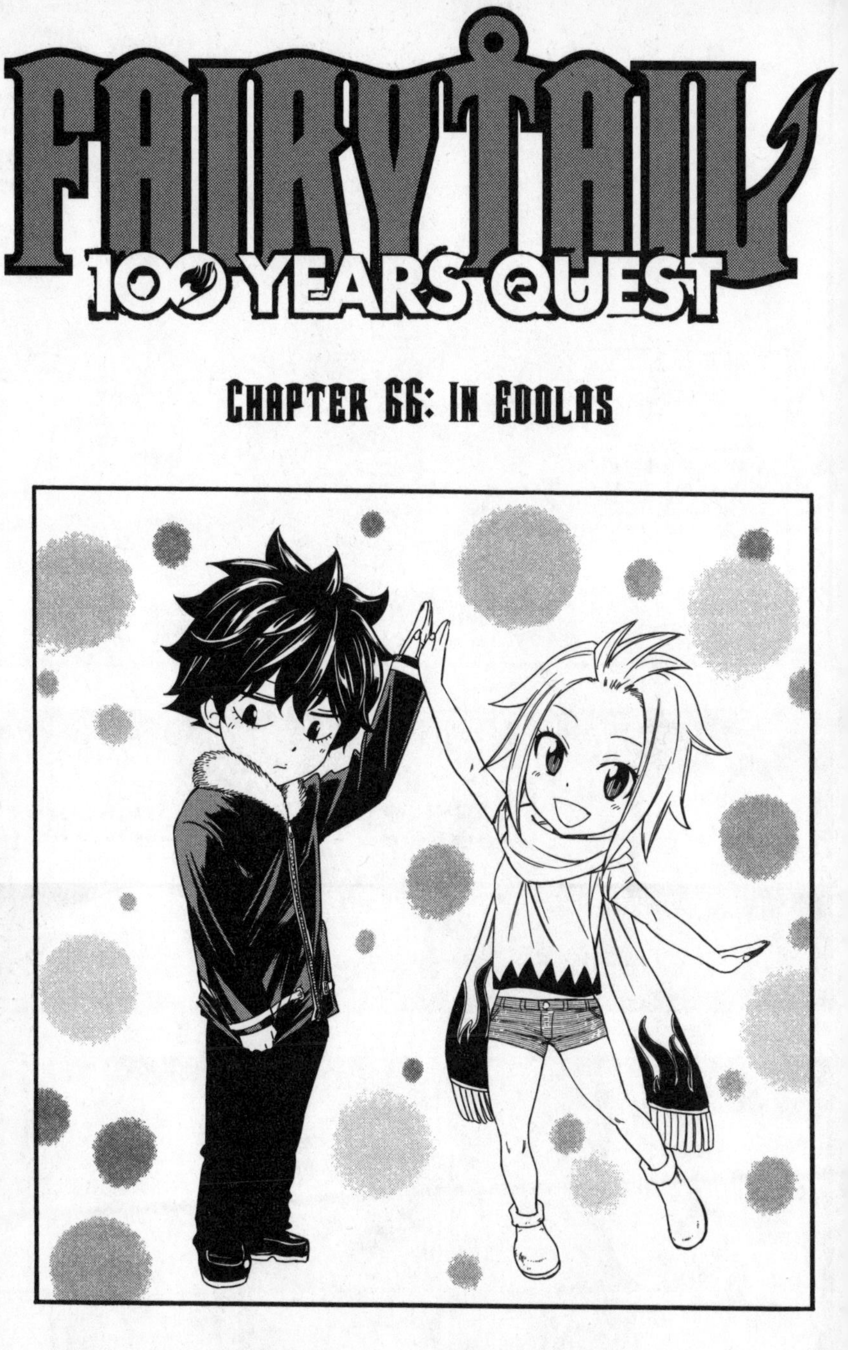

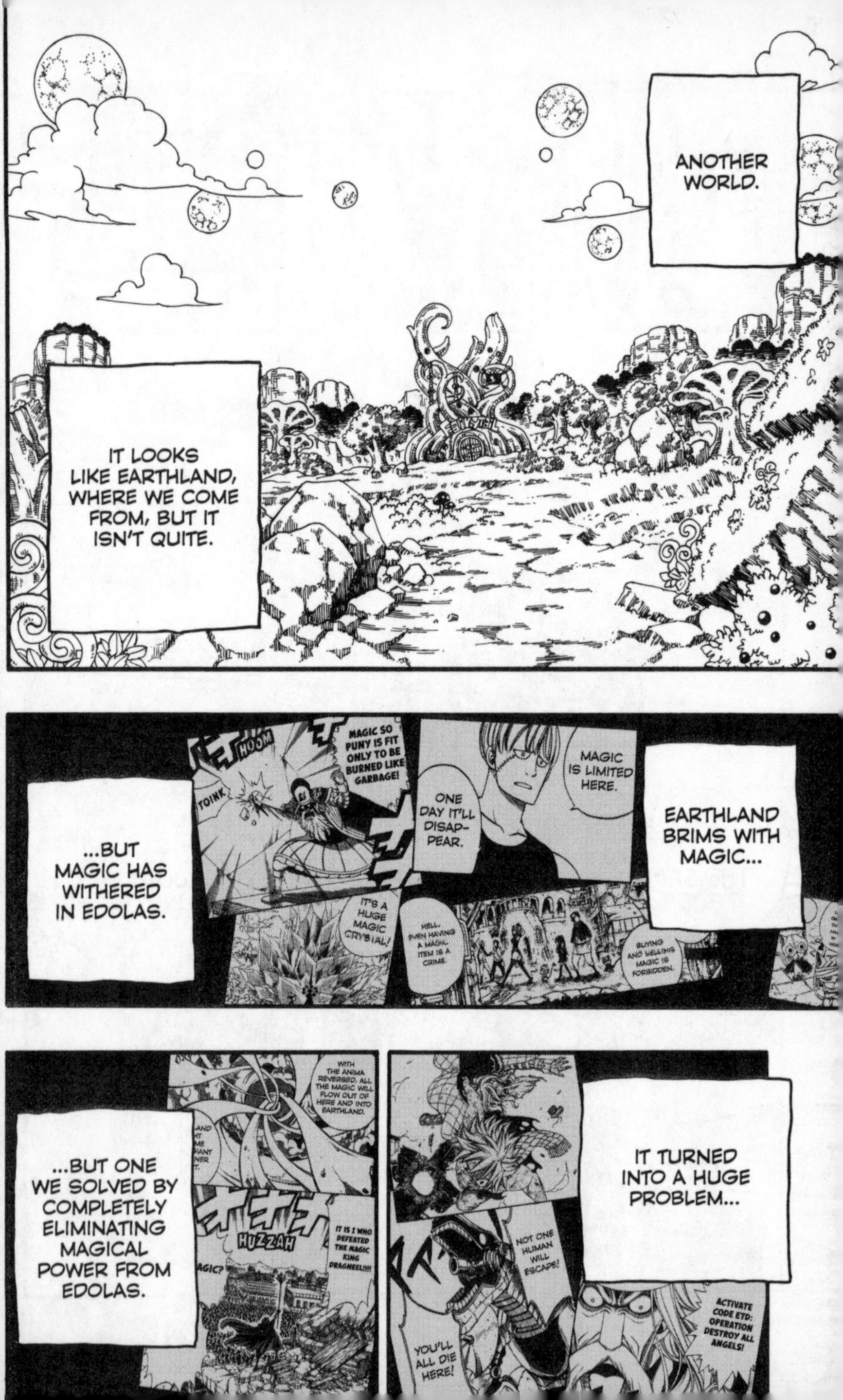
ANOTHER WORLD.
IT LOOKS LIKE EARTHLAND, WHERE WE COME FROM, BUT IT ISN'T QUITE.
EARTHLAND BRIMS WITH MAGIC...
MAGIC IS LIMITED HERE.
ONE DAY IT'LL DISAPPEAR.
MAGIC SO PUNY IS FIT ONLY TO BE BURNED LIKE GARBAGE!
HOOM
TOINK
BUYING AND SELLING MAGIC IS FORBIDDEN.
HELL, EVEN HAVING A MAGIC ITEM IS A CRIME.
IT'S A HUGE MAGIC CRYSTAL!
...BUT MAGIC HAS WITHERED IN EDOLAS.
IT TURNED INTO A HUGE PROBLEM...
ACTIVATE CODE ETD: OPERATION DESTROY ALL ANGELS!
NOT ONE HUMAN WILL ESCAPE!
YOU'LL ALL DIE HERE!
WITH THE ANIMA REVERSED, ALL THE MAGIC WILL FLOW OUT OF HERE AND INTO EARTHLAND.
IT IS I WHO DEFEATED THE MAGIC KING DRAGNEEL!!!!
HUZZAH
...BUT ONE WE SOLVED BY COMPLETELY ELIMINATING MAGICAL POWER FROM EDOLAS.

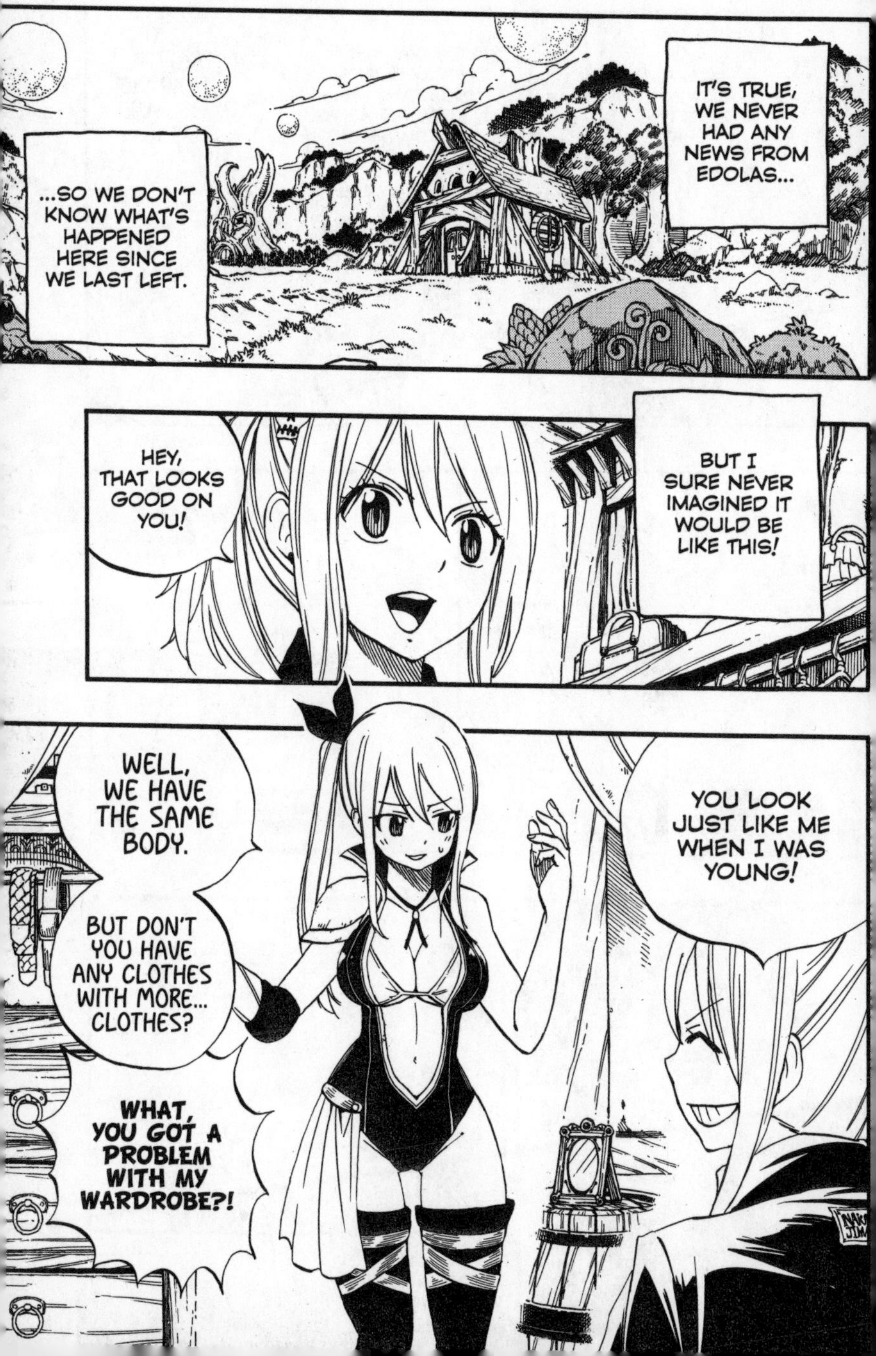
IT'S TRUE, WE NEVER HAD ANY NEWS FROM EDOLAS...
...SO WE DON'T KNOW WHAT'S HAPPENED HERE SINCE WE LAST LEFT.
BUT I SURE NEVER IMAGINED IT WOULD BE LIKE THIS!
HEY, THAT LOOKS GOOD ON YOU!
YOU LOOK JUST LIKE ME WHEN I WAS YOUNG!
WELL, WE HAVE THE SAME BODY.
BUT DON'T YOU HAVE ANY CLOTHES WITH MORE... CLOTHES?
WHAT, YOU GOT A PROBLEM WITH MY WARDROBE?!

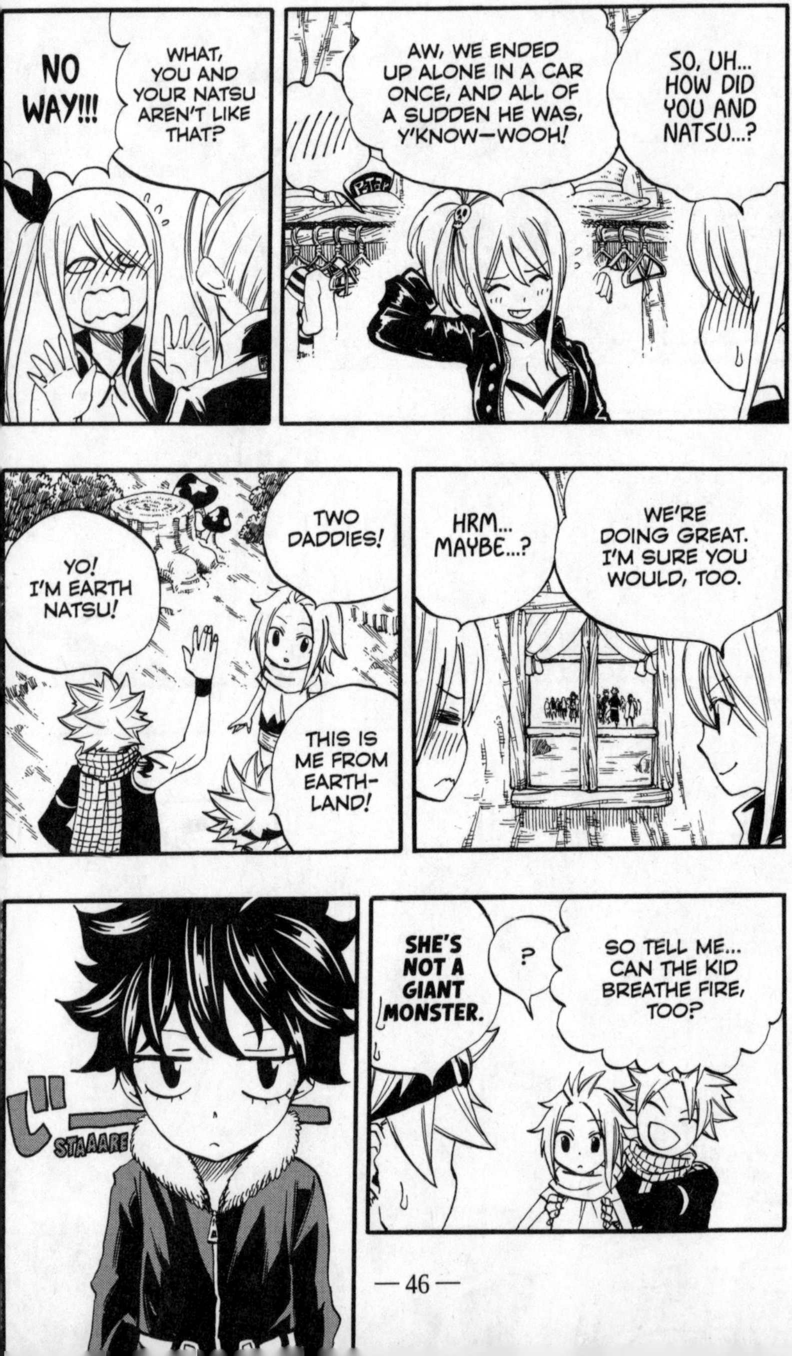
SO, UH... HOW DID YOU AND NATSU...?
AW, WE ENDED UP ALONE IN A CAR ONCE, AND ALL OF A SUDDEN HE WAS, Y'KNOW—WOOH!
WHAT, YOU AND YOUR NATSU AREN'T LIKE THAT?
NO WAY!!!
WE'RE DOING GREAT. I'M SURE YOU WOULD, TOO.
HRM... MAYBE...?
TWO DADDIES!
YO! I'M EARTH NATSU!
THIS IS ME FROM EARTH-LAND!
SO TELL ME... CAN THE KID BREATHE FIRE, TOO?
?
SHE'S NOT A GIANT MONSTER.
STAAARE

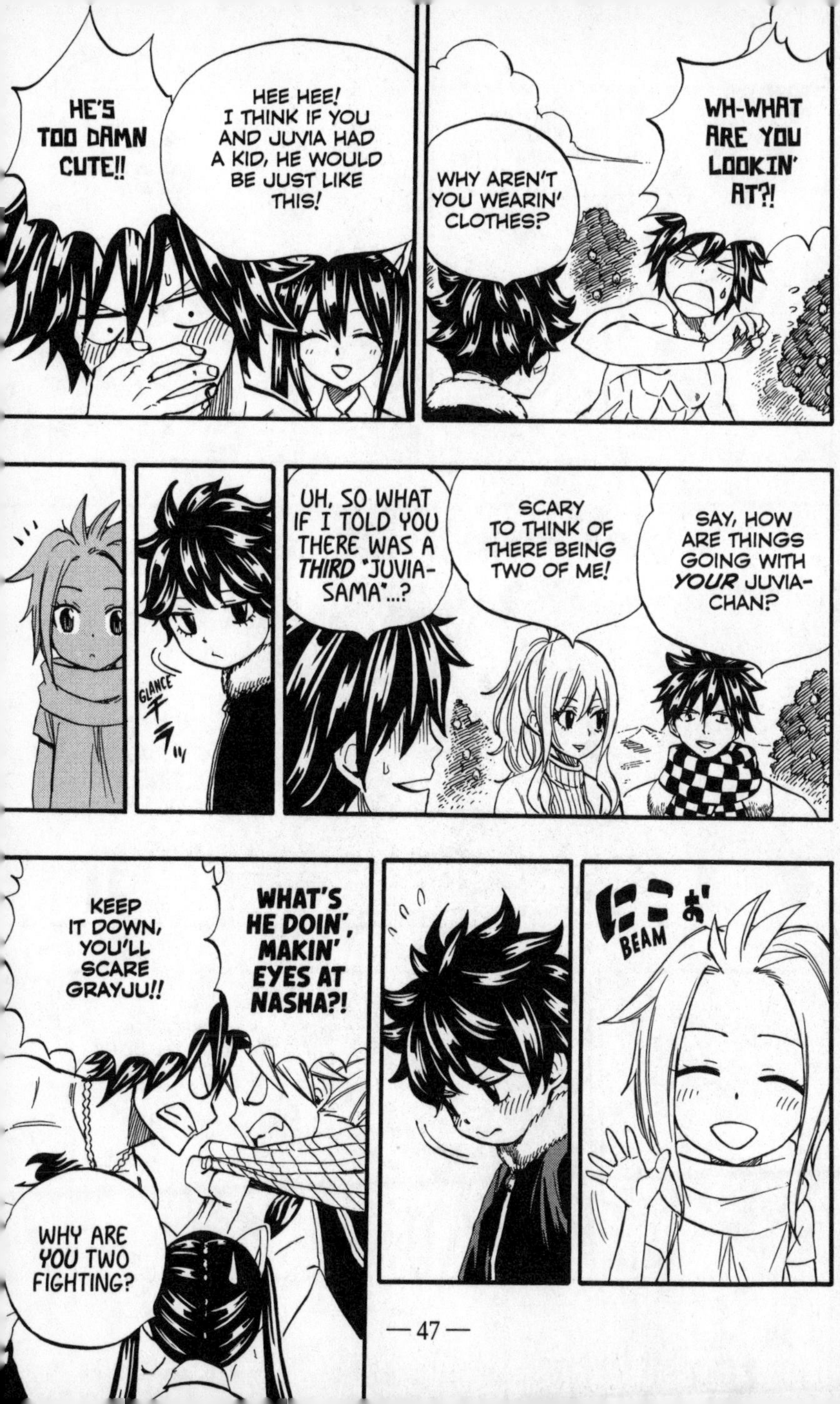
WH-WHAT ARE YOU LOOKIN' AT?!
WHY AREN'T YOU WEARIN' CLOTHES?
HEE HEE! I THINK IF YOU AND JUVIA HAD A KID, HE WOULD BE JUST LIKE THIS!
HE'S TOO DAMN CUTE!!
SAY, HOW ARE THINGS GOING WITH *YOUR* JUVIA-CHAN?
SCARY TO THINK OF THERE BEING TWO OF ME!
UH, SO WHAT IF I TOLD YOU THERE WAS A *THIRD* "JUVIA-SAMA"...?
GLANCE
BEAM
WHAT'S HE DOIN', MAKIN' EYES AT NASHA?!
KEEP IT DOWN, YOU'LL SCARE GRAYJU!!
WHY ARE *YOU* TWO FIGHTING?

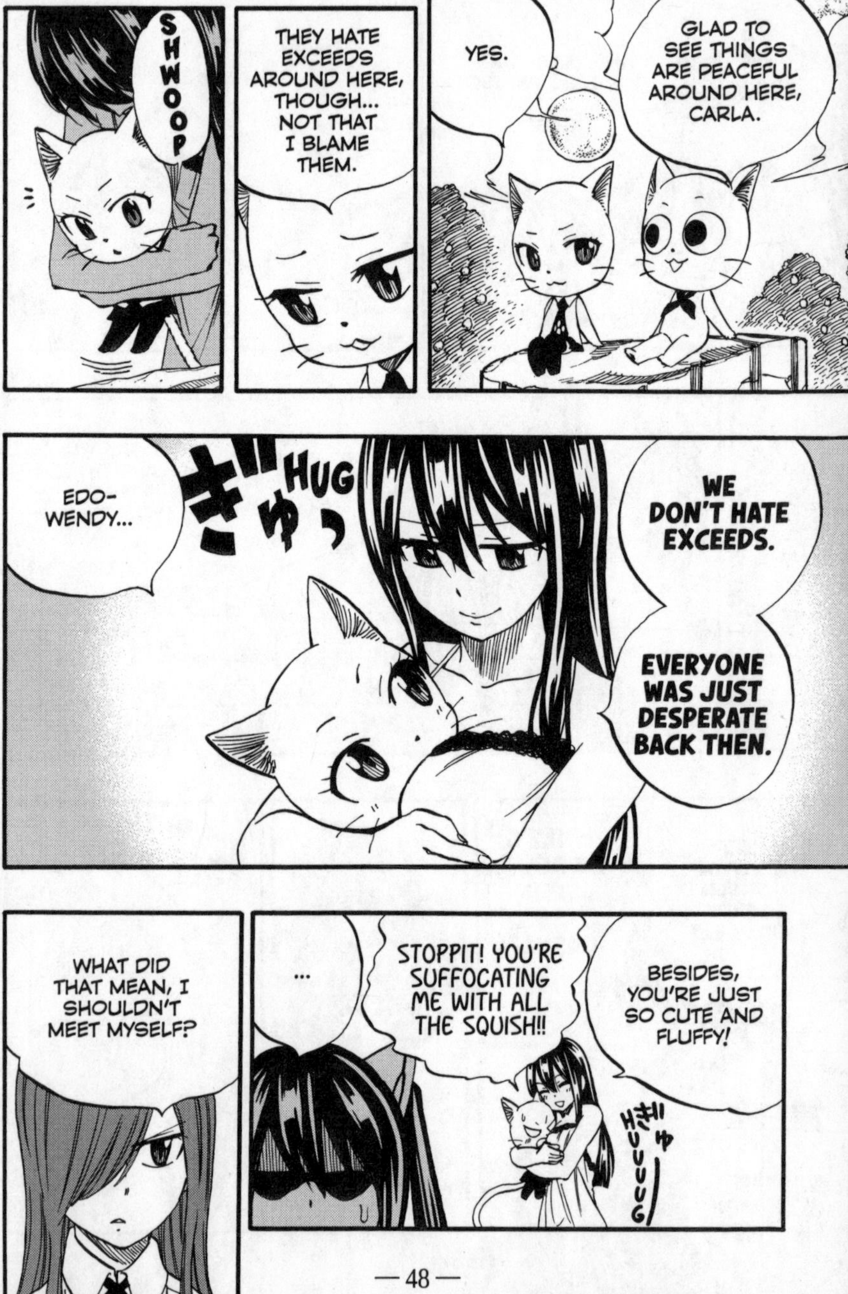
GLAD TO SEE THINGS ARE PEACEFUL AROUND HERE, CARLA.
YES.
THEY HATE EXCEEDS AROUND HERE, THOUGH... NOT THAT I BLAME THEM.
SHWOOP
WE DON'T HATE EXCEEDS.
EVERYONE WAS JUST DESPERATE BACK THEN.
HUG
EDO-WENDY...
BESIDES, YOU'RE JUST SO CUTE AND FLUFFY!
STOPPIT! YOU'RE SUFFOCATING ME WITH ALL THE SQUISH!!
...
HUUUUG
WHAT DID THAT MEAN, I SHOULDN'T MEET MYSELF?

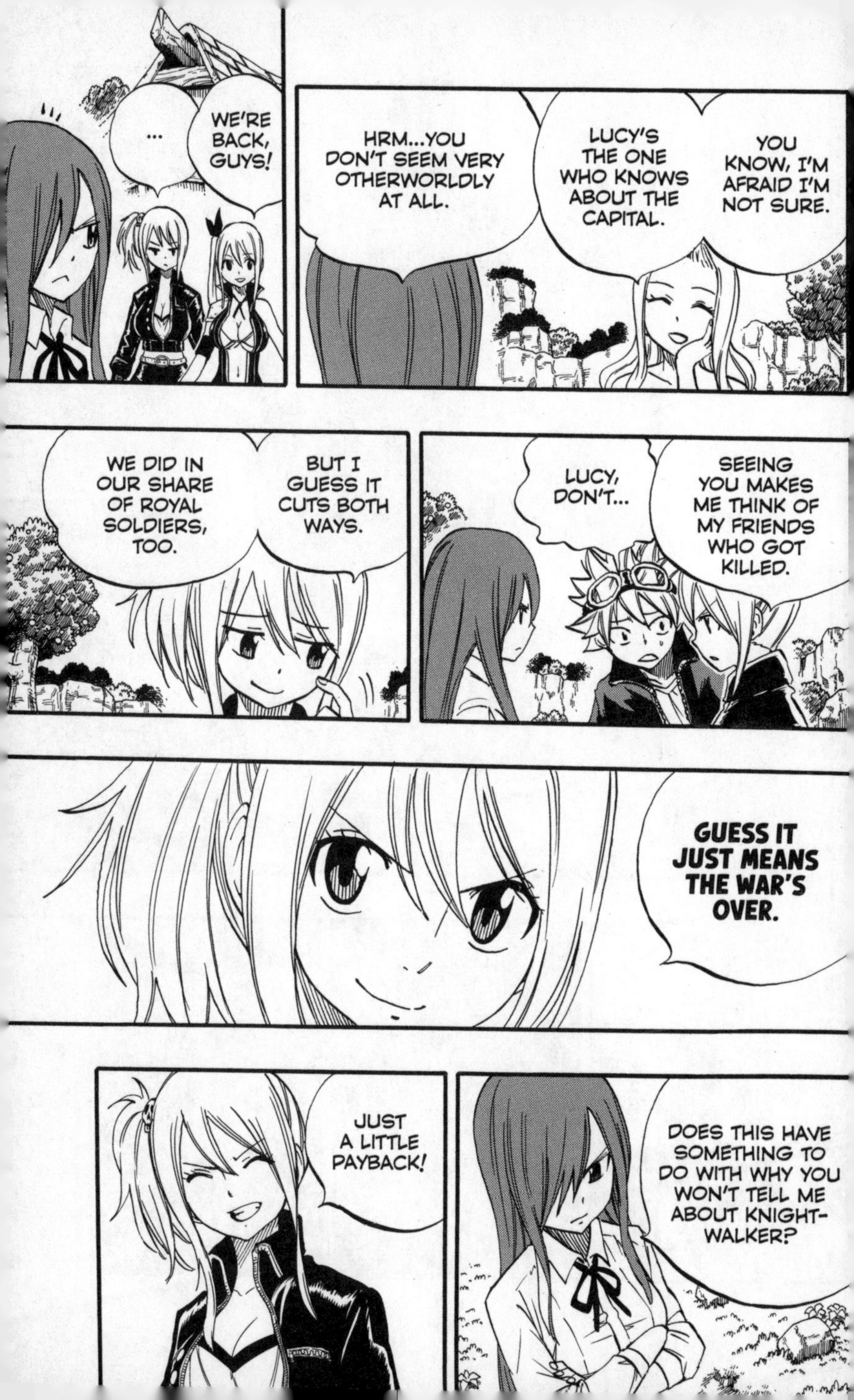
YOU KNOW, I'M AFRAID I'M NOT SURE.
LUCY'S THE ONE WHO KNOWS ABOUT THE CAPITAL.
HRM...YOU DON'T SEEM VERY OTHERWORLDLY AT ALL.
WE'RE BACK, GUYS!
...
SEEING YOU MAKES ME THINK OF MY FRIENDS WHO GOT KILLED.
LUCY, DON'T...
BUT I GUESS IT CUTS BOTH WAYS.
WE DID IN OUR SHARE OF ROYAL SOLDIERS, TOO.
GUESS IT JUST MEANS THE WAR'S OVER.
DOES THIS HAVE SOMETHING TO DO WITH WHY YOU WON'T TELL ME ABOUT KNIGHT-WALKER?
JUST A LITTLE PAYBACK!

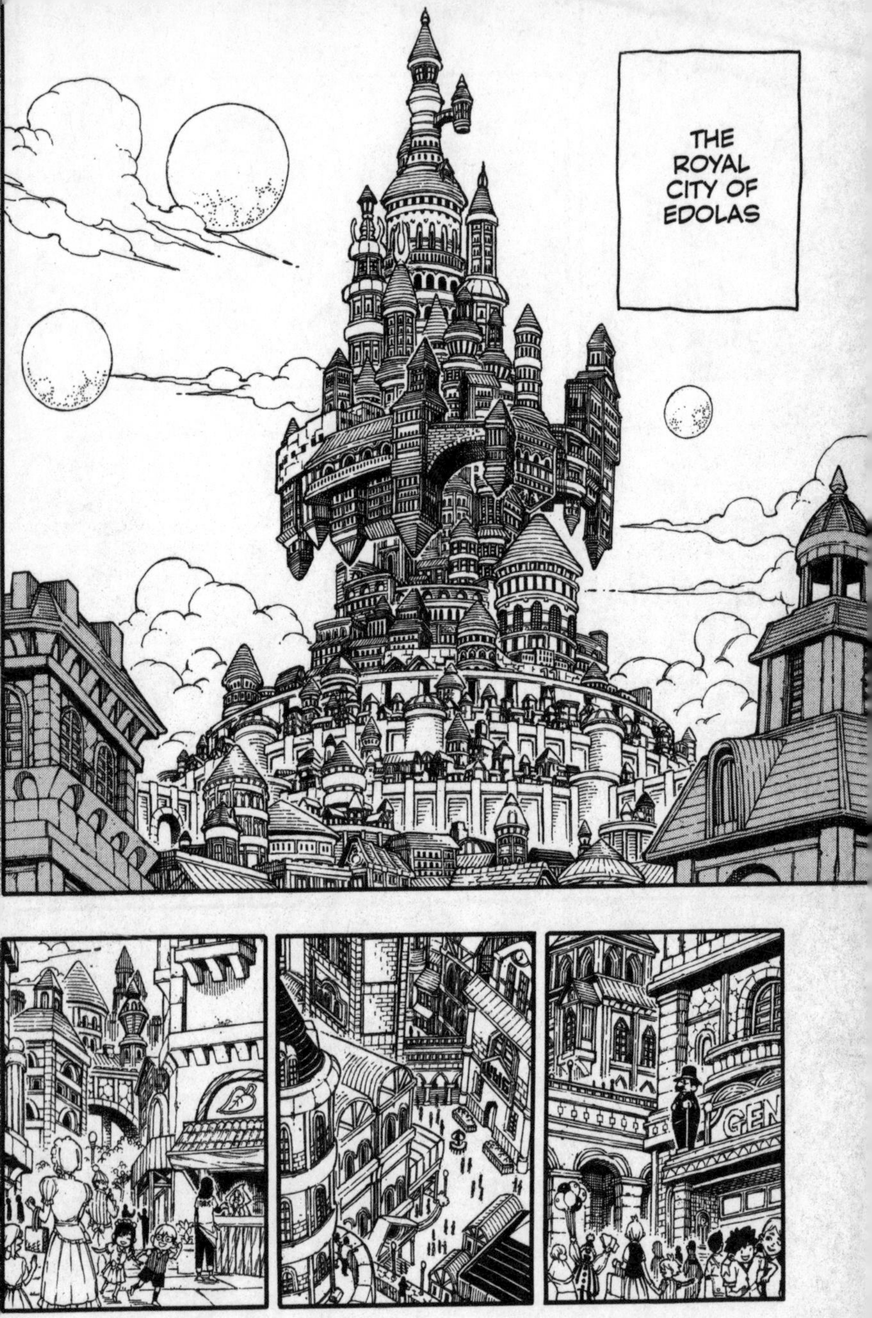
THE ROYAL CITY OF EDOLAS
GEN

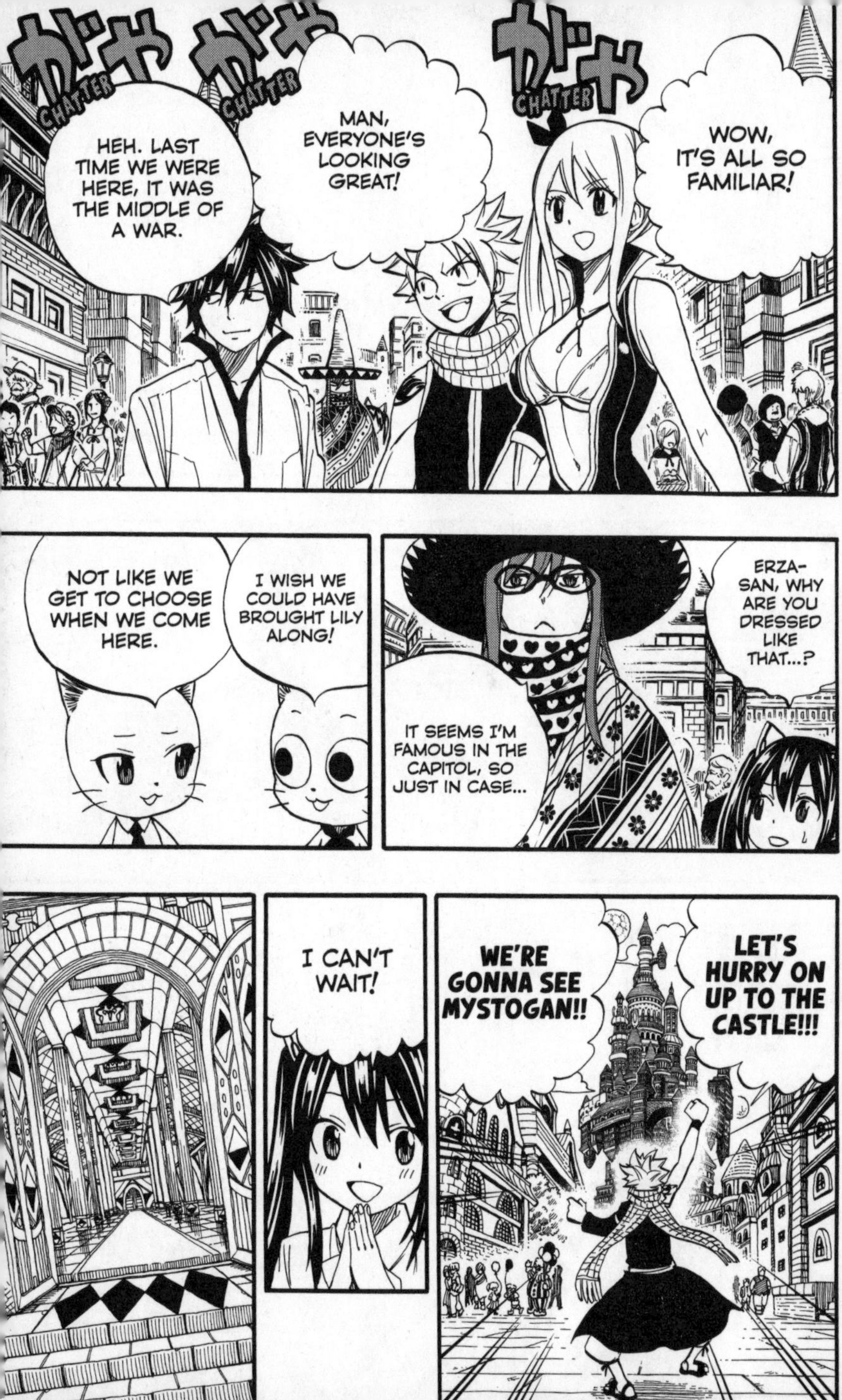
がや CHATTER
WOW, IT'S ALL SO FAMILIAR!
がや CHATTER
MAN, EVERYONE'S LOOKING GREAT!
がや CHATTER
HEH. LAST TIME WE WERE HERE, IT WAS THE MIDDLE OF A WAR.
ERZA-SAN, WHY ARE YOU DRESSED LIKE THAT...?
IT SEEMS I'M FAMOUS IN THE CAPITOL, SO JUST IN CASE...
I WISH WE COULD HAVE BROUGHT LILY ALONG!
NOT LIKE WE GET TO CHOOSE WHEN WE COME HERE.
LET'S HURRY ON UP TO THE CASTLE!!!
WE'RE GONNA SEE MYSTOGAN!!
I CAN'T WAIT!

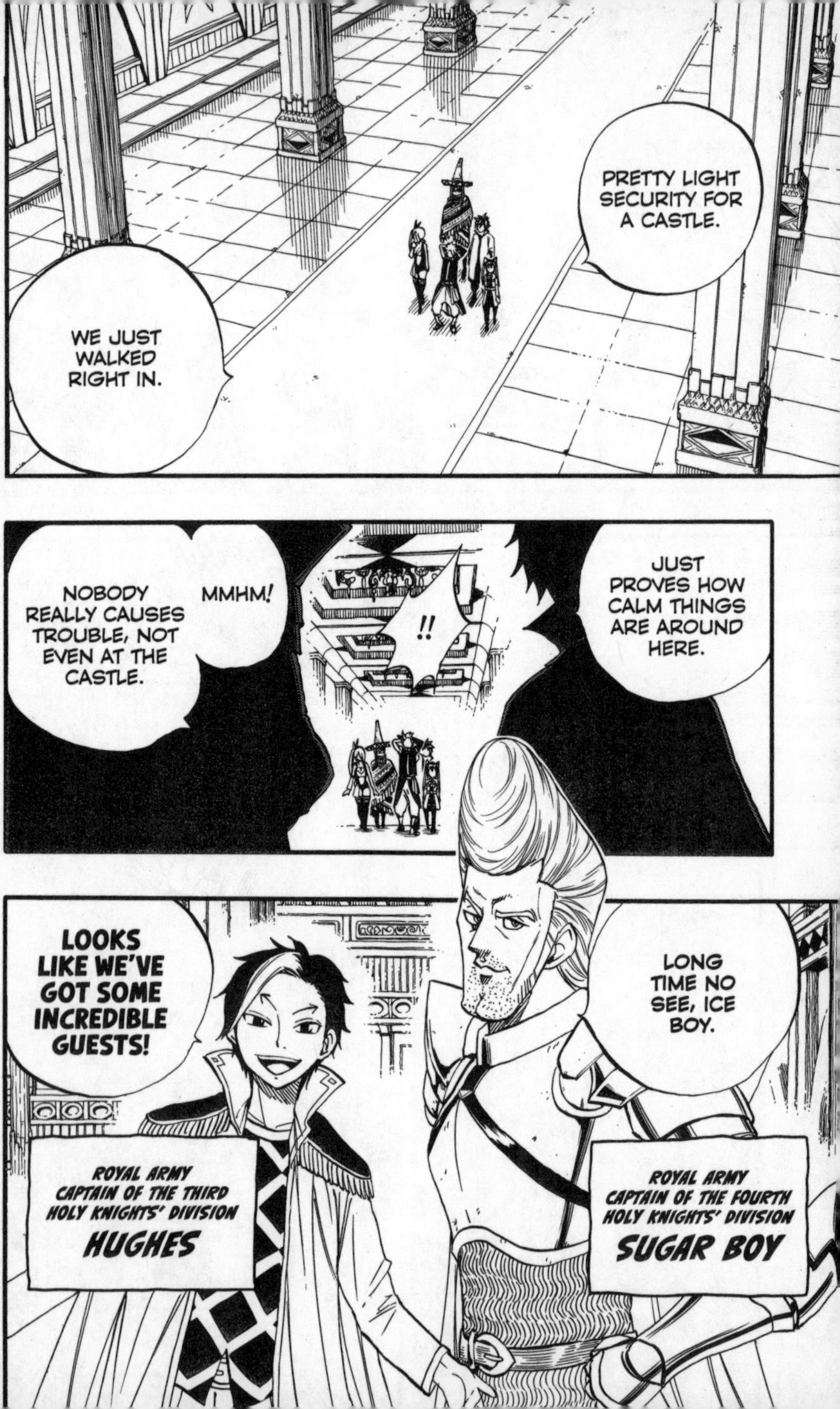
PRETTY LIGHT SECURITY FOR A CASTLE.
WE JUST WALKED RIGHT IN.
JUST PROVES HOW CALM THINGS ARE AROUND HERE.
MMHM!
NOBODY REALLY CAUSES TROUBLE, NOT EVEN AT THE CASTLE.
!!
LONG TIME NO SEE, ICE BOY.
LOOKS LIKE WE'VE GOT SOME INCREDIBLE GUESTS!
ROYAL ARMY CAPTAIN OF THE FOURTH HOLY KNIGHTS' DIVISION SUGAR BOY
ROYAL ARMY CAPTAIN OF THE THIRD HOLY KNIGHTS' DIVISION HUGHES

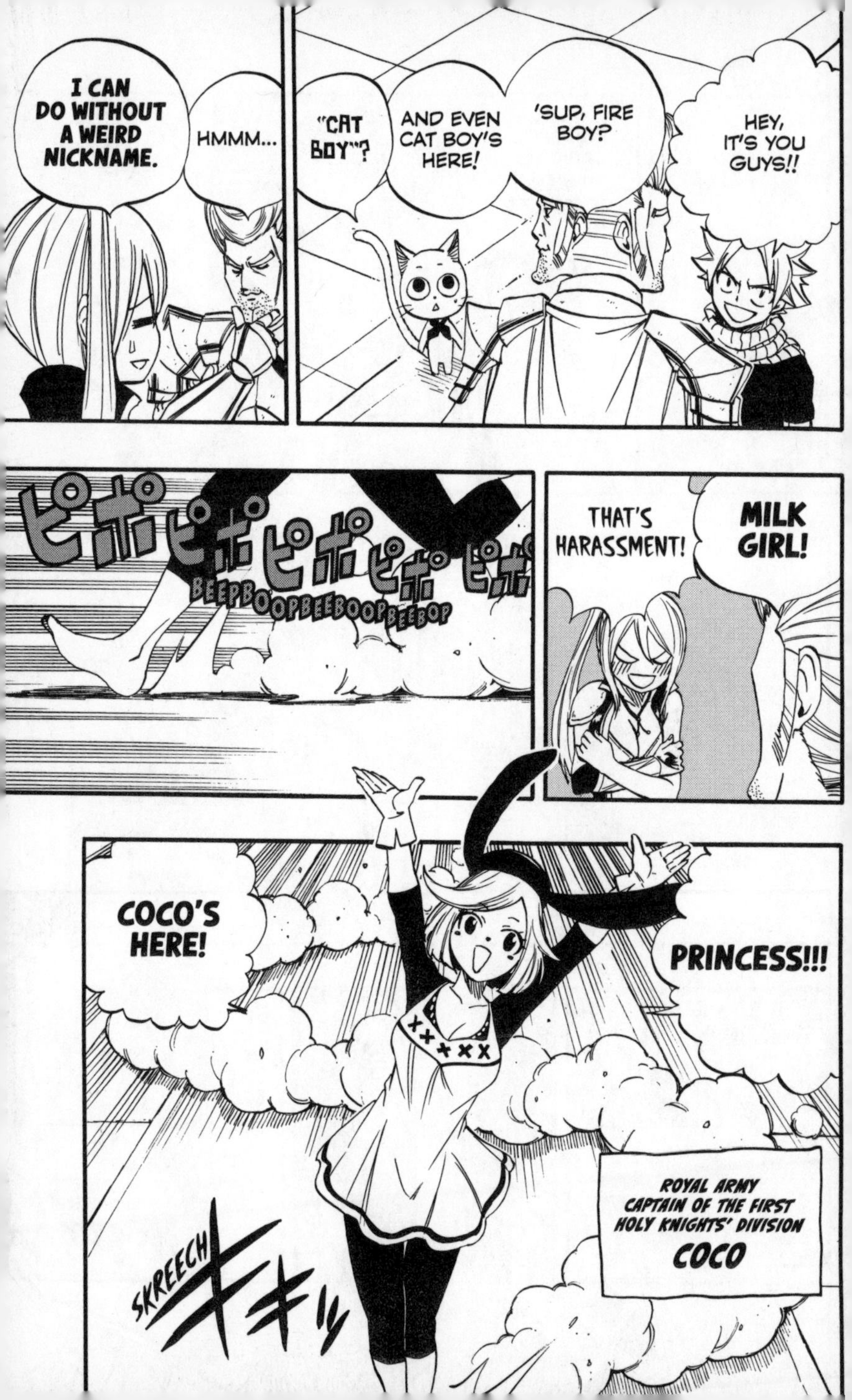
HEY, IT'S YOU GUYS!!
'SUP, FIRE BOY?
AND EVEN CAT BOY'S HERE!
"CAT BOY"?
HMMM...
I CAN DO WITHOUT A WEIRD NICKNAME.
MILK GIRL!
THAT'S HARASSMENT!
BEEPBOOPBEEBOOPBEEBOP
PRINCESS!!!
COCO'S HERE!
ROYAL ARMY CAPTAIN OF THE FIRST HOLY KNIGHTS' DIVISION COCO
SKREECH

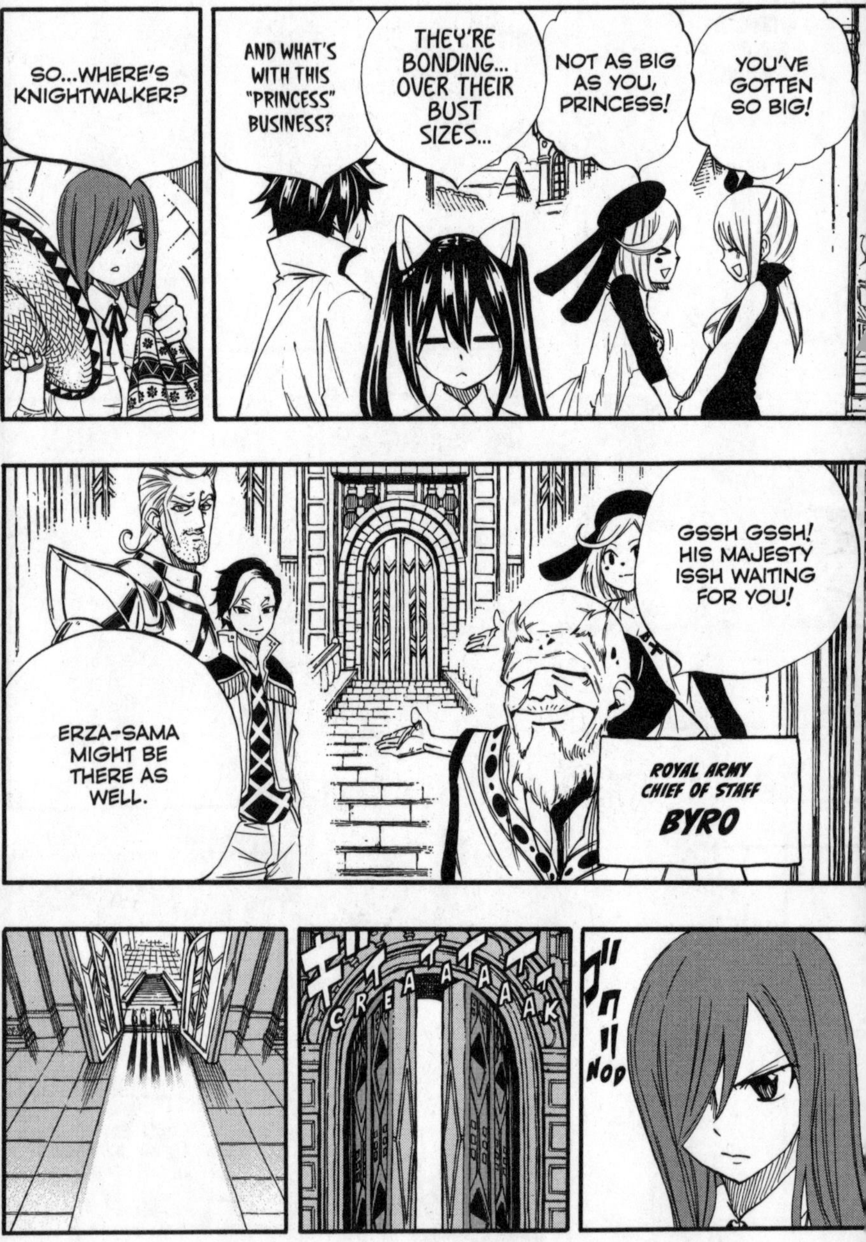
YOU'VE GOTTEN SO BIG!
NOT AS BIG AS YOU, PRINCESS!
THEY'RE BONDING... OVER THEIR BUST SIZES...
AND WHAT'S WITH THIS "PRINCESS" BUSINESS?
SO...WHERE'S KNIGHTWALKER?
GSSH GSSH! HIS MAJESTY ISSH WAITING FOR YOU!
ROYAL ARMY CHIEF OF STAFF BYRO
ERZA-SAMA MIGHT BE THERE AS WELL.
NOD
CREATAAAK

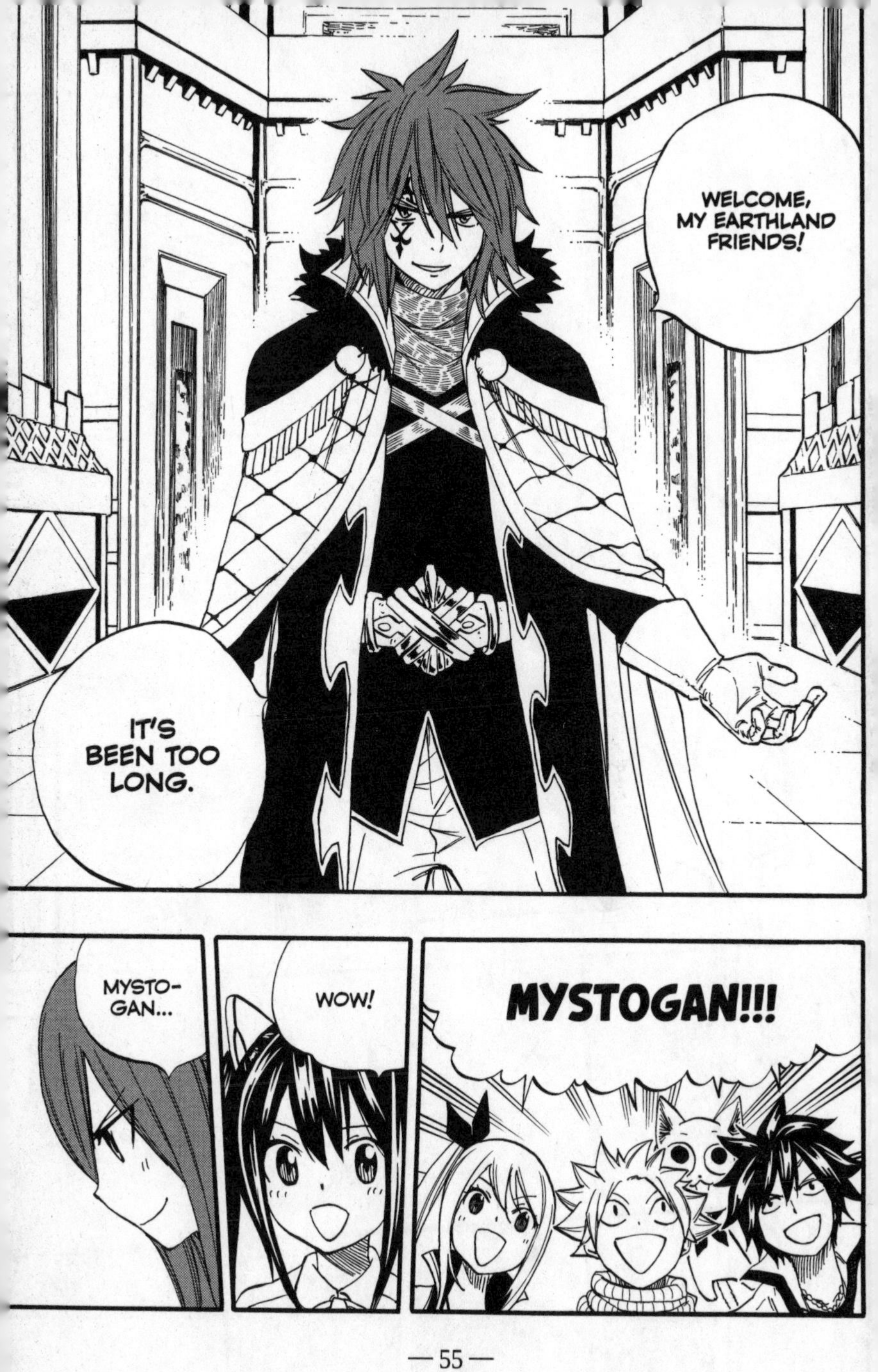
WELCOME, MY EARTHLAND FRIENDS!
IT'S BEEN TOO LONG.
MYSTOGAN!!!
WOW!
MYSTO-GAN...

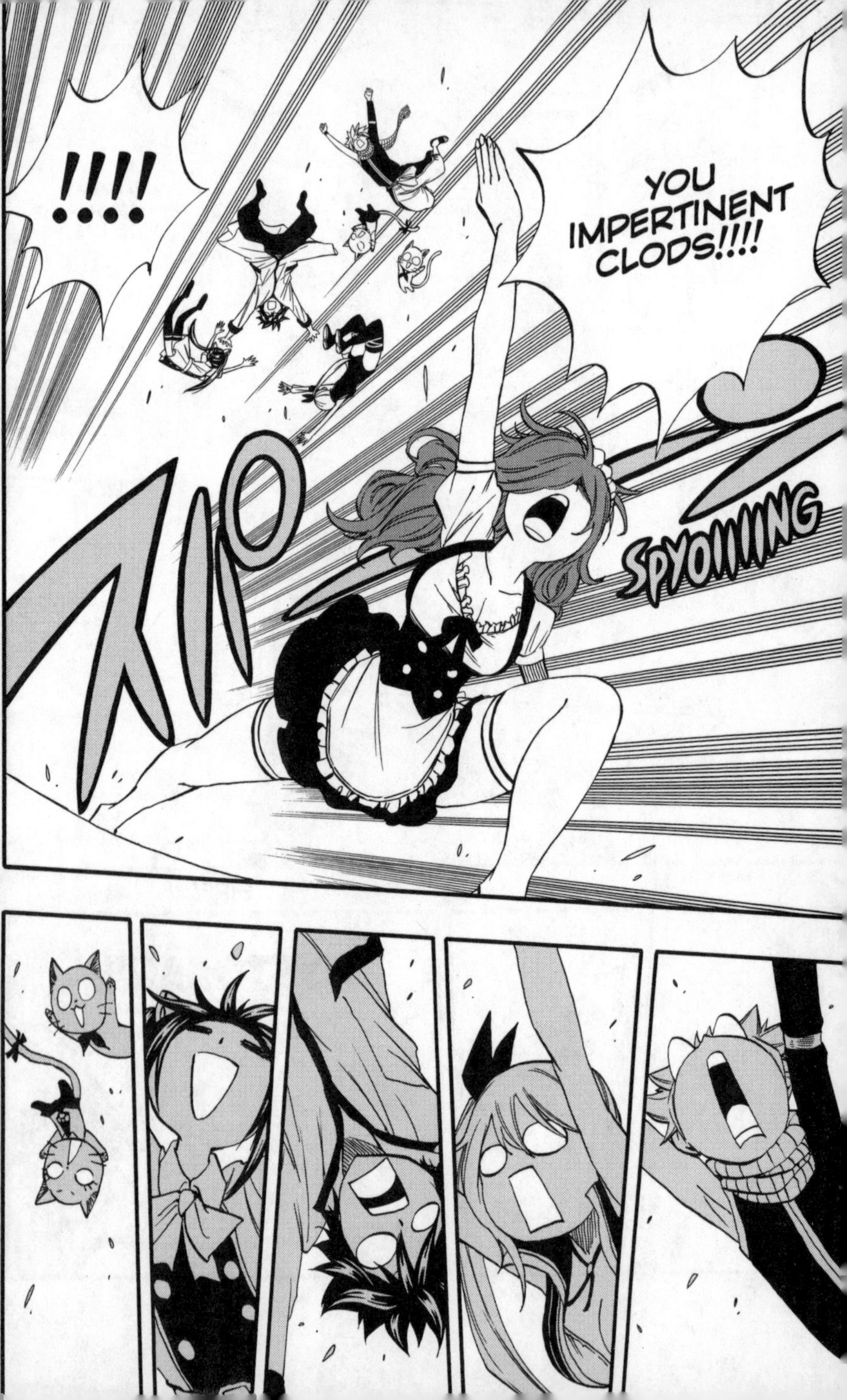
YOU IMPERTINENT CLODS!!!!
SPYOIIIING
!!!!
ZIP

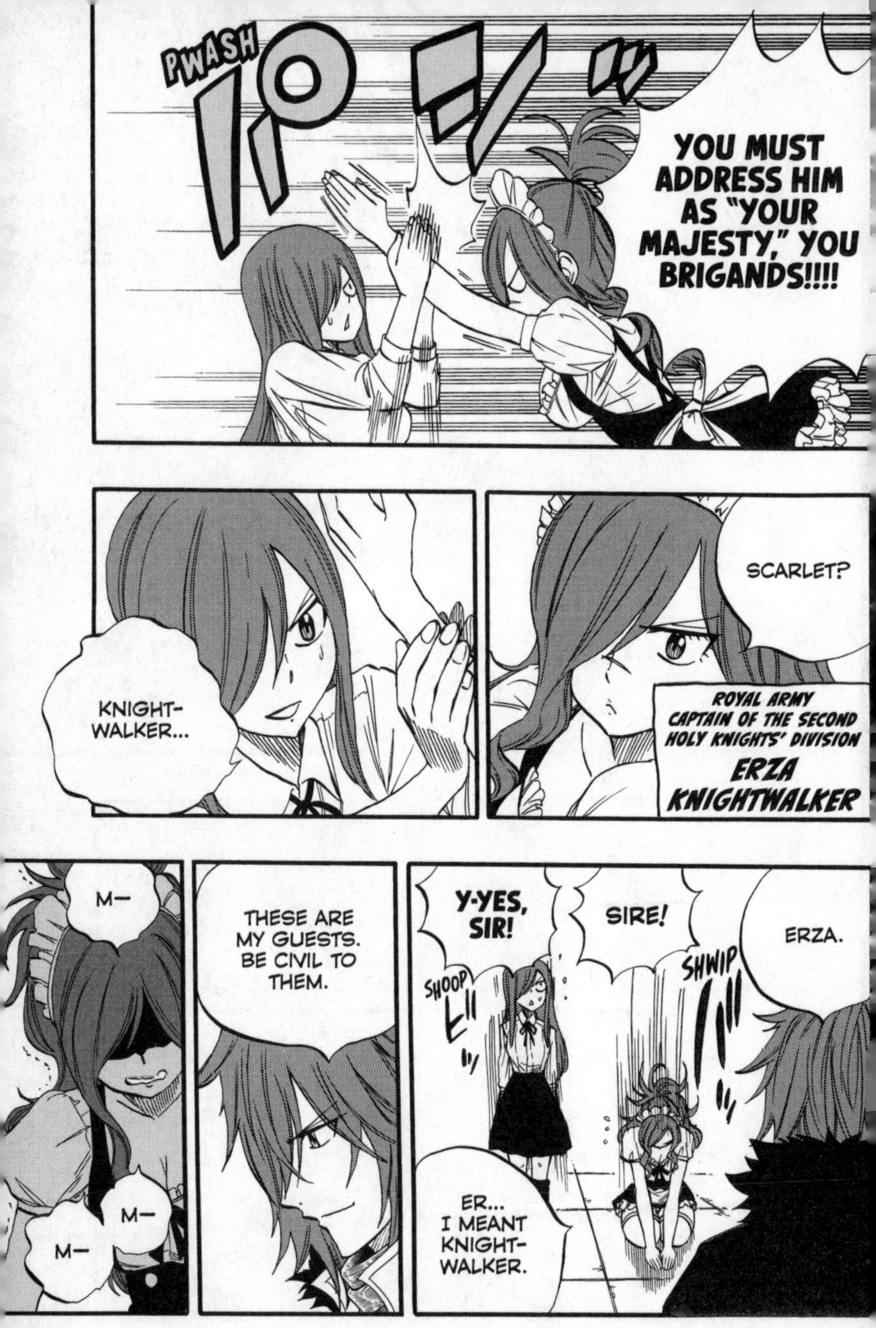
YOU MUST ADDRESS HIM AS "YOUR MAJESTY," YOU BRIGANDS!!!!
PWASH
SCARLET?
ROYAL ARMY
CAPTAIN OF THE SECOND HOLY KNIGHTS' DIVISION
ERZA KNIGHTWALKER
KNIGHT-WALKER...
ERZA.
SHWIP
SIRE!
Y-YES, SIR!
SHOOP
ER... I MEANT KNIGHT-WALKER.
THESE ARE MY GUESTS. BE CIVIL TO THEM.
M—
M—
M—

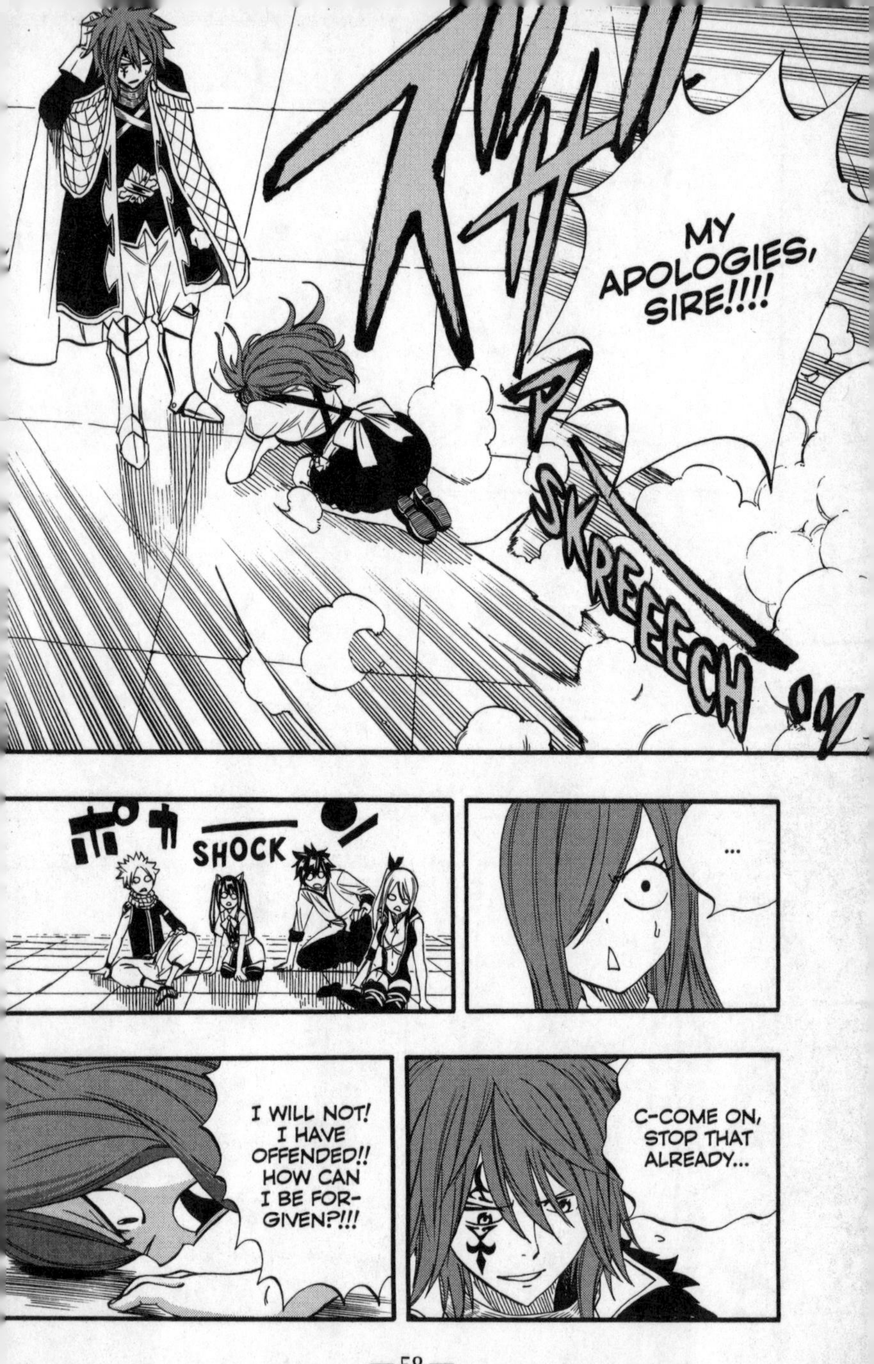
MY APOLOGIES, SIRE!!!!
SKREEECH
...
ポカ
SHOCK
C-COME ON, STOP THAT ALREADY...
I WILL NOT! I HAVE OFFENDED!! HOW CAN I BE FOR-GIVEN?!!!

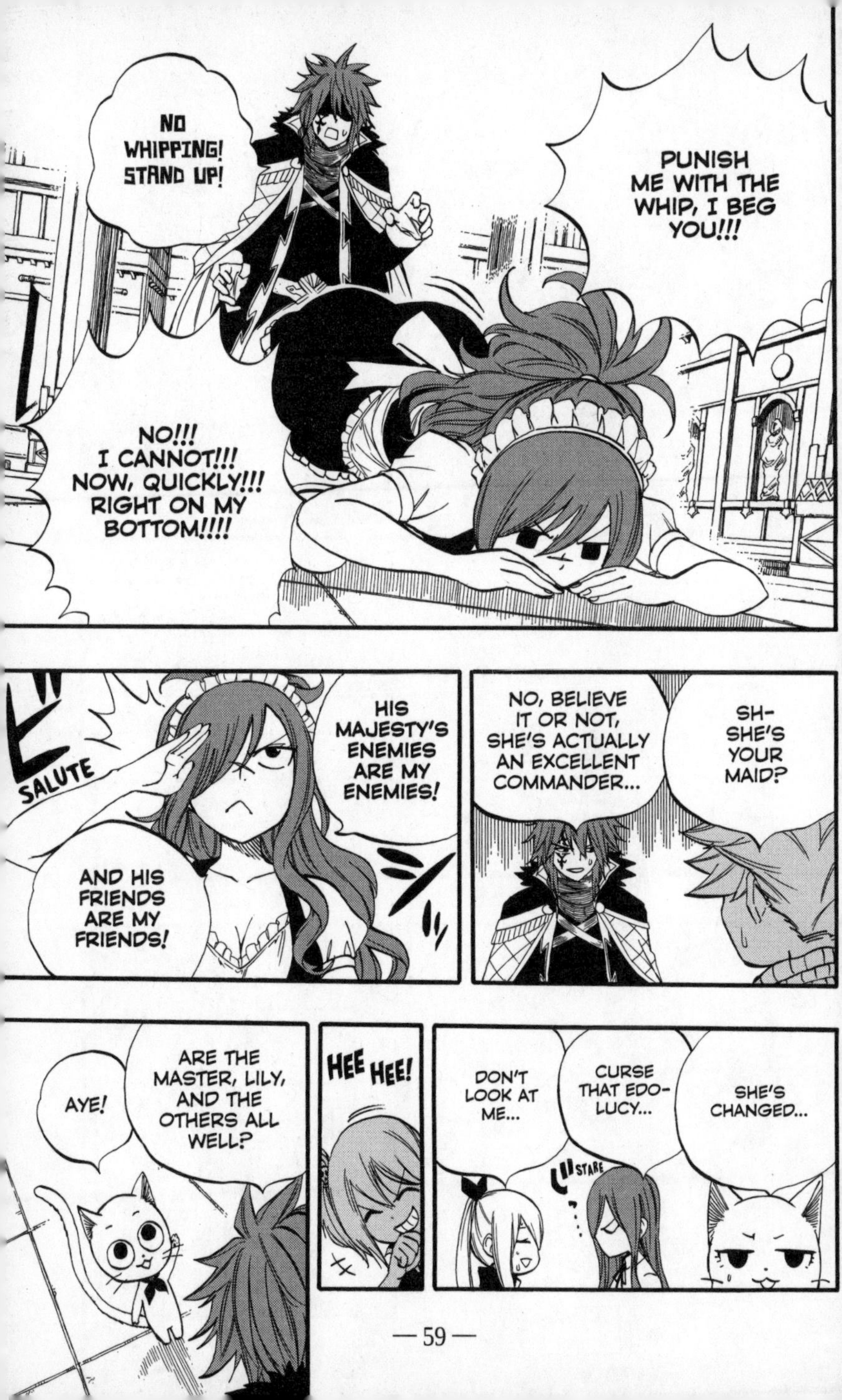
PUNISH ME WITH THE WHIP, I BEG YOU!!!
NO WHIPPING! STAND UP!
NO!!! I CANNOT!!! NOW, QUICKLY!!! RIGHT ON MY BOTTOM!!!!
SH- SHE'S YOUR MAID?
NO, BELIEVE IT OR NOT, SHE'S ACTUALLY AN EXCELLENT COMMANDER...
HIS MAJESTY'S ENEMIES ARE MY ENEMIES!
SALUTE
AND HIS FRIENDS ARE MY FRIENDS!
SHE'S CHANGED...
CURSE THAT EDO-LUCY...
DON'T LOOK AT ME...
STARE
HEE HEE!
ARE THE MASTER, LILY, AND THE OTHERS ALL WELL?
AYE!

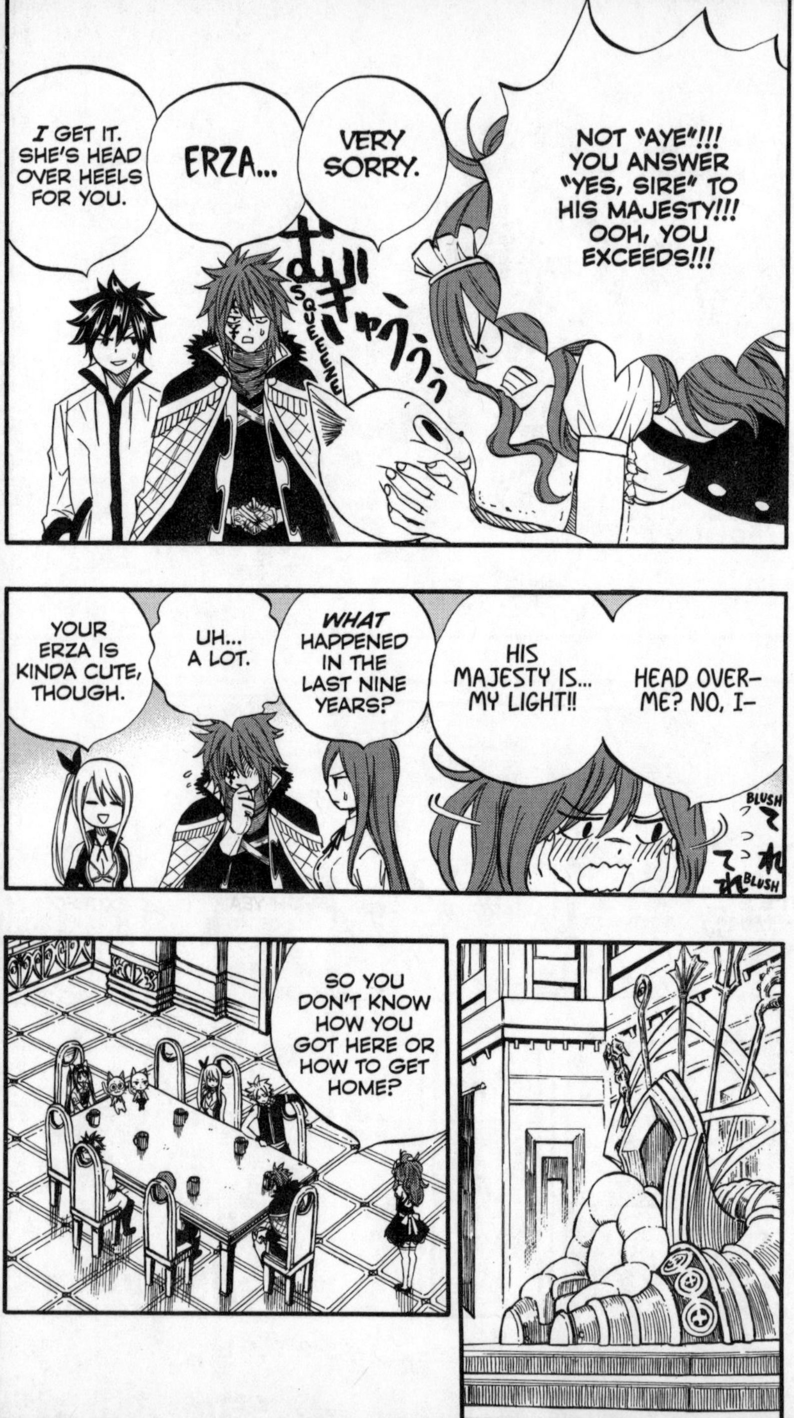
NOT "AYE"!!! YOU ANSWER "YES, SIRE" TO HIS MAJESTY!!! OOH, YOU EXCEEDS!!!
VERY SORRY.
SQUEEEEZE
ERZA...
I GET IT. SHE'S HEAD OVER HEELS FOR YOU.
HEAD OVER-ME? NO, I-
BLUSH
BLUSH
HIS MAJESTY IS... MY LIGHT!!
WHAT HAPPENED IN THE LAST NINE YEARS?
UH... A LOT.
YOUR ERZA IS KINDA CUTE, THOUGH.
SO YOU DON'T KNOW HOW YOU GOT HERE OR HOW TO GET HOME?

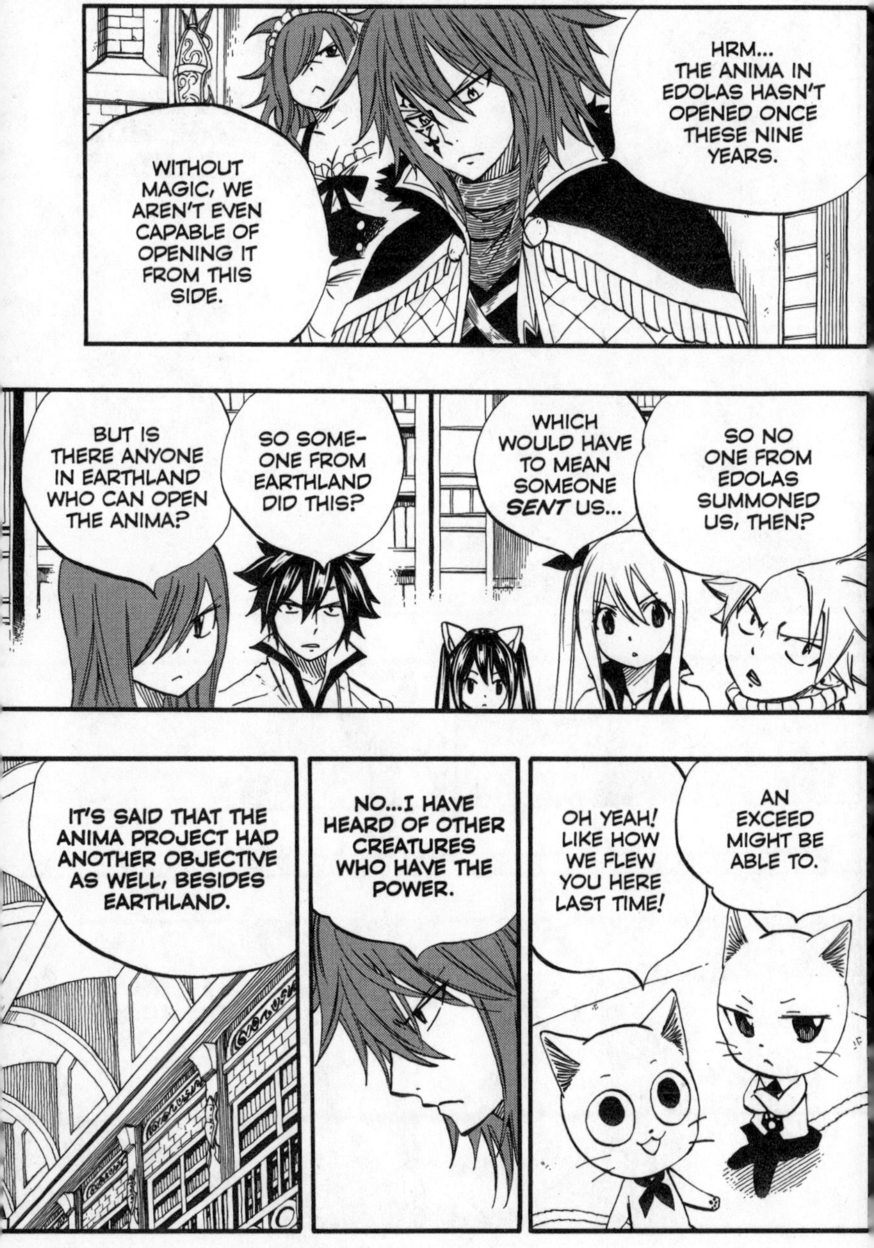
HRM... THE ANIMA IN EDOLAS HASN'T OPENED ONCE THESE NINE YEARS.
WITHOUT MAGIC, WE AREN'T EVEN CAPABLE OF OPENING IT FROM THIS SIDE.
SO NO ONE FROM EDOLAS SUMMONED US, THEN?
WHICH WOULD HAVE TO MEAN SOMEONE *SENT* US...
SO SOME-ONE FROM EARTHLAND DID THIS?
BUT IS THERE ANYONE IN EARTHLAND WHO CAN OPEN THE ANIMA?
AN EXCEED MIGHT BE ABLE TO.
OH YEAH! LIKE HOW WE FLEW YOU HERE LAST TIME!
NO...I HAVE HEARD OF OTHER CREATURES WHO HAVE THE POWER.
IT'S SAID THAT THE ANIMA PROJECT HAD ANOTHER OBJECTIVE AS WELL, BESIDES EARTHLAND.

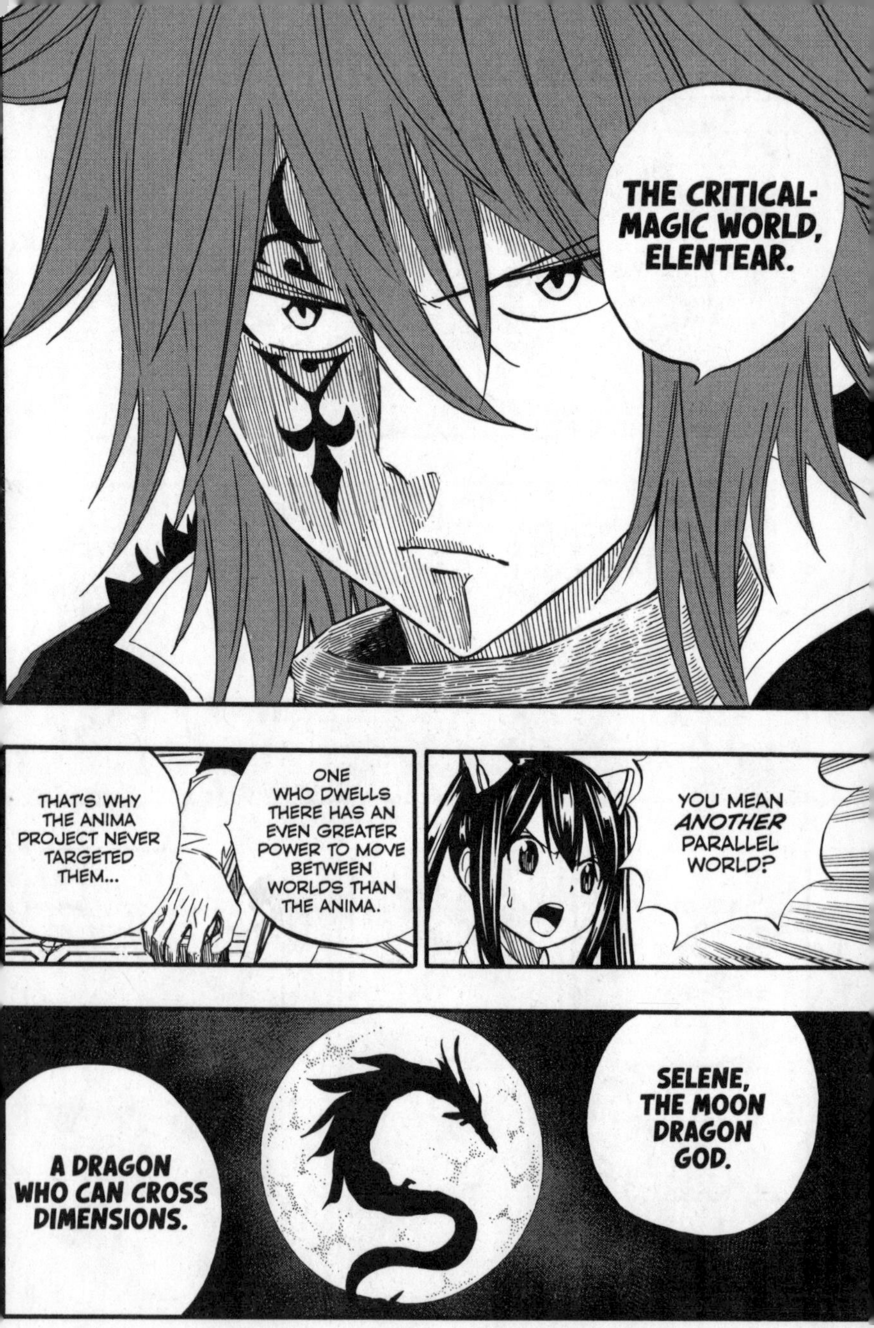
THE CRITICAL-MAGIC WORLD, ELENTEAR.
YOU MEAN *ANOTHER* PARALLEL WORLD?
ONE WHO DWELLS THERE HAS AN EVEN GREATER POWER TO MOVE BETWEEN WORLDS THAN THE ANIMA.
THAT'S WHY THE ANIMA PROJECT NEVER TARGETED THEM...
SELENE, THE MOON DRAGON GOD.
A DRAGON WHO CAN CROSS DIMENSIONS.

FAIRY TAIL
100 YEARS QUEST

Chapter 67: Aqua Aera

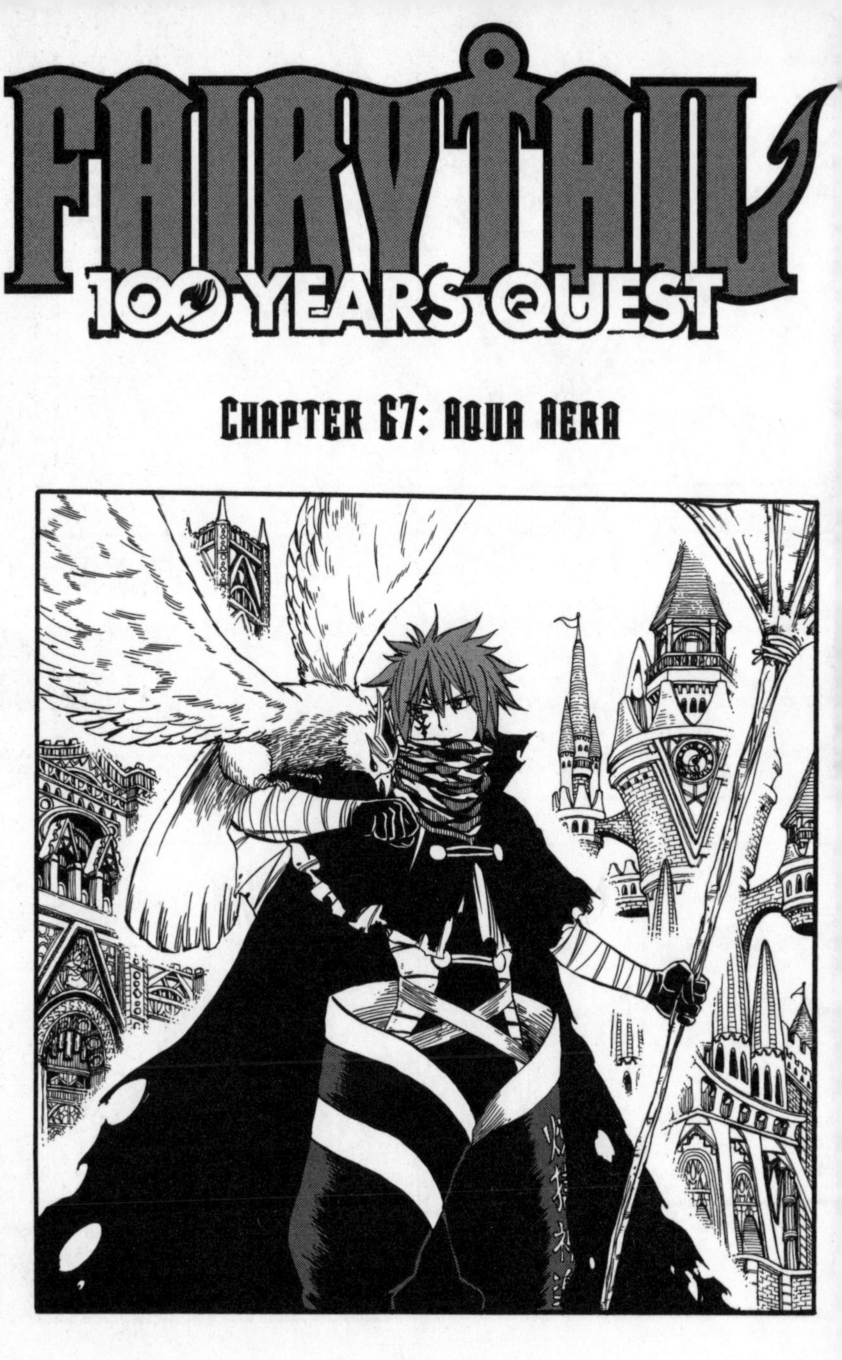

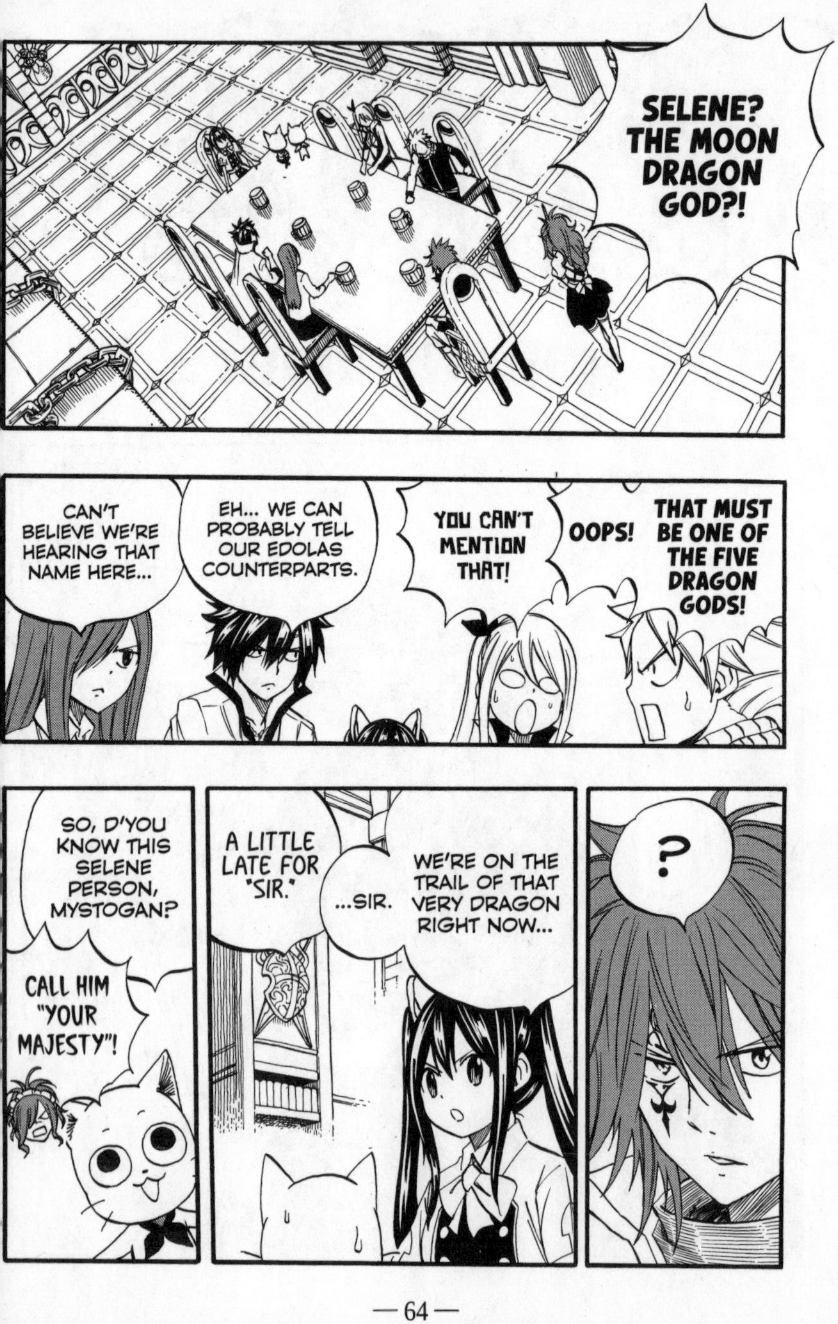
SELENE? THE MOON DRAGON GOD?!
THAT MUST BE ONE OF THE FIVE DRAGON GODS!
OOPS!
YOU CAN'T MENTION THAT!
EH... WE CAN PROBABLY TELL OUR EDOLAS COUNTERPARTS.
CAN'T BELIEVE WE'RE HEARING THAT NAME HERE...
?
WE'RE ON THE TRAIL OF THAT VERY DRAGON RIGHT NOW...
...SIR.
A LITTLE LATE FOR "SIR."
SO, D'YOU KNOW THIS SELENE PERSON, MYSTOGAN?
CALL HIM "YOUR MAJESTY"!

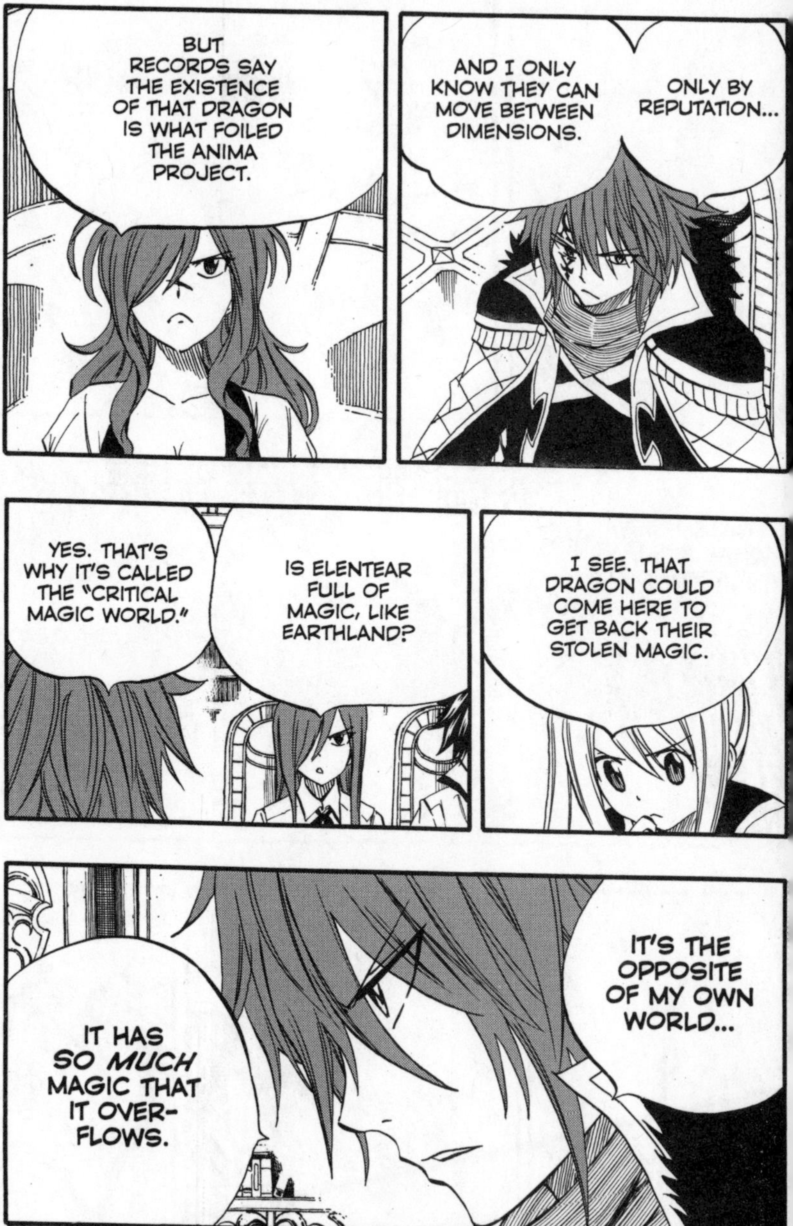
AND I ONLY KNOW THEY CAN MOVE BETWEEN DIMENSIONS.
ONLY BY REPUTATION...
BUT RECORDS SAY THE EXISTENCE OF THAT DRAGON IS WHAT FOILED THE ANIMA PROJECT.
I SEE. THAT DRAGON COULD COME HERE TO GET BACK THEIR STOLEN MAGIC.
IS ELENTEAR FULL OF MAGIC, LIKE EARTHLAND?
YES. THAT'S WHY IT'S CALLED THE "CRITICAL MAGIC WORLD."
IT'S THE OPPOSITE OF MY OWN WORLD...
IT HAS *SO MUCH* MAGIC THAT IT OVER-FLOWS.

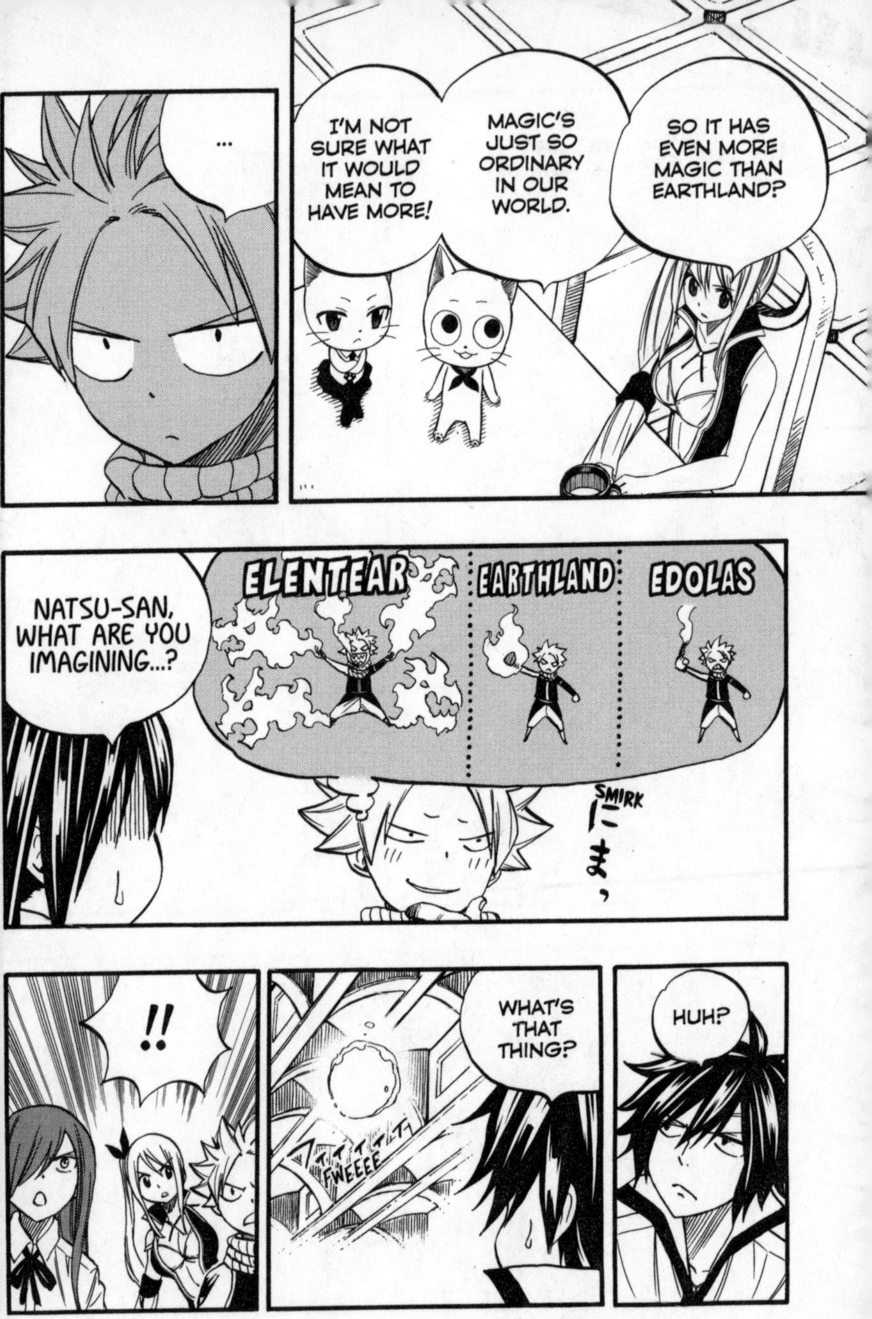
SO IT HAS EVEN MORE MAGIC THAN EARTHLAND?
MAGIC'S JUST SO ORDINARY IN OUR WORLD.
I'M NOT SURE WHAT IT WOULD MEAN TO HAVE MORE!
...
...
EDOLAS
EARTHLAND
ELENTEAR
SMIRK
NATSU-SAN, WHAT ARE YOU IMAGINING...?
HUH?
WHAT'S THAT THING?
FWEEEE
!!

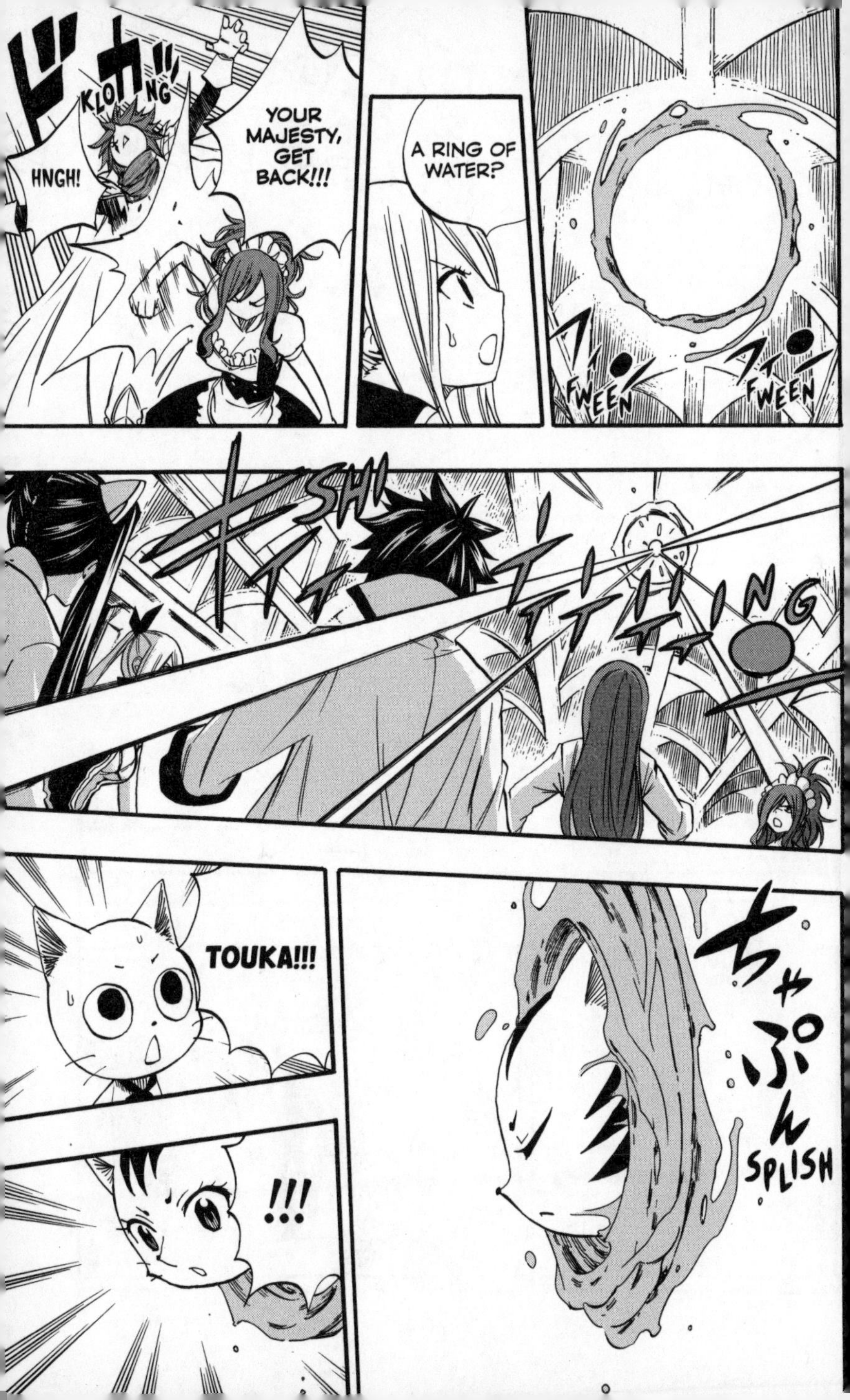
FWEEN
FWEEN
A RING OF WATER?
YOUR MAJESTY, GET BACK!!!
ドカ!!!
KLONG
HNGH!
SHIIIIING
ちゃぷん
SPLISH
TOUKA!!!
!!!

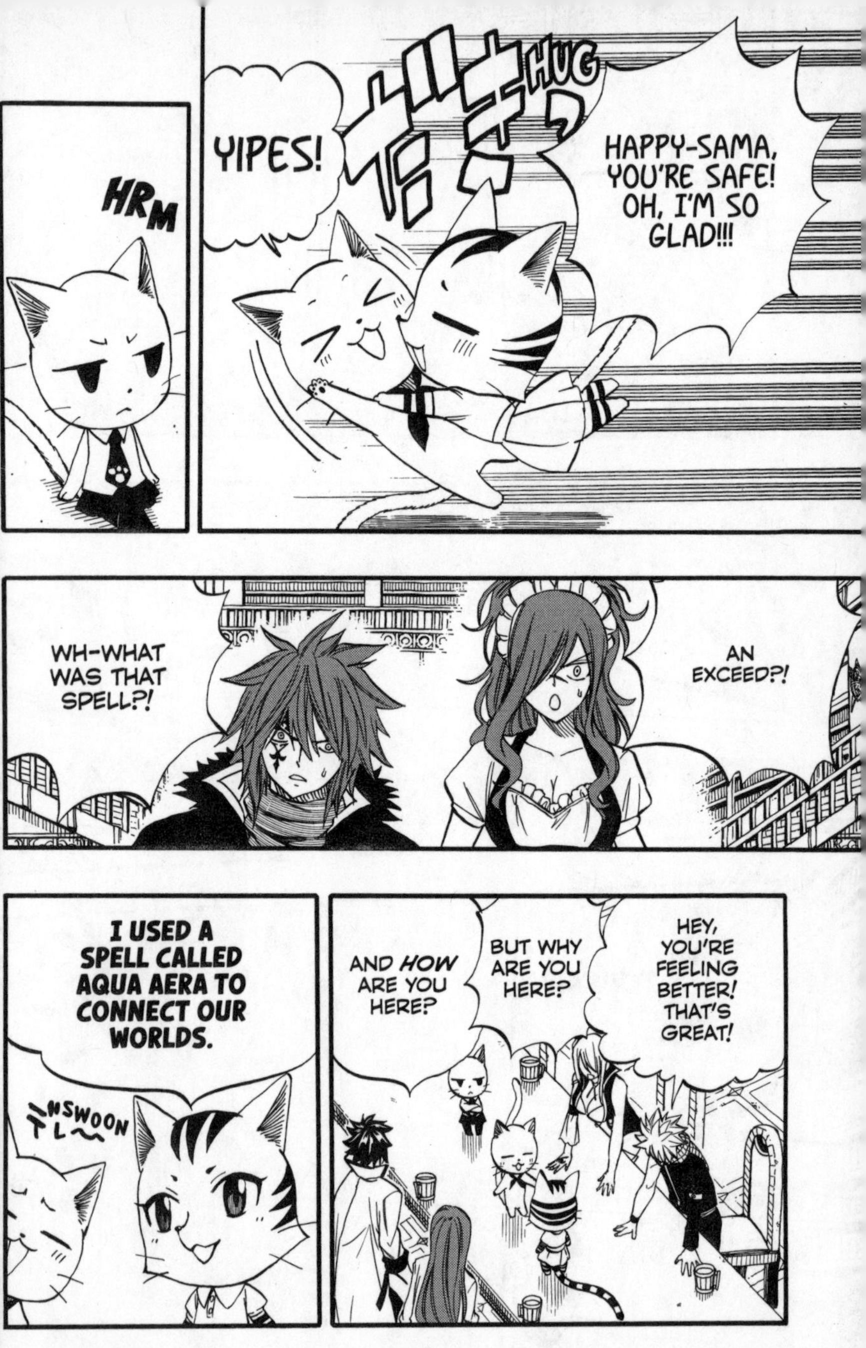
HUG
HAPPY-SAMA, YOU'RE SAFE! OH, I'M SO GLAD!!!
YIPES!
HRM
AN EXCEED?!
WH-WHAT WAS THAT SPELL?!
HEY, YOU'RE FEELING BETTER! THAT'S GREAT!
BUT WHY ARE YOU HERE?
AND *HOW* ARE YOU HERE?
I USED A SPELL CALLED AQUA AERA TO CONNECT OUR WORLDS.
SWOON

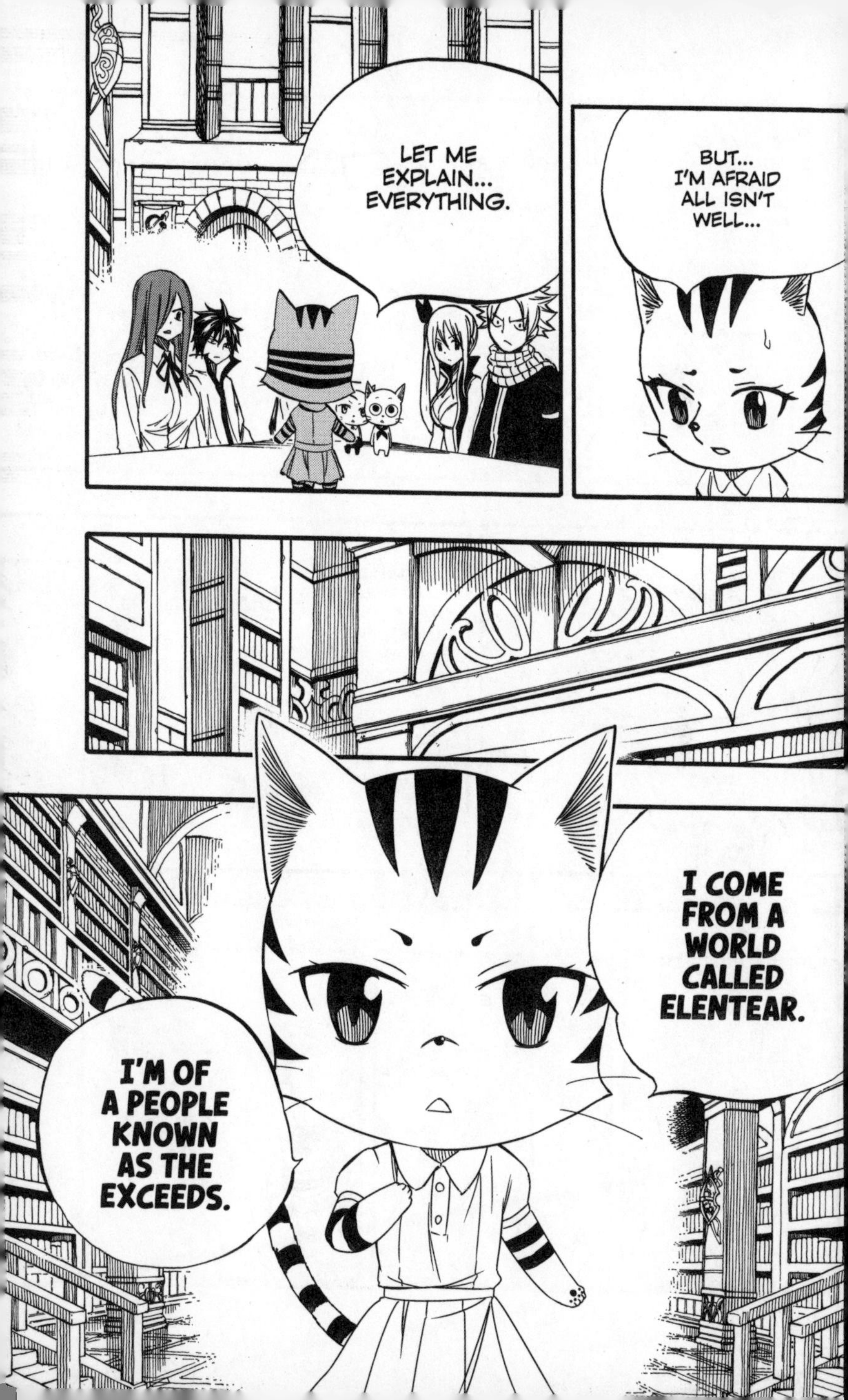
BUT... I'M AFRAID ALL ISN'T WELL...
LET ME EXPLAIN... EVERYTHING.
I COME FROM A WORLD CALLED ELENTEAR.
I'M OF A PEOPLE KNOWN AS THE EXCEEDS.

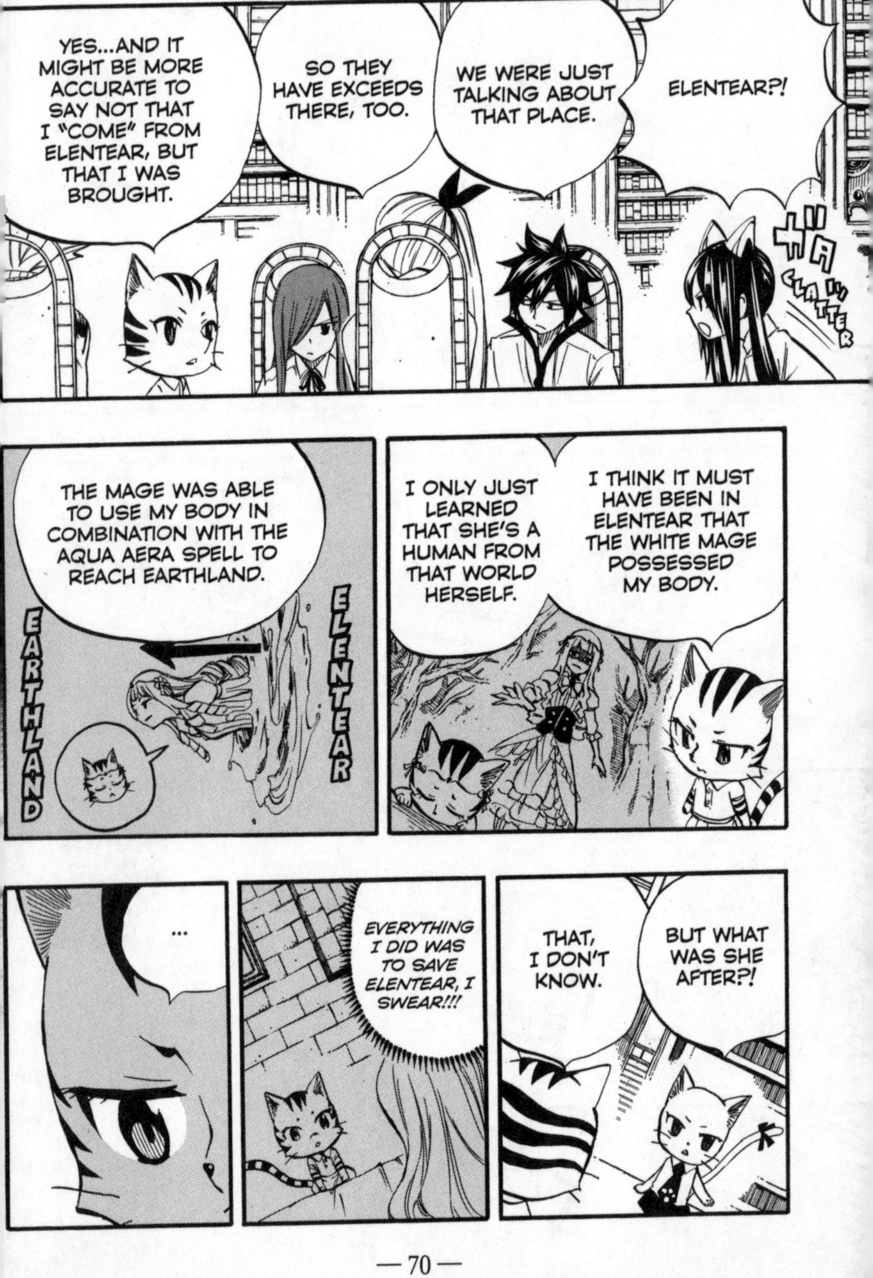
ELENTEAR?!
ガタ
CLATTER
WE WERE JUST TALKING ABOUT THAT PLACE.
SO THEY HAVE EXCEEDS THERE, TOO.
YES...AND IT MIGHT BE MORE ACCURATE TO SAY NOT THAT I "COME" FROM ELENTEAR, BUT THAT I WAS BROUGHT.
I THINK IT MUST HAVE BEEN IN ELENTEAR THAT THE WHITE MAGE POSSESSED MY BODY.
I ONLY JUST LEARNED THAT SHE'S A HUMAN FROM THAT WORLD HERSELF.
THE MAGE WAS ABLE TO USE MY BODY IN COMBINATION WITH THE AQUA AERA SPELL TO REACH EARTHLAND.
ELENTEAR
EARTHLAND
BUT WHAT WAS SHE AFTER?!
THAT, I DON'T KNOW.
EVERYTHING I DID WAS TO SAVE ELENTEAR, I SWEAR!!!
...

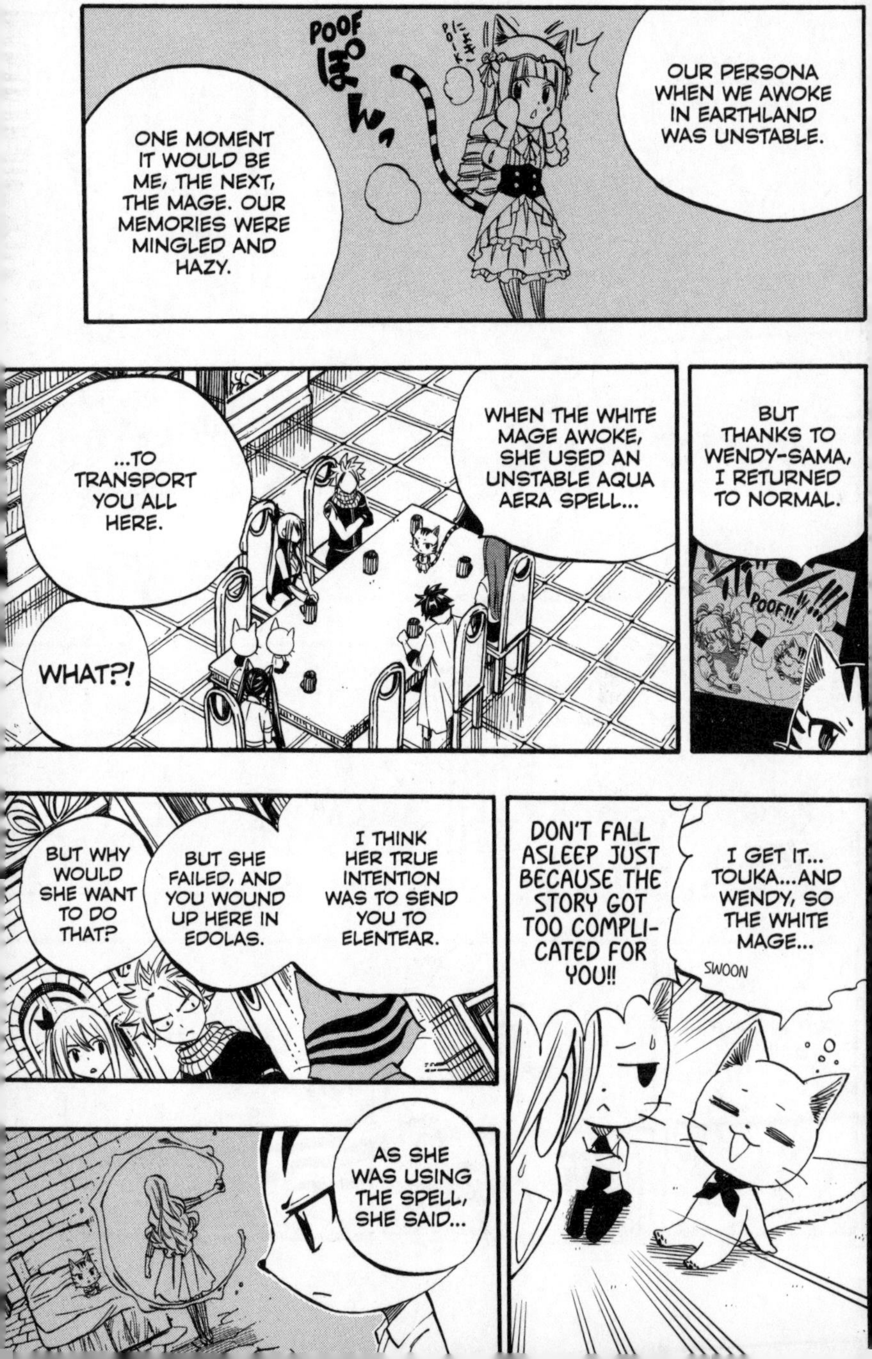
OUR PERSONA WHEN WE AWOKE IN EARTHLAND WAS UNSTABLE.
POOF
ぽん
ONE MOMENT IT WOULD BE ME, THE NEXT, THE MAGE. OUR MEMORIES WERE MINGLED AND HAZY.
BUT THANKS TO WENDY-SAMA, I RETURNED TO NORMAL.
POOF!!!
WHEN THE WHITE MAGE AWOKE, SHE USED AN UNSTABLE AQUA AERA SPELL...
...TO TRANSPORT YOU ALL HERE.
WHAT?!
I GET IT... TOUKA...AND WENDY, SO THE WHITE MAGE...
SWOON
DON'T FALL ASLEEP JUST BECAUSE THE STORY GOT TOO COMPLI-CATED FOR YOU!!
I THINK HER TRUE INTENTION WAS TO SEND YOU TO ELENTEAR.
BUT SHE FAILED, AND YOU WOUND UP HERE IN EDOLAS.
BUT WHY WOULD SHE WANT TO DO THAT?
AS SHE WAS USING THE SPELL, SHE SAID...

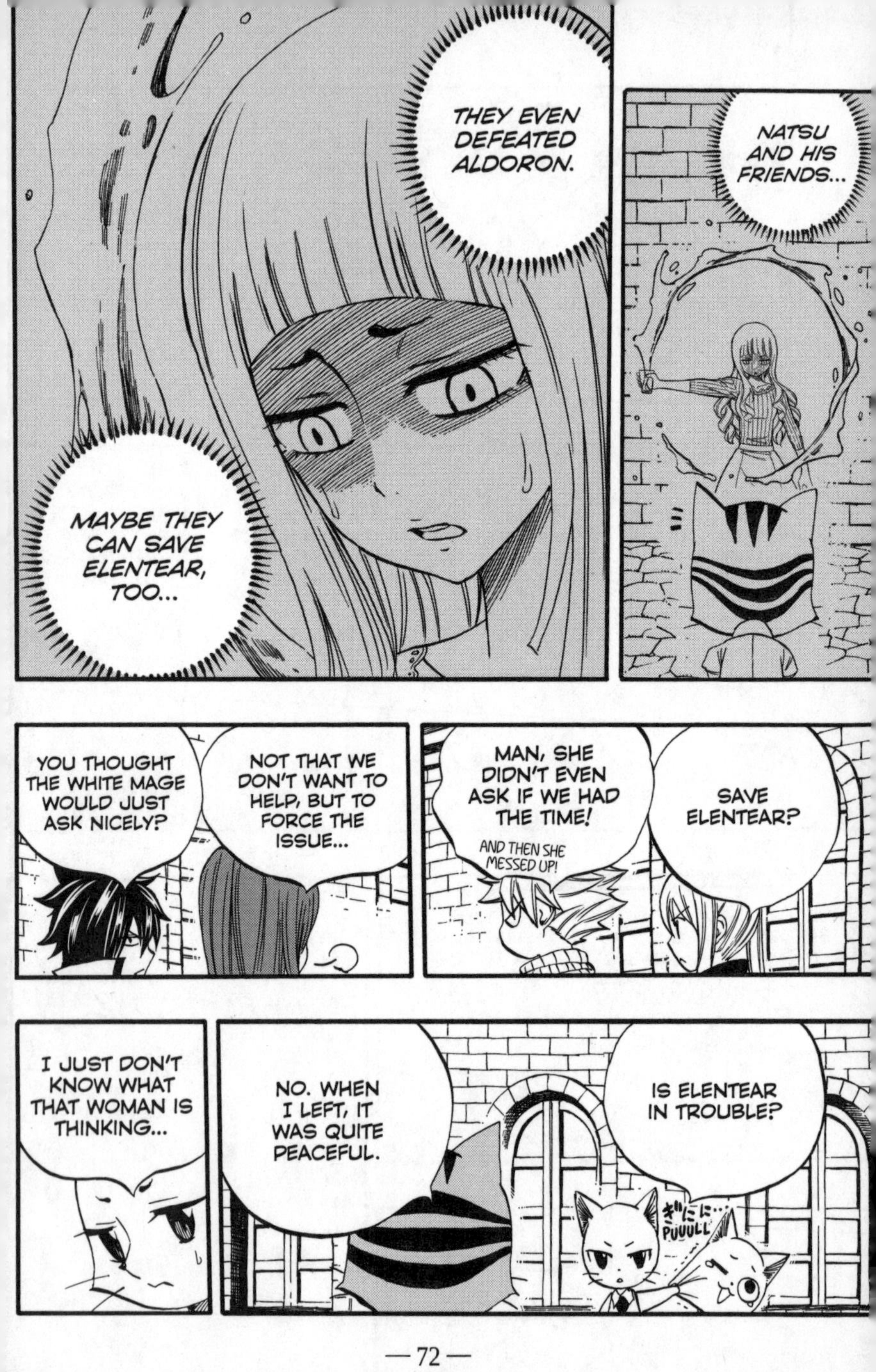
NATSU AND HIS FRIENDS...
THEY EVEN DEFEATED ALDORON.
MAYBE THEY CAN SAVE ELENTEAR, TOO...
SAVE ELENTEAR?
MAN, SHE DIDN'T EVEN ASK IF WE HAD THE TIME!
AND THEN SHE MESSED UP!
NOT THAT WE DON'T WANT TO HELP, BUT TO FORCE THE ISSUE...
YOU THOUGHT THE WHITE MAGE WOULD JUST ASK NICELY?
IS ELENTEAR IN TROUBLE?
NO. WHEN I LEFT, IT WAS QUITE PEACEFUL.
ぎにに… PUUULL
I JUST DON'T KNOW WHAT THAT WOMAN IS THINKING...

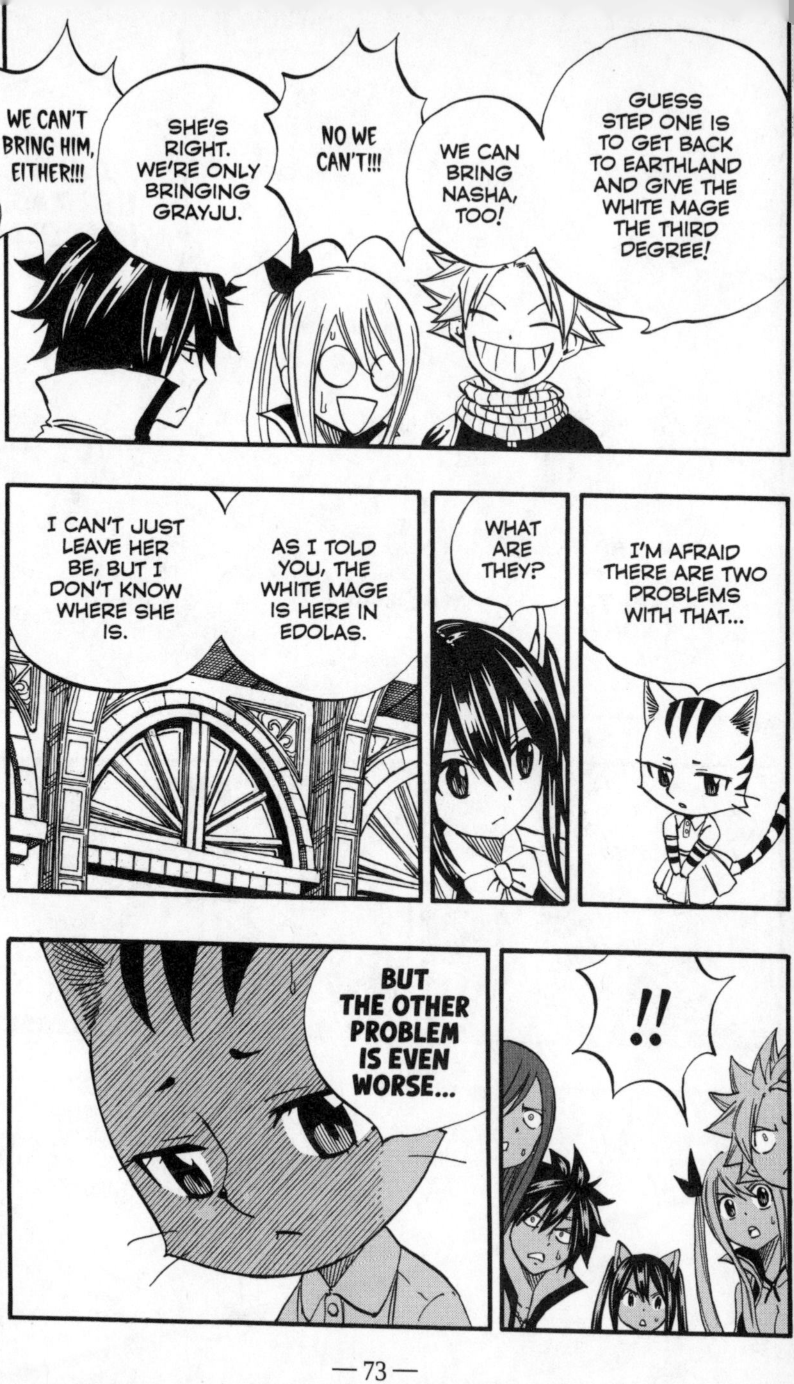
GUESS STEP ONE IS TO GET BACK TO EARTHLAND AND GIVE THE WHITE MAGE THE THIRD DEGREE!
WE CAN BRING NASHA, TOO!
NO WE CAN'T!!!
SHE'S RIGHT. WE'RE ONLY BRINGING GRAYJU.
WE CAN'T BRING HIM, EITHER!!!
I'M AFRAID THERE ARE TWO PROBLEMS WITH THAT...
WHAT ARE THEY?
AS I TOLD YOU, THE WHITE MAGE IS HERE IN EDOLAS.
I CAN'T JUST LEAVE HER BE, BUT I DON'T KNOW WHERE SHE IS.
!!
BUT THE OTHER PROBLEM IS EVEN WORSE...

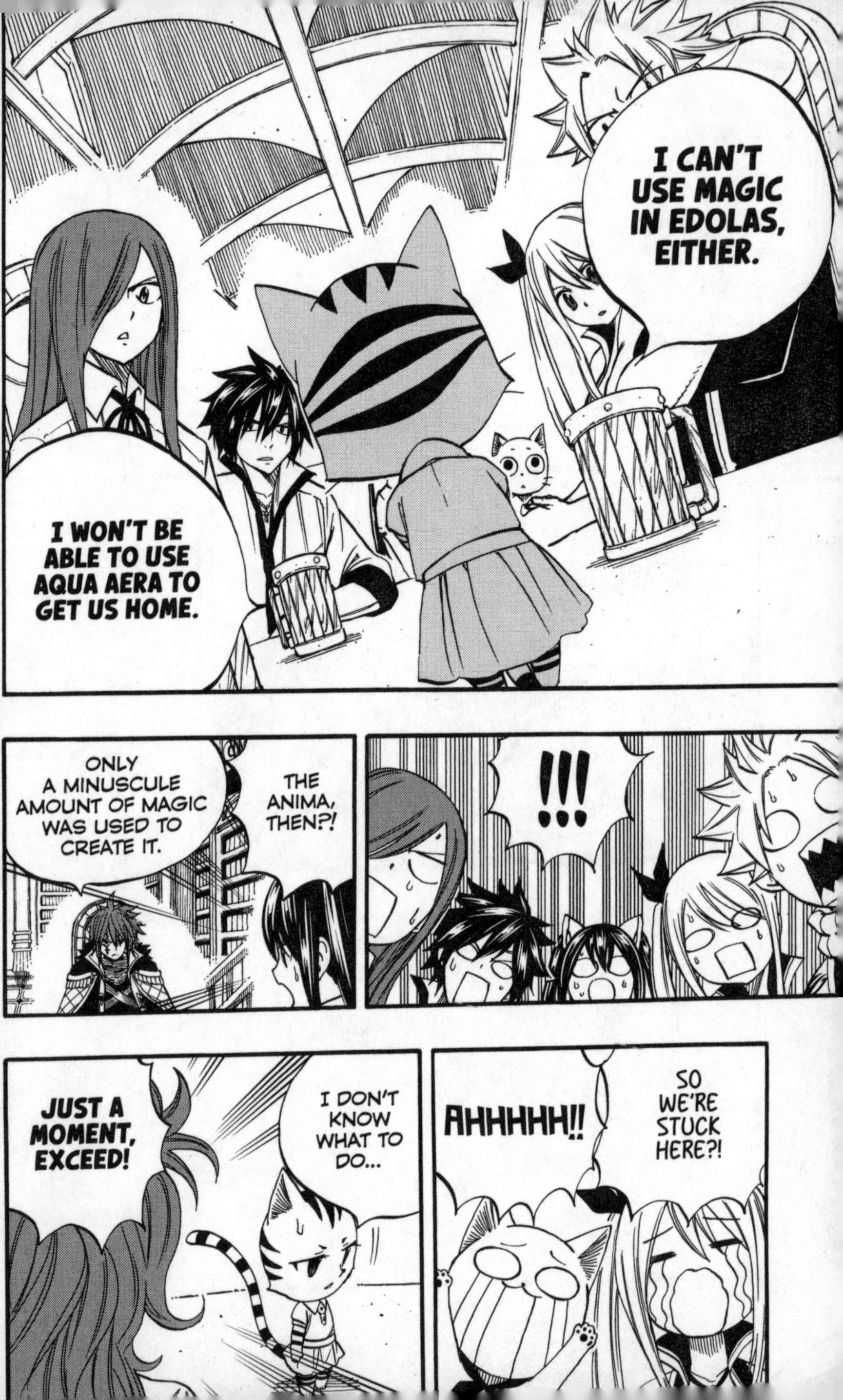
I CAN'T USE MAGIC IN EDOLAS, EITHER.
I WON'T BE ABLE TO USE AQUA AERA TO GET US HOME.
!!!
THE ANIMA, THEN?!
ONLY A MINUSCULE AMOUNT OF MAGIC WAS USED TO CREATE IT.
SO WE'RE STUCK HERE?!
AHHHHH!!
I DON'T KNOW WHAT TO DO...
JUST A MOMENT, EXCEED!

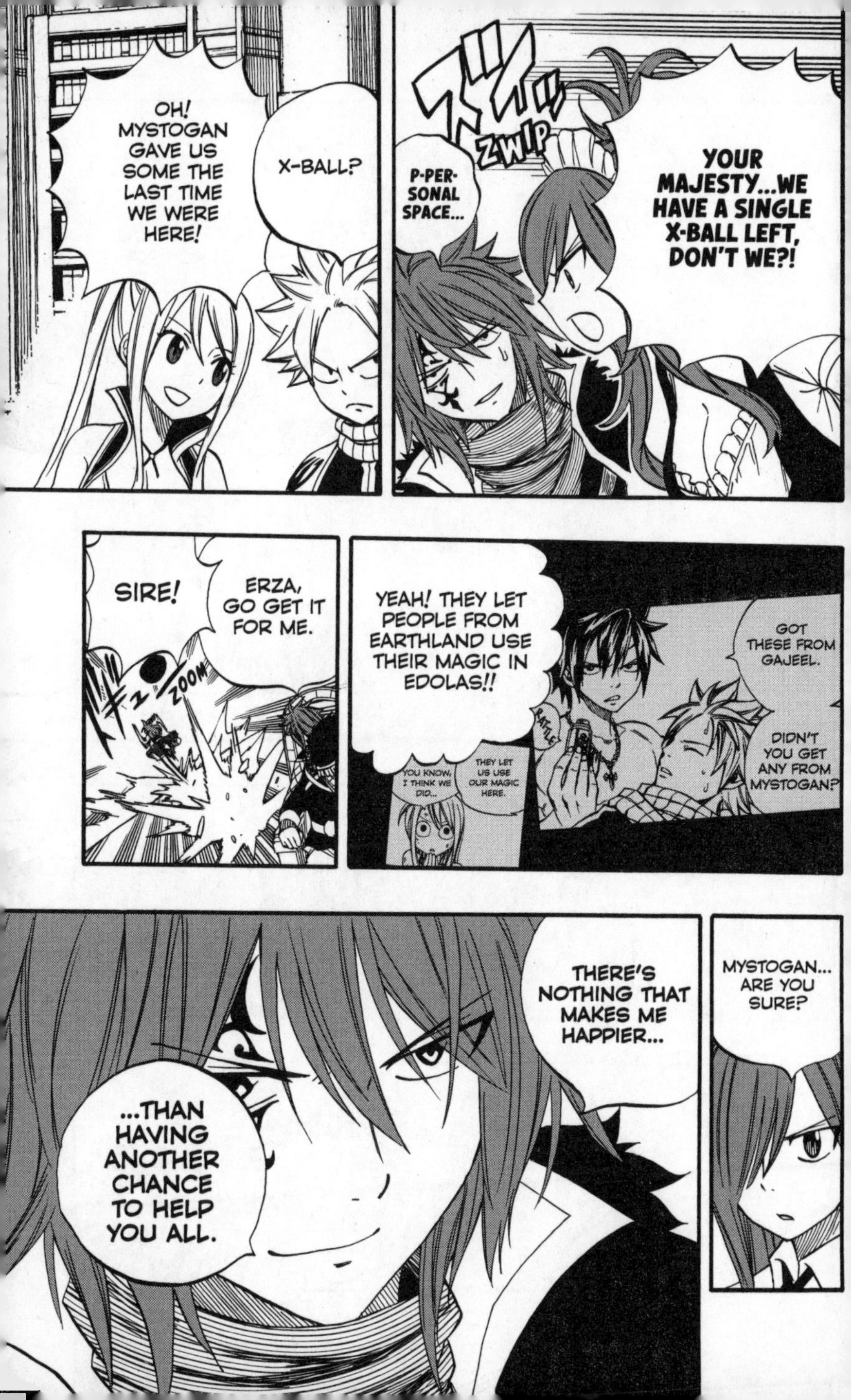
ZWIP
YOUR MAJESTY...WE HAVE A SINGLE X-BALL LEFT, DON'T WE?!
P-PERSONAL SPACE...
X-BALL?
OH! MYSTOGAN GAVE US SOME THE LAST TIME WE WERE HERE!
GOT THESE FROM GAJEEL.
DIDN'T YOU GET ANY FROM MYSTOGAN?
RATTLE
YEAH! THEY LET PEOPLE FROM EARTHLAND USE THEIR MAGIC IN EDOLAS!!
THEY LET US USE OUR MAGIC HERE.
YOU KNOW, I THINK WE DID...
ERZA, GO GET IT FOR ME.
SIRE!
ZOOM
MYSTOGAN... ARE YOU SURE?
THERE'S NOTHING THAT MAKES ME HAPPIER...
...THAN HAVING ANOTHER CHANCE TO HELP YOU ALL.

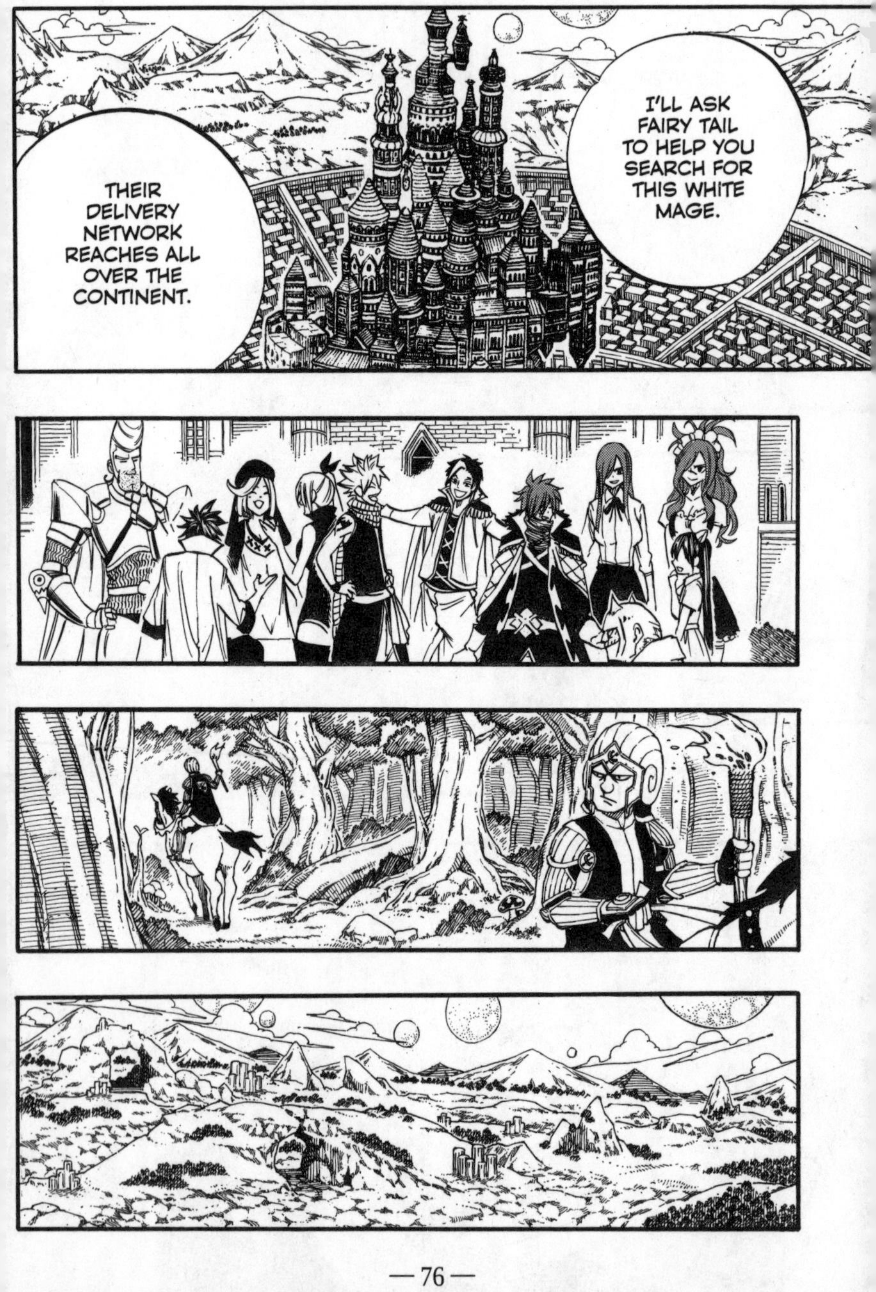
I'LL ASK FAIRY TAIL TO HELP YOU SEARCH FOR THIS WHITE MAGE.
THEIR DELIVERY NETWORK REACHES ALL OVER THE CONTINENT.

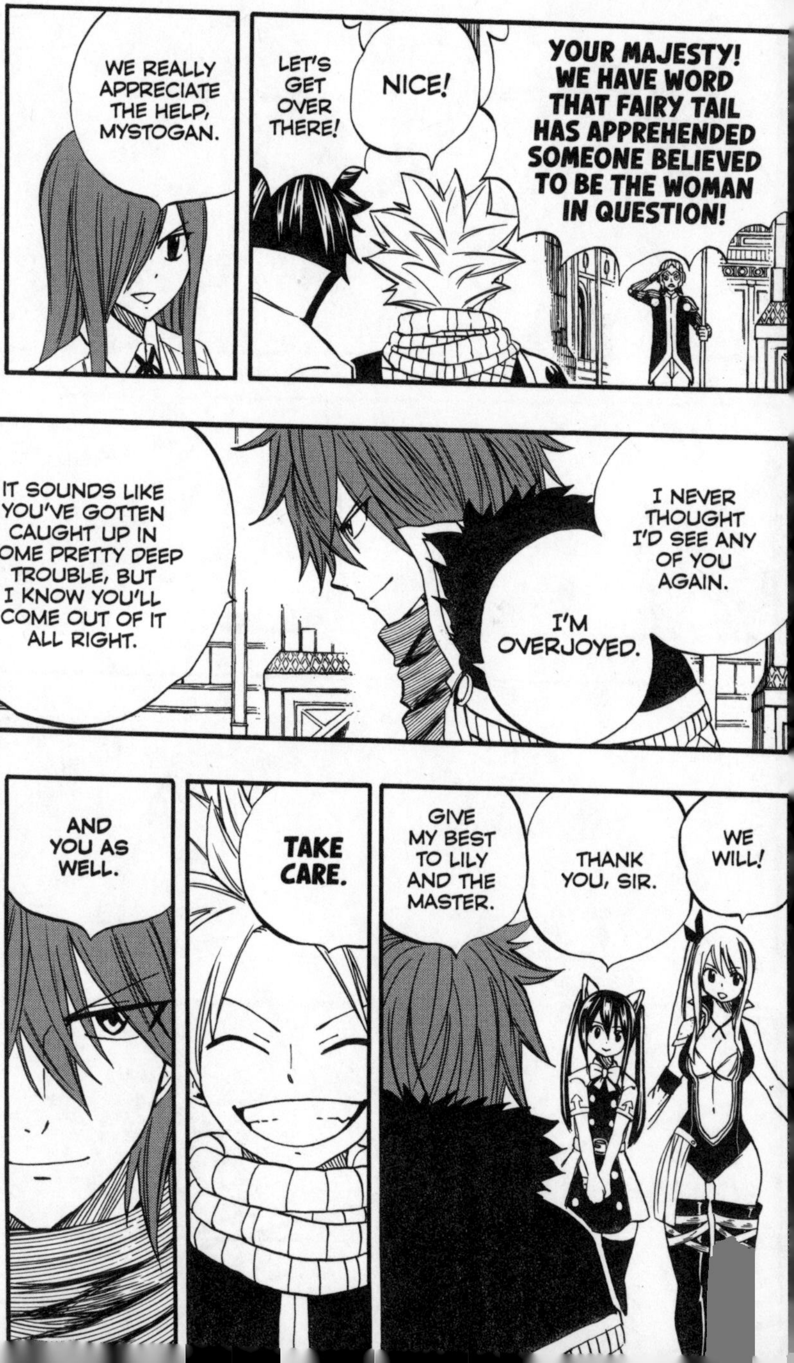

YOUR MAJESTY! WE HAVE WORD THAT FAIRY TAIL HAS APPREHENDED SOMEONE BELIEVED TO BE THE WOMAN IN QUESTION!
NICE!
LET'S GET OVER THERE!
WE REALLY APPRECIATE THE HELP, MYSTOGAN.
I NEVER THOUGHT I'D SEE ANY OF YOU AGAIN.
I'M OVERJOYED.
IT SOUNDS LIKE YOU'VE GOTTEN CAUGHT UP IN SOME PRETTY DEEP TROUBLE, BUT I KNOW YOU'LL COME OUT OF IT ALL RIGHT.
WE WILL!
THANK YOU, SIR.
GIVE MY BEST TO LILY AND THE MASTER.
TAKE CARE.
AND YOU AS WELL.

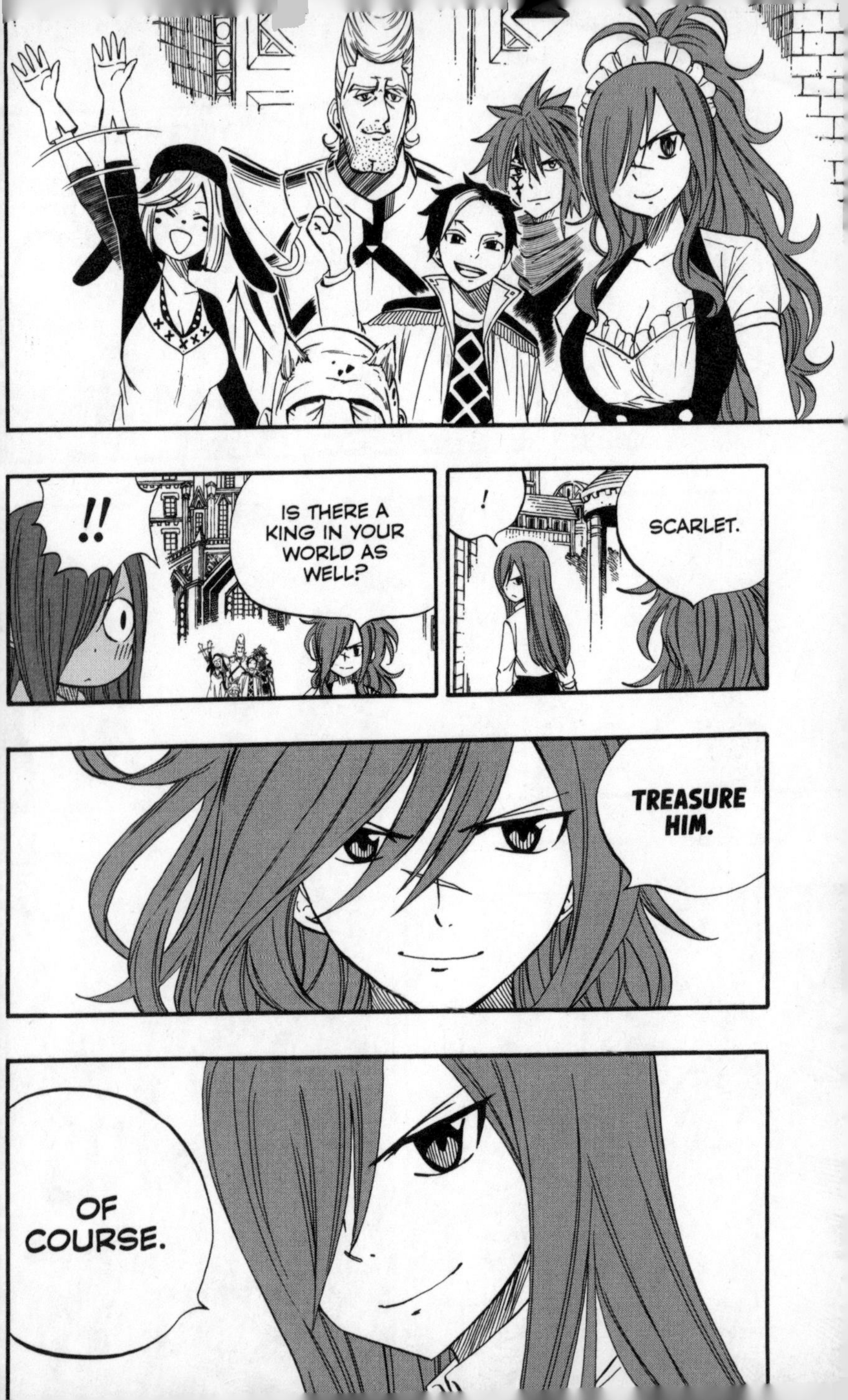
SCARLET.
!
IS THERE A KING IN YOUR WORLD AS WELL?
!!
TREASURE HIM.
OF COURSE.

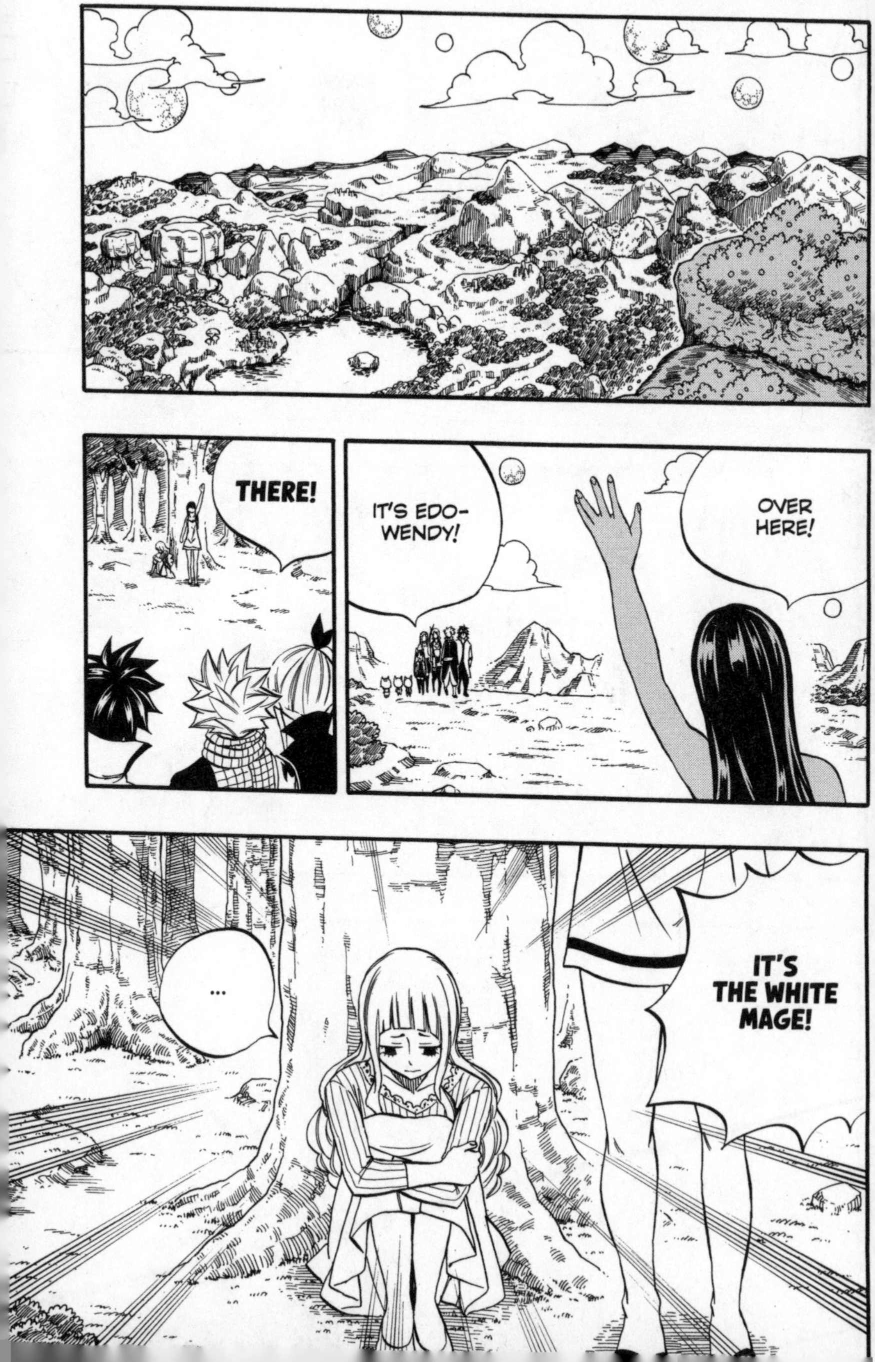
OVER HERE!
IT'S EDO-WENDY!
THERE!
IT'S THE WHITE MAGE!
...

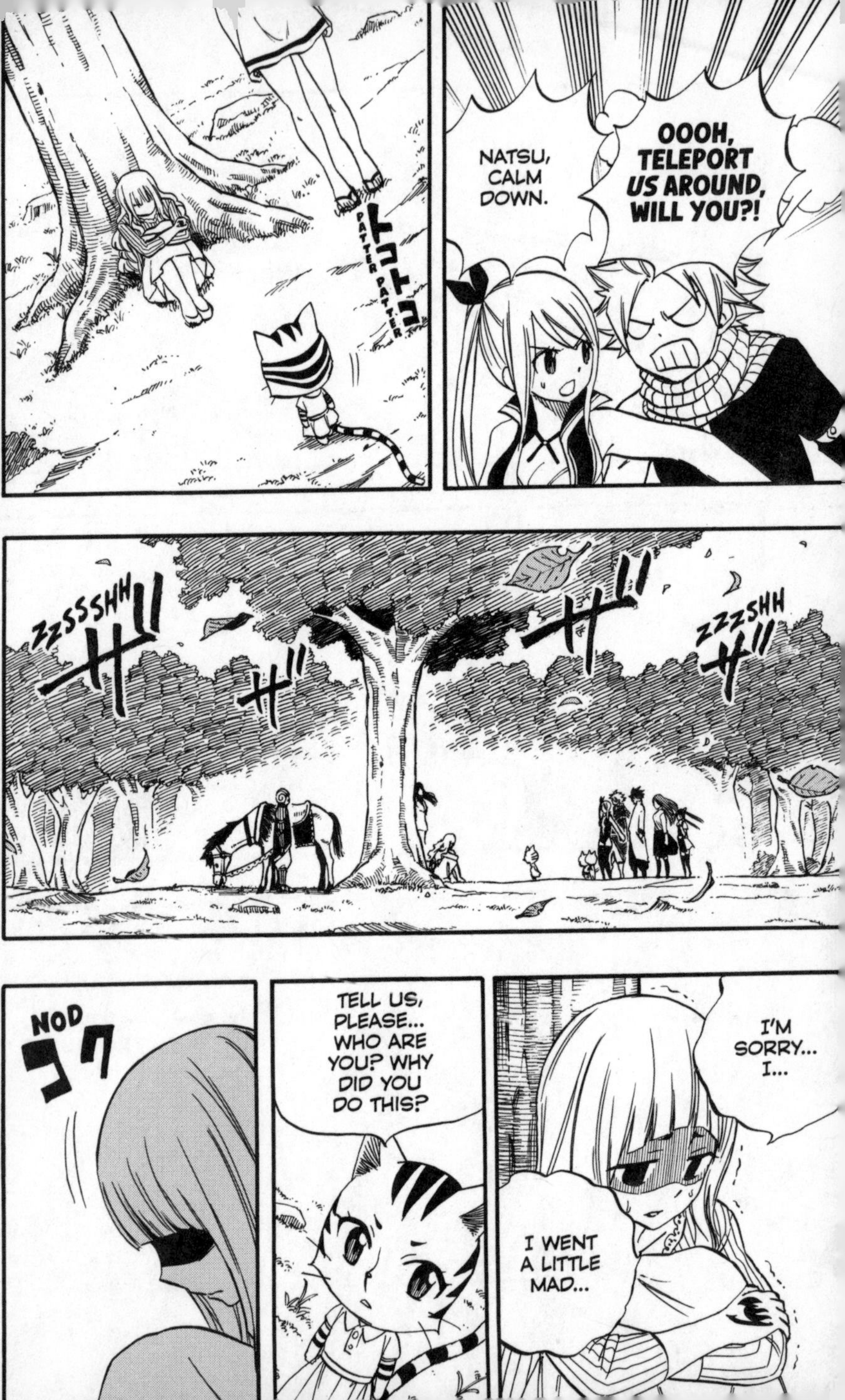
OOOH, TELEPORT US AROUND, WILL YOU?!
NATSU, CALM DOWN.
PATTER PATTER
トコトコ
ZZZSHH
ザ
ザザ
ZZSSSHH
ザ
I'M SORRY... I...
I WENT A LITTLE MAD...
TELL US, PLEASE... WHO ARE YOU? WHY DID YOU DO THIS?
NOD
コク

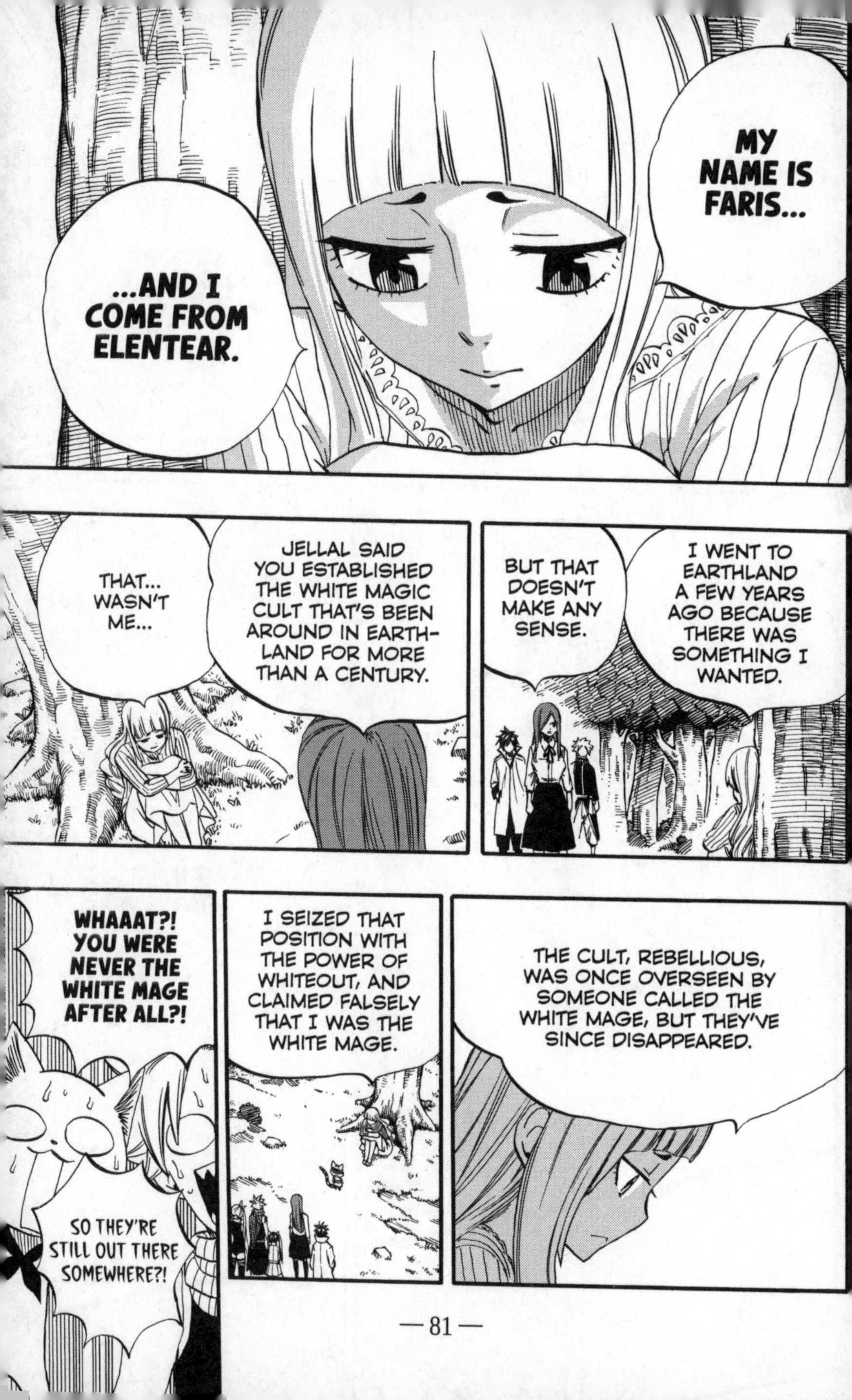
MY NAME IS FARIS...
...AND I COME FROM ELENTEAR.
I WENT TO EARTHLAND A FEW YEARS AGO BECAUSE THERE WAS SOMETHING I WANTED.
BUT THAT DOESN'T MAKE ANY SENSE.
JELLAL SAID YOU ESTABLISHED THE WHITE MAGIC CULT THAT'S BEEN AROUND IN EARTH-LAND FOR MORE THAN A CENTURY.
THAT... WASN'T ME...
THE CULT, REBELLIOUS, WAS ONCE OVERSEEN BY SOMEONE CALLED THE WHITE MAGE, BUT THEY'VE SINCE DISAPPEARED.
I SEIZED THAT POSITION WITH THE POWER OF WHITEOUT, AND CLAIMED FALSELY THAT I WAS THE WHITE MAGE.
WHAAAT?! YOU WERE NEVER THE WHITE MAGE AFTER ALL?!
SO THEY'RE STILL OUT THERE SOMEWHERE?!

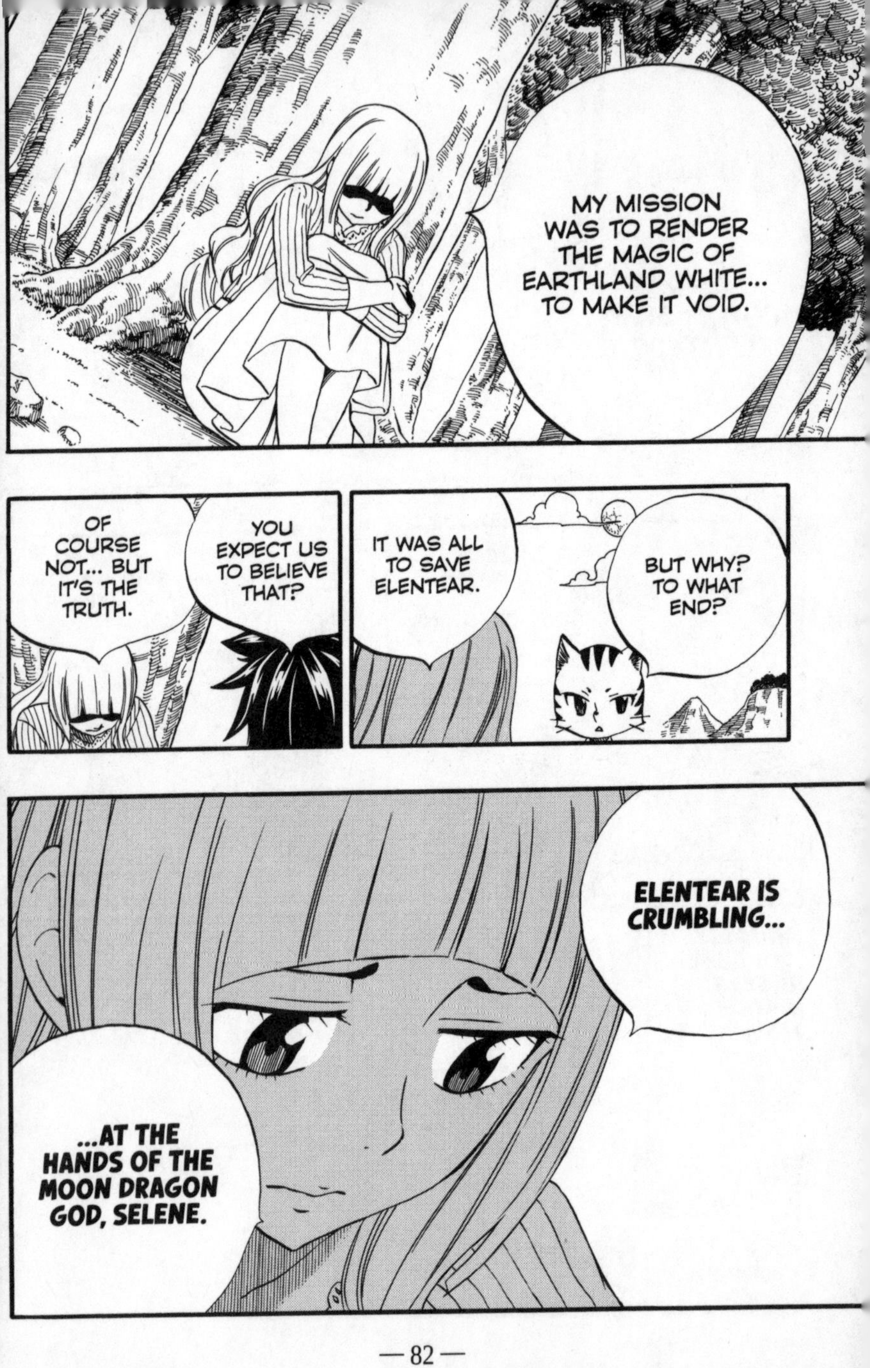
MY MISSION WAS TO RENDER THE MAGIC OF EARTHLAND WHITE... TO MAKE IT VOID.
BUT WHY? TO WHAT END?
IT WAS ALL TO SAVE ELENTEAR.
YOU EXPECT US TO BELIEVE THAT?
OF COURSE NOT... BUT IT'S THE TRUTH.
ELENTEAR IS CRUMBLING...
...AT THE HANDS OF THE MOON DRAGON GOD, SELENE.

FAIRY TAIL
100 YEARS QUEST

Chapter 68: Selene, the Moon Dragon God

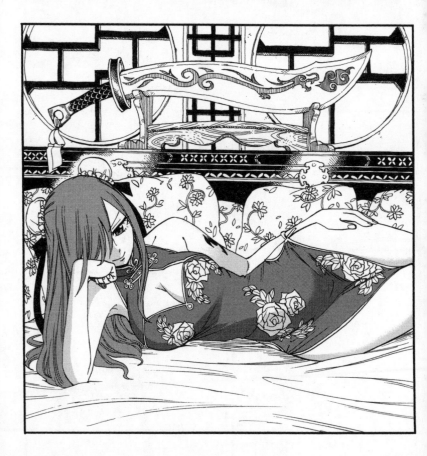

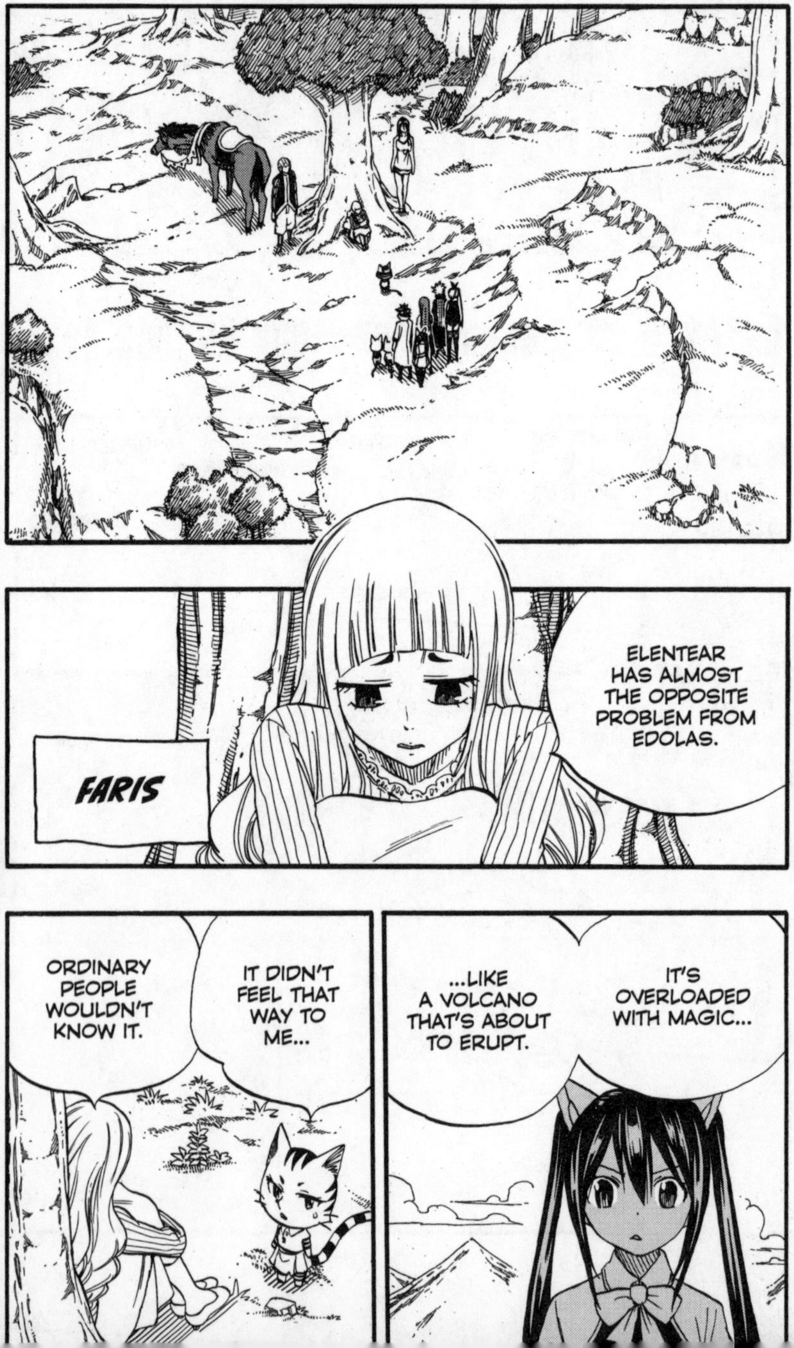
ELENTEAR HAS ALMOST THE OPPOSITE PROBLEM FROM EDOLAS.
FARIS
IT'S OVERLOADED WITH MAGIC...
...LIKE A VOLCANO THAT'S ABOUT TO ERUPT.
IT DIDN'T FEEL THAT WAY TO ME...
ORDINARY PEOPLE WOULDN'T KNOW IT.

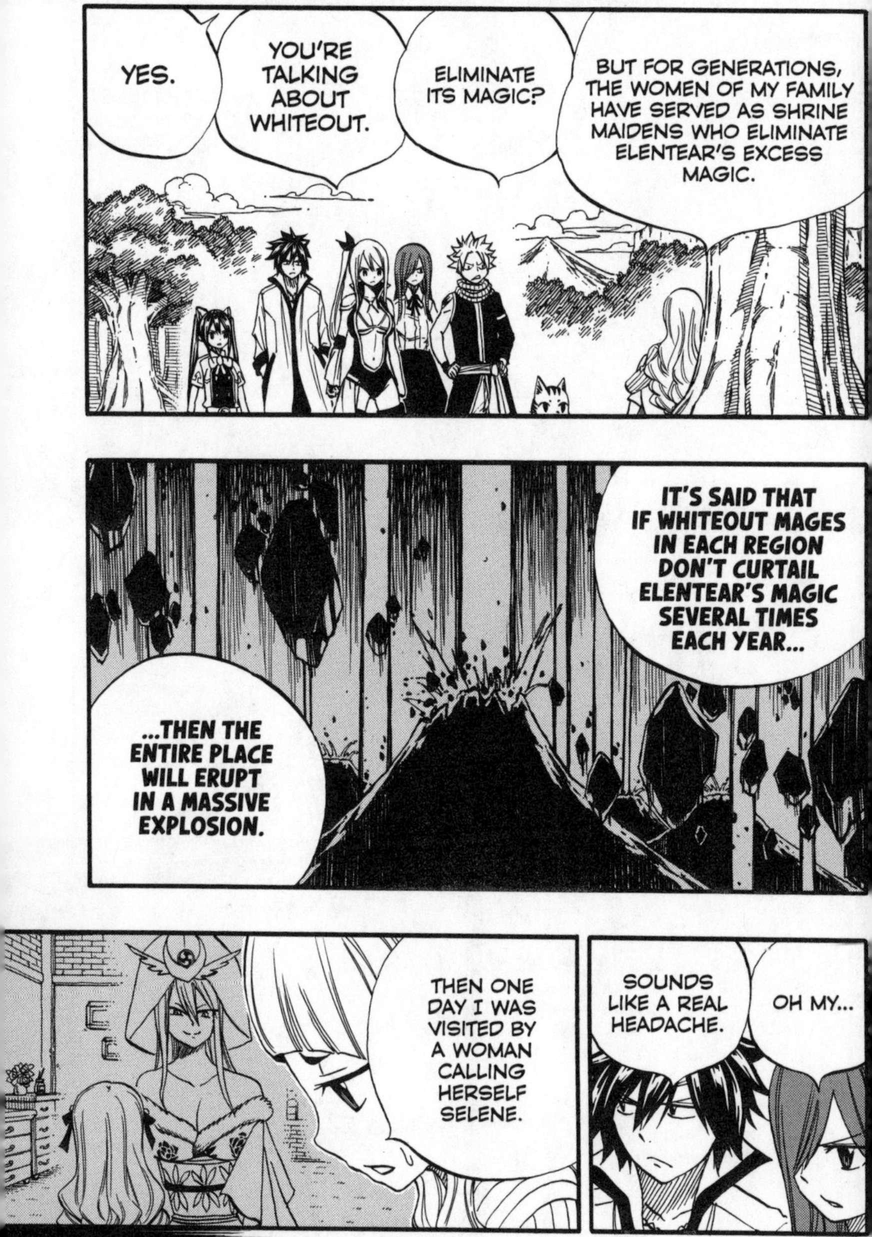
BUT FOR GENERATIONS, THE WOMEN OF MY FAMILY HAVE SERVED AS SHRINE MAIDENS WHO ELIMINATE ELENTEAR'S EXCESS MAGIC.
ELIMINATE ITS MAGIC?
YOU'RE TALKING ABOUT WHITEOUT.
YES.
IT'S SAID THAT IF WHITEOUT MAGES IN EACH REGION DON'T CURTAIL ELENTEAR'S MAGIC SEVERAL TIMES EACH YEAR...
...THEN THE ENTIRE PLACE WILL ERUPT IN A MASSIVE EXPLOSION.
OH MY...
SOUNDS LIKE A REAL HEADACHE.
THEN ONE DAY I WAS VISITED BY A WOMAN CALLING HERSELF SELENE.

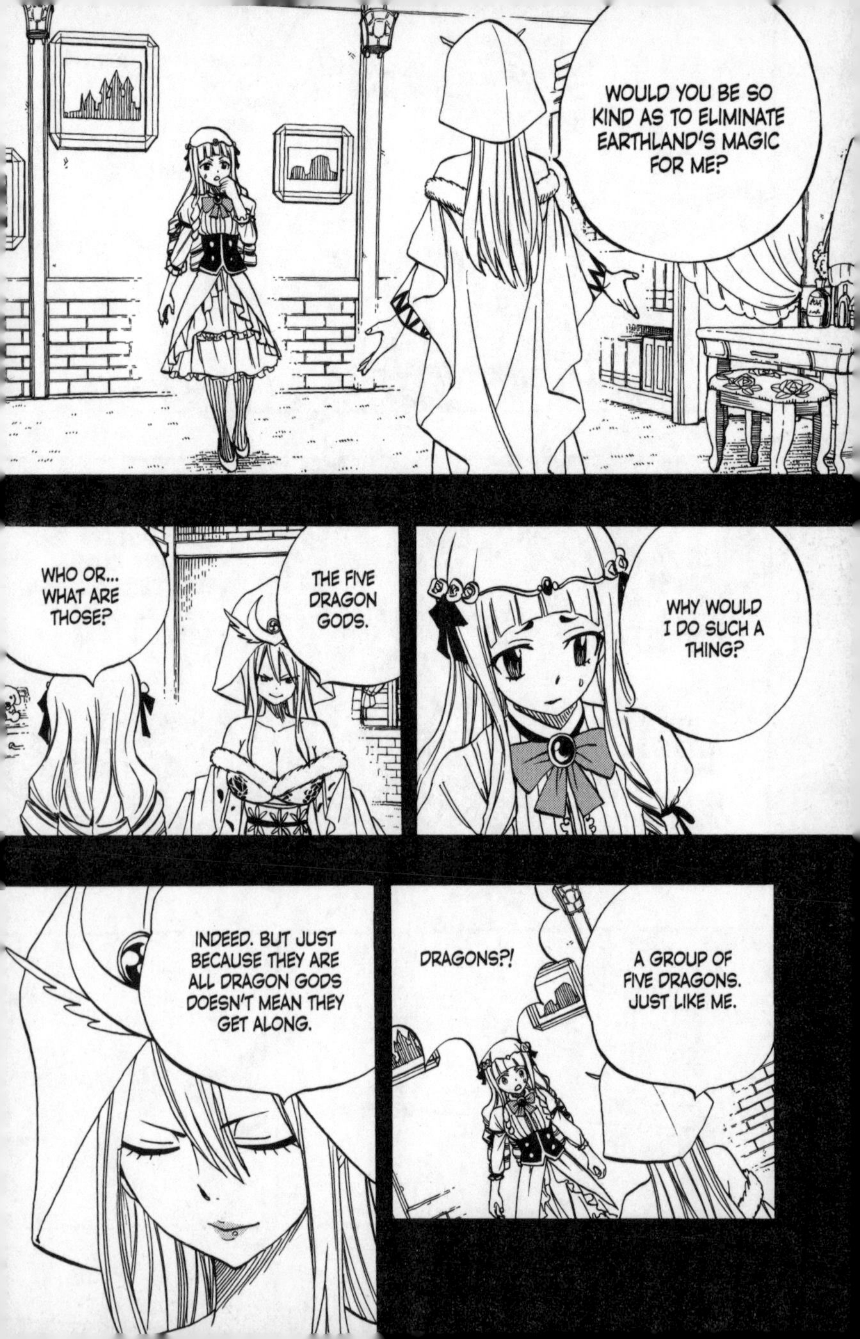
WOULD YOU BE SO KIND AS TO ELIMINATE EARTHLAND'S MAGIC FOR ME?
WHY WOULD I DO SUCH A THING?
THE FIVE DRAGON GODS.
WHO OR... WHAT ARE THOSE?
A GROUP OF FIVE DRAGONS. JUST LIKE ME.
DRAGONS?!
INDEED. BUT JUST BECAUSE THEY ARE ALL DRAGON GODS DOESN'T MEAN THEY GET ALONG.

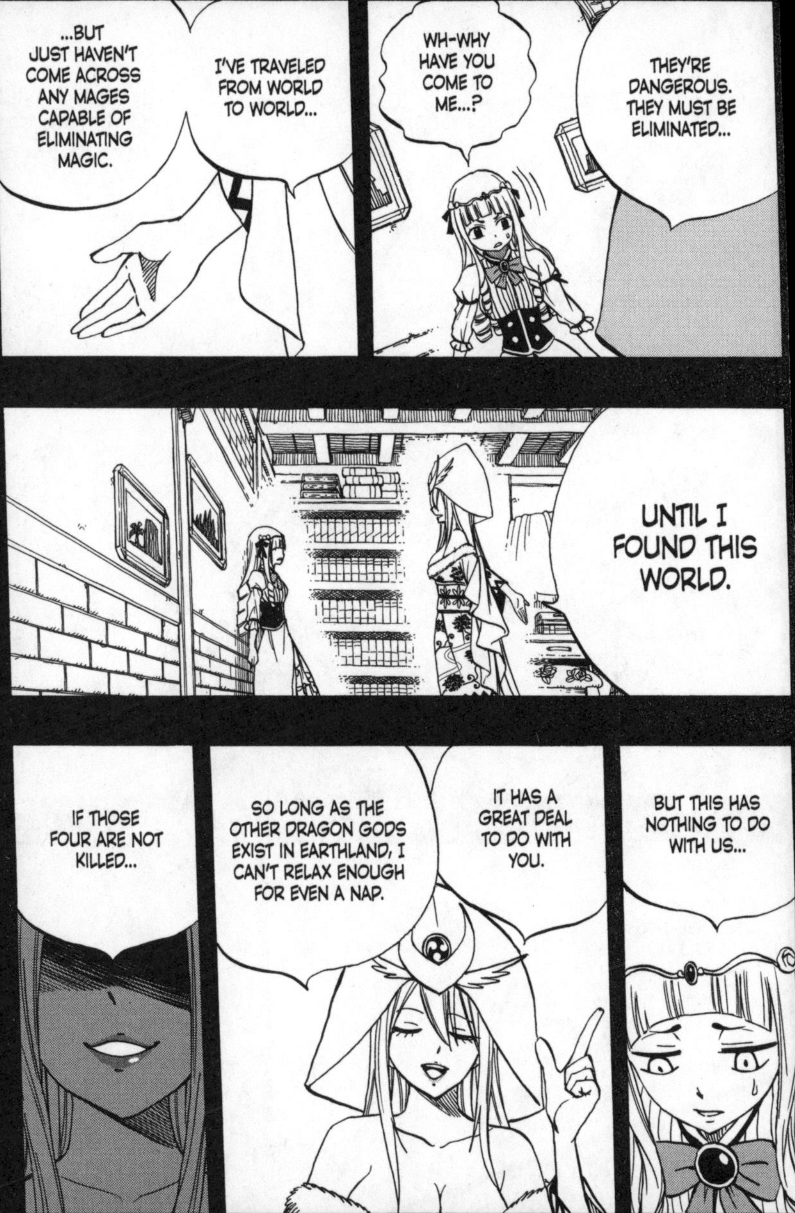
THEY'RE DANGEROUS. THEY MUST BE ELIMINATED...
WH-WHY HAVE YOU COME TO ME...?
I'VE TRAVELED FROM WORLD TO WORLD...
...BUT JUST HAVEN'T COME ACROSS ANY MAGES CAPABLE OF ELIMINATING MAGIC.
UNTIL I FOUND THIS WORLD.
BUT THIS HAS NOTHING TO DO WITH US...
IT HAS A GREAT DEAL TO DO WITH YOU.
SO LONG AS THE OTHER DRAGON GODS EXIST IN EARTHLAND, I CAN'T RELAX ENOUGH FOR EVEN A NAP.
IF THOSE FOUR ARE NOT KILLED...

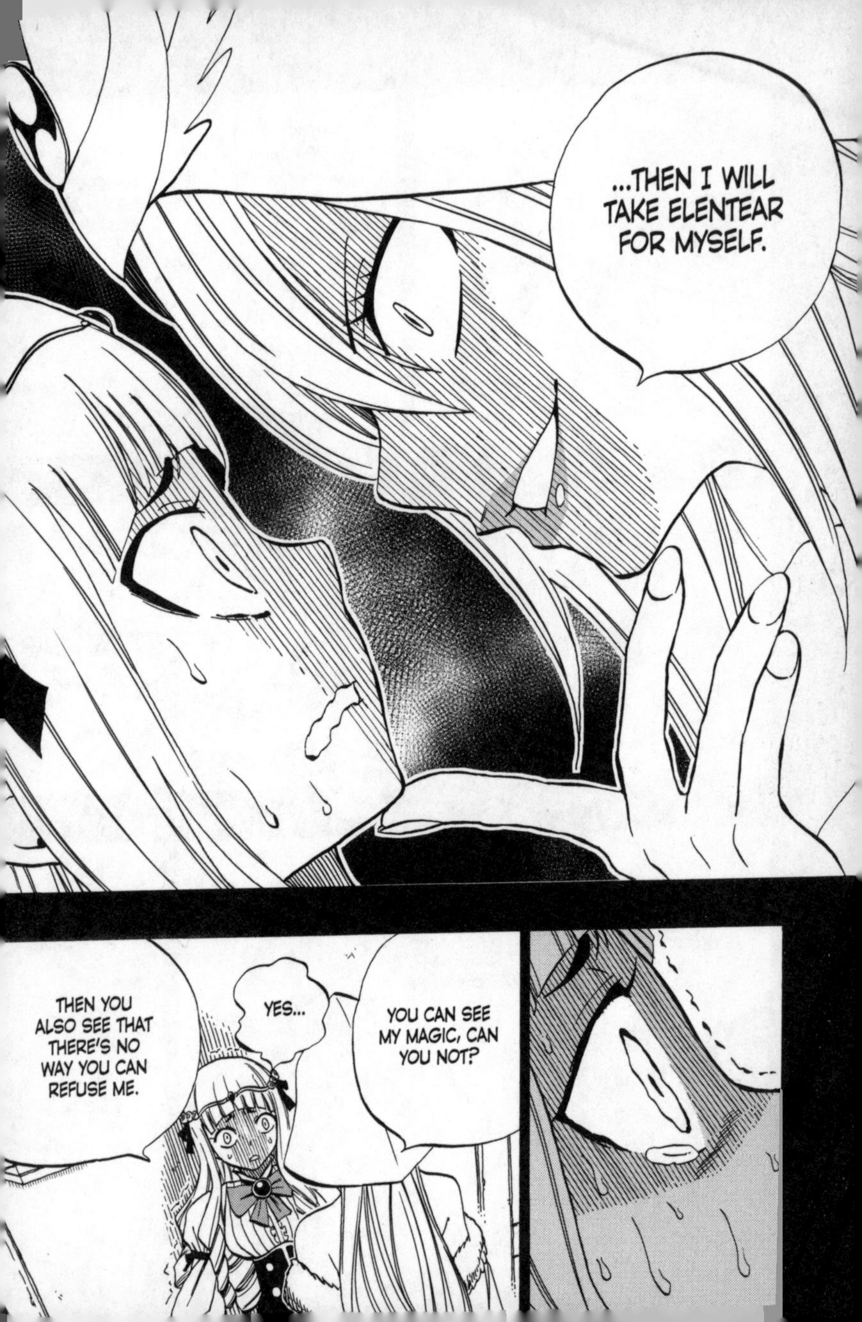
...THEN I WILL TAKE ELENTEAR FOR MYSELF.
YOU CAN SEE MY MAGIC, CAN YOU NOT?
YES...
THEN YOU ALSO SEE THAT THERE'S NO WAY YOU CAN REFUSE ME.

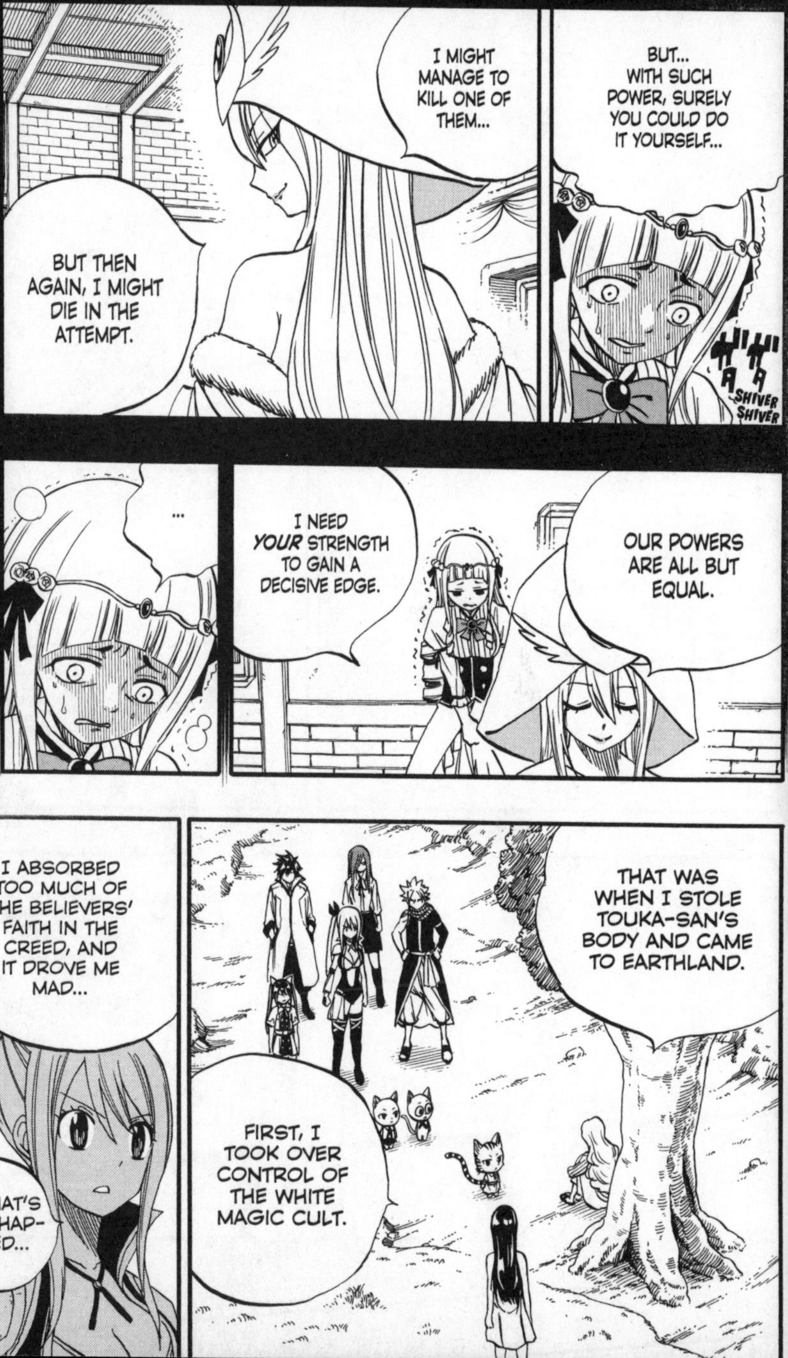
BUT... WITH SUCH POWER, SURELY YOU COULD DO IT YOURSELF...
SHIVER SHIVER
I MIGHT MANAGE TO KILL ONE OF THEM...
BUT THEN AGAIN, I MIGHT DIE IN THE ATTEMPT.
OUR POWERS ARE ALL BUT EQUAL.
I NEED *YOUR* STRENGTH TO GAIN A DECISIVE EDGE.
...
THAT WAS WHEN I STOLE TOUKA-SAN'S BODY AND CAME TO EARTHLAND.
FIRST, I TOOK OVER CONTROL OF THE WHITE MAGIC CULT.
I ABSORBED TOO MUCH OF THE BELIEVERS' FAITH IN THE CREED, AND IT DROVE ME MAD...
SO THAT'S WHAT HAP-PENED...

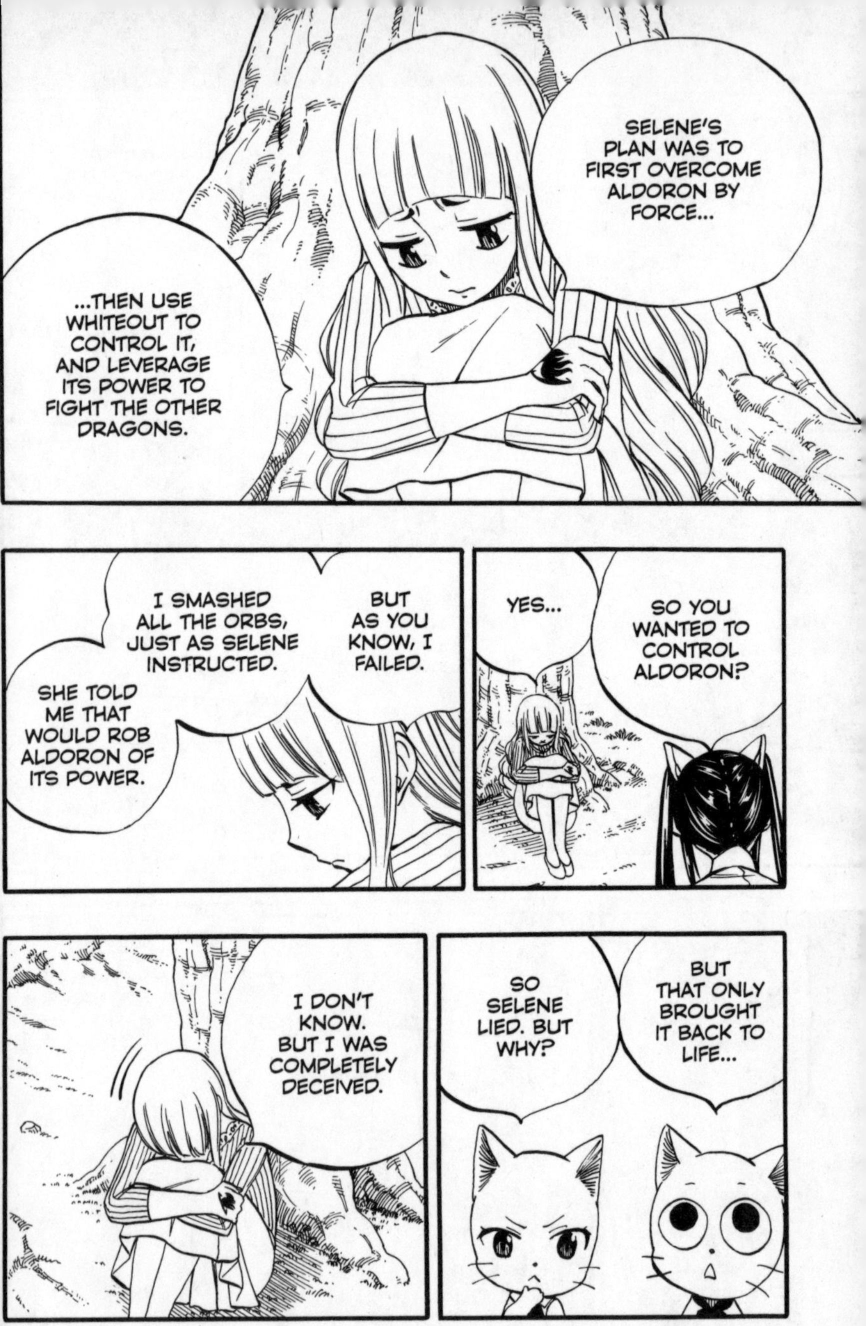
SELENE'S PLAN WAS TO FIRST OVERCOME ALDORON BY FORCE...
...THEN USE WHITEOUT TO CONTROL IT, AND LEVERAGE ITS POWER TO FIGHT THE OTHER DRAGONS.
SO YOU WANTED TO CONTROL ALDORON?
YES...
BUT AS YOU KNOW, I FAILED.
I SMASHED ALL THE ORBS, JUST AS SELENE INSTRUCTED.
SHE TOLD ME THAT WOULD ROB ALDORON OF ITS POWER.
BUT THAT ONLY BROUGHT IT BACK TO LIFE...
SO SELENE LIED. BUT WHY?
I DON'T KNOW. BUT I WAS COMPLETELY DECEIVED.

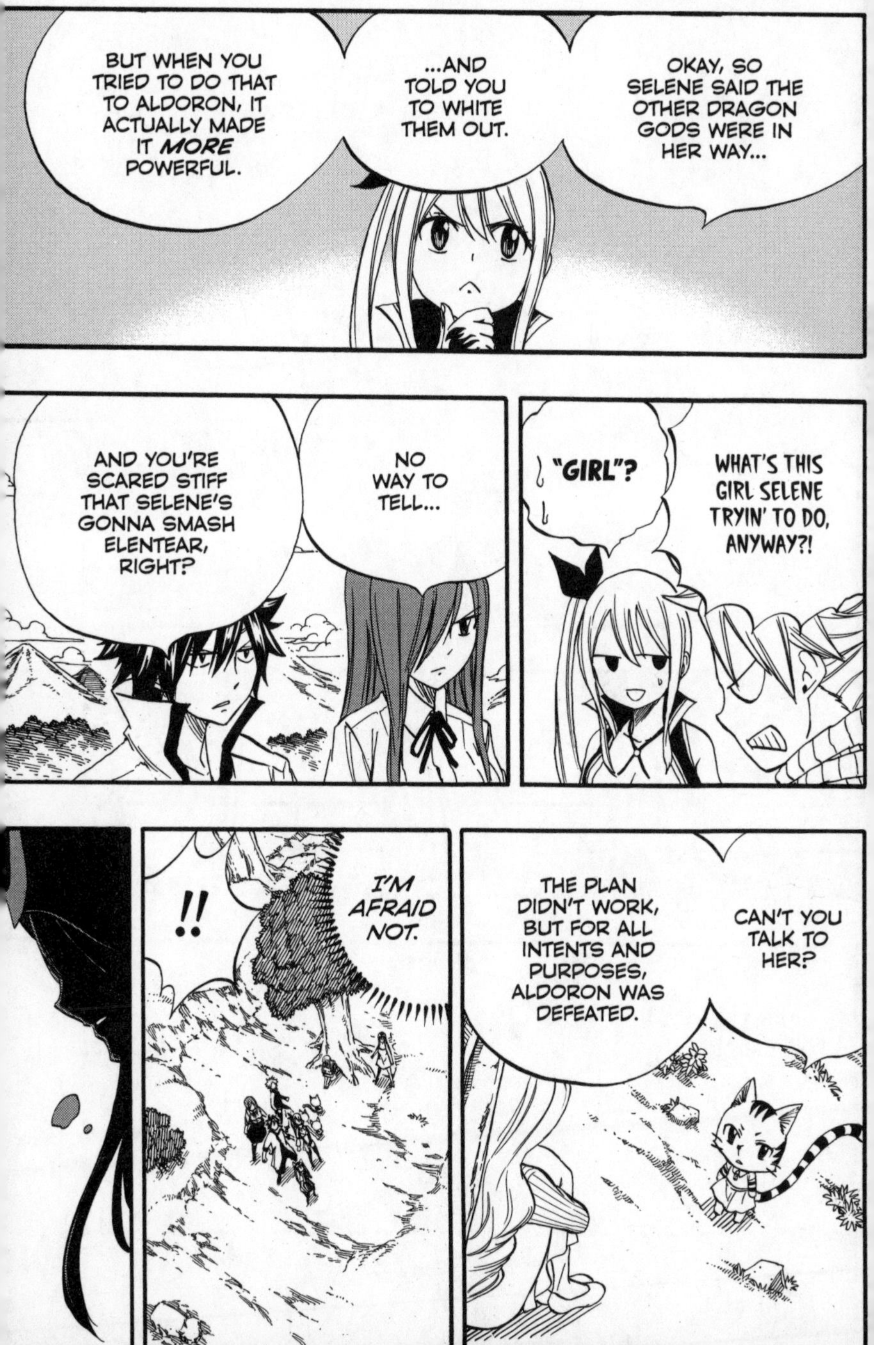
OKAY, SO SELENE SAID THE OTHER DRAGON GODS WERE IN HER WAY...
...AND TOLD YOU TO WHITE THEM OUT.
BUT WHEN YOU TRIED TO DO THAT TO ALDORON, IT ACTUALLY MADE IT *MORE* POWERFUL.
WHAT'S THIS GIRL SELENE TRYIN' TO DO, ANYWAY?!
"GIRL"?
NO WAY TO TELL...
AND YOU'RE SCARED STIFF THAT SELENE'S GONNA SMASH ELENTEAR, RIGHT?
CAN'T YOU TALK TO HER?
THE PLAN DIDN'T WORK, BUT FOR ALL INTENTS AND PURPOSES, ALDORON WAS DEFEATED.
I'M AFRAID NOT.
!!

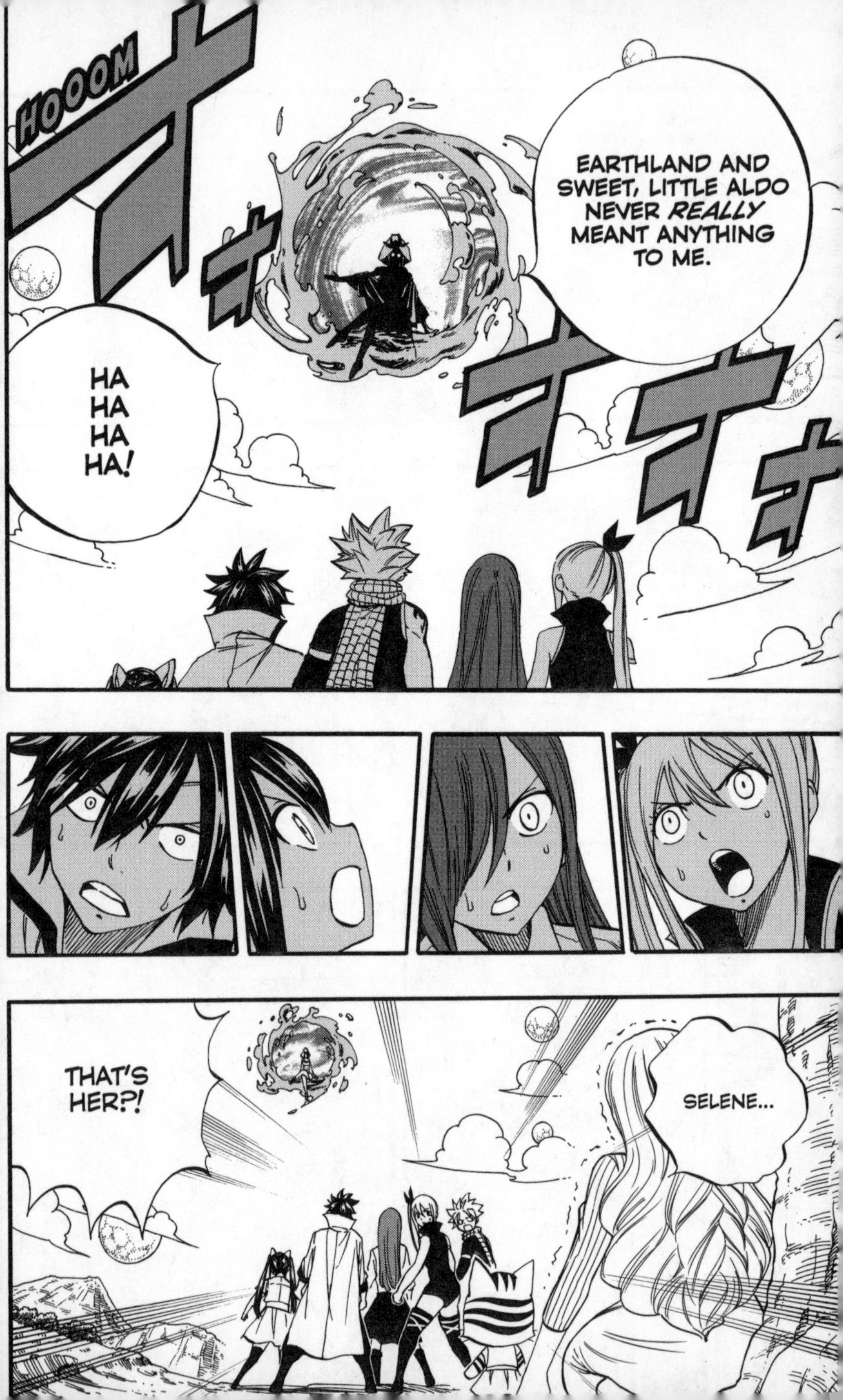
EARTHLAND AND SWEET, LITTLE ALDO NEVER *REALLY* MEANT ANYTHING TO ME.
HOOOM
HA HA HA HA!
SELENE...
THAT'S HER?!

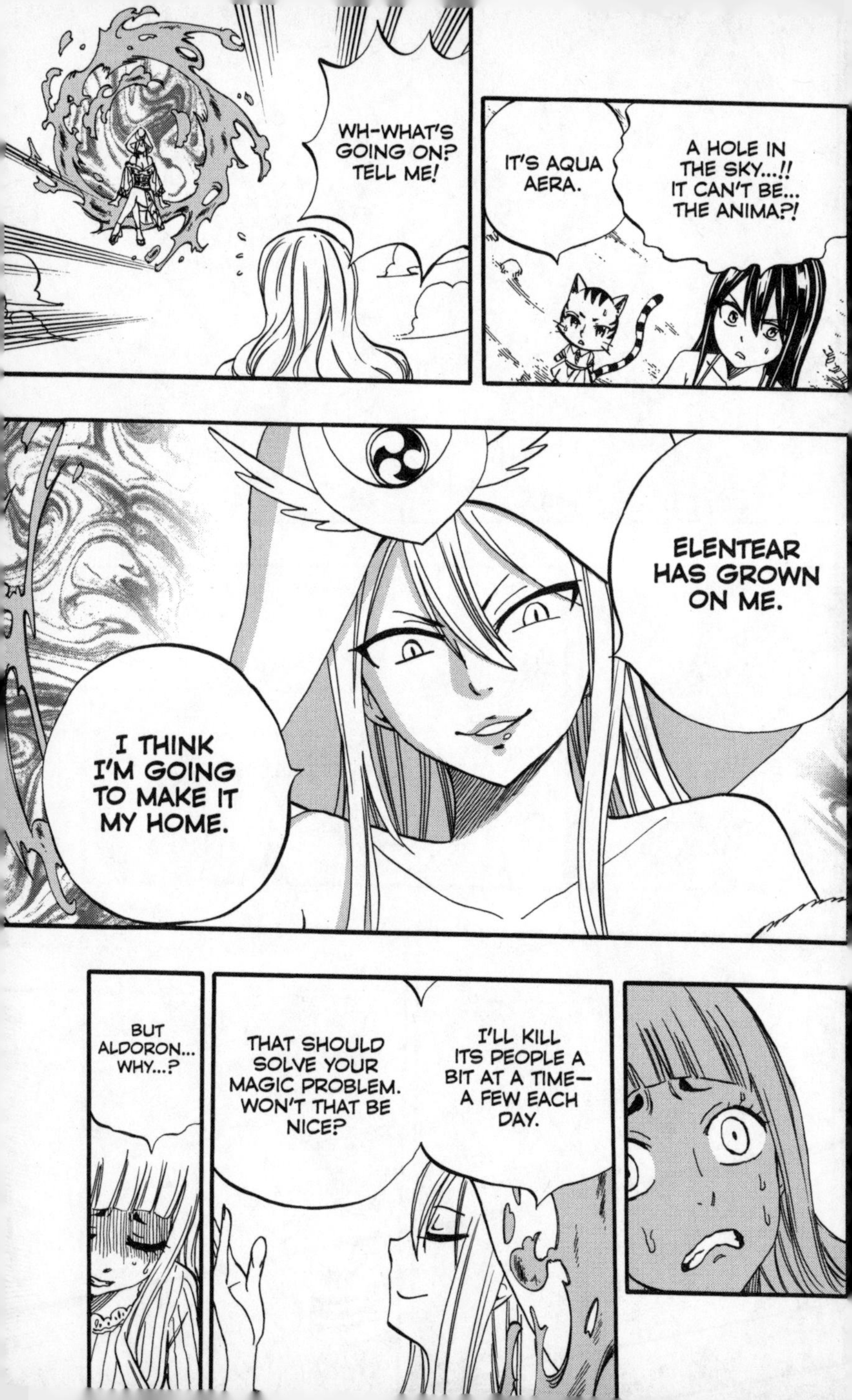
A HOLE IN THE SKY...!! IT CAN'T BE... THE ANIMA?!
IT'S AQUA AERA.
WH-WHAT'S GOING ON? TELL ME!
ELENTEAR HAS GROWN ON ME.
I THINK I'M GOING TO MAKE IT MY HOME.
I'LL KILL ITS PEOPLE A BIT AT A TIME— A FEW EACH DAY.
THAT SHOULD SOLVE YOUR MAGIC PROBLEM. WON'T THAT BE NICE?
BUT ALDORON... WHY...?

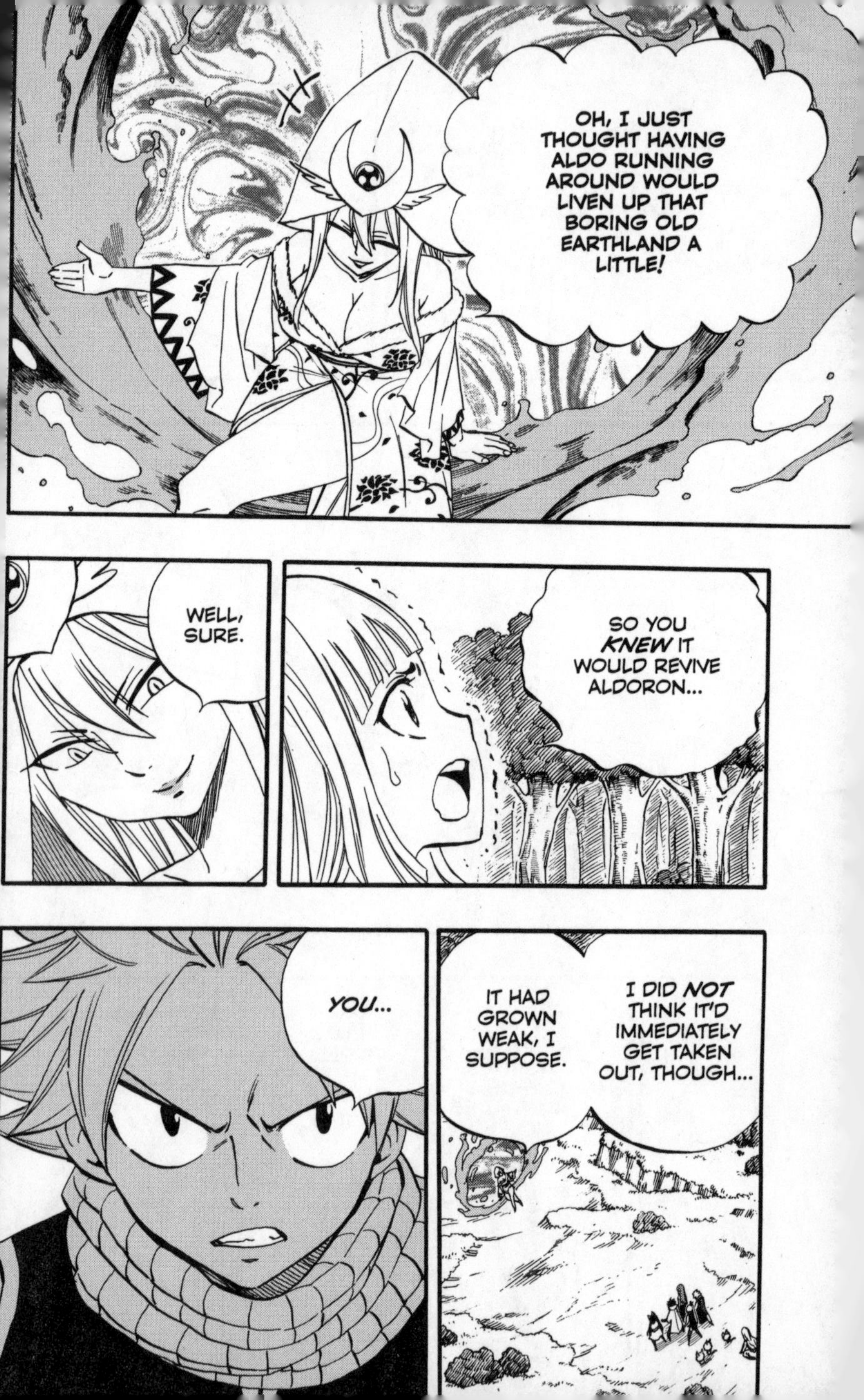
OH, I JUST THOUGHT HAVING ALDO RUNNING AROUND WOULD LIVEN UP THAT BORING OLD EARTHLAND A LITTLE!
SO YOU *KNEW* IT WOULD REVIVE ALDORON...
WELL, SURE.
I DID *NOT* THINK IT'D IMMEDIATELY GET TAKEN OUT, THOUGH...
IT HAD GROWN WEAK, I SUPPOSE.
YOU...

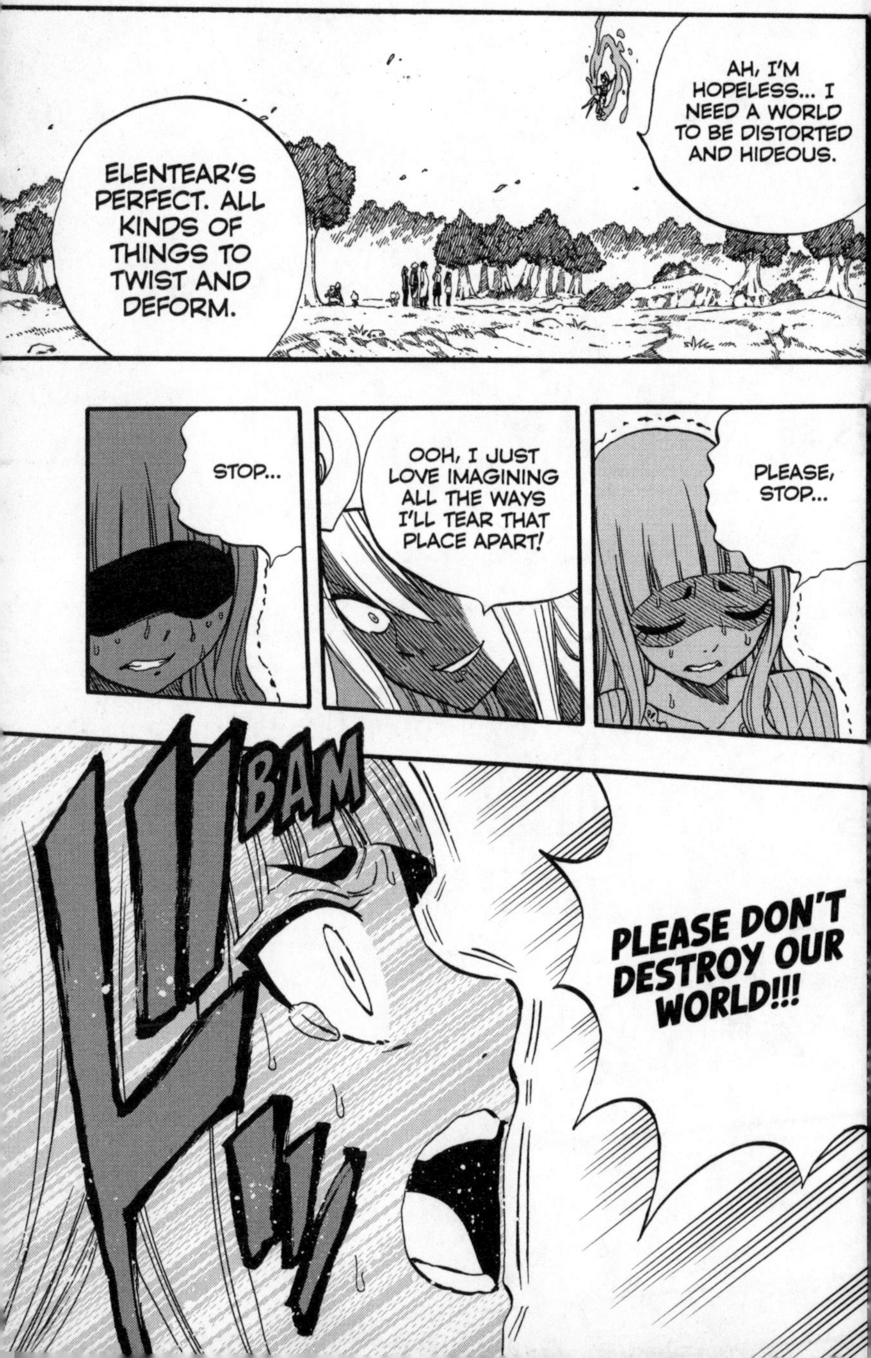
AH, I'M HOPELESS... I NEED A WORLD TO BE DISTORTED AND HIDEOUS.
ELENTEAR'S PERFECT. ALL KINDS OF THINGS TO TWIST AND DEFORM.
PLEASE, STOP...
OOH, I JUST LOVE IMAGINING ALL THE WAYS I'LL TEAR THAT PLACE APART!
STOP...
BAM
PLEASE DON'T DESTROY OUR WORLD!!!

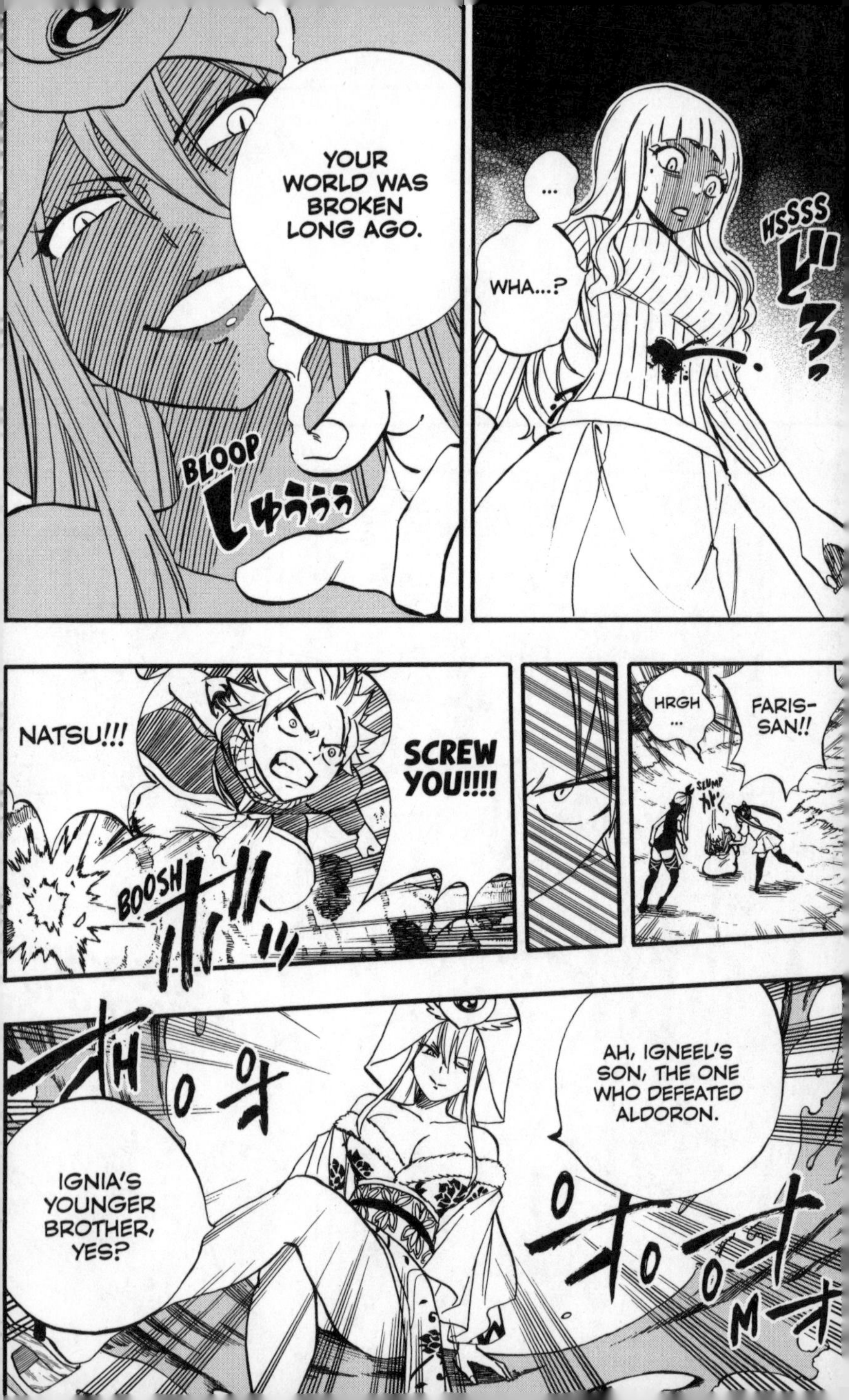
...
WHA...?
HSSSS
YOUR WORLD WAS BROKEN LONG AGO.
BLOOP
しゅうううう
FARIS-SAN!!
HRGH ...
SLUMP
SCREW YOU!!!!
NATSU!!!
BOOSH
AH, IGNEEL'S SON, THE ONE WHO DEFEATED ALDORON.
IGNIA'S YOUNGER BROTHER, YES?

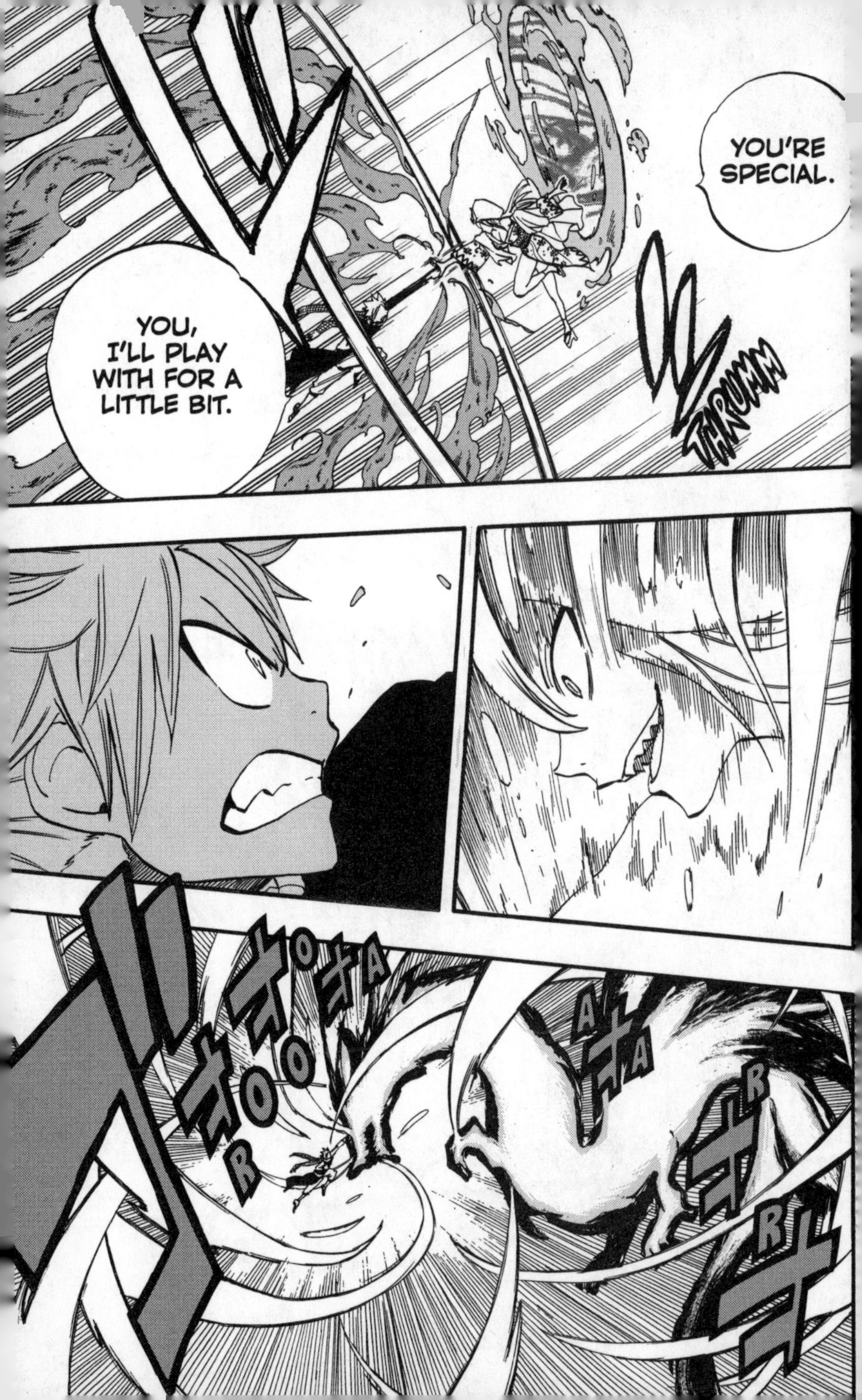
YOU'RE SPECIAL.
YOU, I'LL PLAY WITH FOR A LITTLE BIT.
THRUMM
AARR
ROOOA

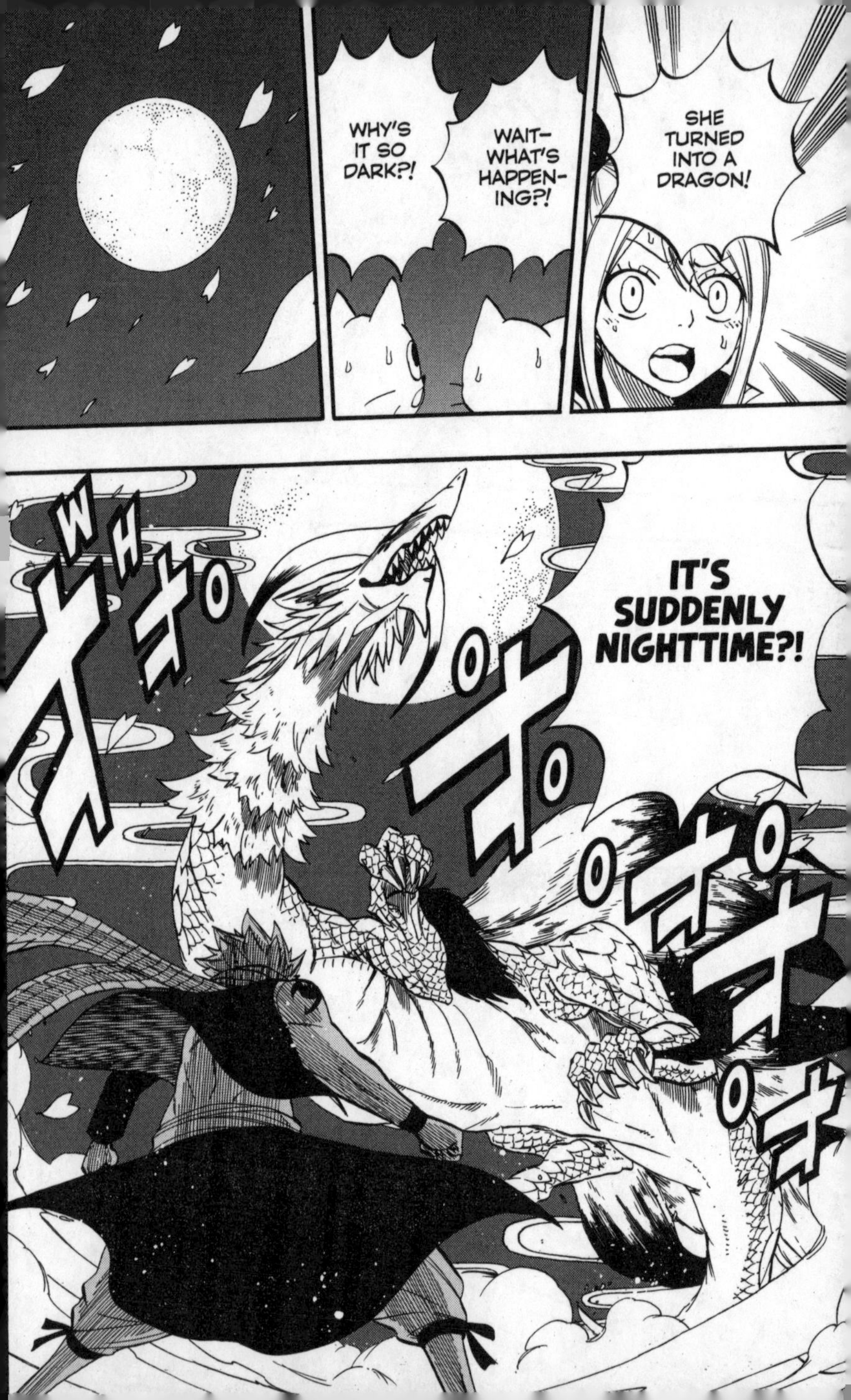
SHE TURNED INTO A DRAGON!
WAIT— WHAT'S HAPPEN-ING?!
WHY'S IT SO DARK?!
IT'S SUDDENLY NIGHTTIME?!

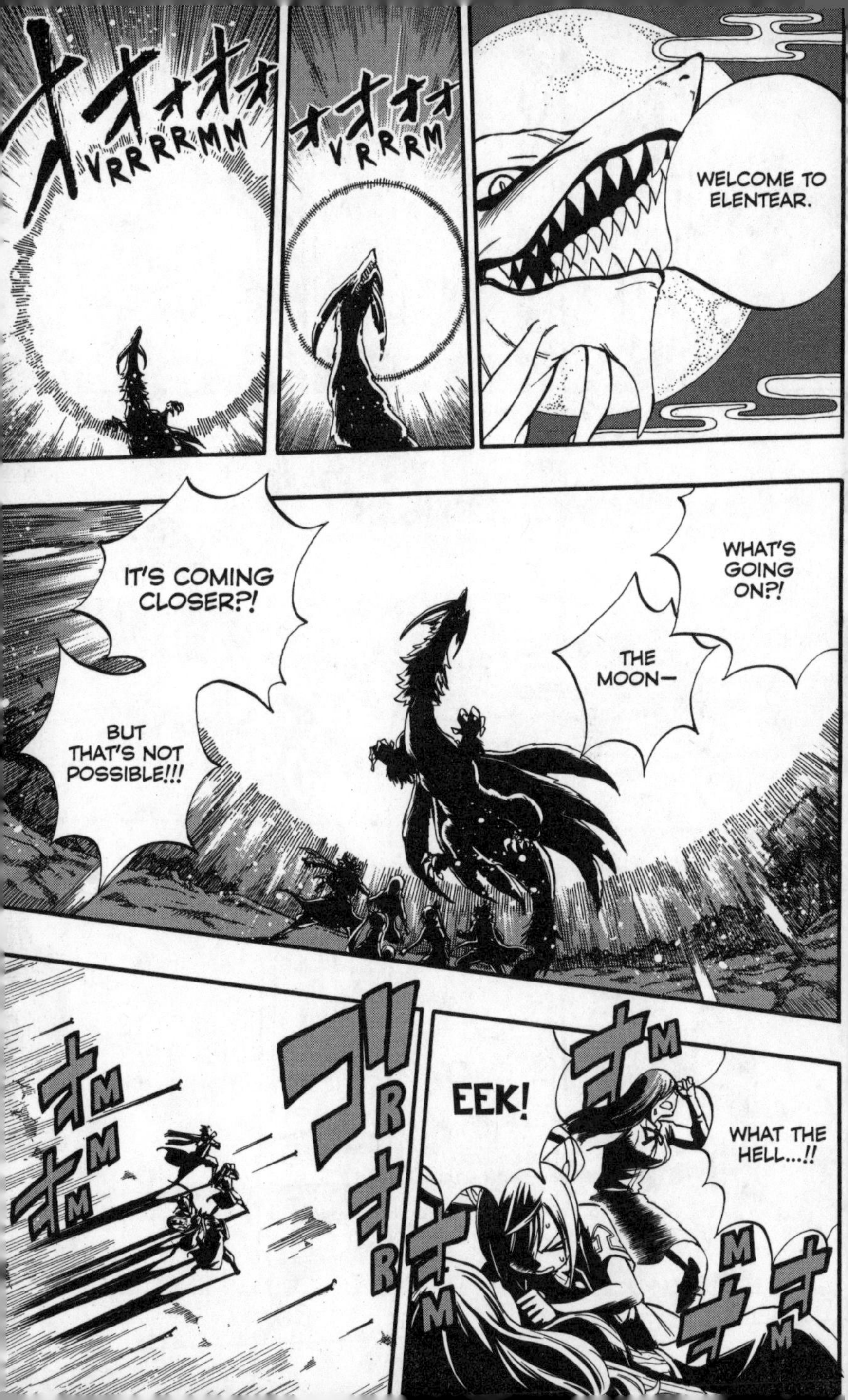
WELCOME TO ELENTEAR.
VRRRM
VRRRRMM
WHAT'S GOING ON?!
THE MOON—
IT'S COMING CLOSER?!
BUT THAT'S NOT POSSIBLE!!!
WHAT THE HELL...!!
EEK!

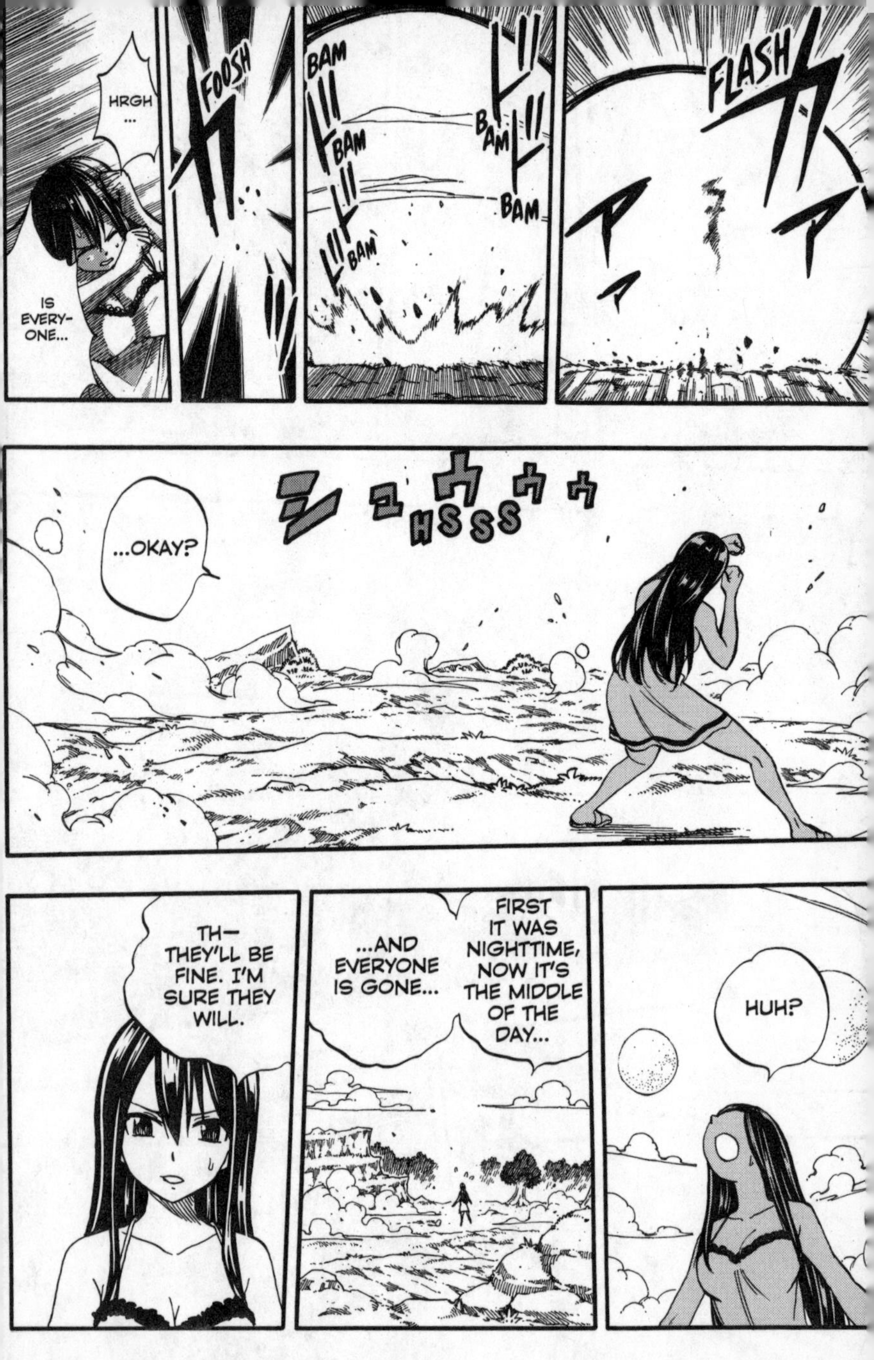
FLASH
BAM
BAM
BAM
BAM
BAM
FOOSH
HRGH ...
IS EVERY-ONE...
シュウウウ
HSSS
...OKAY?
HUH?
FIRST IT WAS NIGHTTIME, NOW IT'S THE MIDDLE OF THE DAY...
...AND EVERYONE IS GONE...
TH— THEY'LL BE FINE. I'M SURE THEY WILL.

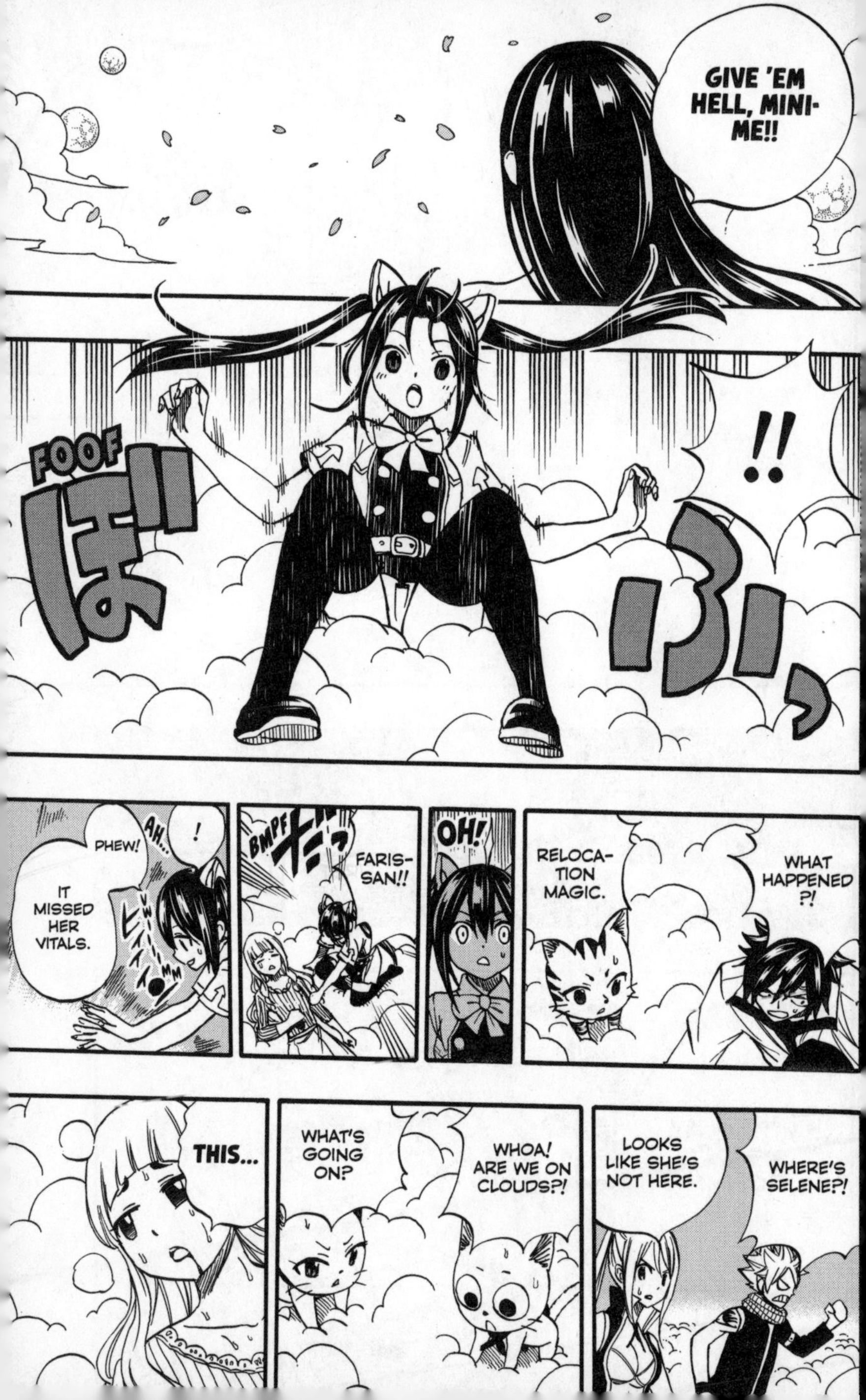
GIVE 'EM HELL, MINI-ME!!
!!
FOOF
WHAT HAPPENED?!
RELOCATION MAGIC.
OH!
FARIS-SAN!!
BMPF
AH...
!
PHEW!
IT MISSED HER VITALS.
VWI-I-IMM
WHERE'S SELENE?!
LOOKS LIKE SHE'S NOT HERE.
WHOA! ARE WE ON CLOUDS?!
WHAT'S GOING ON?
THIS...

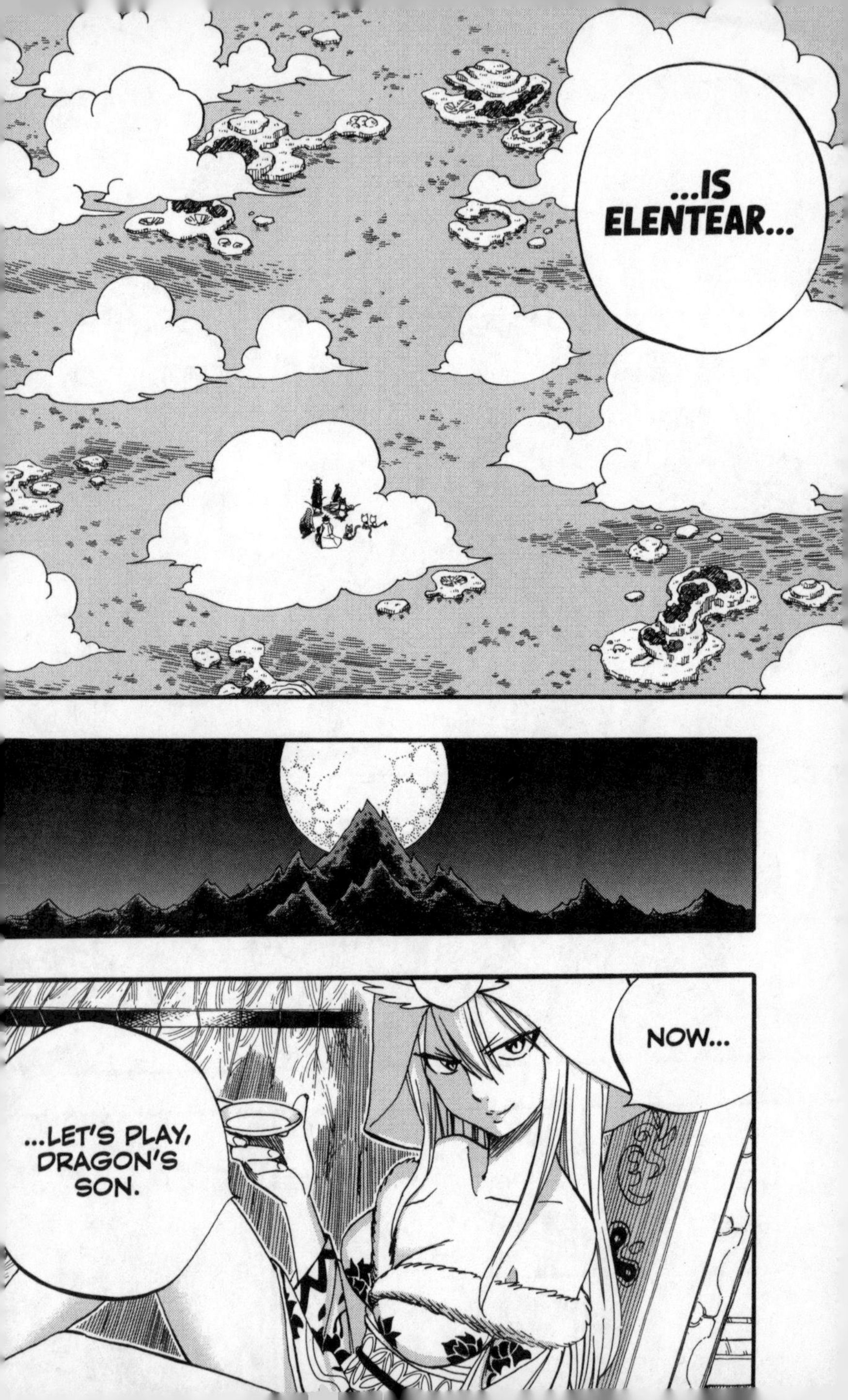
...IS ELENTEAR...
NOW...
...LET'S PLAY, DRAGON'S SON.

FAIRY TAIL 100 YEARS QUEST

Chapter 69: The Hand

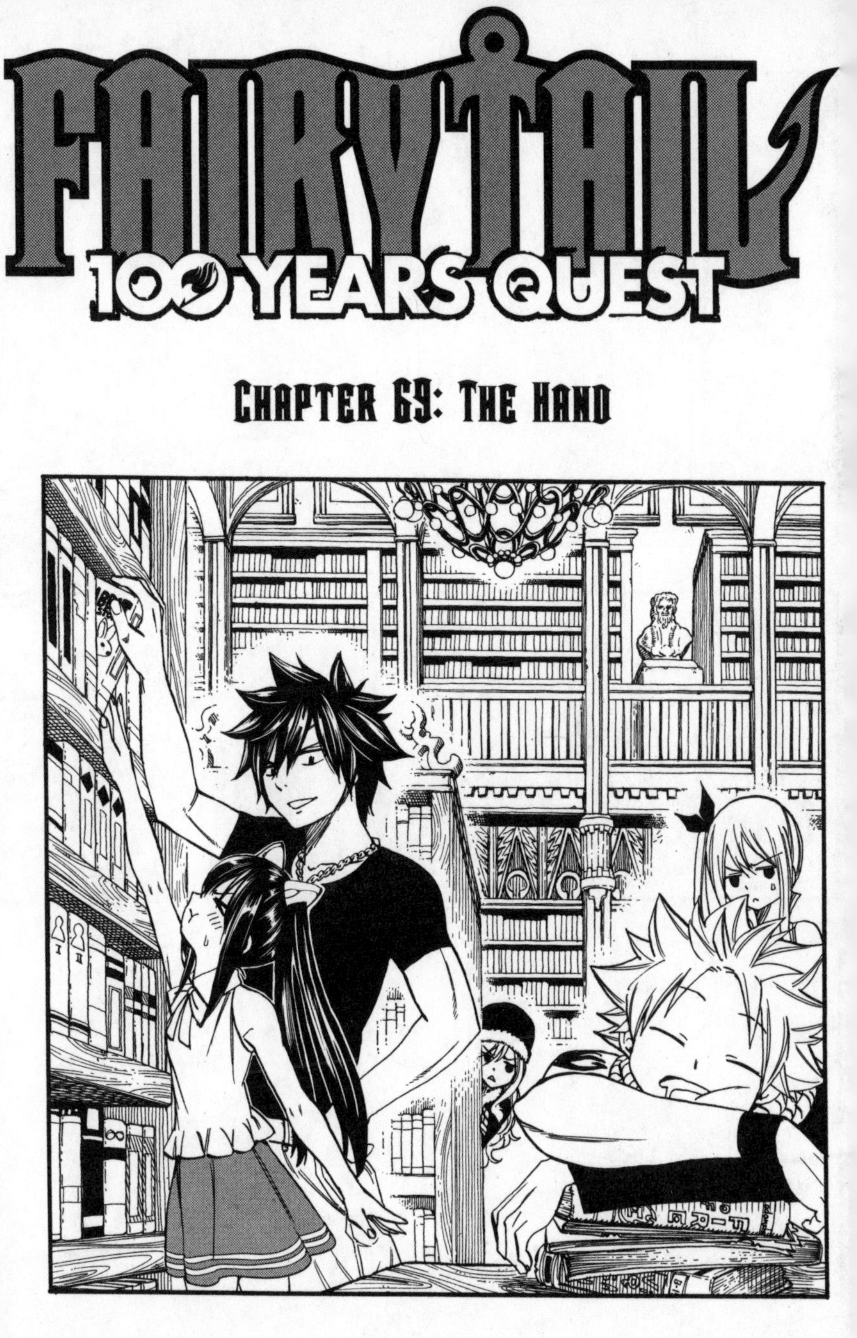

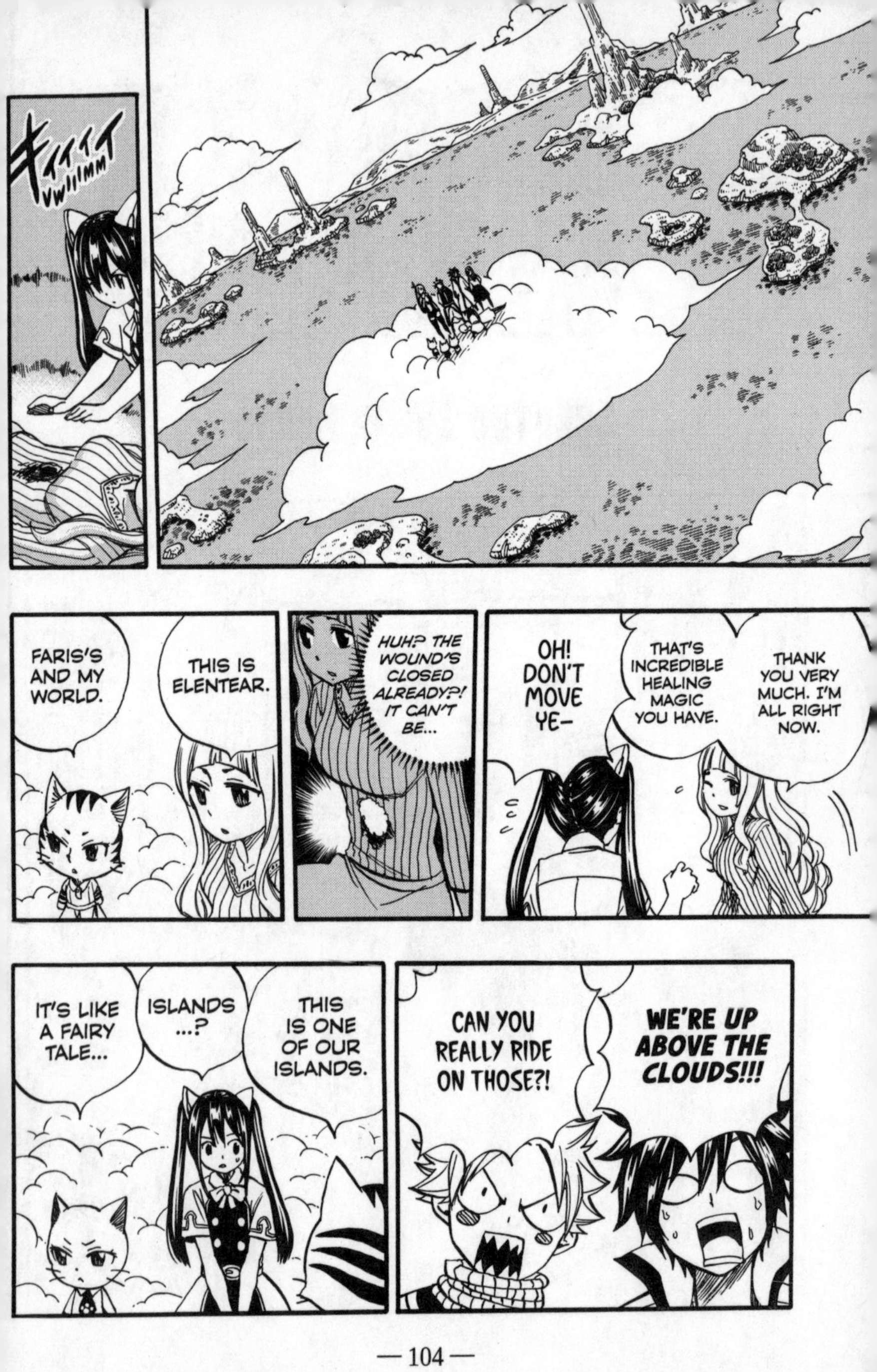
キイイイイ
VWIIIMM
THANK YOU VERY MUCH. I'M ALL RIGHT NOW.
THAT'S INCREDIBLE HEALING MAGIC YOU HAVE.
OH! DON'T MOVE YE–
HUH? THE WOUND'S CLOSED ALREADY?! IT CAN'T BE...
THIS IS ELENTEAR.
FARIS'S AND MY WORLD.
WE'RE UP ABOVE THE CLOUDS!!!
CAN YOU REALLY RIDE ON THOSE?!
THIS IS ONE OF OUR ISLANDS.
ISLANDS ...?
IT'S LIKE A FAIRY TALE...

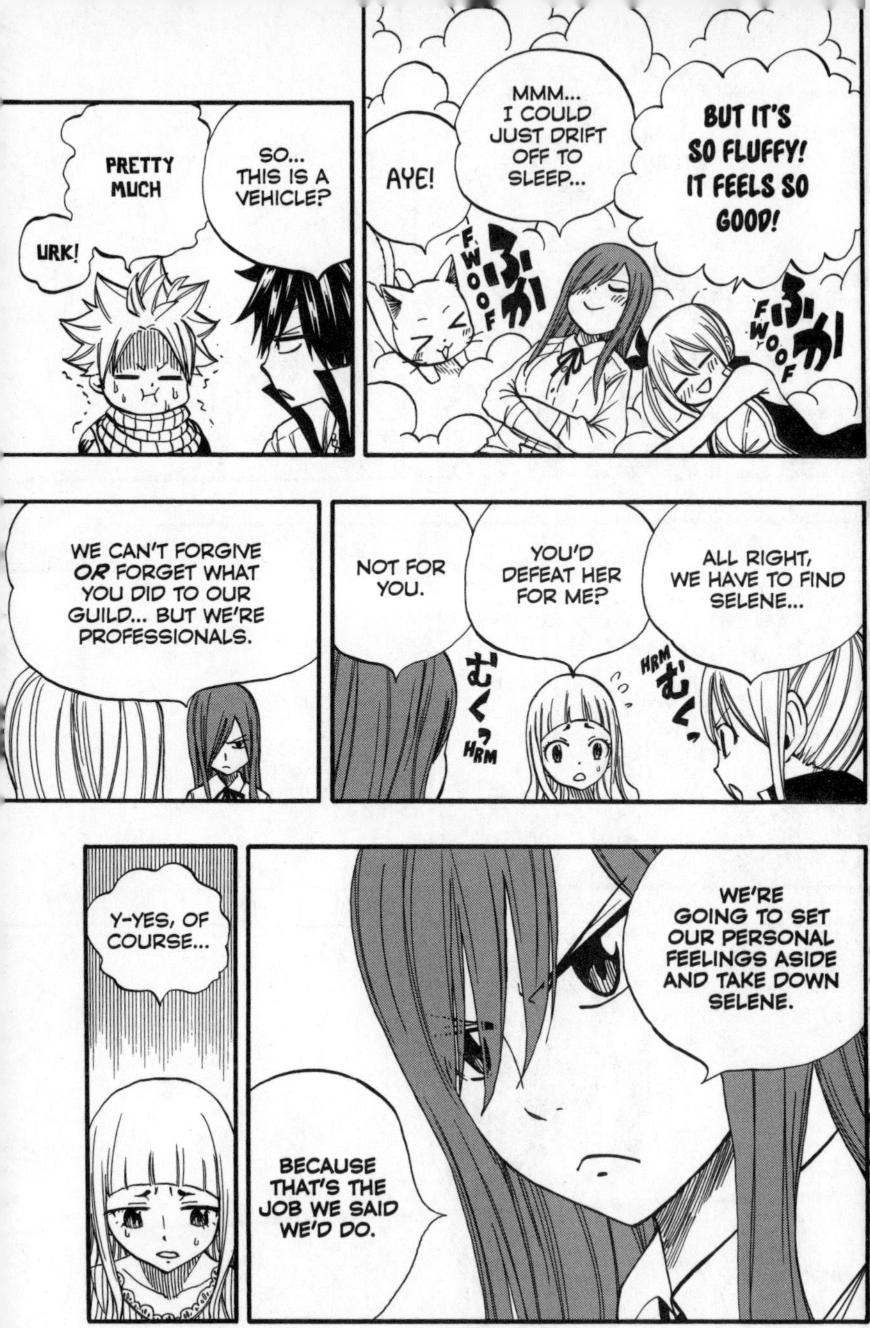
BUT IT'S SO FLUFFY! IT FEELS SO GOOD!
FWOOF
MMM... I COULD JUST DRIFT OFF TO SLEEP...
AYE!
FWOOF
SO... THIS IS A VEHICLE?
PRETTY MUCH
URK!
ALL RIGHT, WE HAVE TO FIND SELENE...
HRM
YOU'D DEFEAT HER FOR ME?
NOT FOR YOU.
HRM
WE CAN'T FORGIVE *OR* FORGET WHAT YOU DID TO OUR GUILD... BUT WE'RE PROFESSIONALS.
WE'RE GOING TO SET OUR PERSONAL FEELINGS ASIDE AND TAKE DOWN SELENE.
BECAUSE THAT'S THE JOB WE SAID WE'D DO.
Y-YES, OF COURSE...

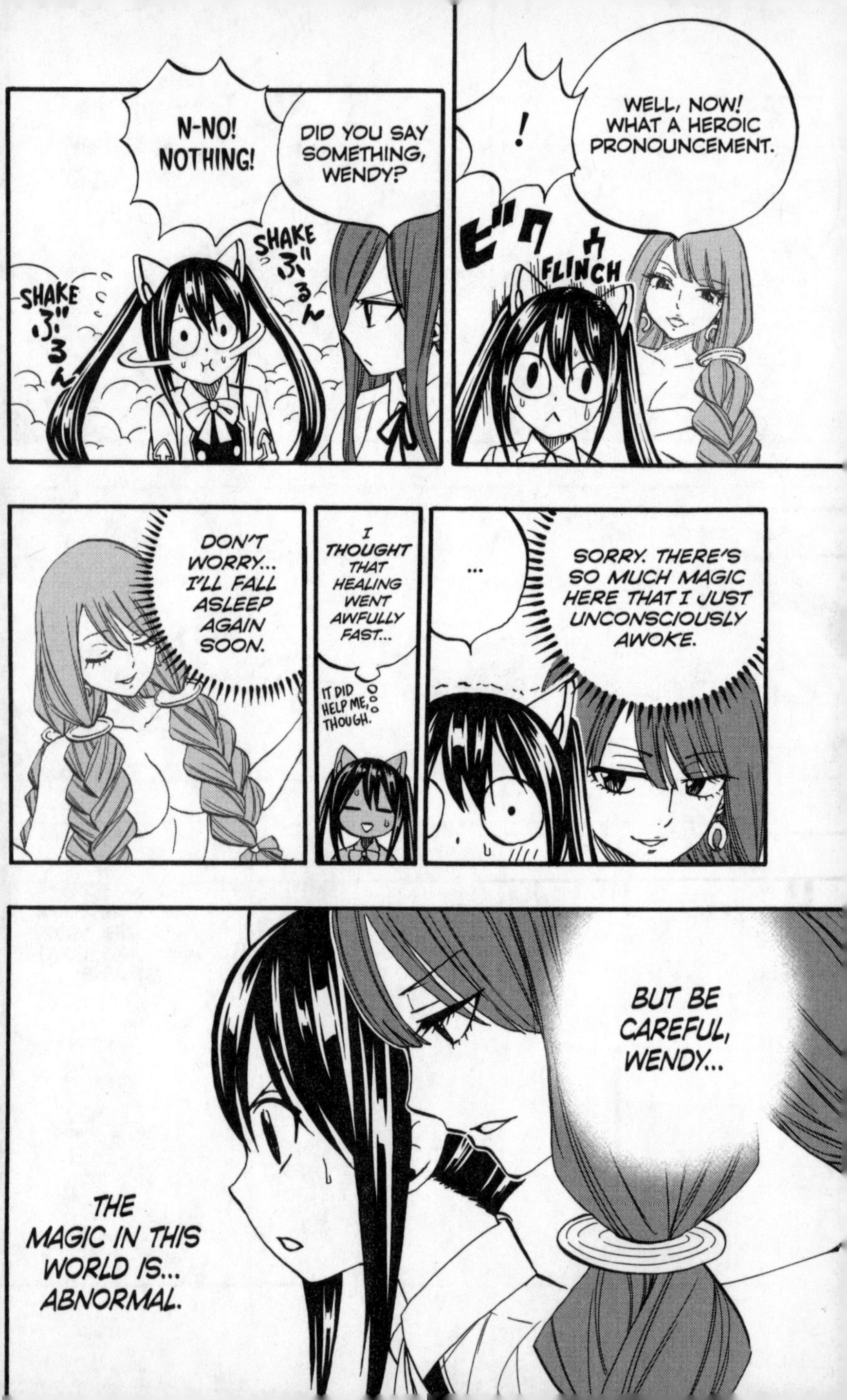
WELL, NOW! WHAT A HEROIC PRONOUNCEMENT.
!
ビクッ
FLINCH
DID YOU SAY SOMETHING, WENDY?
N-NO! NOTHING!
SHAKE ぶるん
SHAKE ぶるん
SORRY. THERE'S SO MUCH MAGIC HERE THAT I JUST UNCONSCIOUSLY AWOKE.
...
I THOUGHT THAT HEALING WENT AWFULLY FAST...
IT DID HELP ME, THOUGH.
DON'T WORRY... I'LL FALL ASLEEP AGAIN SOON.
BUT BE CAREFUL, WENDY...
THE MAGIC IN THIS WORLD IS... ABNORMAL.

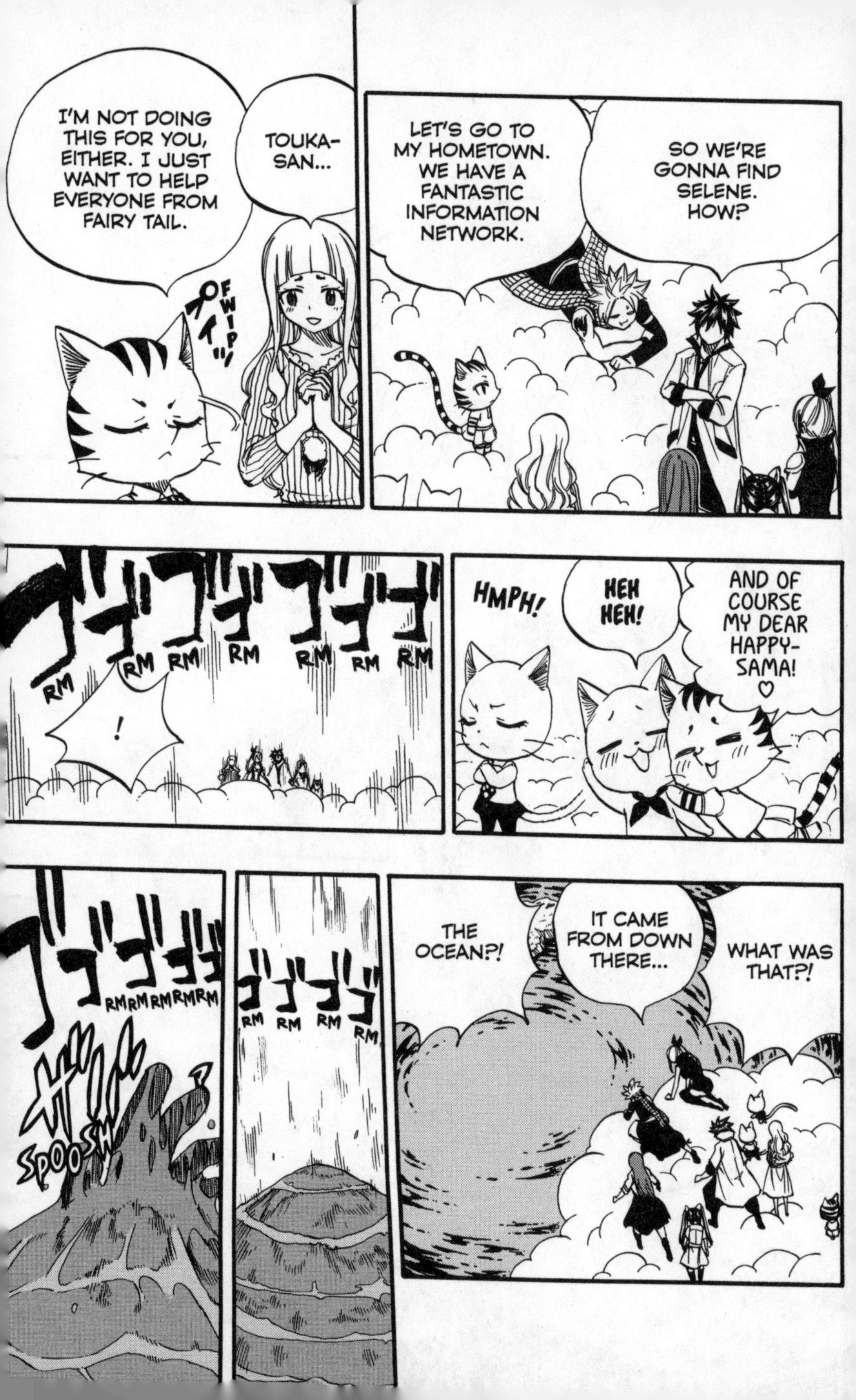
SO WE'RE GONNA FIND SELENE. HOW?
LET'S GO TO MY HOMETOWN. WE HAVE A FANTASTIC INFORMATION NETWORK.
TOUKA-SAN...
I'M NOT DOING THIS FOR YOU, EITHER. I JUST WANT TO HELP EVERYONE FROM FAIRY TAIL.
FWIP
AND OF COURSE MY DEAR HAPPY-SAMA! ♡
HEH HEH!
HMPH!
RM RM RM RM RM RM RM
!
WHAT WAS THAT?!
IT CAME FROM DOWN THERE...
THE OCEAN?!
RM RM RM RM
RMRMRMRMRM
SPOOSH

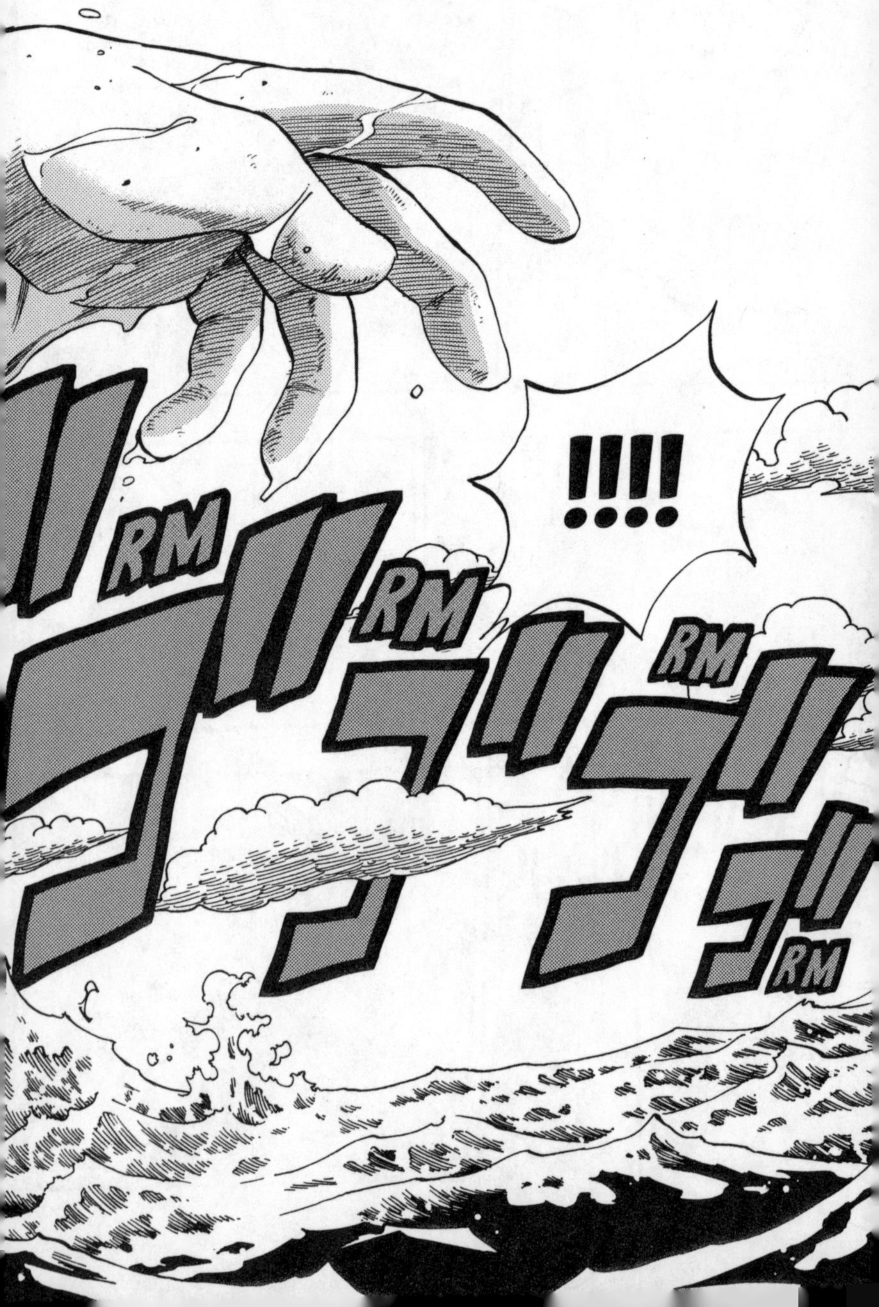
!!!!
RM RM RM RM

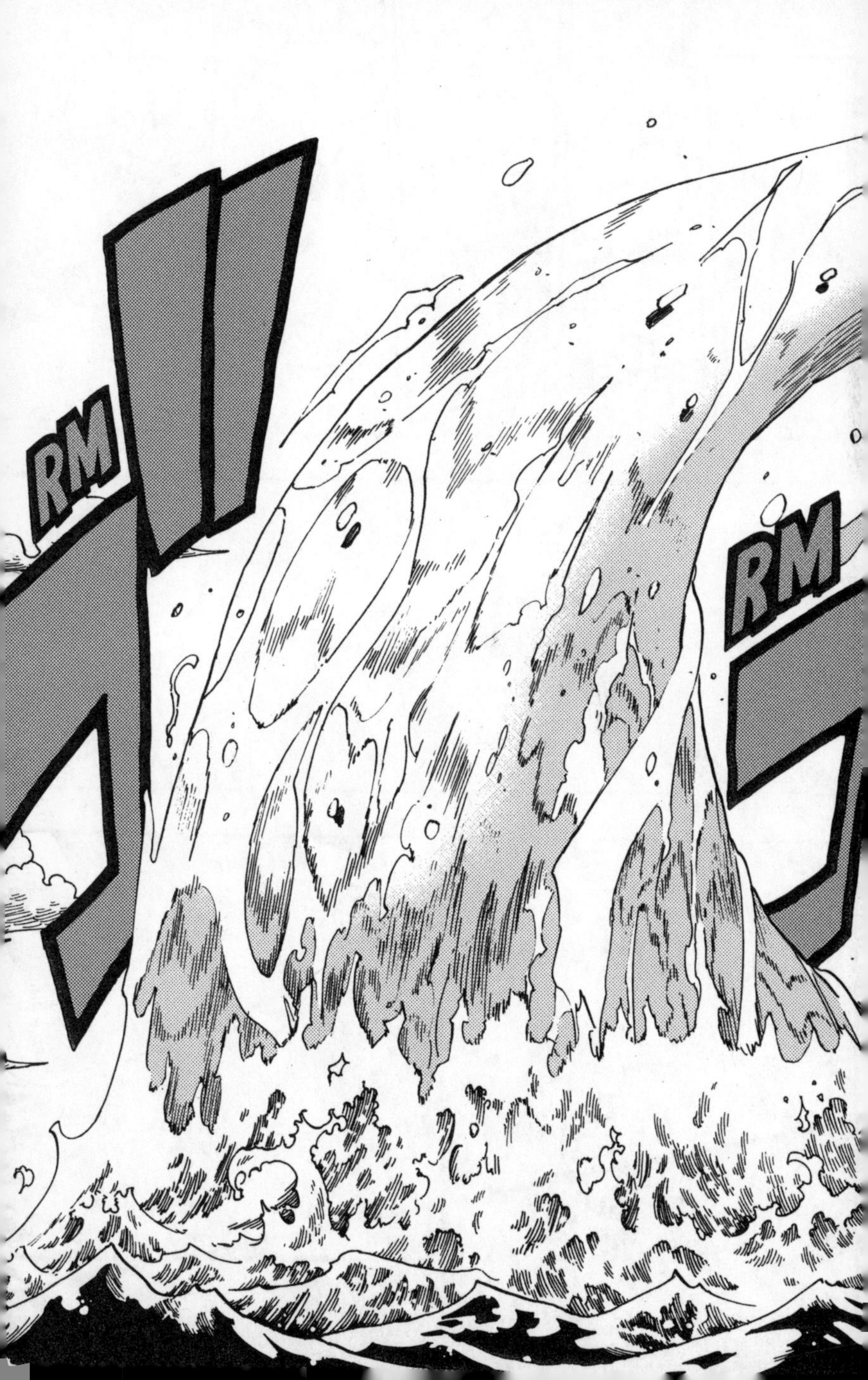
RM
RM

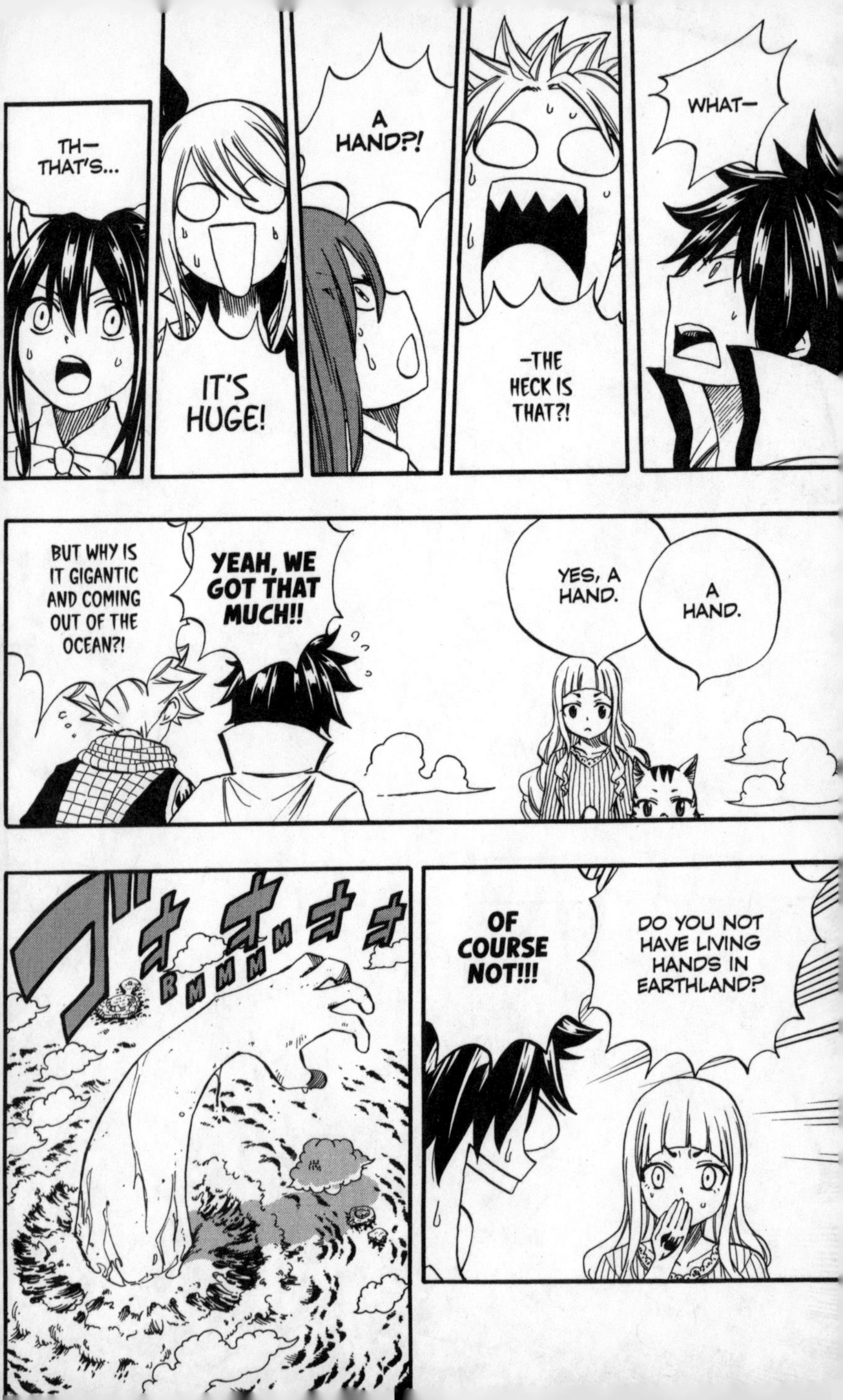
WHAT—
—THE HECK IS THAT?!
A HAND?!
IT'S HUGE!
TH— THAT'S...
A HAND.
YES, A HAND.
YEAH, WE GOT THAT MUCH!!
BUT WHY IS IT GIGANTIC AND COMING OUT OF THE OCEAN?!
DO YOU NOT HAVE LIVING HANDS IN EARTHLAND?
OF COURSE NOT!!!
ゴオオオオ
RMMMM

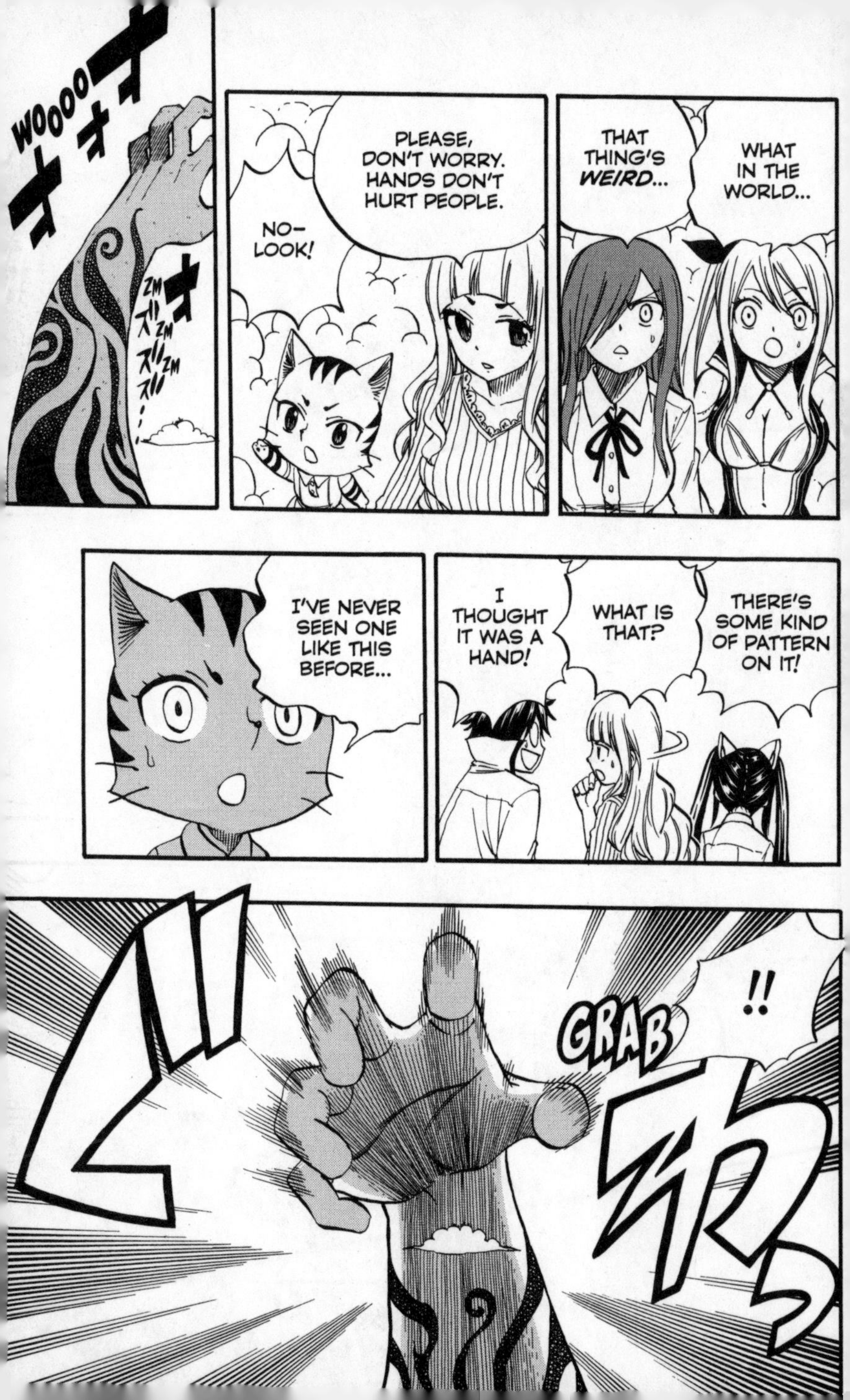
WHAT IN THE WORLD...
THAT THING'S *WEIRD*...
PLEASE, DON'T WORRY. HANDS DON'T HURT PEOPLE.
NO— LOOK!
WOOOO
ZM ZM ZM
THERE'S SOME KIND OF PATTERN ON IT!
WHAT IS THAT?
I THOUGHT IT WAS A HAND!
I'VE NEVER SEEN ONE LIKE THIS BEFORE...
!!
GRAB

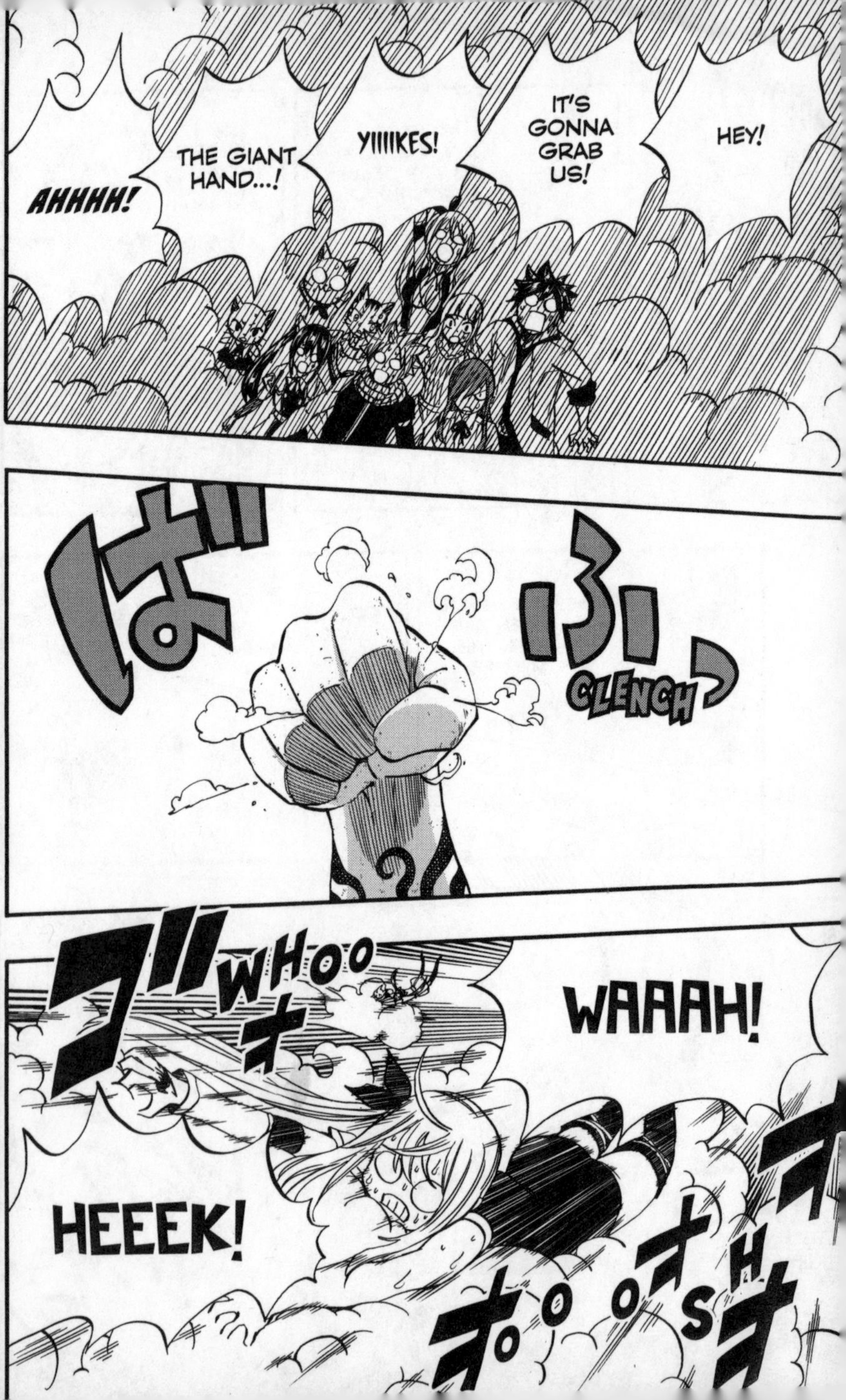
HEY!
IT'S GONNA GRAB US!
YIIIIKES!
THE GIANT HAND...!
AHHHH!
CLENCH
WAAAH!
WHOO
HEEEK!
OOSH

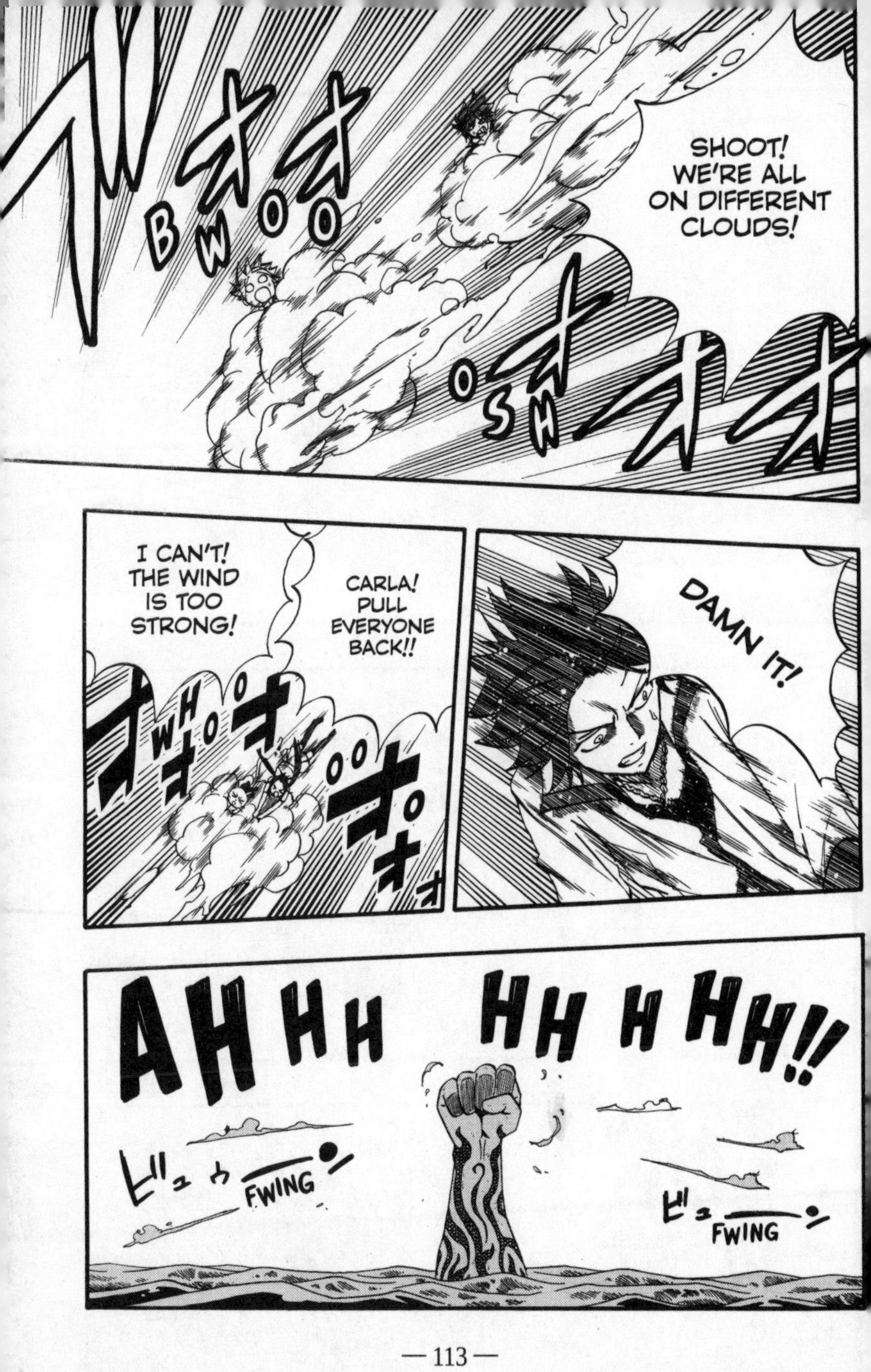

BWOO
SHOOT! WE'RE ALL ON DIFFERENT CLOUDS!
WOOSH
DAMN IT!
CARLA! PULL EVERYONE BACK!!
I CAN'T! THE WIND IS TOO STRONG!
WHOOOO
AHHHHHHHHHH!!
FWING
FWING

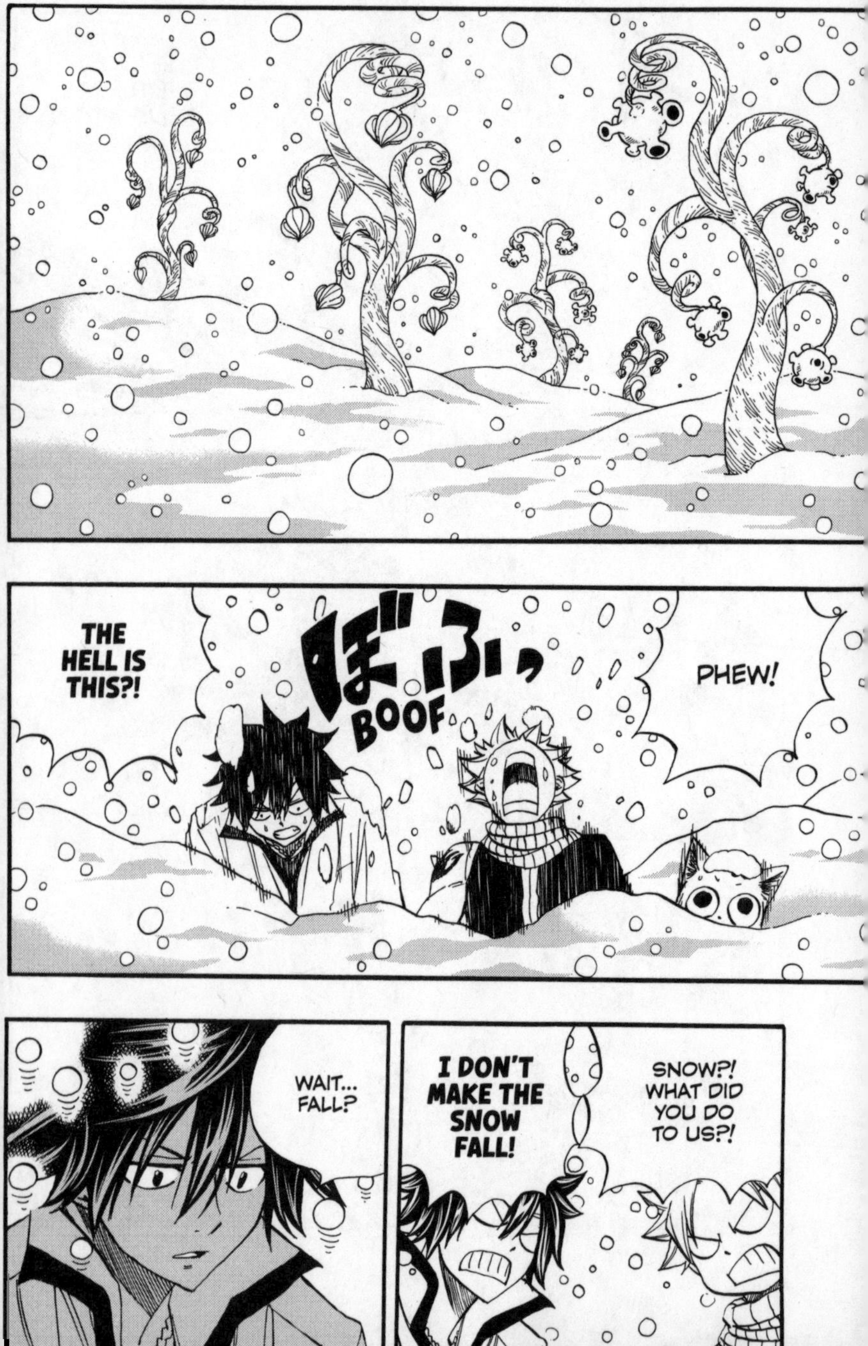
PHEW!
ぼふっ BOOF
THE HELL IS THIS?!
SNOW?! WHAT DID YOU DO TO US?!
I DON'T MAKE THE SNOW FALL!
WAIT... FALL?

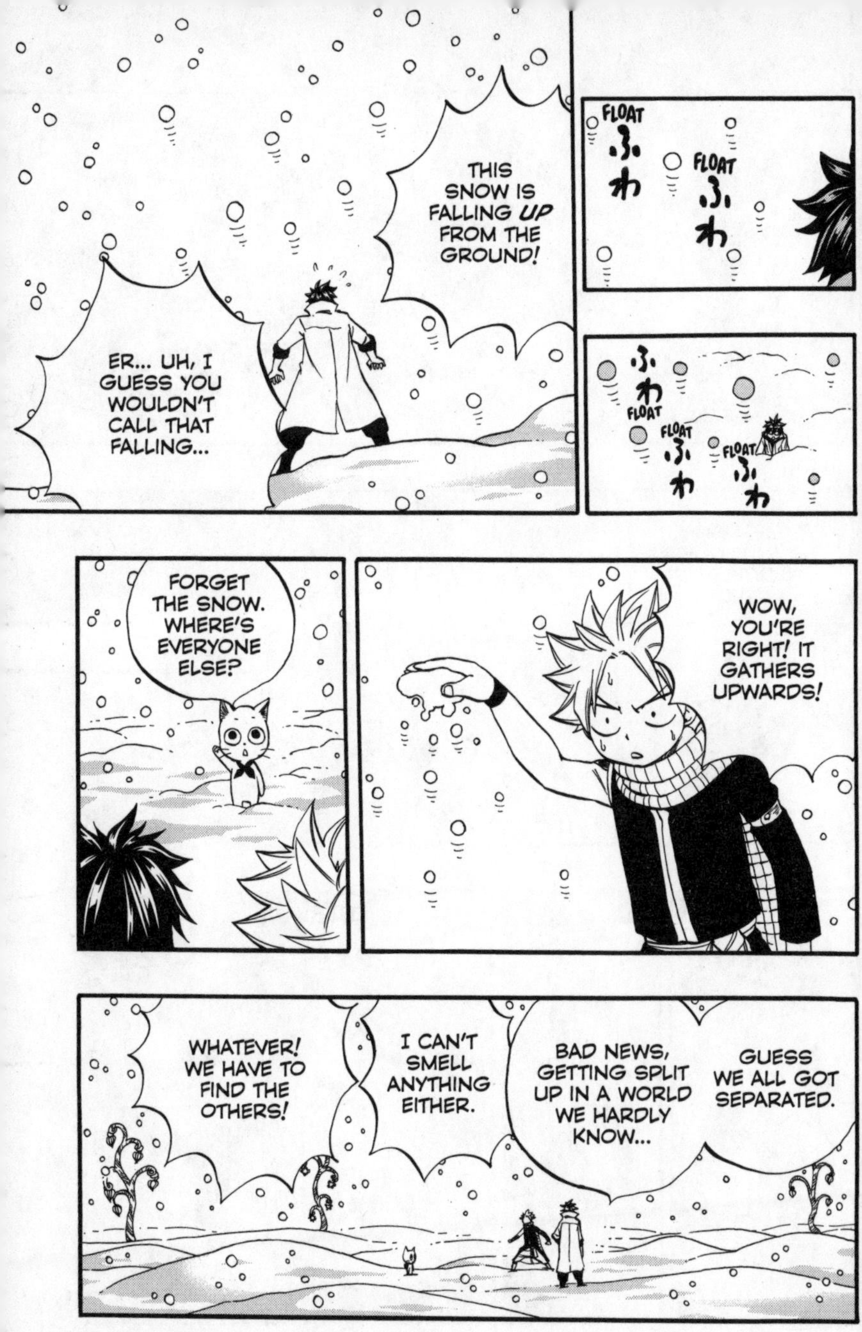
FLOAT
ふわ
FLOAT
ふわ
ふわ
FLOAT
FLOAT
ふわ
FLOAT
ふわ
THIS SNOW IS FALLING *UP* FROM THE GROUND!
ER... UH, I GUESS YOU WOULDN'T CALL THAT FALLING...
WOW, YOU'RE RIGHT! IT GATHERS UPWARDS!
FORGET THE SNOW. WHERE'S EVERYONE ELSE?
GUESS WE ALL GOT SEPARATED.
BAD NEWS, GETTING SPLIT UP IN A WORLD WE HARDLY KNOW...
I CAN'T SMELL ANYTHING EITHER.
WHATEVER! WE HAVE TO FIND THE OTHERS!

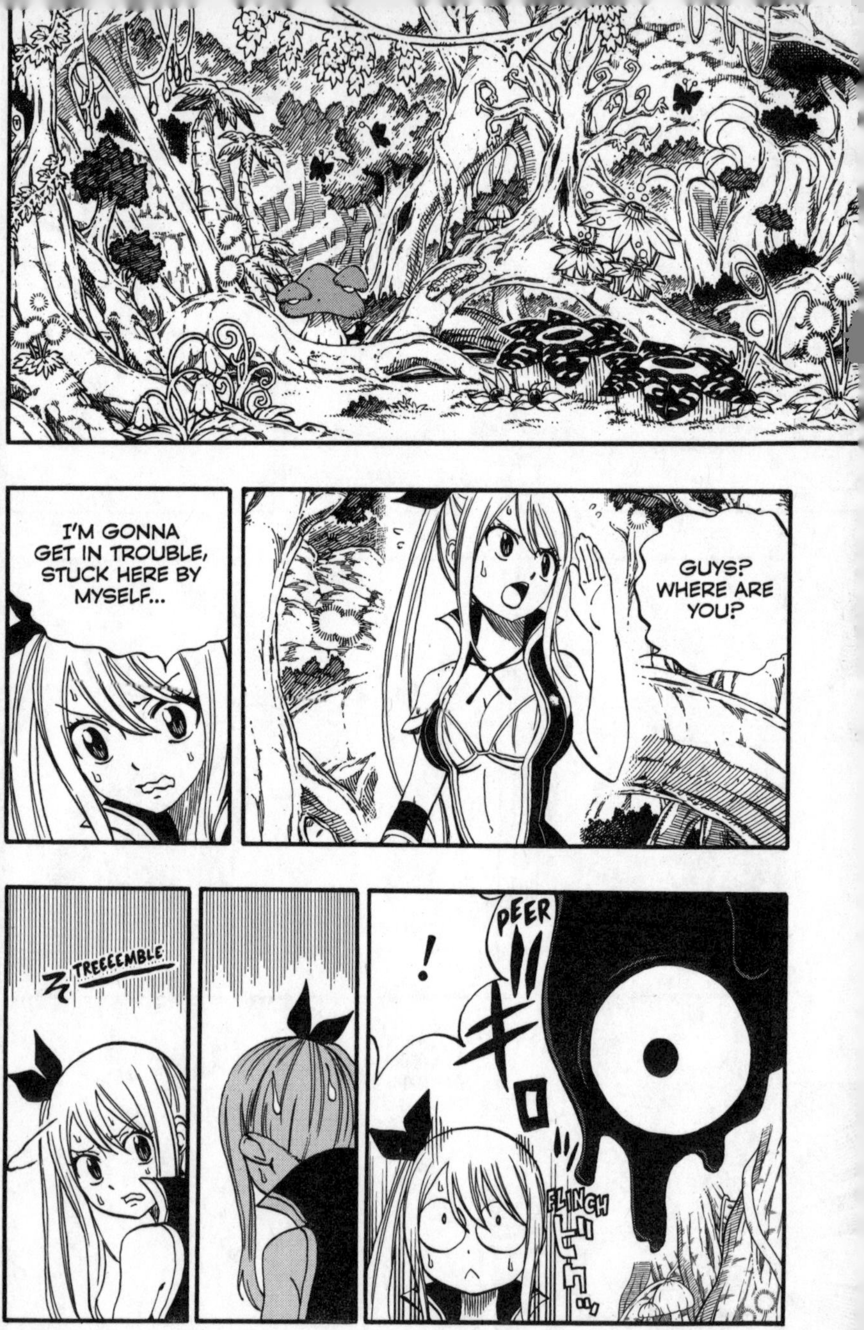
GUYS? WHERE ARE YOU?
I'M GONNA GET IN TROUBLE, STUCK HERE BY MYSELF...
PEER
!
FLINCH
TREEEEMBLE

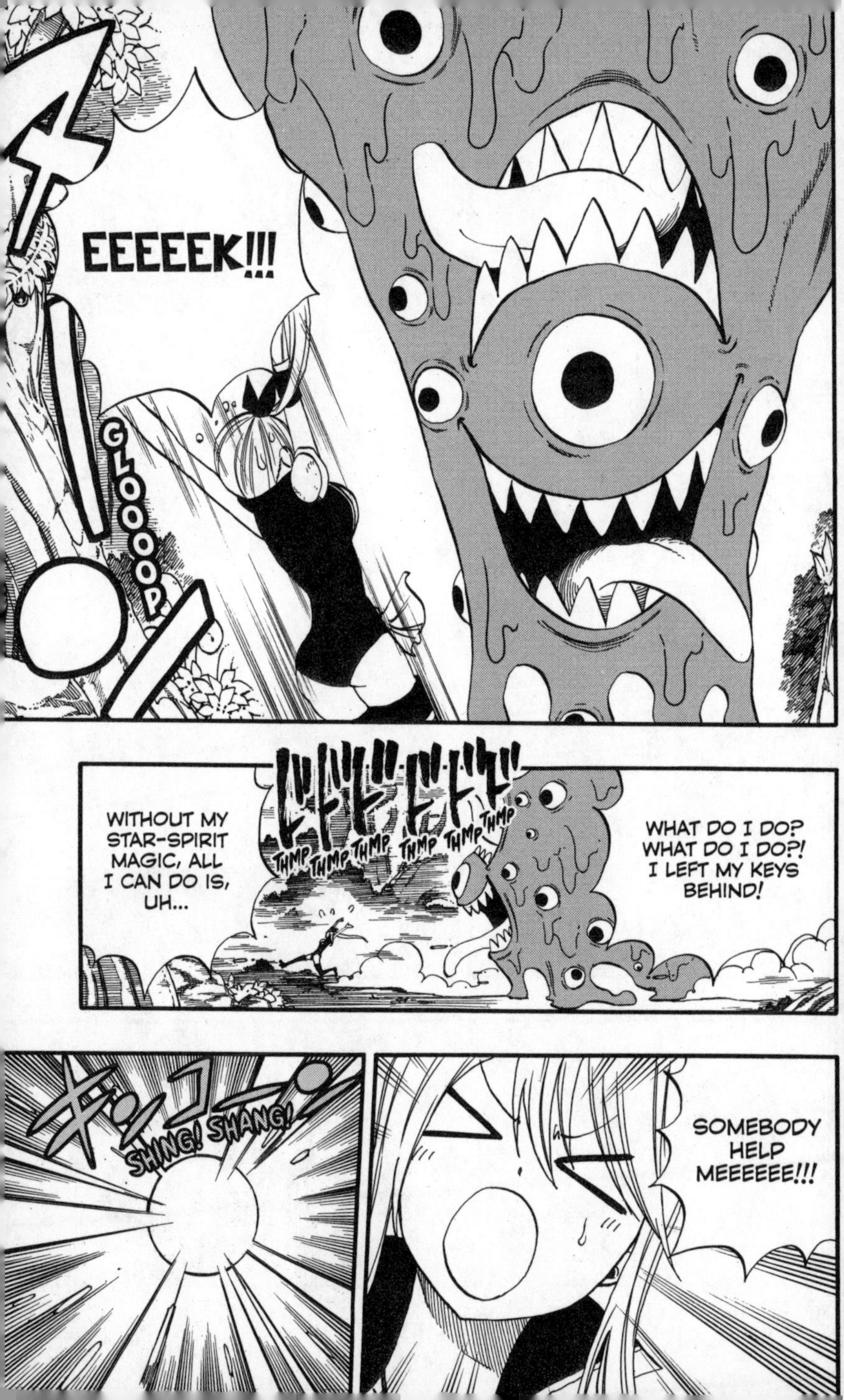
EEEEEK!!!
GLOOOOP
WHAT DO I DO? WHAT DO I DO?! I LEFT MY KEYS BEHIND!
WITHOUT MY STAR-SPIRIT MAGIC, ALL I CAN DO IS, UH...
THMP THMP THMP THMP THMP THMP
SOMEBODY HELP MEEEEEE!!!
SHING! SHANG!

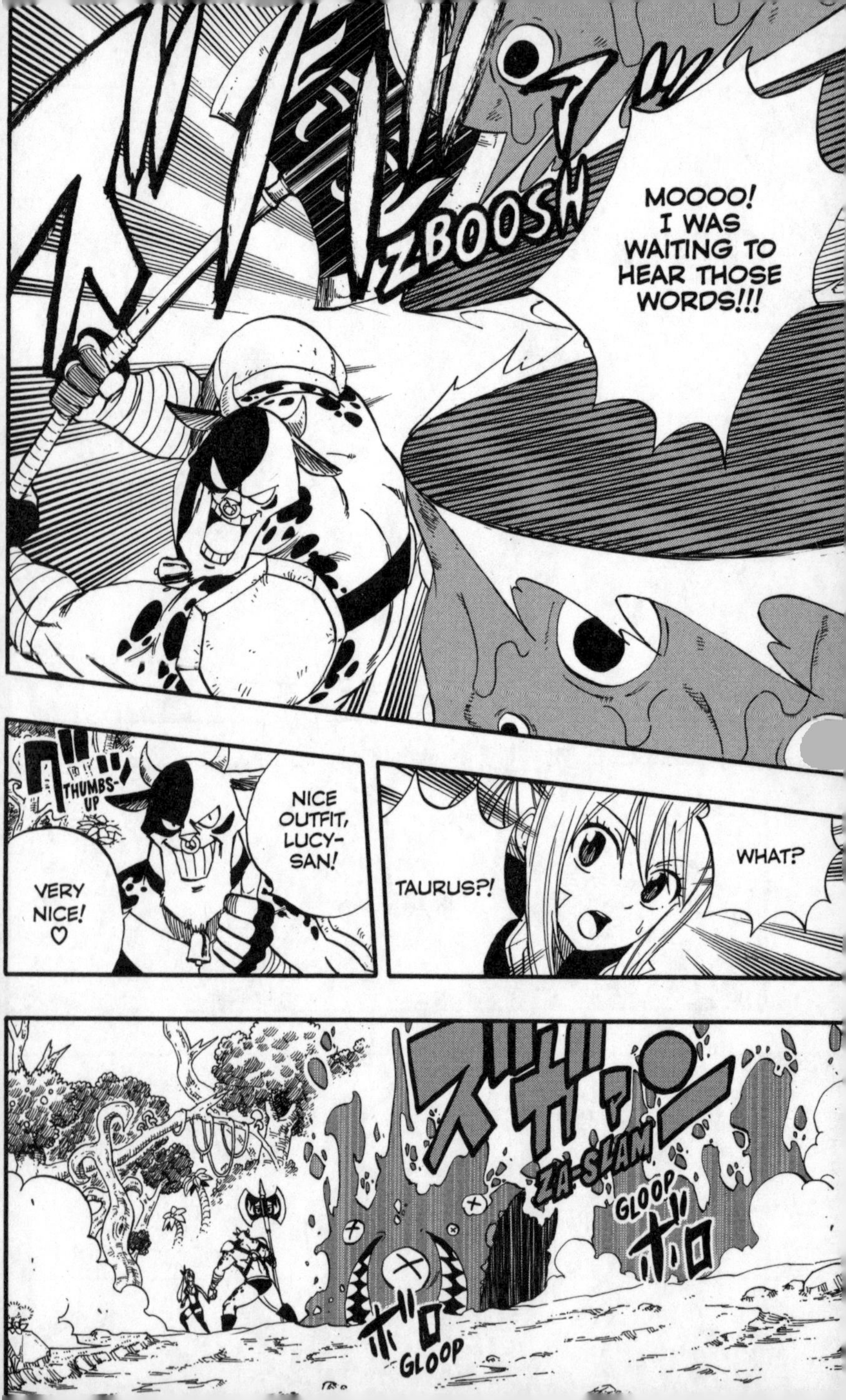
MOOOO! I WAS WAITING TO HEAR THOSE WORDS!!!
ZBOOSH
WHAT?
TAURUS?!
NICE OUTFIT, LUCY-SAN!
THUMBS-UP
VERY NICE! ♡
ZA-SLAM
GLOOP
GLOOP

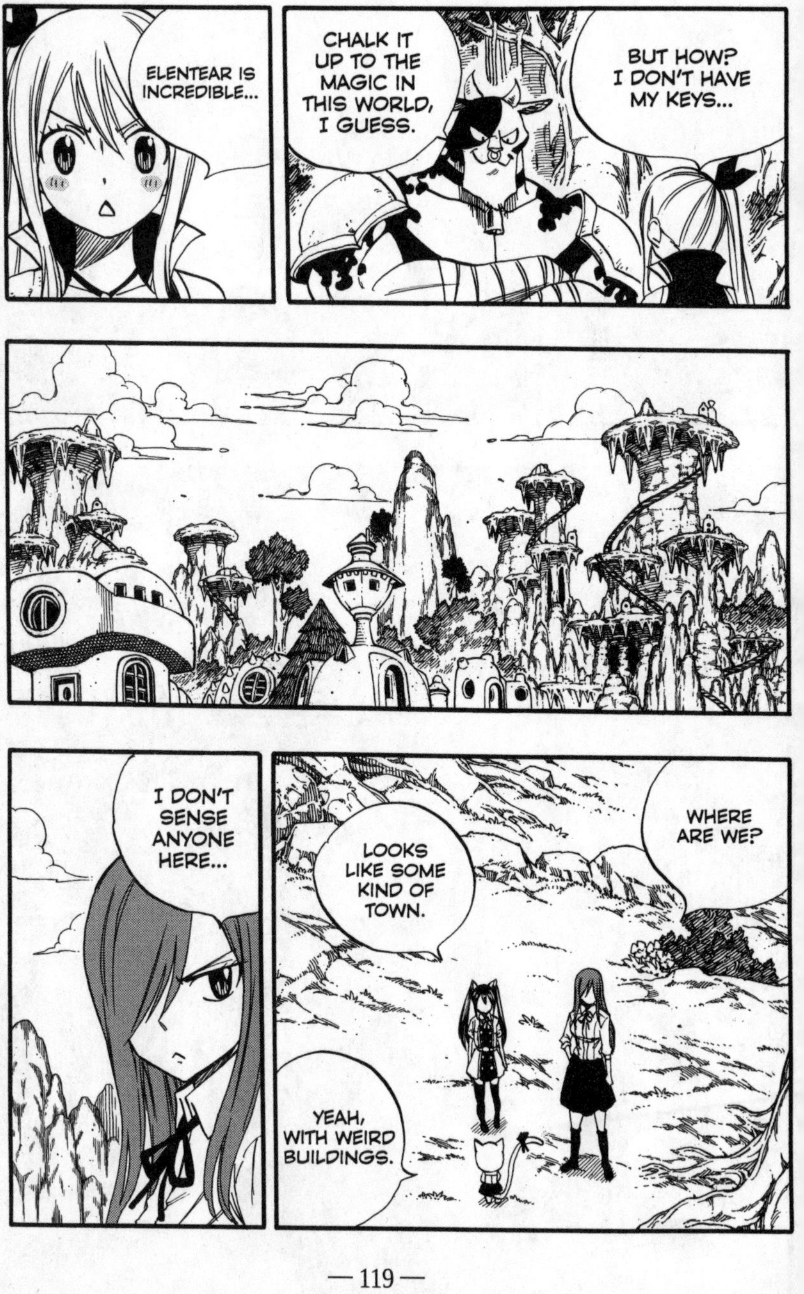
BUT HOW? I DON'T HAVE MY KEYS...
CHALK IT UP TO THE MAGIC IN THIS WORLD, I GUESS.
ELENTEAR IS INCREDIBLE...
WHERE ARE WE?
LOOKS LIKE SOME KIND OF TOWN.
YEAH, WITH WEIRD BUILDINGS.
I DON'T SENSE ANYONE HERE...

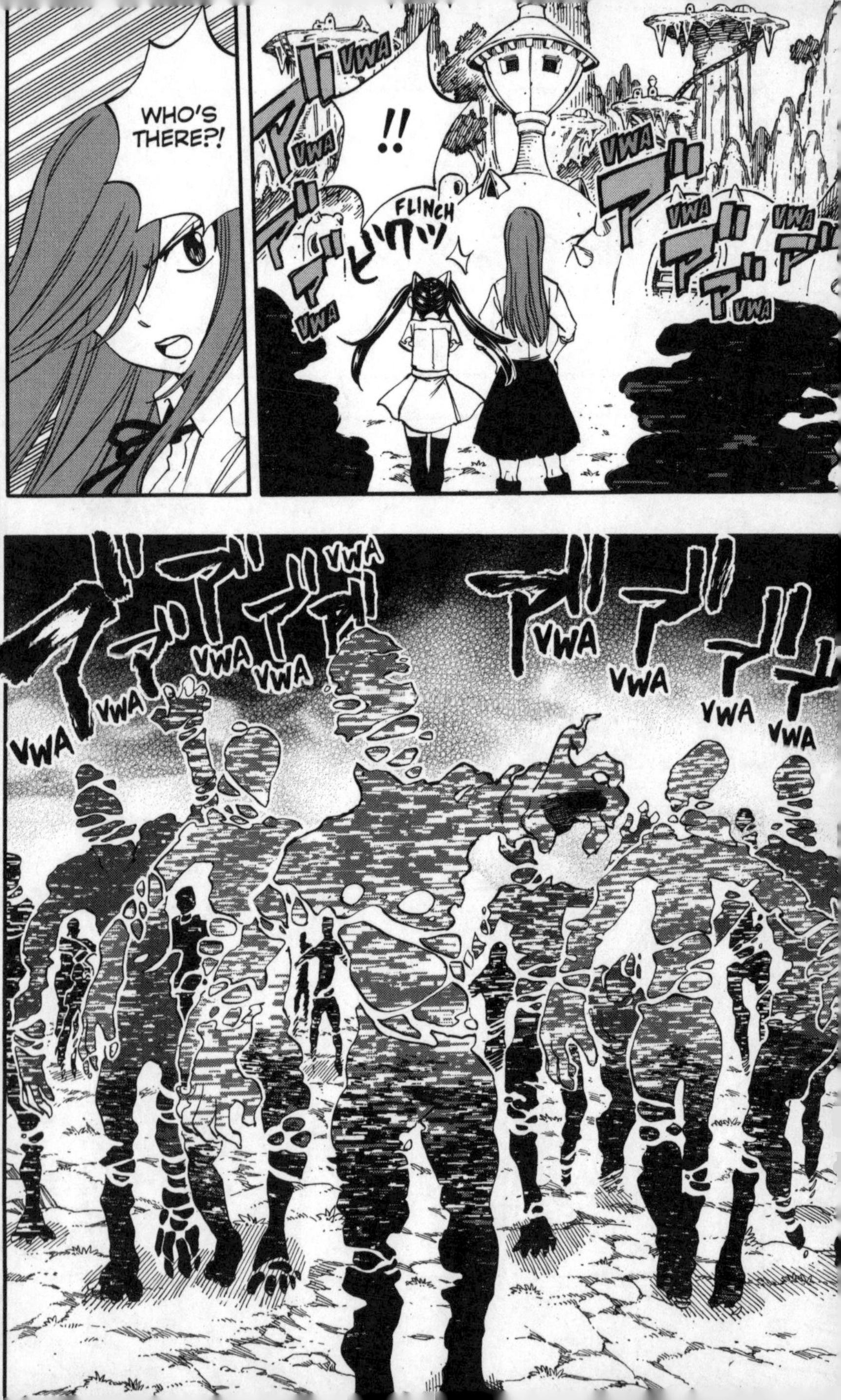
VWA
VWA
VWA
!!
FLINCH
VWA
VWA
VWA
VWA
WHO'S THERE?!
VWA
VWA
VWA
VWA
VWA
VWA
VWA
VWA
VWA

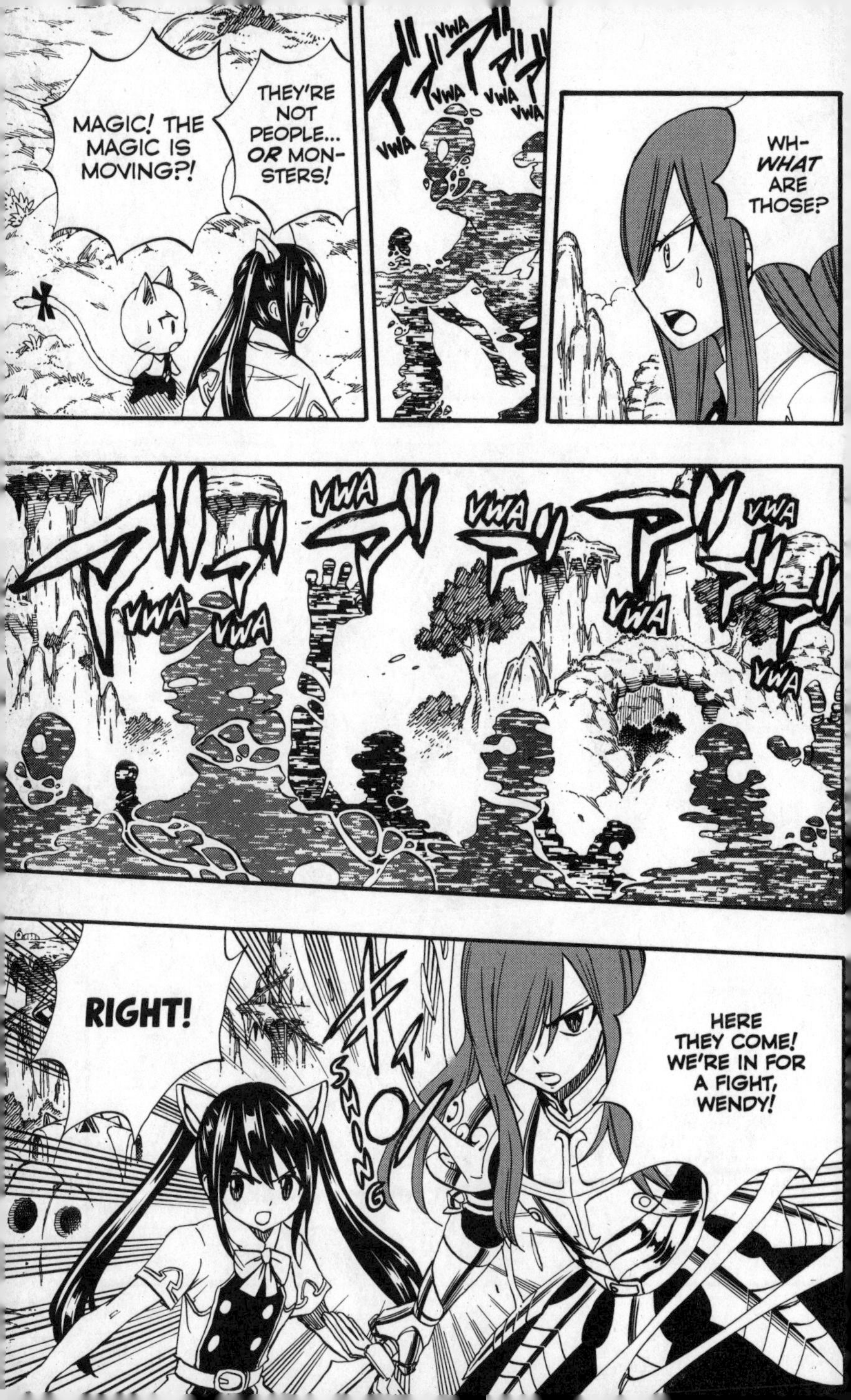
WH-WHAT ARE THOSE?
VWA VWA VWA VWA VWA
THEY'RE NOT PEOPLE... OR MONSTERS!
MAGIC! THE MAGIC IS MOVING?!
VWA VWA VWA VWA VWA VWA VWA VWA
HERE THEY COME! WE'RE IN FOR A FIGHT, WENDY!
SHING
RIGHT!

FLAP
バサ
FLAP
バサ
SO THOSE ARE THE HUMANS SELENE-SAMA BROUGHT.
NOW, SHOW ME, MY DEARS...
ONE OF THE MOONLIGHT DIVINITIES
YOKO
SHOW ME WHETHER YOU'RE FIT TO BE SELENE-SAMA'S TOYS...

FAIRY TAIL
100 YEARS QUEST

Chapter 78: Spiria

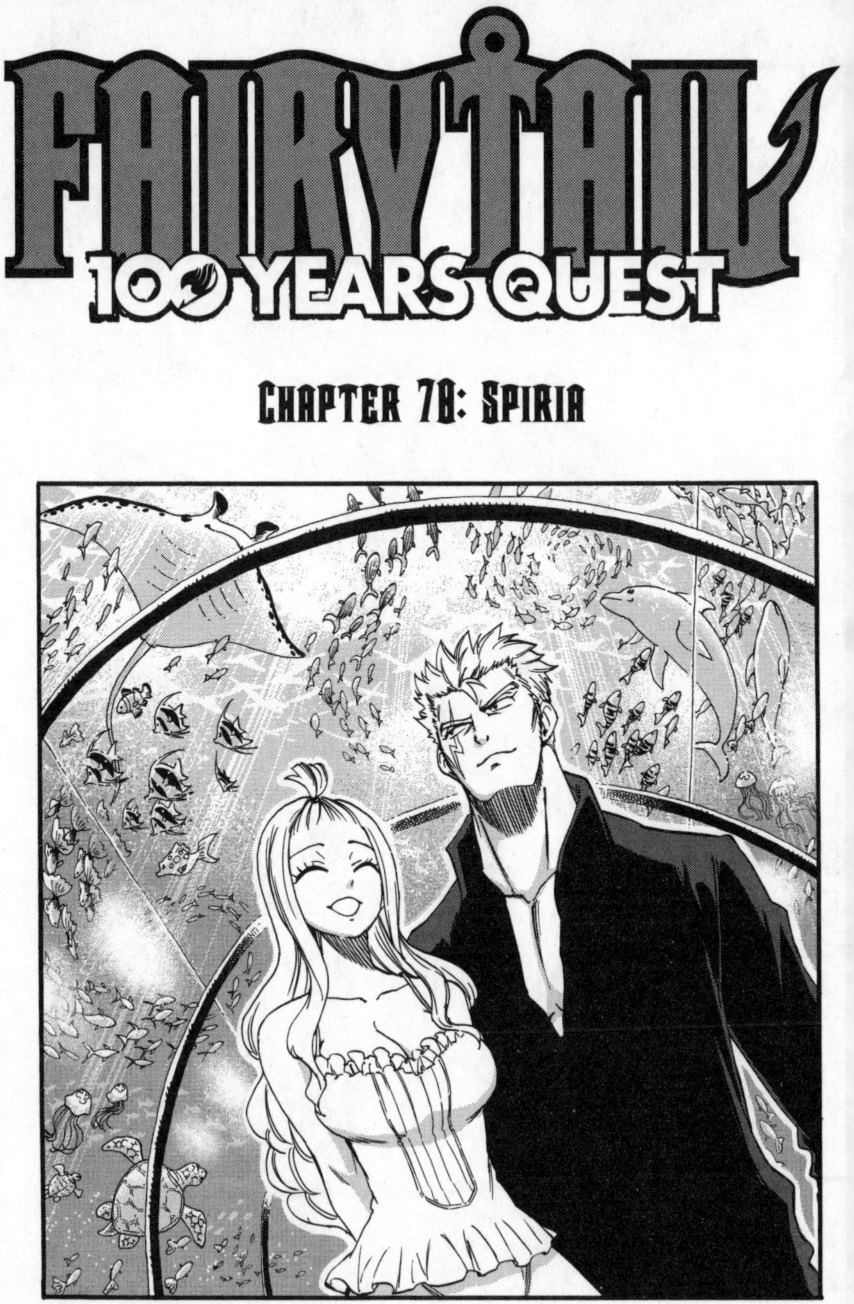

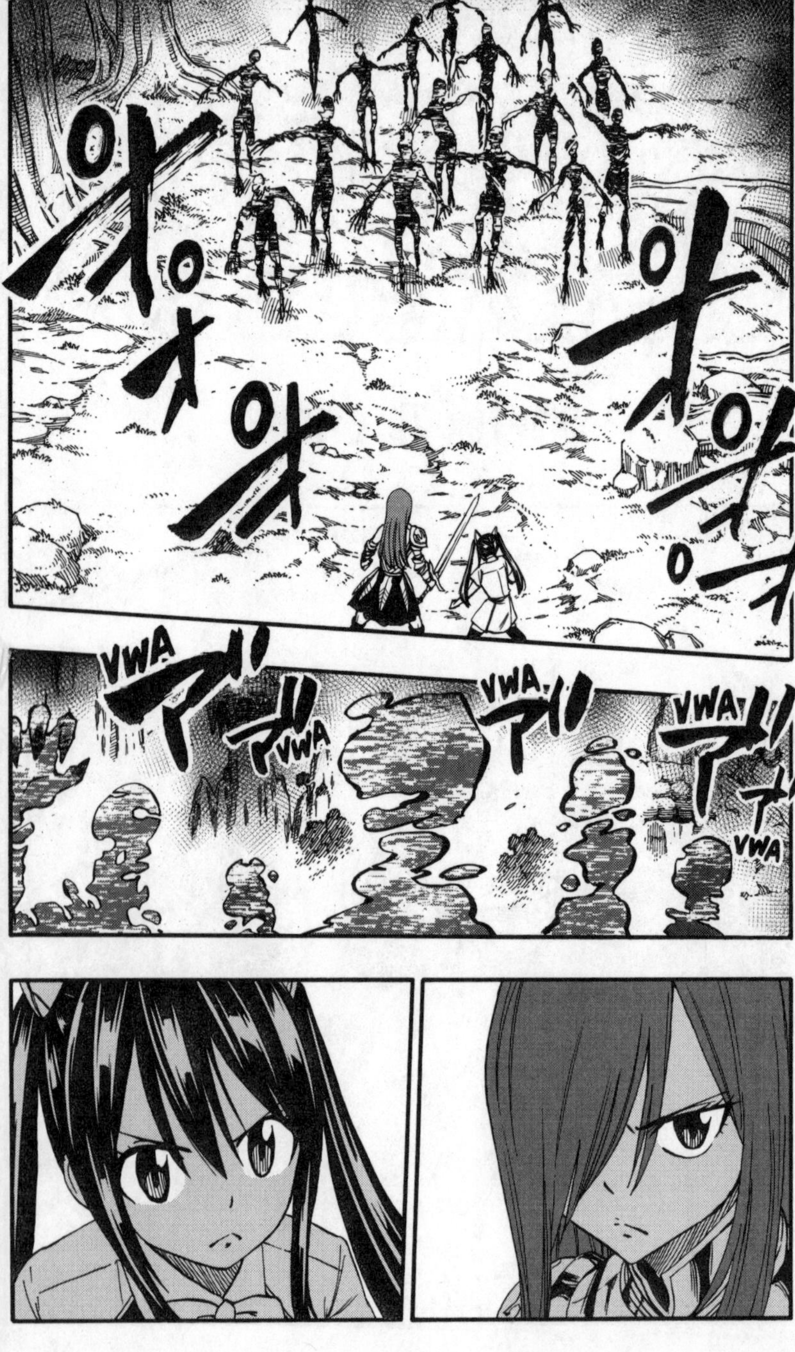
VWA
VWA
VWA
VWA
VWA

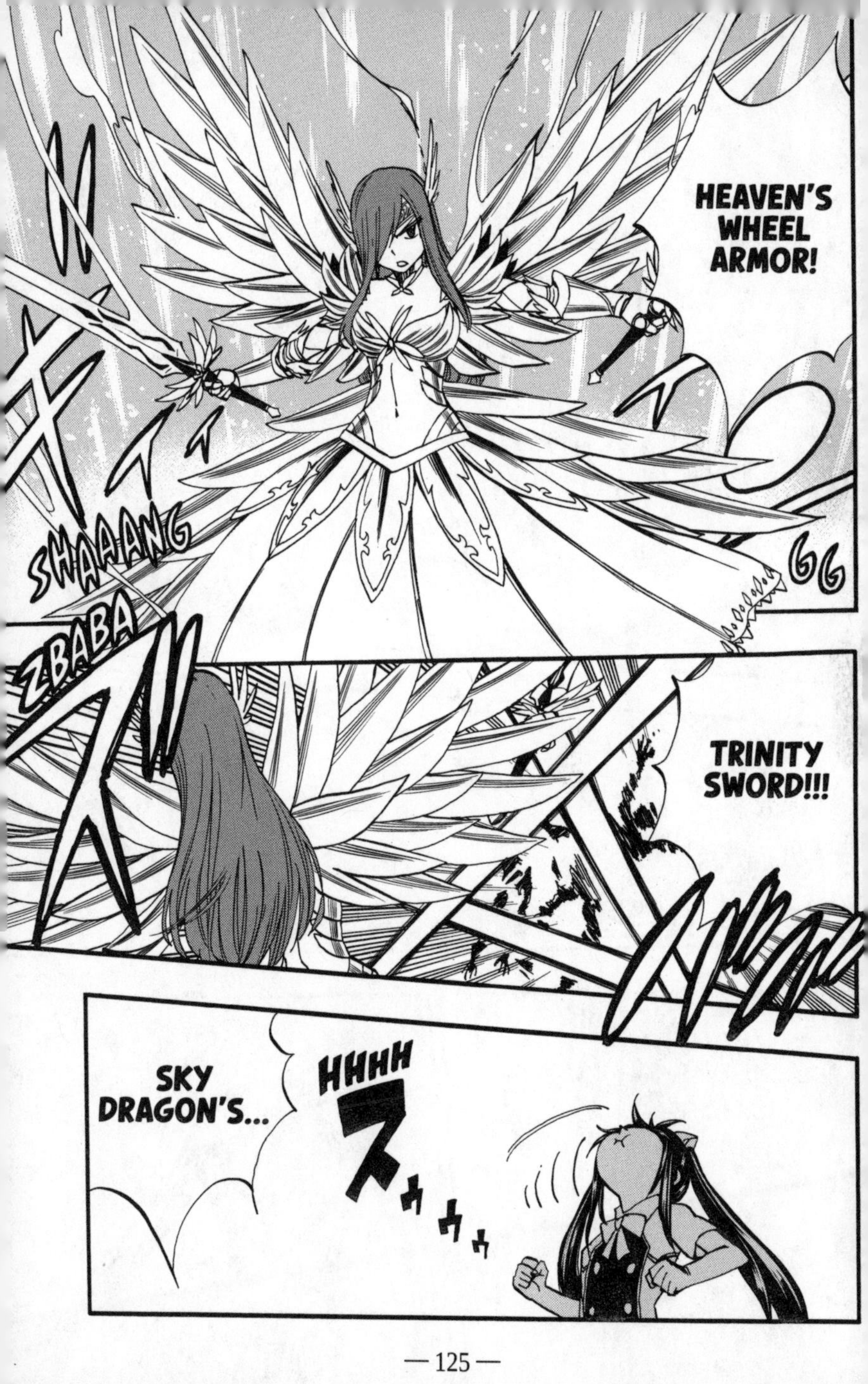
HEAVEN'S WHEEL ARMOR!
GG
SHAAANG
TRINITY SWORD!!!
ZBABA
HHHH
SKY DRAGON'S...

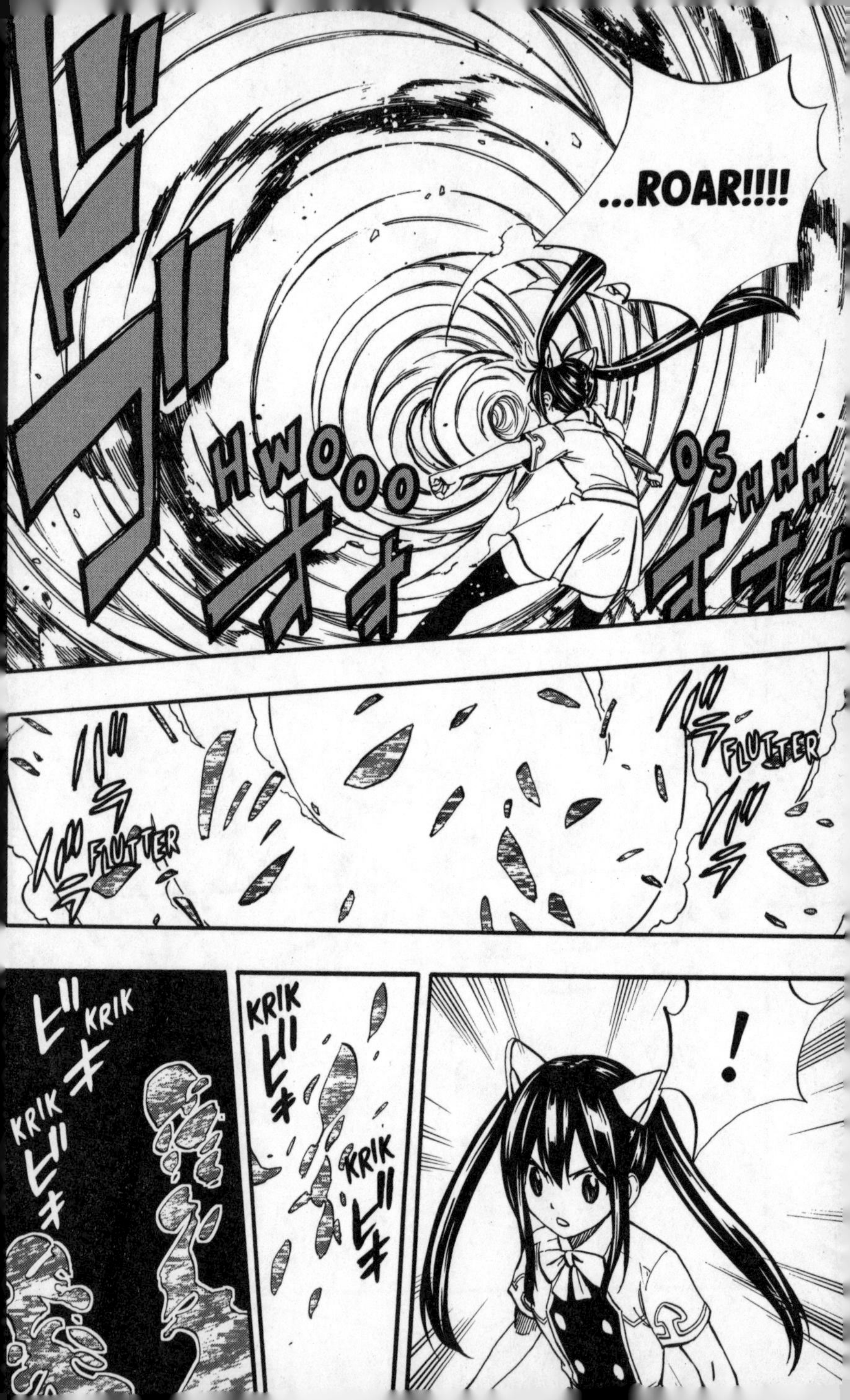
...ROAR!!!!
HWOOO
OSHHH
FLUTTER
FLUTTER
!
KRIK
KRIK
KRIK
KRIK

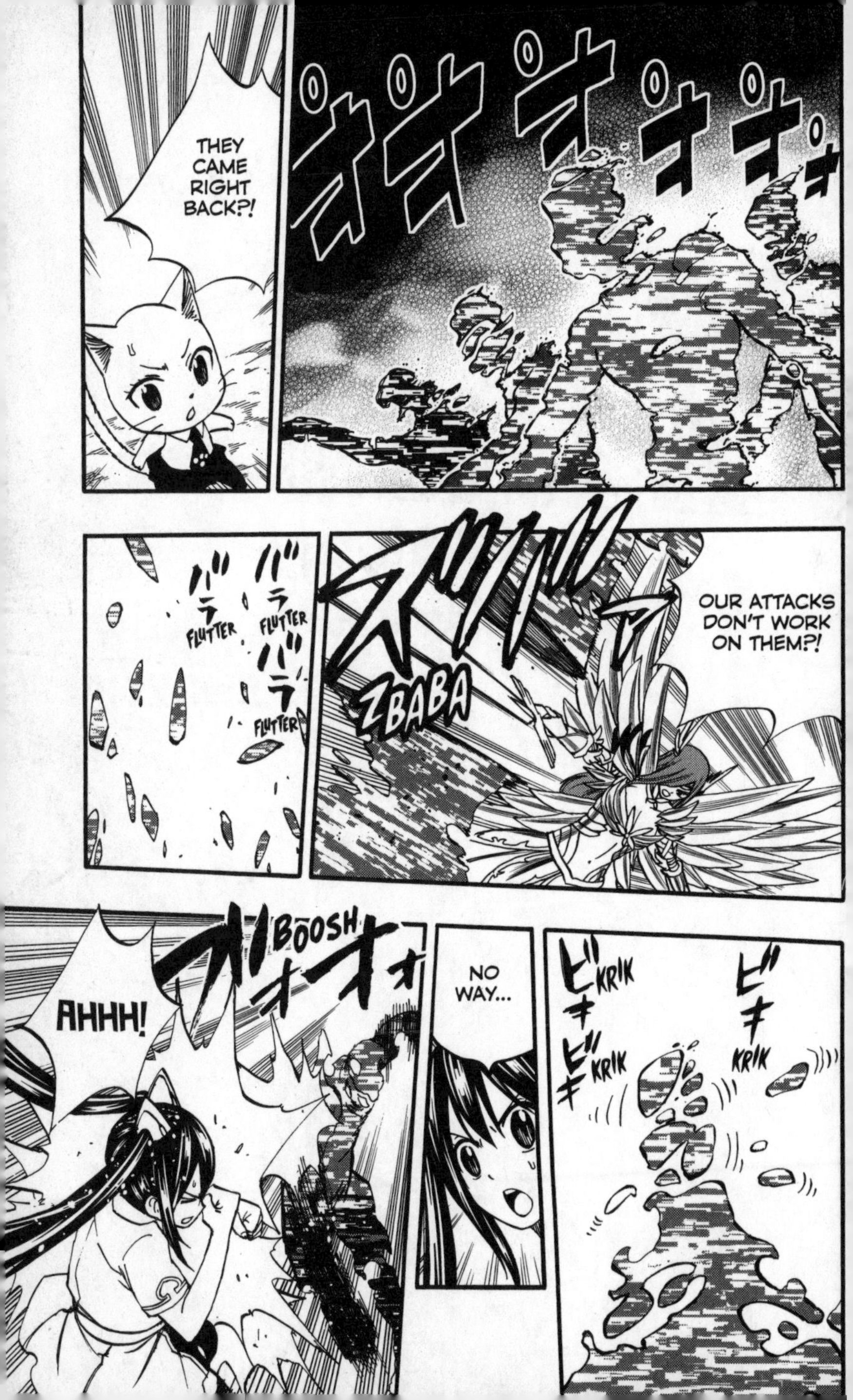
THEY CAME RIGHT BACK?!
ZBABA
OUR ATTACKS DON'T WORK ON THEM?!
FLUTTER
FLUTTER
FLUTTER
KRIK
KRIK
KRIK
NO WAY...
BOOSH
AHHH!

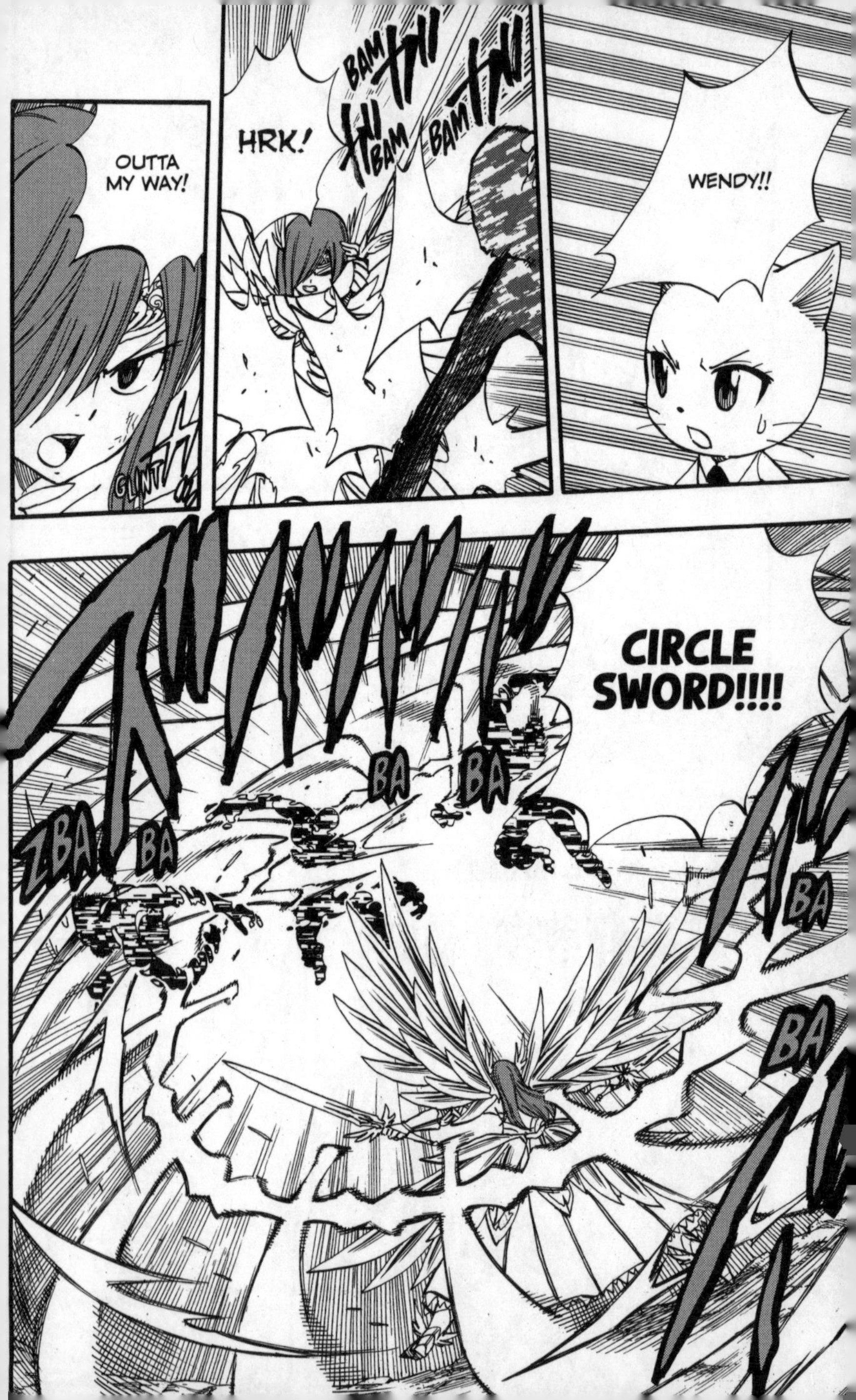
WENDY!!
BAM
BAM
BAM
BAM
HRK!
OUTTA MY WAY!
GLINT
CIRCLE SWORD!!!!
BA
BA
BA
BA
ZBA
BA

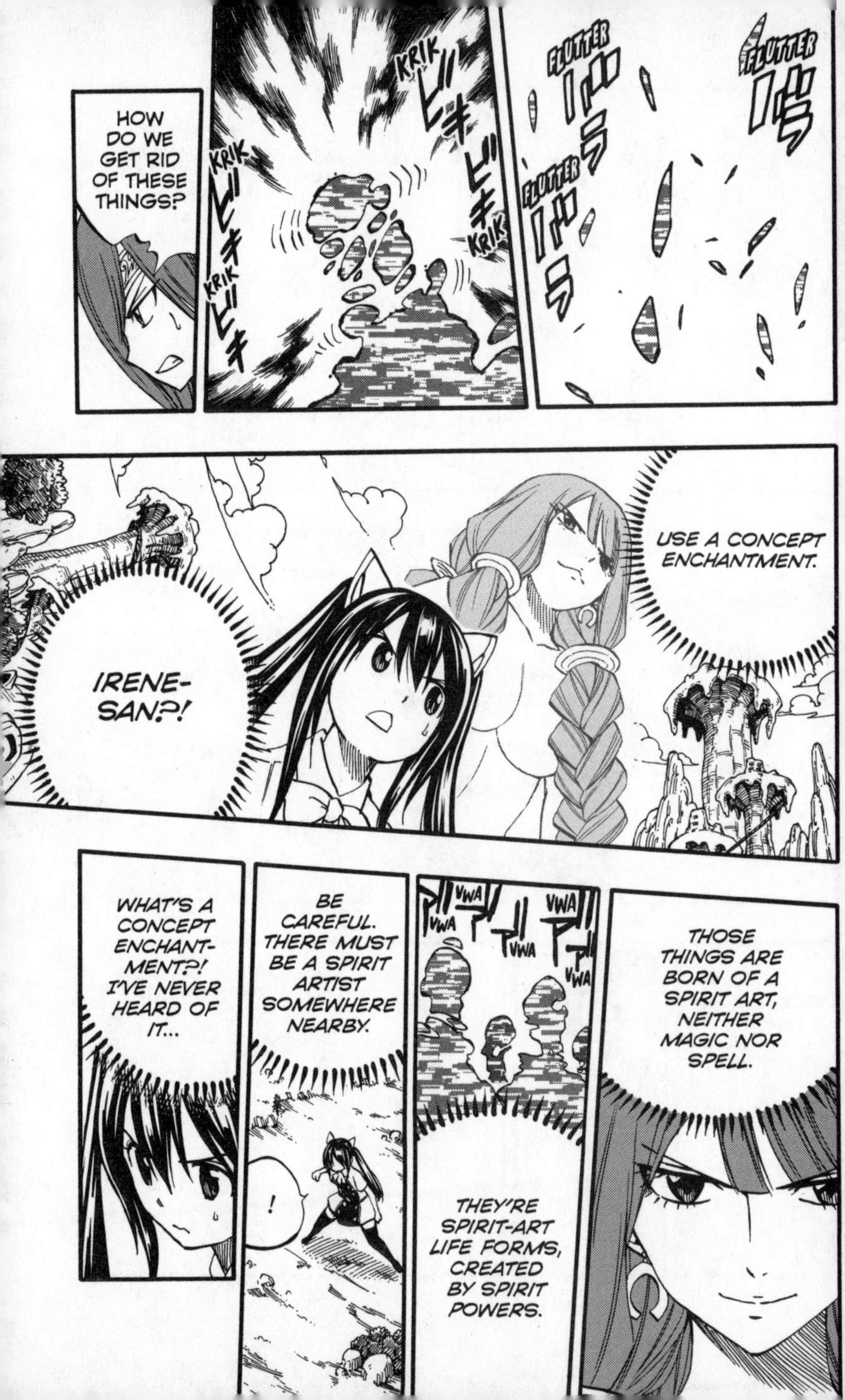
FLUTTER
FLUTTER
FLUTTER
KRIK
KRIK
KRIK
KRIK
HOW DO WE GET RID OF THESE THINGS?
USE A CONCEPT ENCHANTMENT.
IRENE-SAN?!
THOSE THINGS ARE BORN OF A SPIRIT ART, NEITHER MAGIC NOR SPELL.
VWA
VWA
VWA
VWA
VWA
THEY'RE SPIRIT-ART LIFE FORMS, CREATED BY SPIRIT POWERS.
BE CAREFUL. THERE MUST BE A SPIRIT ARTIST SOMEWHERE NEARBY.
!
WHAT'S A CONCEPT ENCHANT-MENT?! I'VE NEVER HEARD OF IT...

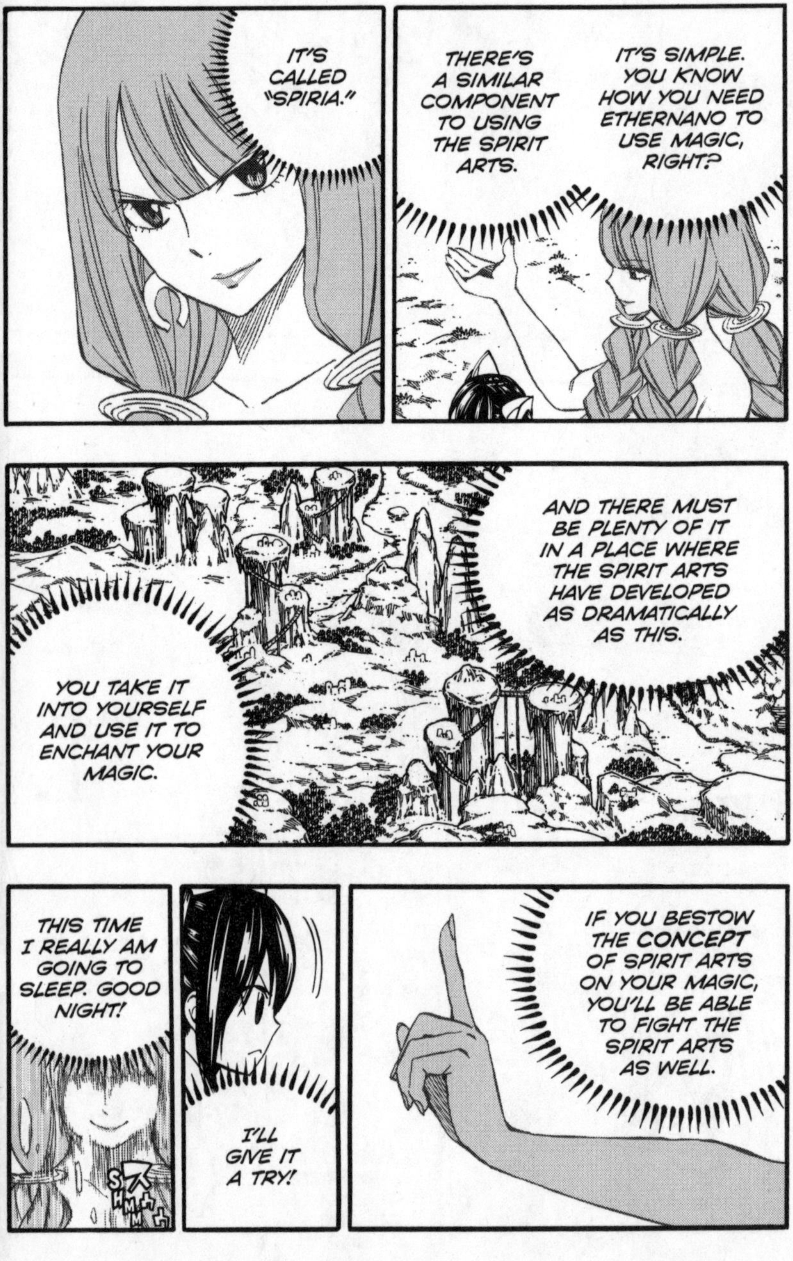
IT'S SIMPLE. YOU KNOW HOW YOU NEED ETHERNANO TO USE MAGIC, RIGHT?
THERE'S A SIMILAR COMPONENT TO USING THE SPIRIT ARTS.
IT'S CALLED "SPIRIA."
AND THERE MUST BE PLENTY OF IT IN A PLACE WHERE THE SPIRIT ARTS HAVE DEVELOPED AS DRAMATICALLY AS THIS.
YOU TAKE IT INTO YOURSELF AND USE IT TO ENCHANT YOUR MAGIC.
IF YOU BESTOW THE CONCEPT OF SPIRIT ARTS ON YOUR MAGIC, YOU'LL BE ABLE TO FIGHT THE SPIRIT ARTS AS WELL.
I'LL GIVE IT A TRY!
THIS TIME I REALLY AM GOING TO SLEEP. GOOD NIGHT!
SHMM

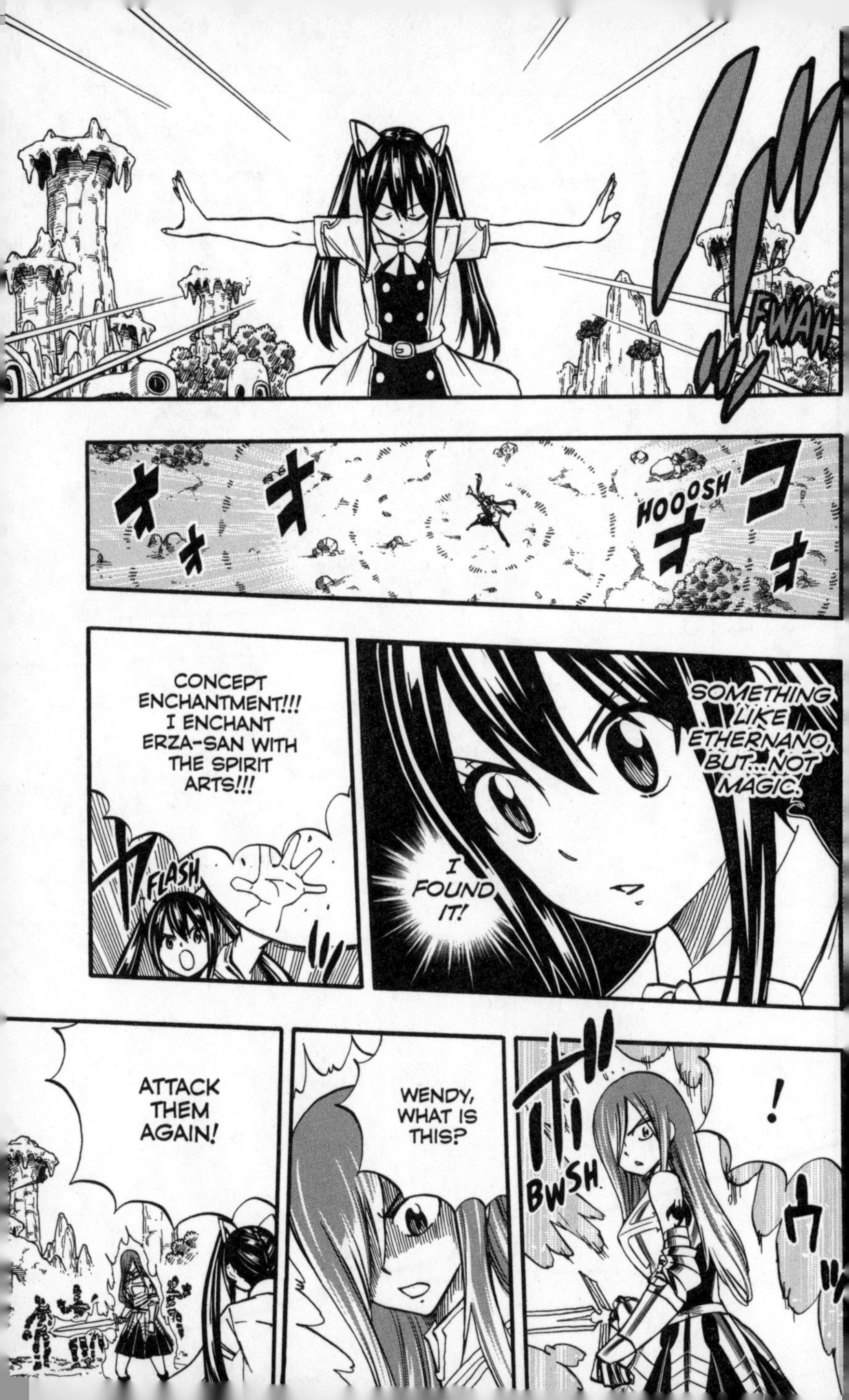

FWAH
HOOOSH
SOMETHING LIKE ETHERNANO, BUT... NOT MAGIC.
I FOUND IT!
CONCEPT ENCHANTMENT!!! I ENCHANT ERZA-SAN WITH THE SPIRIT ARTS!!!
FLASH
!
BWSH
WENDY, WHAT IS THIS?
ATTACK THEM AGAIN!

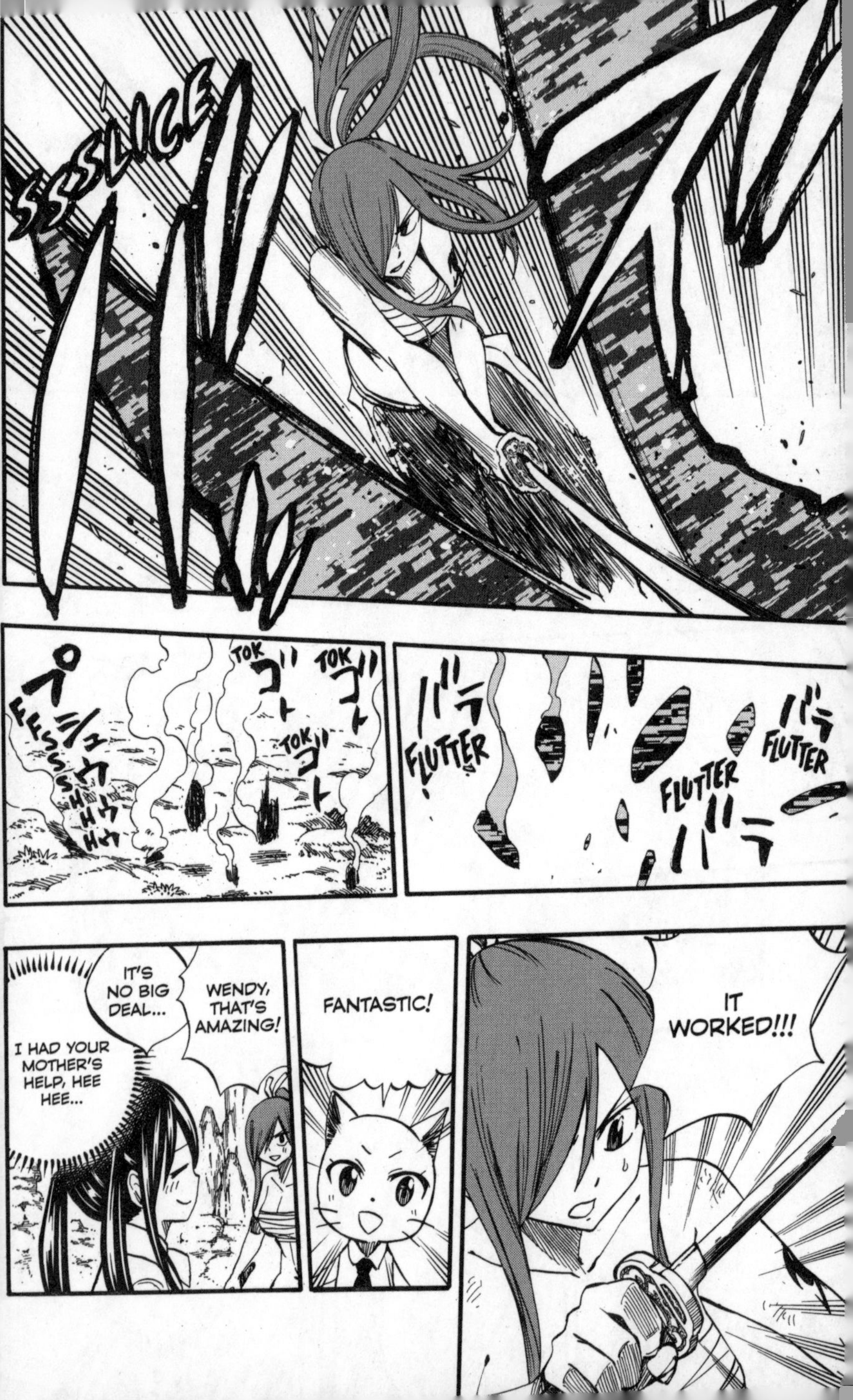
SSSLICE
バラ
FLUTTER
FLUTTER
バラ
FLUTTER
バラ
TOK
ゴト
TOK
ゴト
TOK
ゴト
プシュウウウ
FFSSSSHHH
IT WORKED!!!
FANTASTIC!
WENDY, THAT'S AMAZING!
IT'S NO BIG DEAL...
I HAD YOUR MOTHER'S HELP, HEE HEE...

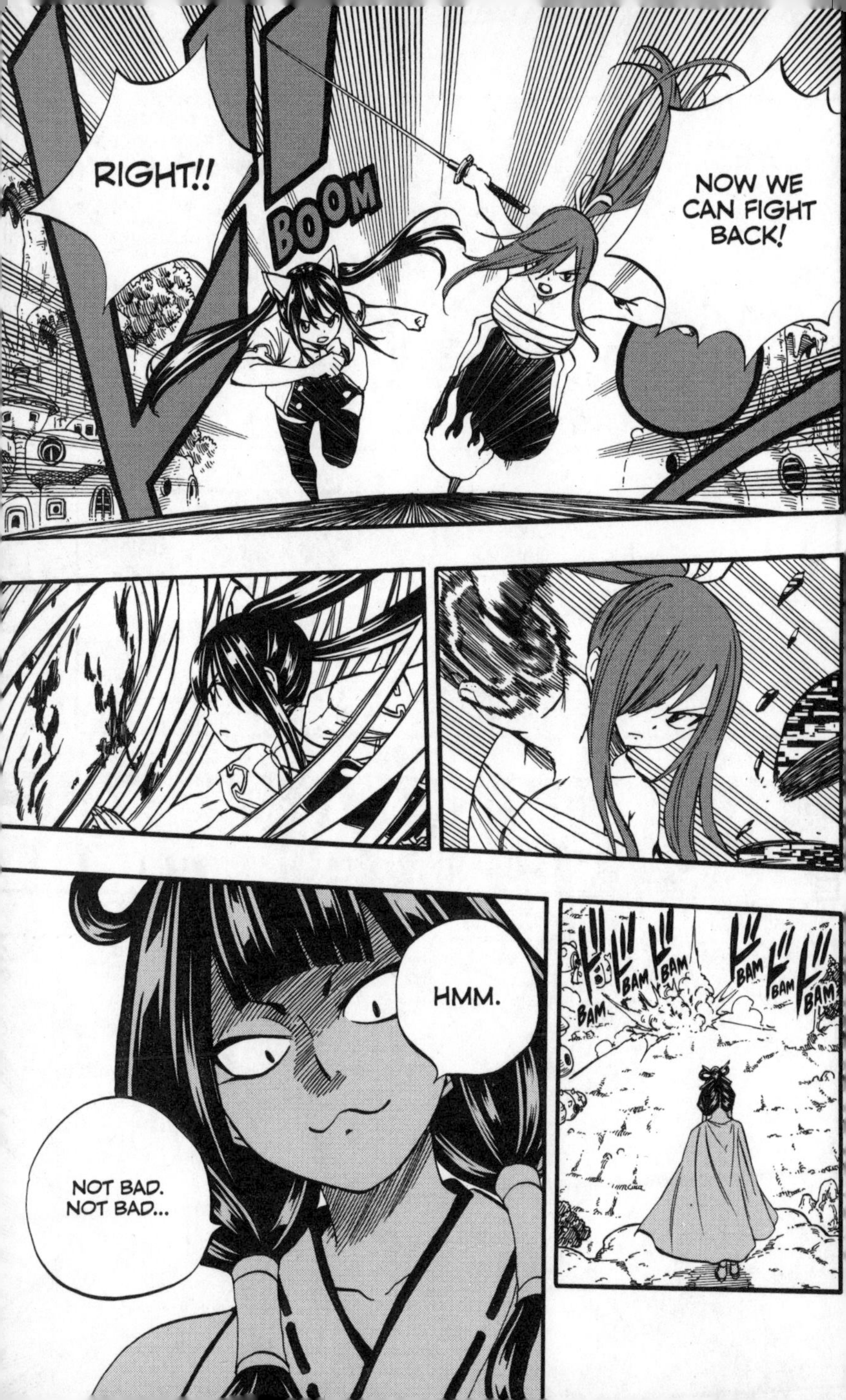
NOW WE CAN FIGHT BACK!
BOOM
RIGHT!!
BAM
BAM
BAM
BAM
BAM
BAM
HMM.
NOT BAD. NOT BAD...

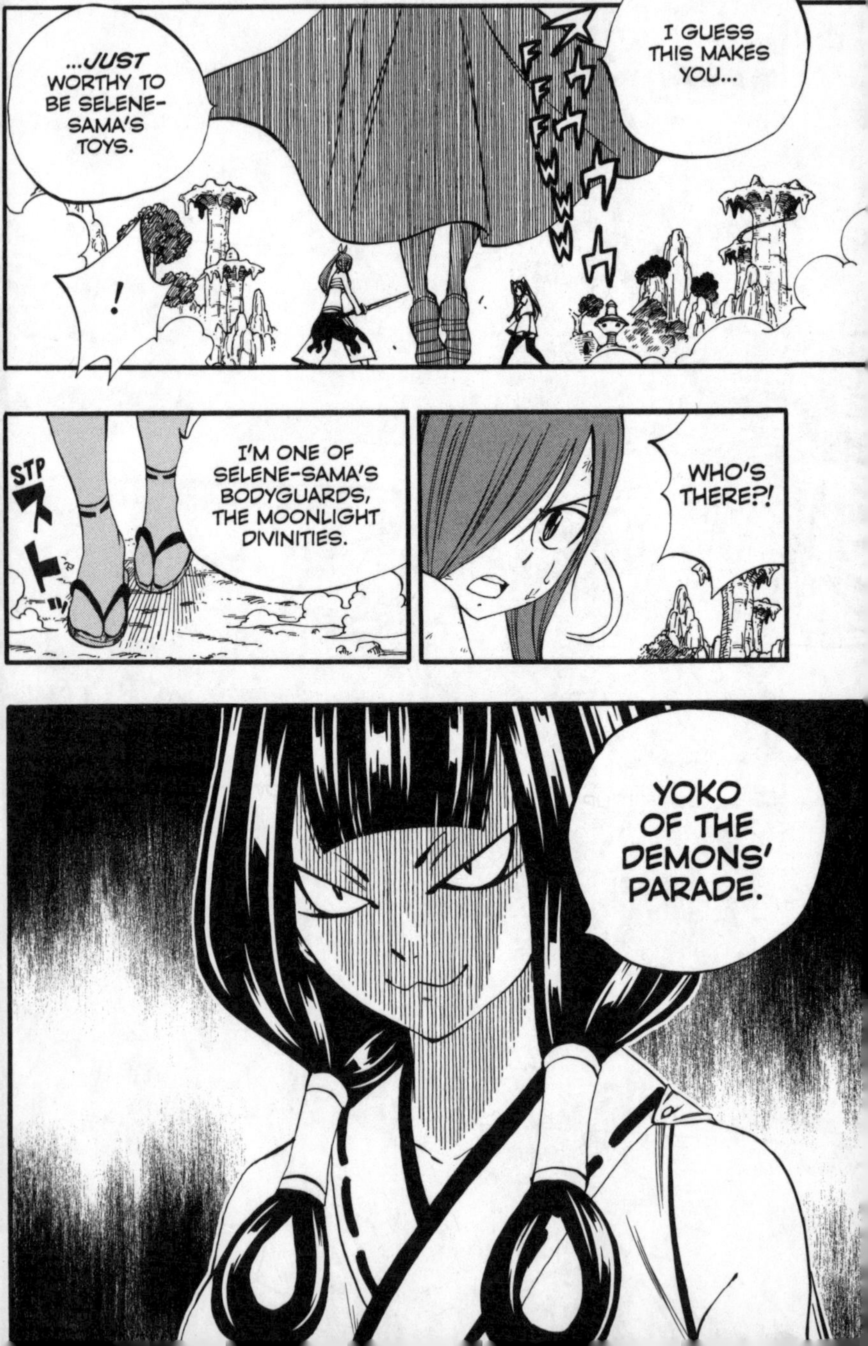
I GUESS THIS MAKES YOU...
FFFWWWW
...*JUST* WORTHY TO BE SELENE-SAMA'S TOYS.
!
WHO'S THERE?!
I'M ONE OF SELENE-SAMA'S BODYGUARDS, THE MOONLIGHT DIVINITIES.
STP
YOKO OF THE DEMONS' PARADE.

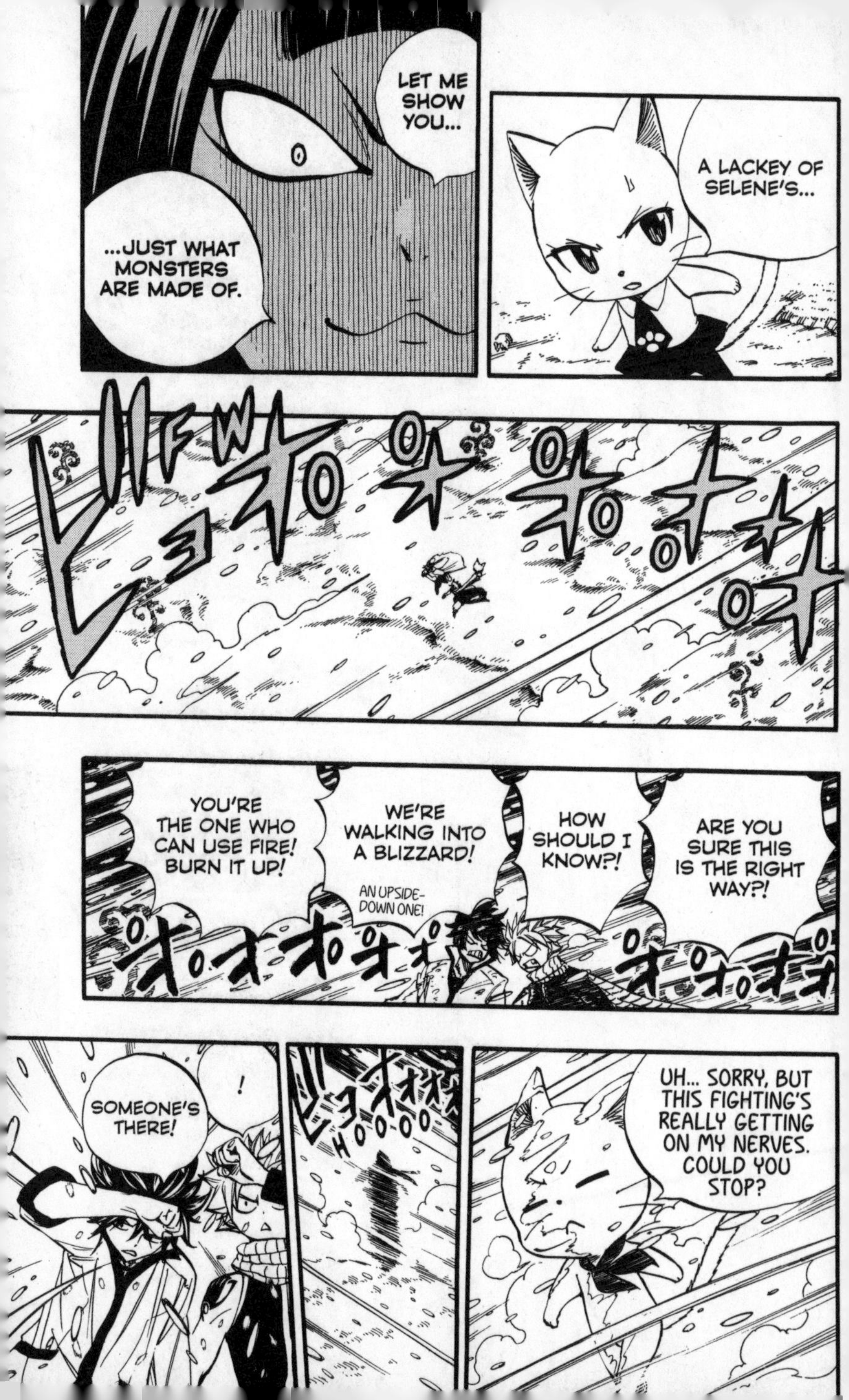
A LACKEY OF SELENE'S...
LET ME SHOW YOU...
...JUST WHAT MONSTERS ARE MADE OF.
ARE YOU SURE THIS IS THE RIGHT WAY?!
HOW SHOULD I KNOW?!
WE'RE WALKING INTO A BLIZZARD!
AN UPSIDE-DOWN ONE!
YOU'RE THE ONE WHO CAN USE FIRE! BURN IT UP!
UH... SORRY, BUT THIS FIGHTING'S REALLY GETTING ON MY NERVES. COULD YOU STOP?
HOOOO
!
SOMEONE'S THERE!

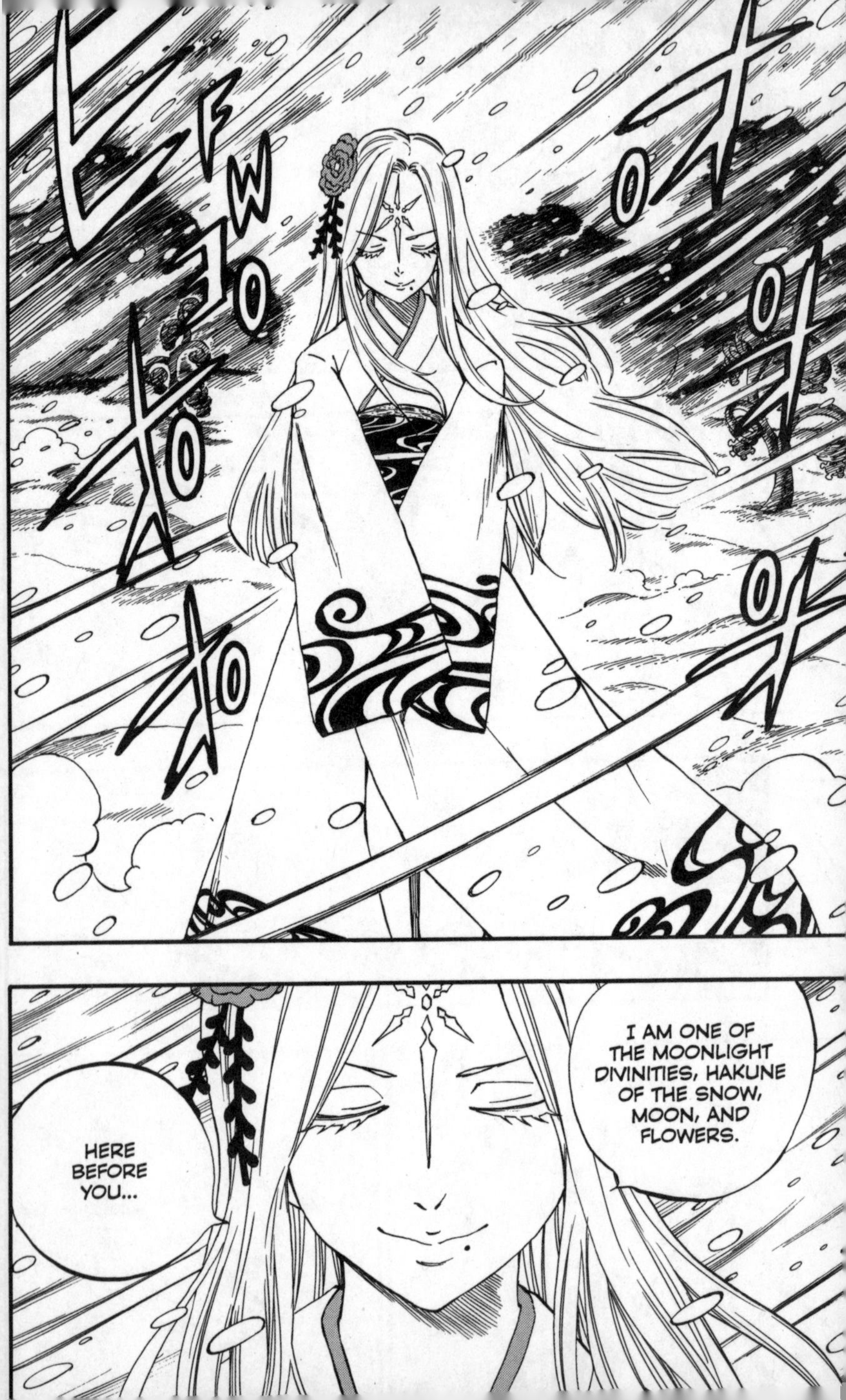
FWOOO
OOO
HERE BEFORE YOU...
I AM ONE OF THE MOONLIGHT DIVINITIES, HAKUNE OF THE SNOW, MOON, AND FLOWERS.

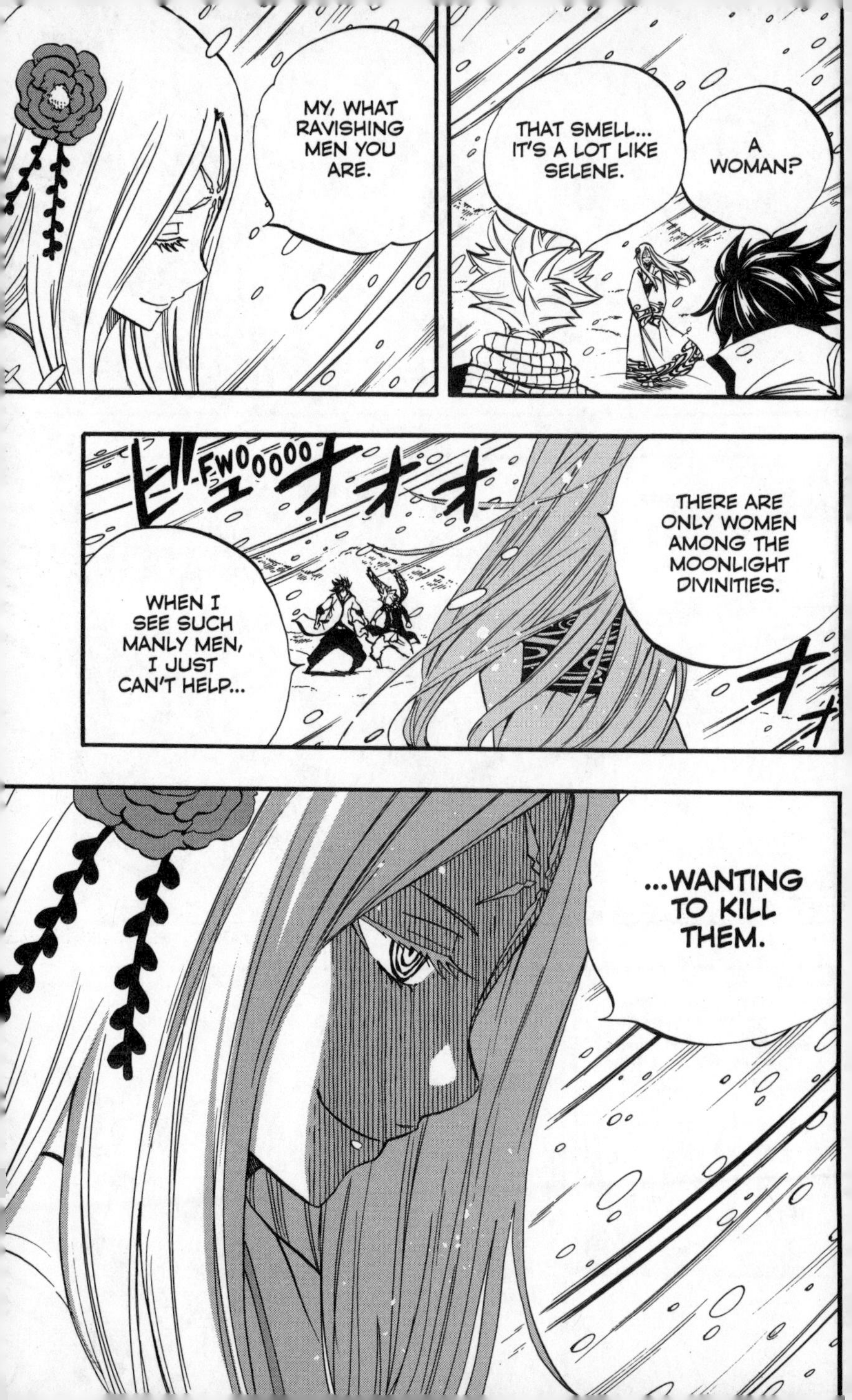
A WOMAN?
THAT SMELL... IT'S A LOT LIKE SELENE.
MY, WHAT RAVISHING MEN YOU ARE.
THERE ARE ONLY WOMEN AMONG THE MOONLIGHT DIVINITIES.
FWOOOOO
WHEN I SEE SUCH MANLY MEN, I JUST CAN'T HELP...
...WANTING TO KILL THEM.

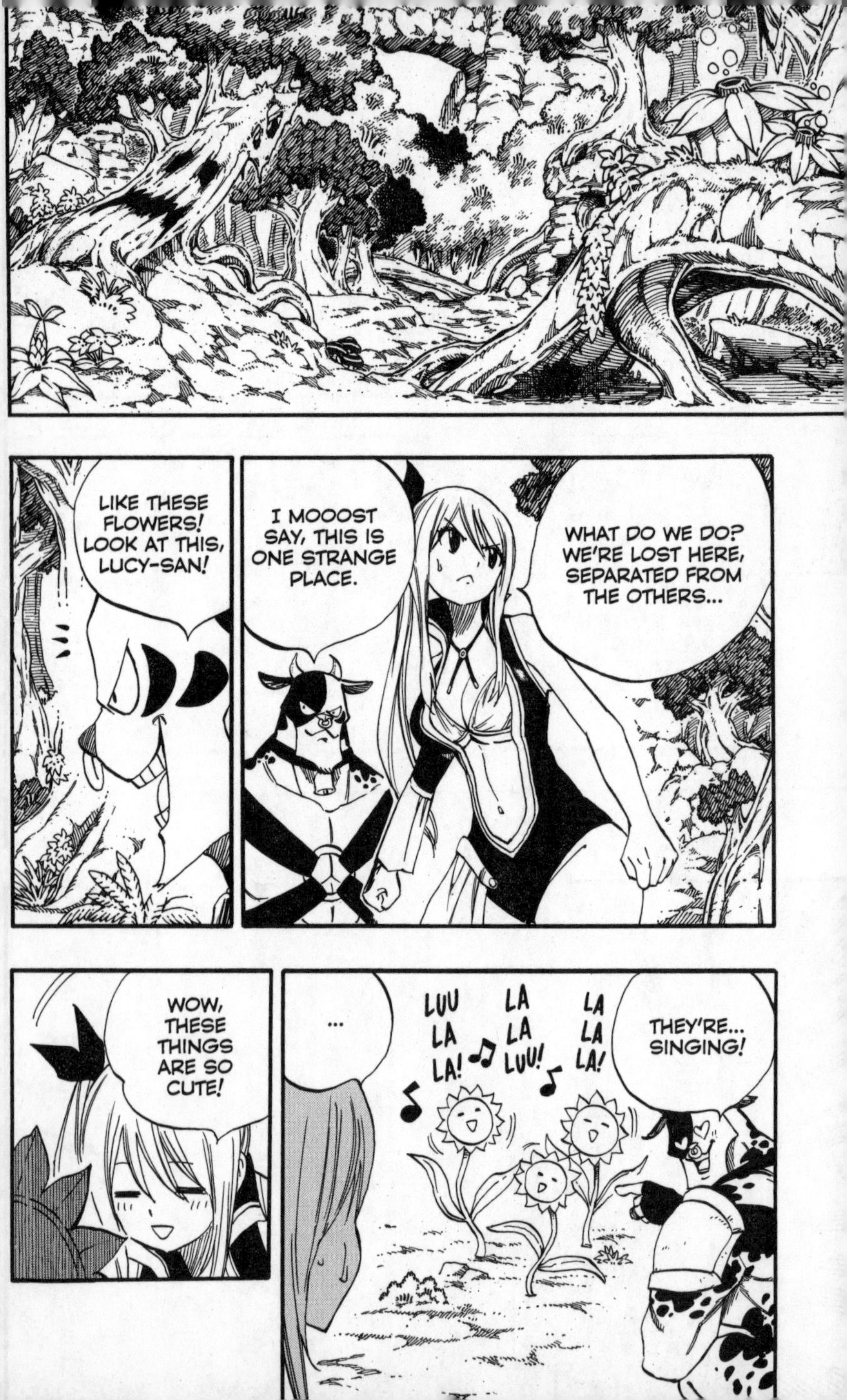
WHAT DO WE DO? WE'RE LOST HERE, SEPARATED FROM THE OTHERS...
I MOOOST SAY, THIS IS ONE STRANGE PLACE.
LIKE THESE FLOWERS! LOOK AT THIS, LUCY-SAN!
THEY'RE... SINGING!
LA LA LA!
LA LA LUU!
LUU LA LA!
...
WOW, THESE THINGS ARE SO CUTE!

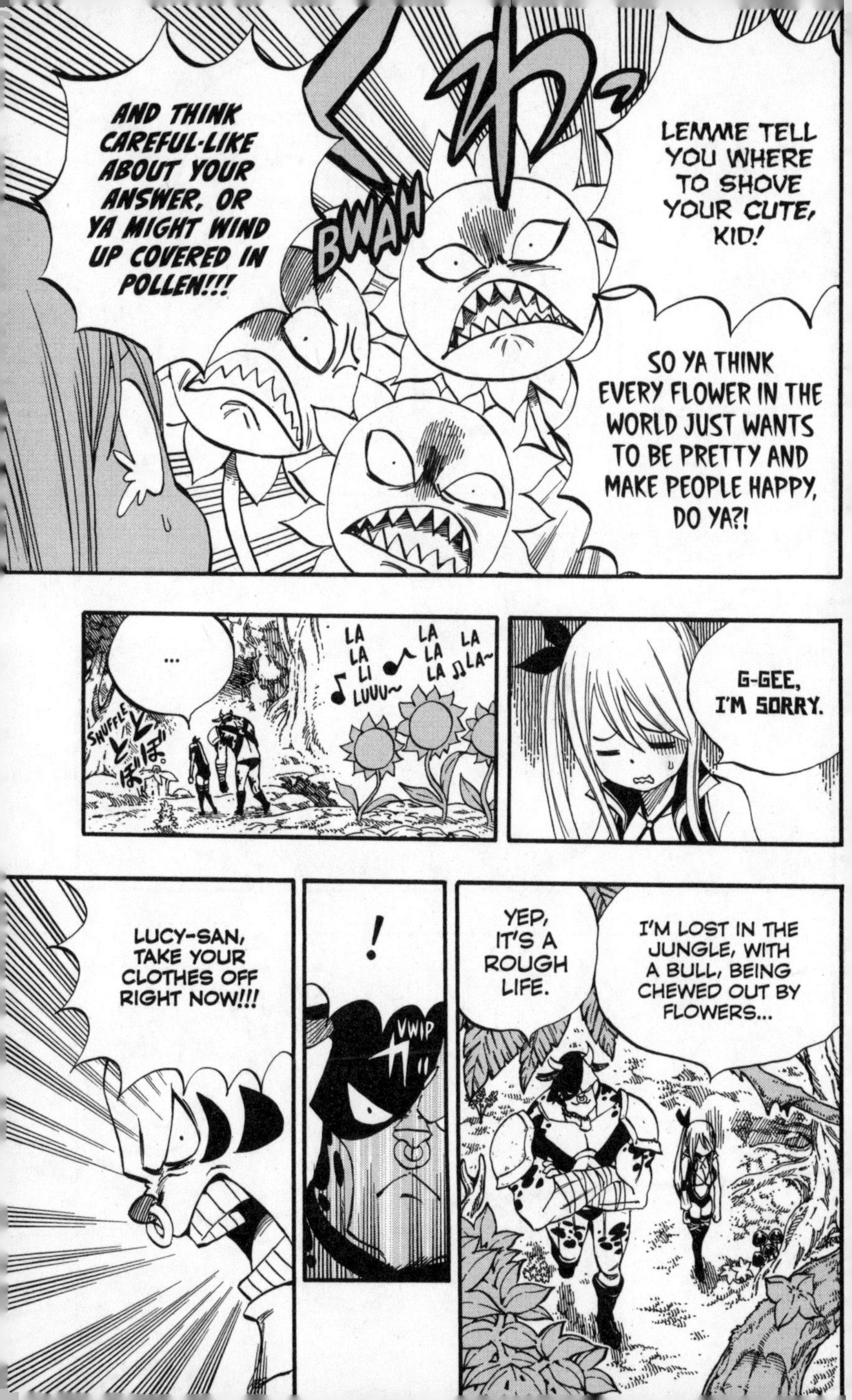
LEMME TELL YOU WHERE TO SHOVE YOUR CUTE, KID!
SO YA THINK EVERY FLOWER IN THE WORLD JUST WANTS TO BE PRETTY AND MAKE PEOPLE HAPPY, DO YA?!
BWAH
AND THINK CAREFUL-LIKE ABOUT YOUR ANSWER, OR YA MIGHT WIND UP COVERED IN POLLEN!!!
G-GEE, I'M SORRY.
LA LA LA
LA LA~
LA LA LI LUUU~
...
SHUFFLE
I'M LOST IN THE JUNGLE, WITH A BULL, BEING CHEWED OUT BY FLOWERS...
YEP, IT'S A ROUGH LIFE.
!
VWIP
LUCY-SAN, TAKE YOUR CLOTHES OFF RIGHT NOW!!!

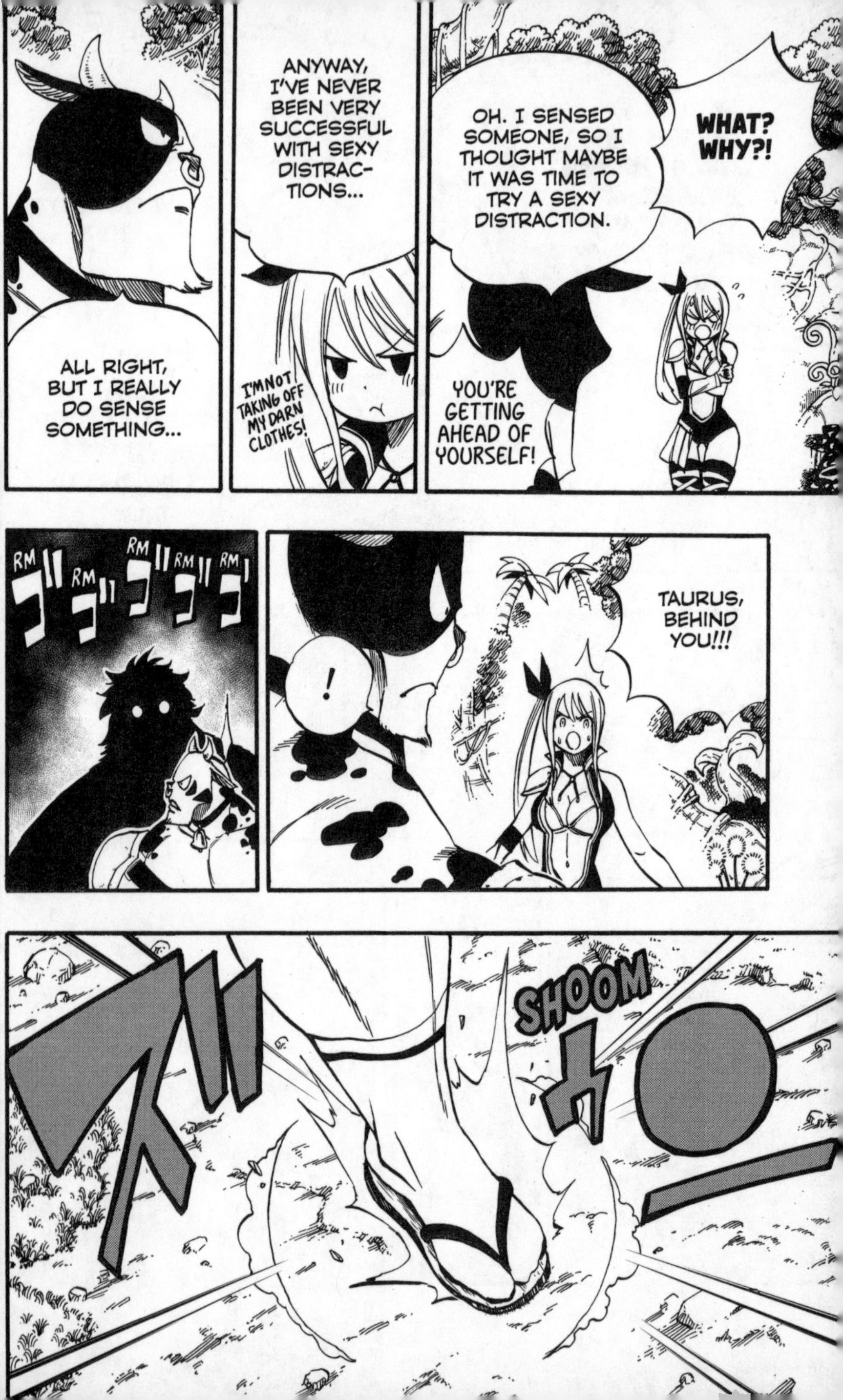

WHAT? WHY?!
OH. I SENSED SOMEONE, SO I THOUGHT MAYBE IT WAS TIME TO TRY A SEXY DISTRACTION.
YOU'RE GETTING AHEAD OF YOURSELF!
ANYWAY, I'VE NEVER BEEN VERY SUCCESSFUL WITH SEXY DISTRACTIONS...
I'M NOT TAKING OFF MY DARN CLOTHES!
ALL RIGHT, BUT I REALLY DO SENSE SOMETHING...
TAURUS, BEHIND YOU!!!
!
RM RM RM RM RM
SHOOM

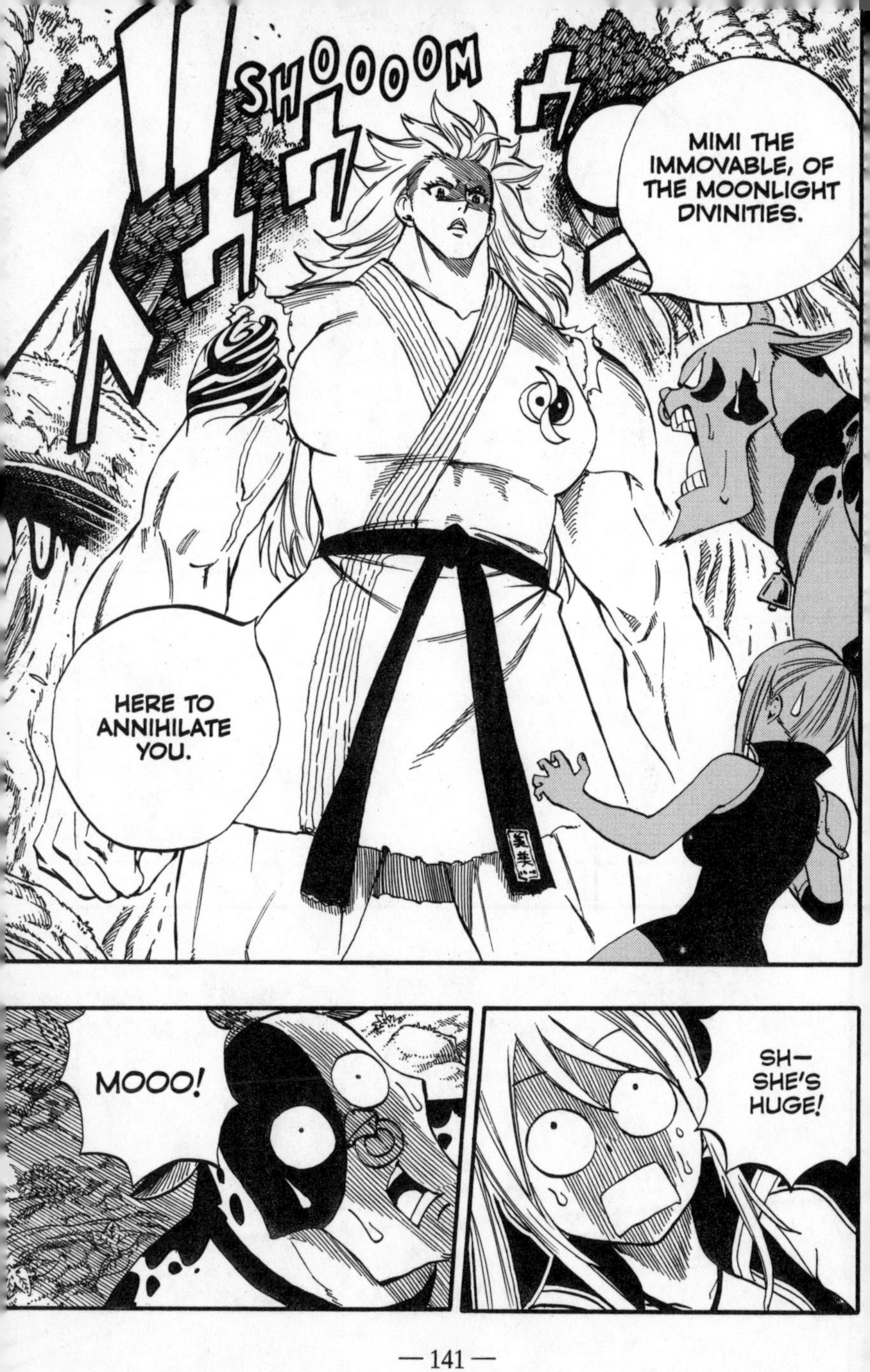
SHOOOOM
MIMI THE IMMOVABLE, OF THE MOONLIGHT DIVINITIES.
HERE TO ANNIHILATE YOU.
SH— SHE'S HUGE!
MOOO!

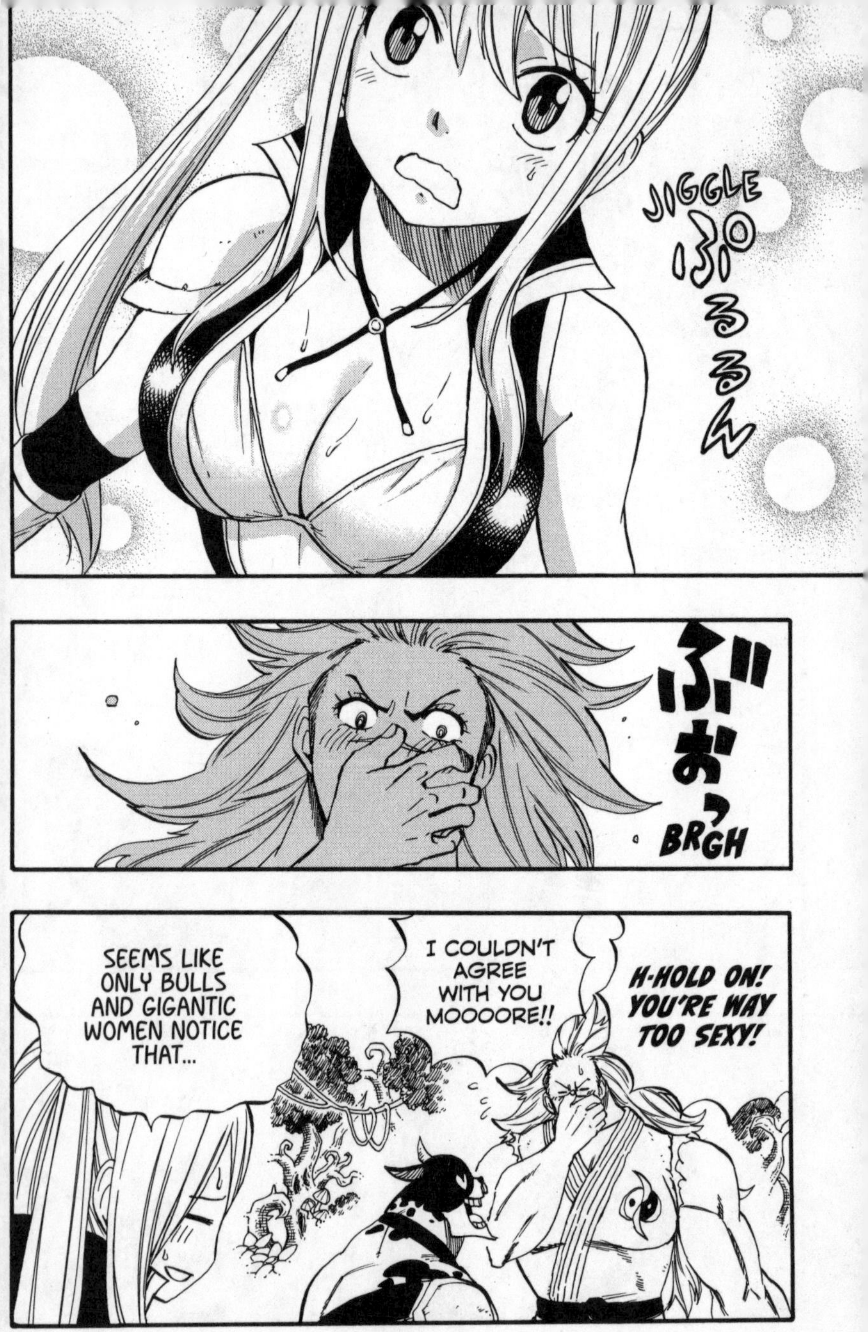
JIGGLE
ぷるるん
ぶおっ
BRGH
H-HOLD ON! YOU'RE WAY TOO SEXY!
I COULDN'T AGREE WITH YOU MOOOORE!!
SEEMS LIKE ONLY BULLS AND GIGANTIC WOMEN NOTICE THAT...

Chapter 71: The Spirit Arts

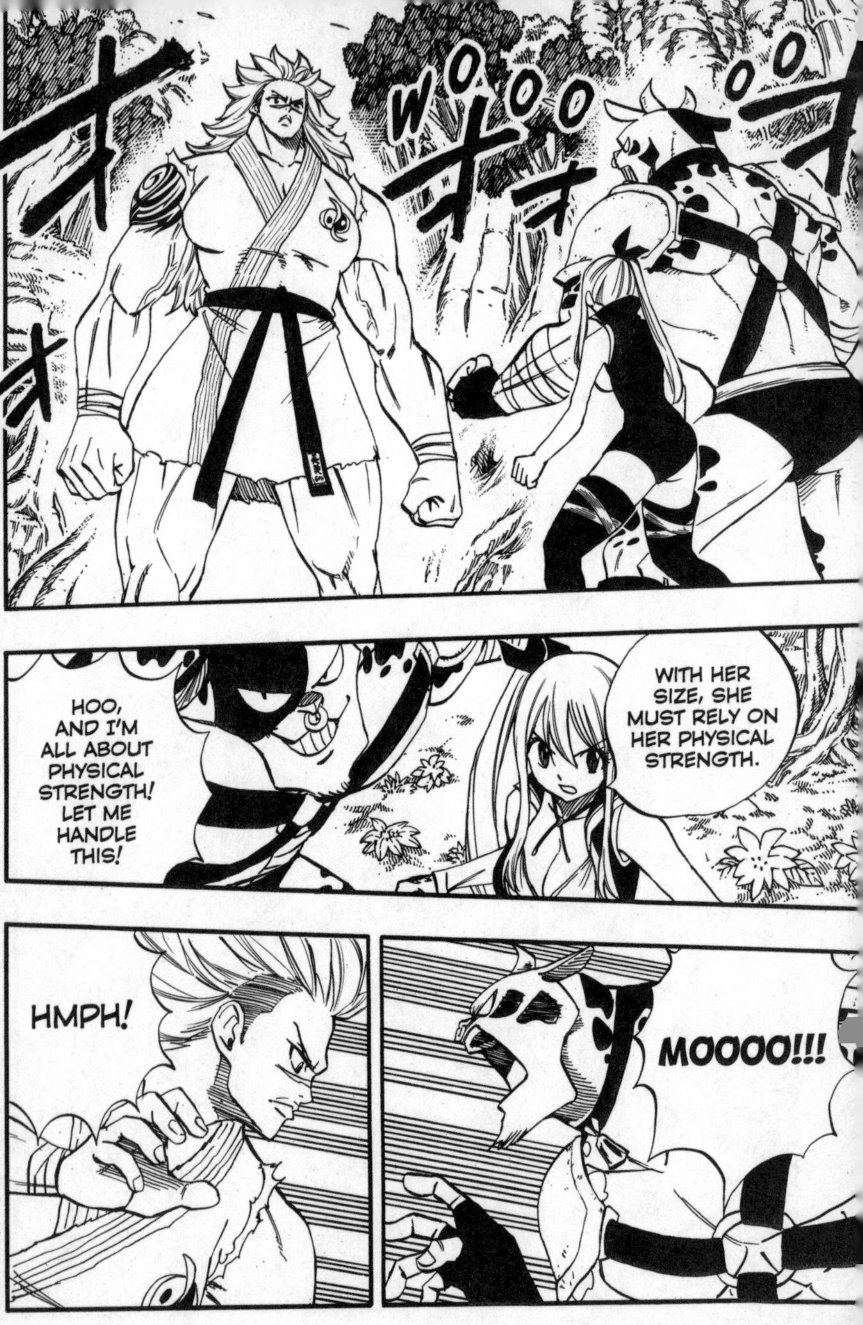
WOOOOO
オォォォ
WITH HER SIZE, SHE MUST RELY ON HER PHYSICAL STRENGTH.
HOO, AND I'M ALL ABOUT PHYSICAL STRENGTH! LET ME HANDLE THIS!
MOOOO!!!
HMPH!

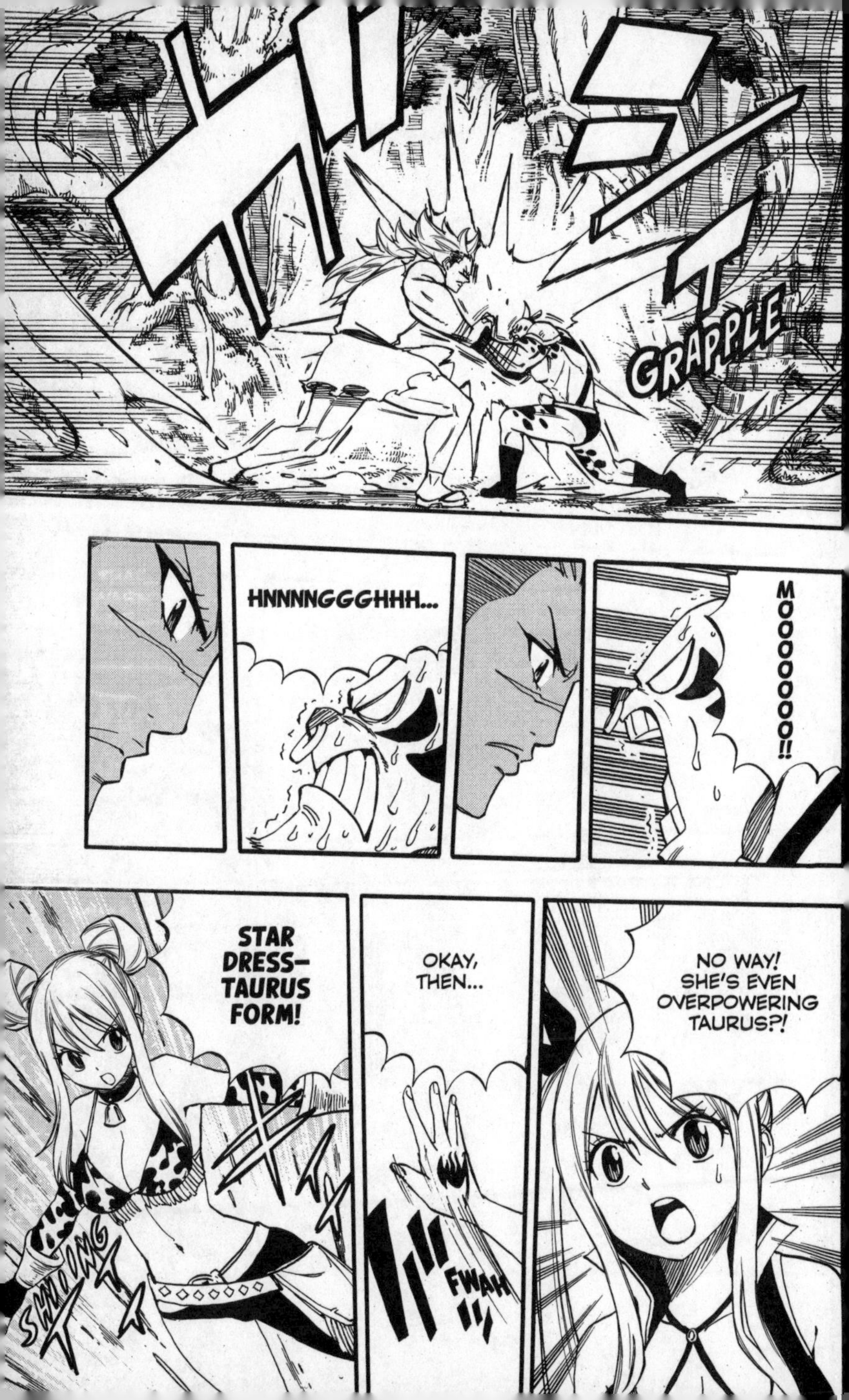
GRAPPLE
MOOOOOOOO!!
HNNNNGGGHHH...
NO WAY! SHE'S EVEN OVERPOWERING TAURUS?!
OKAY, THEN...
FWAH
STAR DRESS—TAURUS FORM!
SHIING

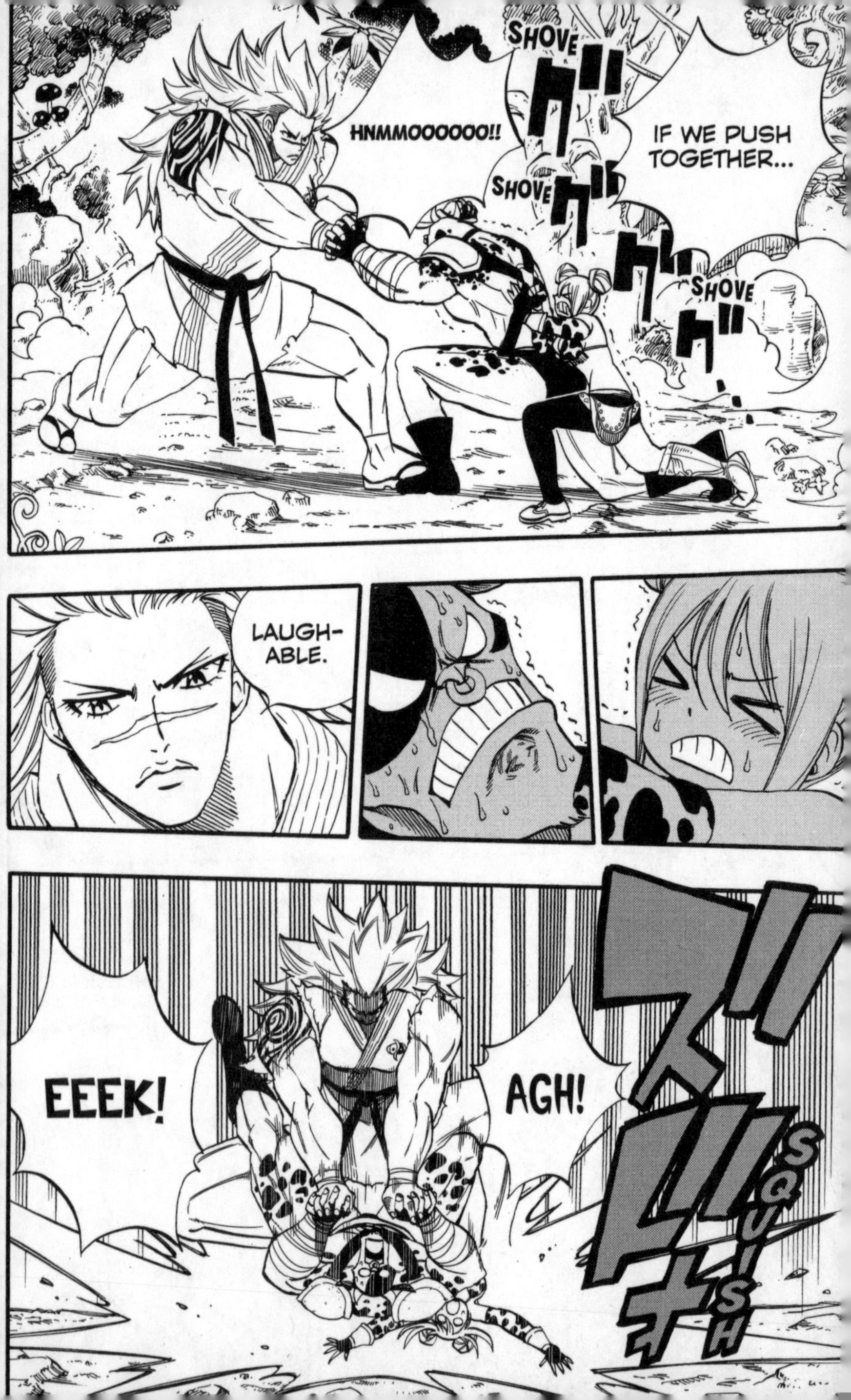
IF WE PUSH TOGETHER...
SHOVE
SHOVE
SHOVE
HNMMOOOOOO!!
LAUGH-ABLE.
SQUISH
AGH!
EEEK!

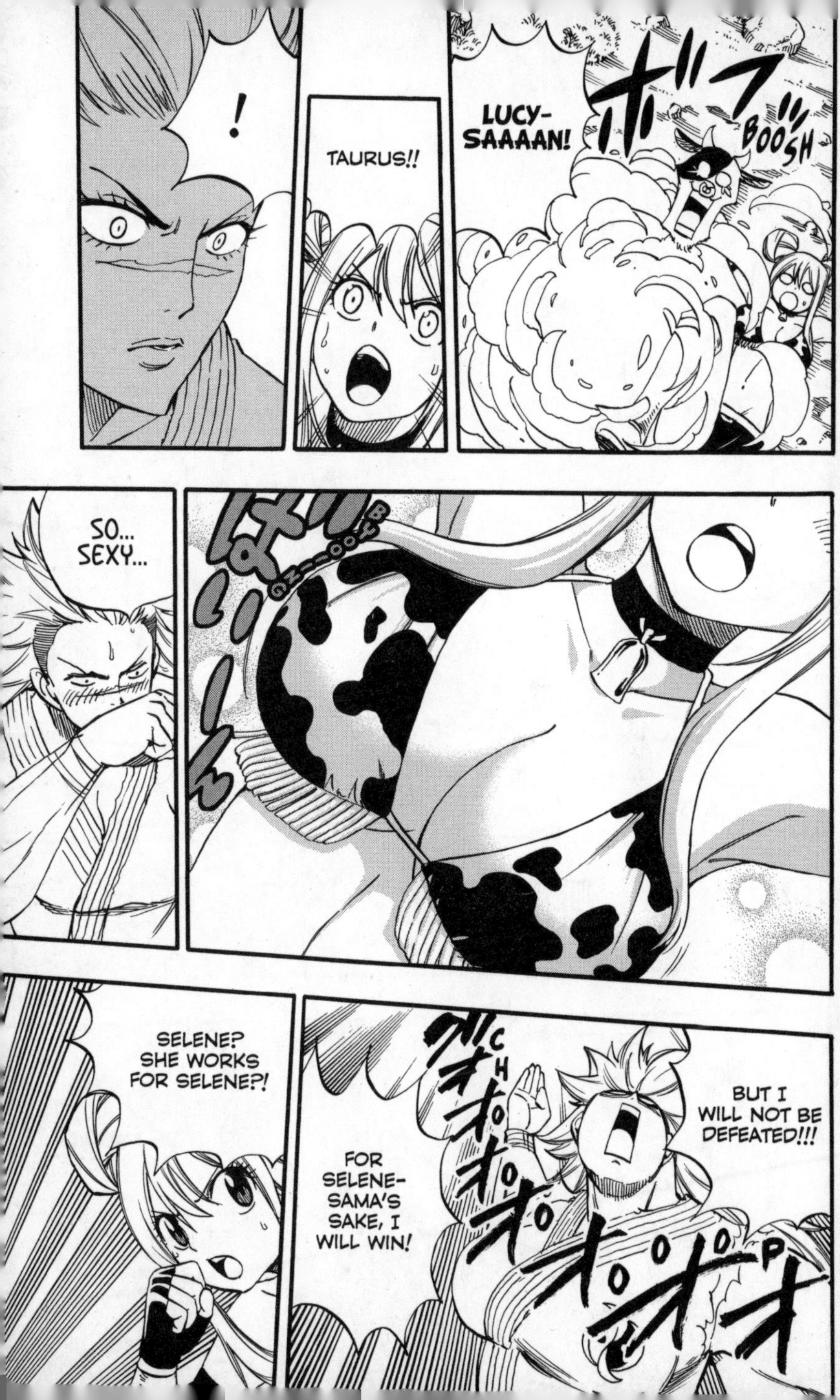
LUCY-SAAAAN!
BOOSH
TAURUS!!
!
SO... SEXY...
BUT I WILL NOT BE DEFEATED!!!
FOR SELENE-SAMA'S SAKE, I WILL WIN!
SELENE? SHE WORKS FOR SELENE?!

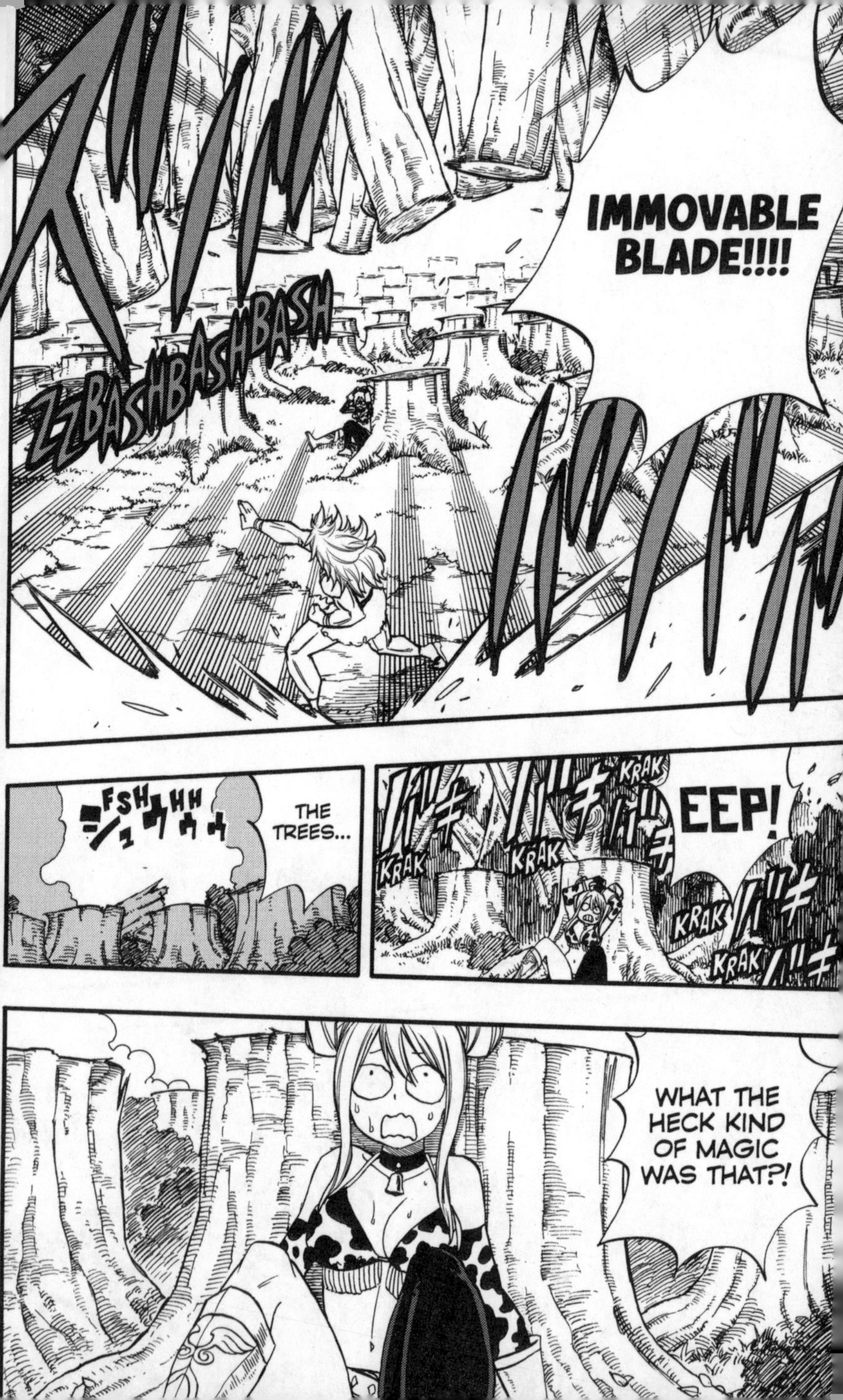
IMMOVABLE BLADE!!!!
ZZBASHBASHBASH
KRAK
KRAK
EEP!
KRAK
KRAK
KRAK
FSHHH
THE TREES...
WHAT THE HECK KIND OF MAGIC WAS THAT?!

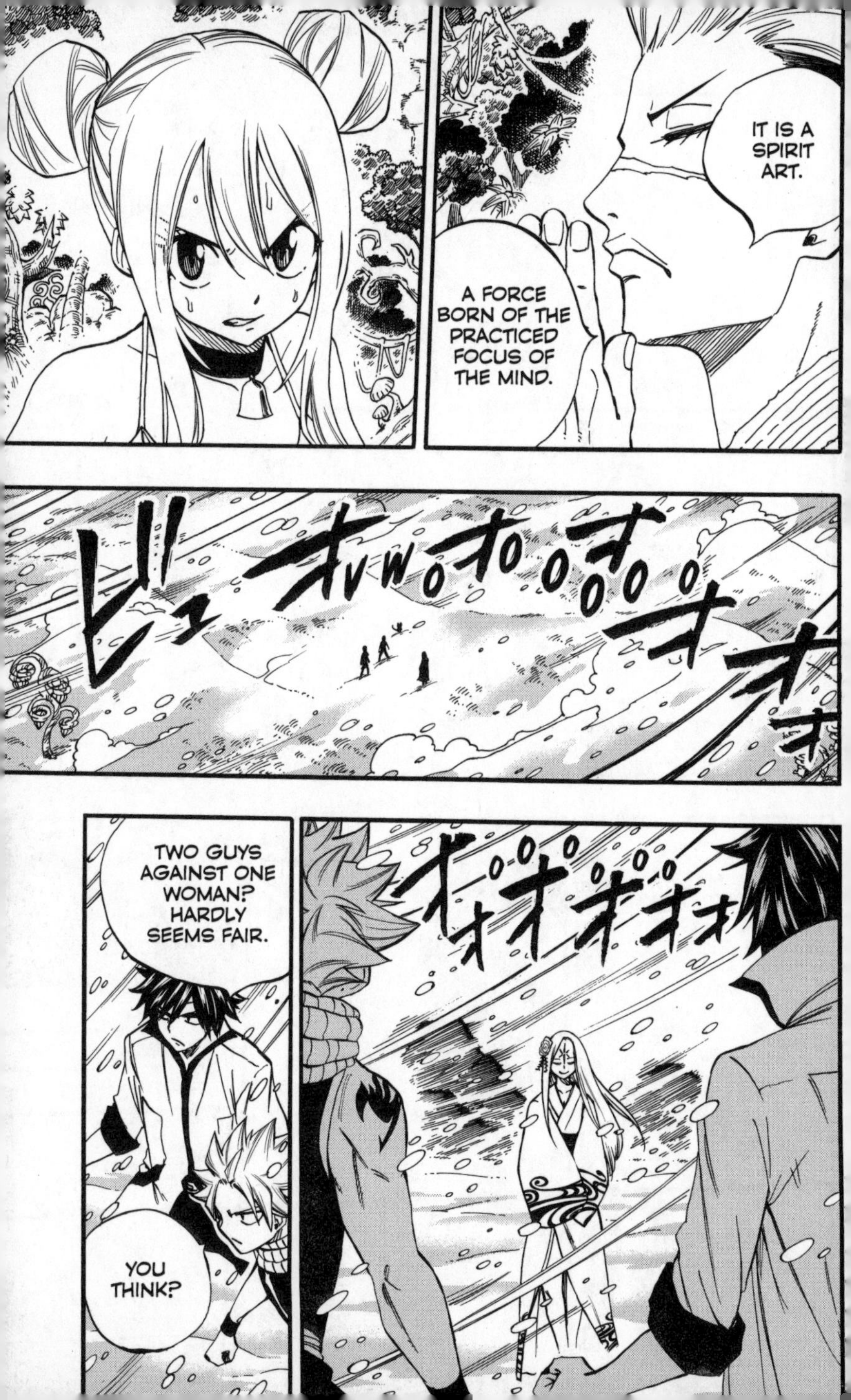
IT IS A SPIRIT ART.
A FORCE BORN OF THE PRACTICED FOCUS OF THE MIND.
TWO GUYS AGAINST ONE WOMAN? HARDLY SEEMS FAIR.
YOU THINK?

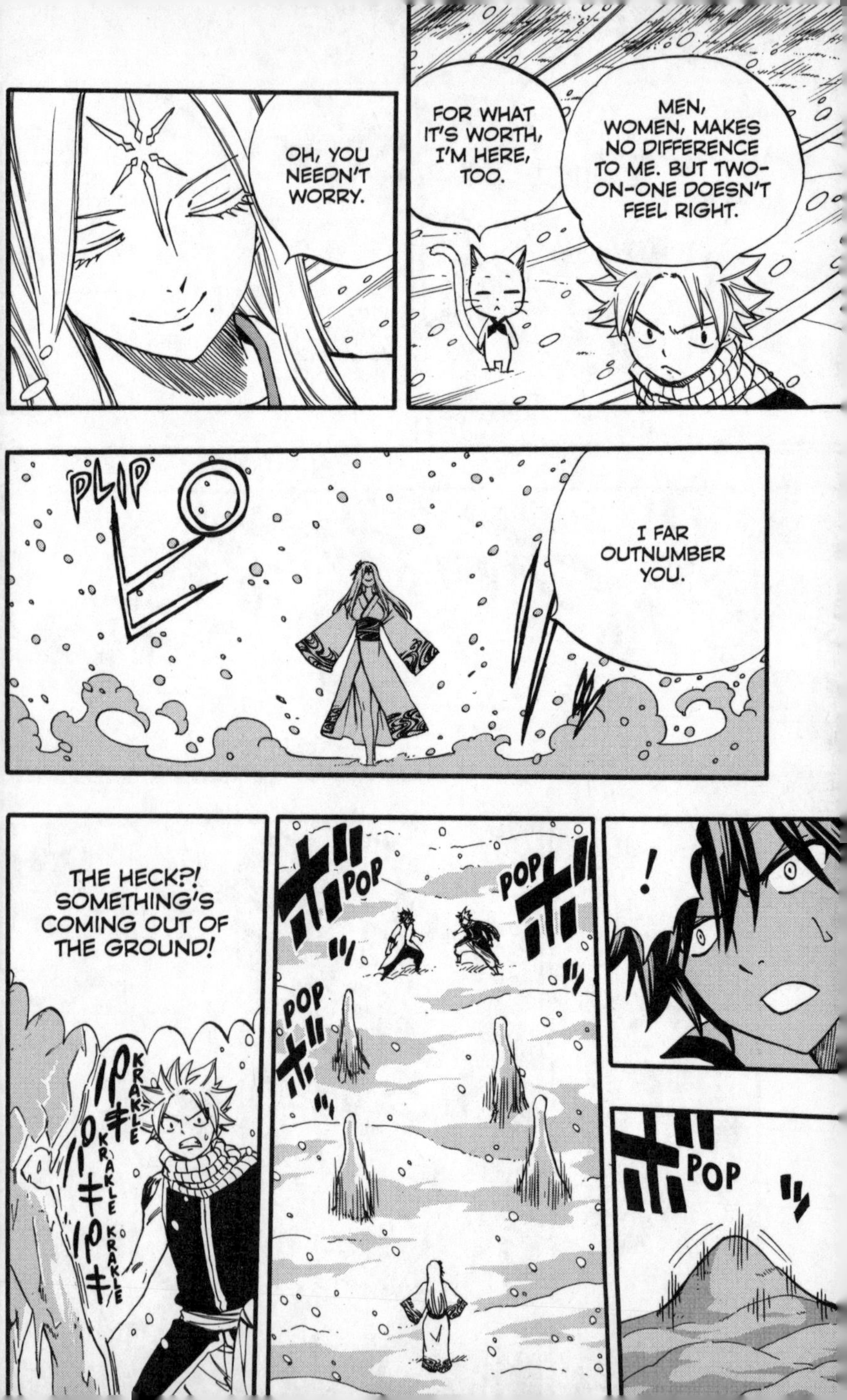
MEN, WOMEN, MAKES NO DIFFERENCE TO ME. BUT TWO-ON-ONE DOESN'T FEEL RIGHT.
FOR WHAT IT'S WORTH, I'M HERE, TOO.
OH, YOU NEEDN'T WORRY.
I FAR OUTNUMBER YOU.
PLIP
!
POP
POP
POP
POP
THE HECK?! SOMETHING'S COMING OUT OF THE GROUND!
KRAKLE
KRAKLE
KRAKLE

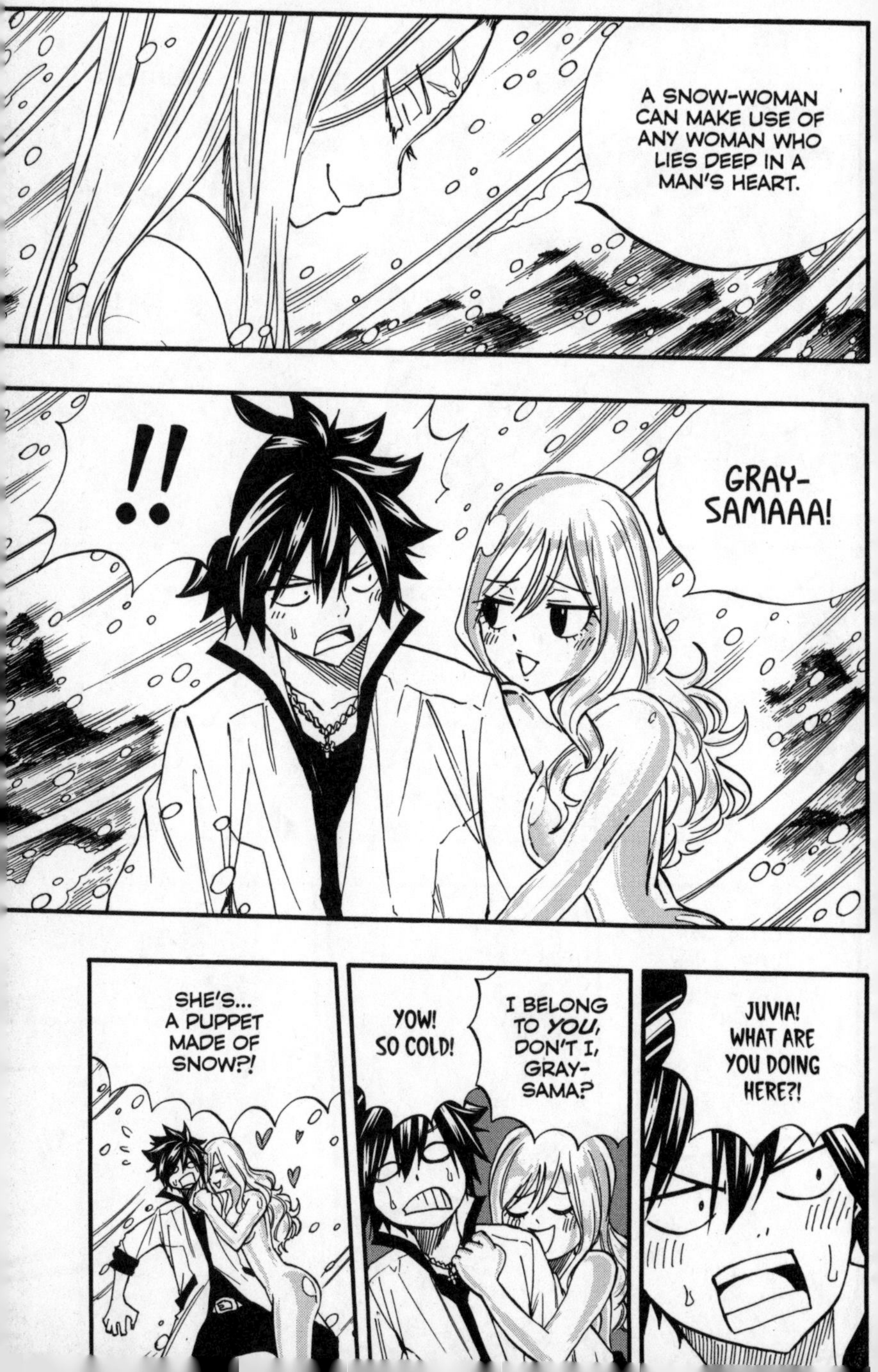
A SNOW-WOMAN CAN MAKE USE OF ANY WOMAN WHO LIES DEEP IN A MAN'S HEART.
GRAY-SAMAAA!
!!
JUVIA! WHAT ARE YOU DOING HERE?!
I BELONG TO *YOU*, DON'T I, GRAY-SAMA?
YOW! SO COLD!
SHE'S... A PUPPET MADE OF SNOW?!

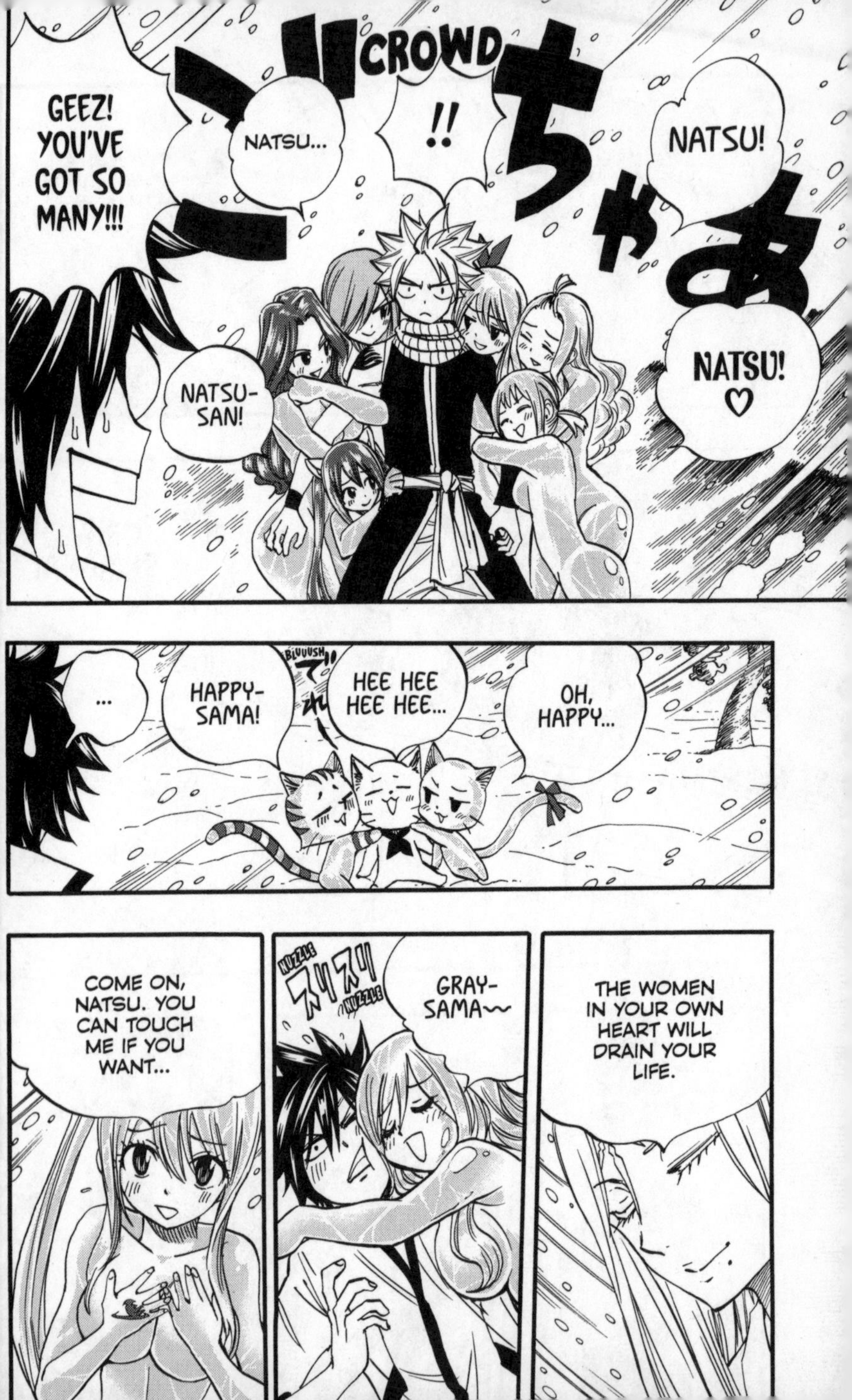
CROWD
NATSU!
!!
NATSU...
GEEZ! YOU'VE GOT SO MANY!!!
NATSU! ♡
NATSU-SAN!
OH, HAPPY...
HEE HEE HEE HEE...
BLUUUSH
HAPPY-SAMA!
...
THE WOMEN IN YOUR OWN HEART WILL DRAIN YOUR LIFE.
GRAY-SAMA~
NUZZLE
NUZZLE
COME ON, NATSU. YOU CAN TOUCH ME IF YOU WANT...

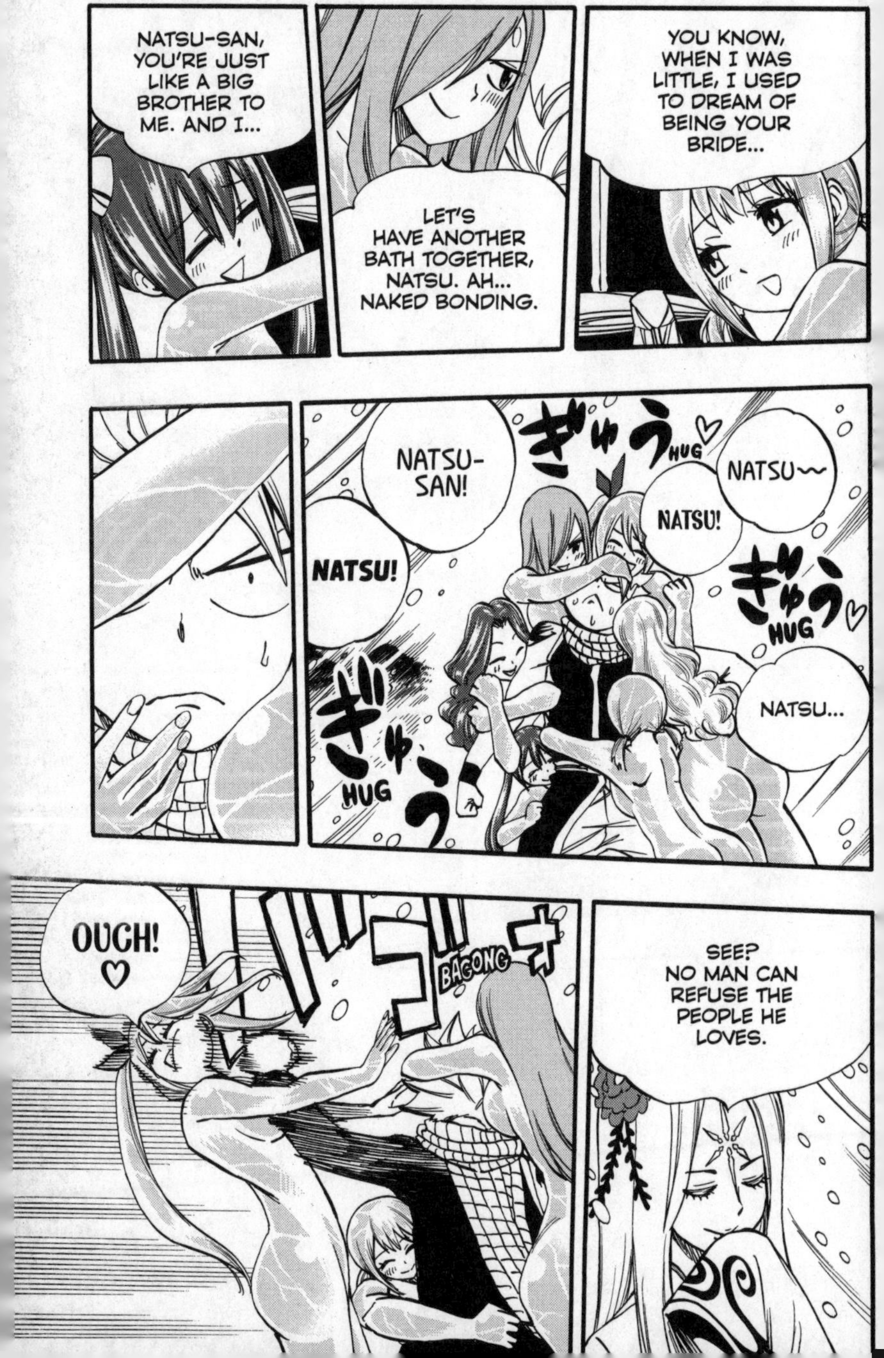
YOU KNOW, WHEN I WAS LITTLE, I USED TO DREAM OF BEING YOUR BRIDE...
LET'S HAVE ANOTHER BATH TOGETHER, NATSU. AH... NAKED BONDING.
NATSU-SAN, YOU'RE JUST LIKE A BIG BROTHER TO ME. AND I...
NATSU~~
NATSU!
ぎゅう HUG
NATSU-SAN!
ぎゅう HUG
NATSU...
NATSU!
ぎゅう HUG
SEE? NO MAN CAN REFUSE THE PEOPLE HE LOVES.
BAGONG
OUCH! ♡

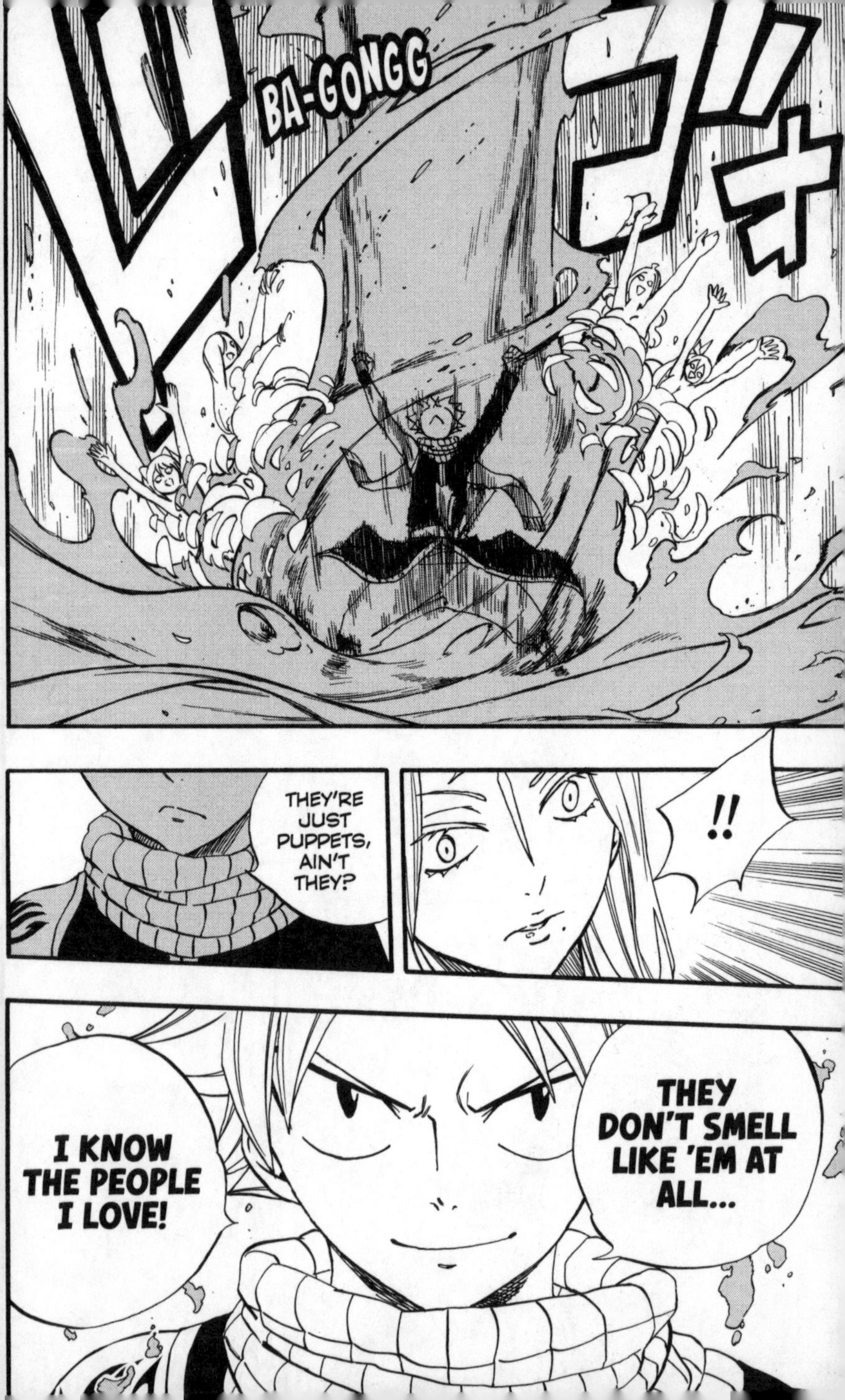
BA-GONGG
!!
THEY'RE JUST PUPPETS, AIN'T THEY?
THEY DON'T SMELL LIKE 'EM AT ALL...
I KNOW THE PEOPLE I LOVE!

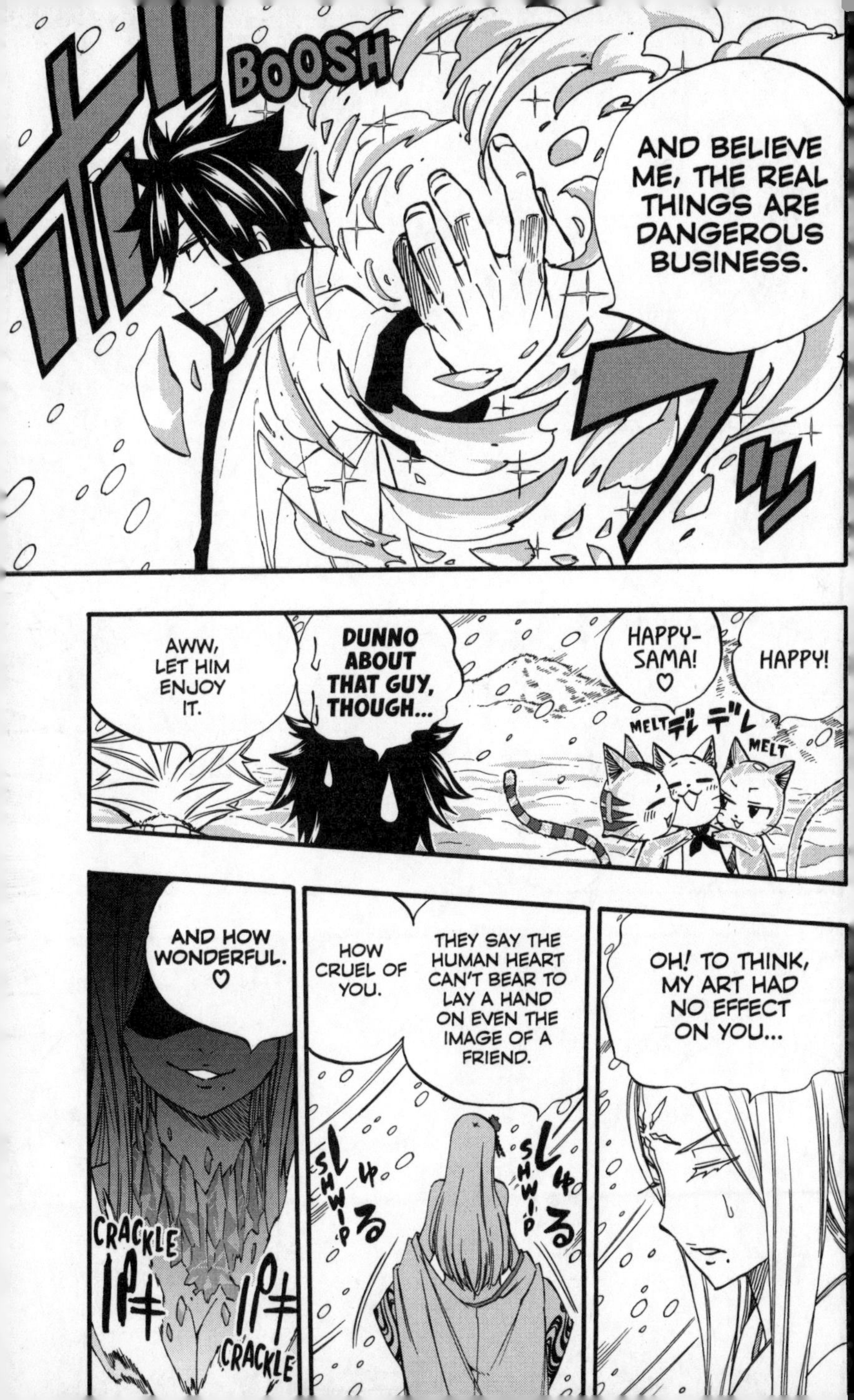
BOOSH
AND BELIEVE ME, THE REAL THINGS ARE DANGEROUS BUSINESS.
HAPPY!
HAPPY-SAMA! ♡
MELT
MELT
DUNNO ABOUT THAT GUY, THOUGH...
AWW, LET HIM ENJOY IT.
OH! TO THINK, MY ART HAD NO EFFECT ON YOU...
THEY SAY THE HUMAN HEART CAN'T BEAR TO LAY A HAND ON EVEN THE IMAGE OF A FRIEND.
HOW CRUEL OF YOU.
SHWIP
SHWIP
AND HOW WONDERFUL. ♡
CRACKLE
CRACKLE

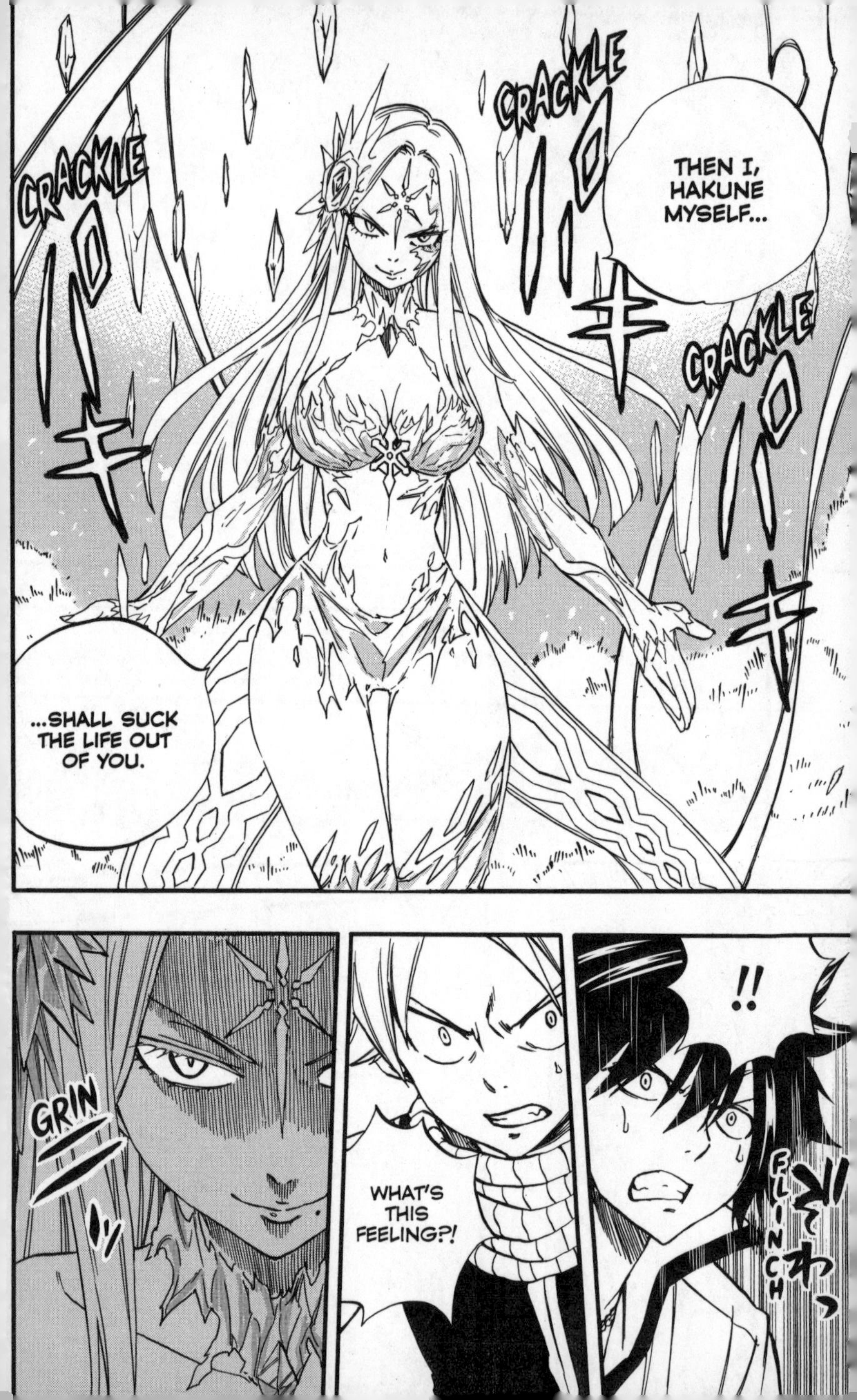
CRACKLE
THEN I, HAKUNE MYSELF...
CRACKLE
CRACKLE
...SHALL SUCK THE LIFE OUT OF YOU.
!!
FLINCH
WHAT'S THIS FEELING?!
GRIN

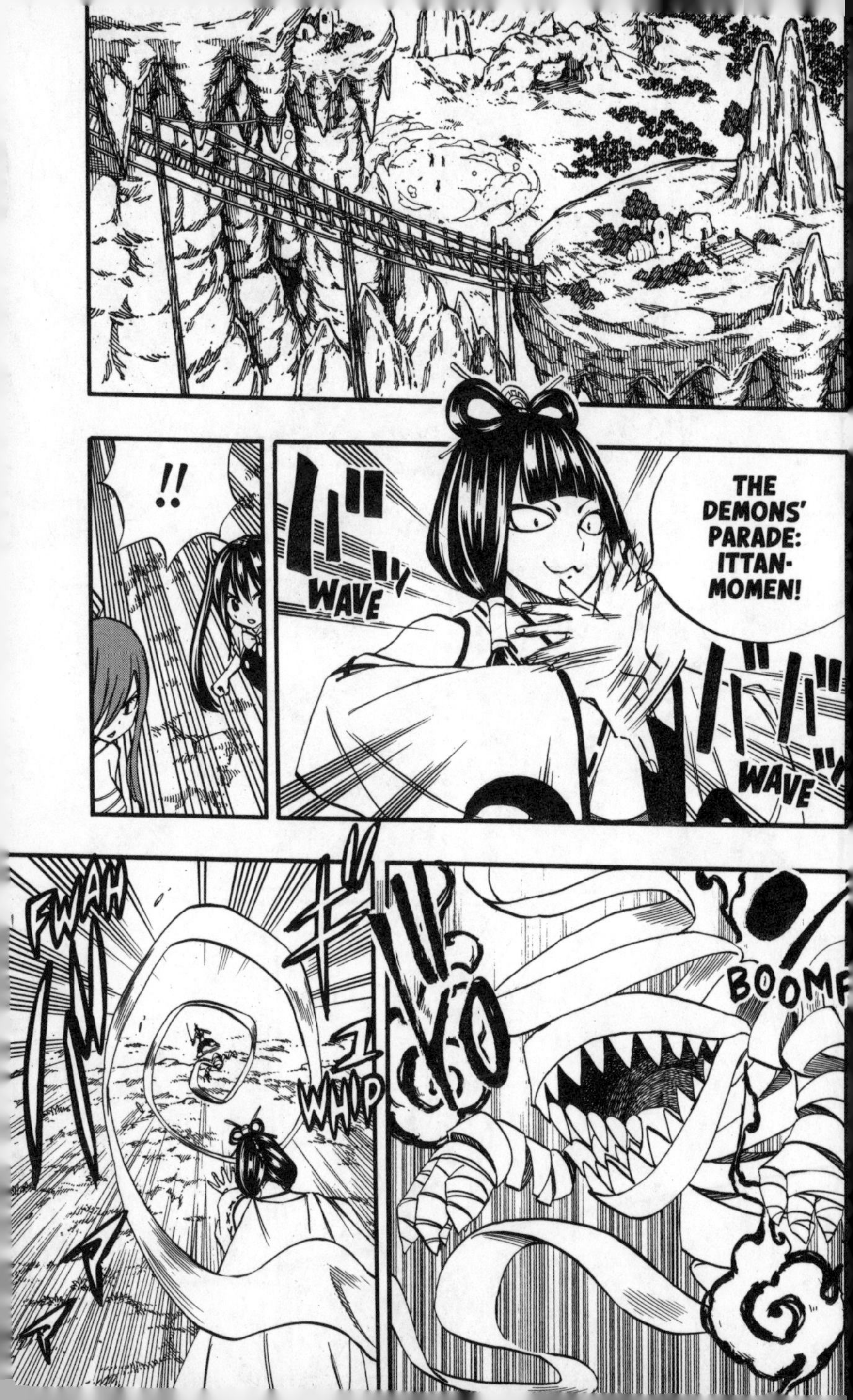
THE DEMONS' PARADE: ITTAN-MOMEN!
WAVE
WAVE
!!
BOOMF
WHIP
FWAH

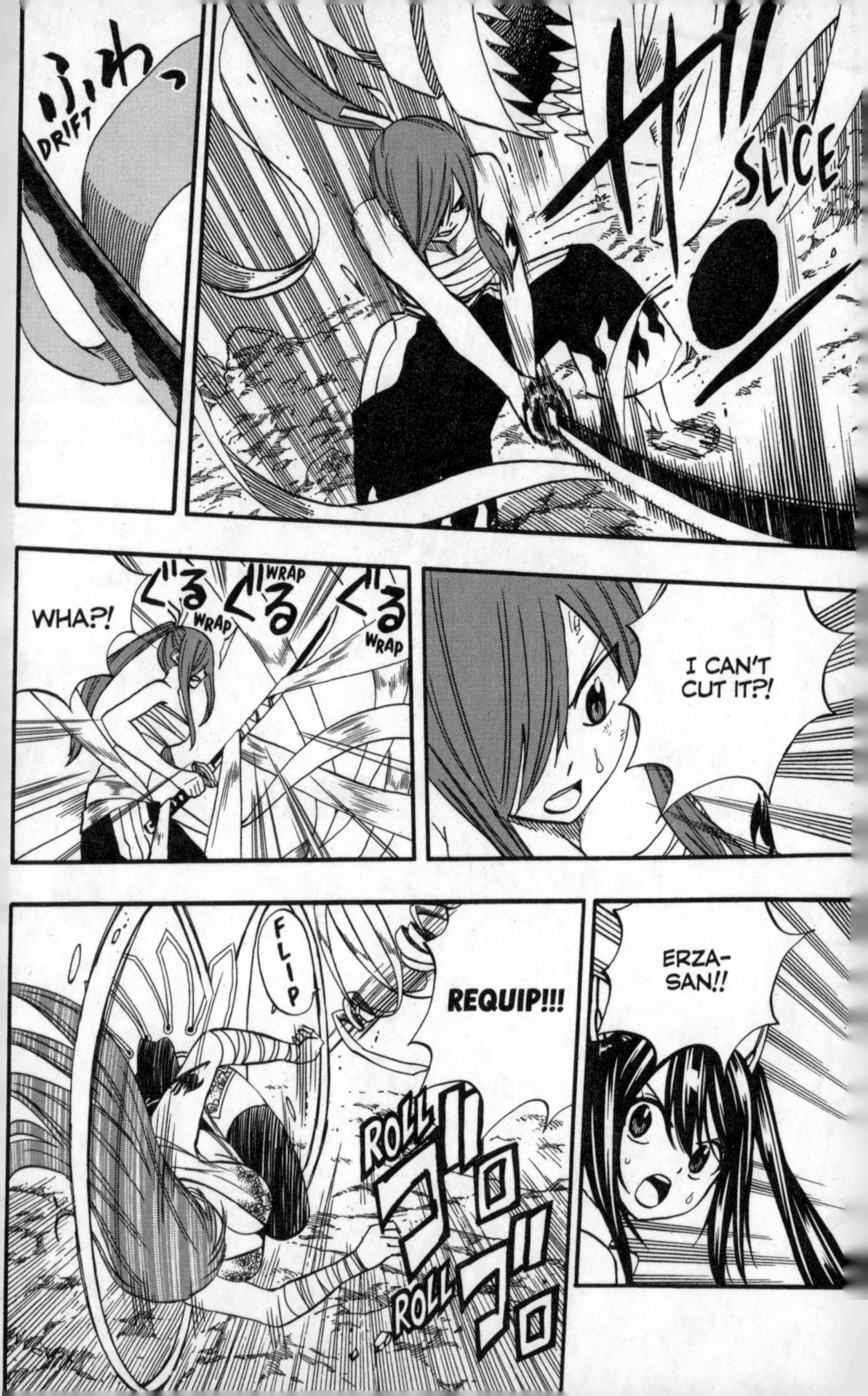
SLICE
ふわっ
DRIFT
I CAN'T CUT IT?!
ぐる
WRAP
ぐる
WRAP
ぐる
WRAP
WHA?!
ERZA-SAN!!
REQUIP!!!
FLIP
ROLL
ゴロ
ROLL
ゴロ

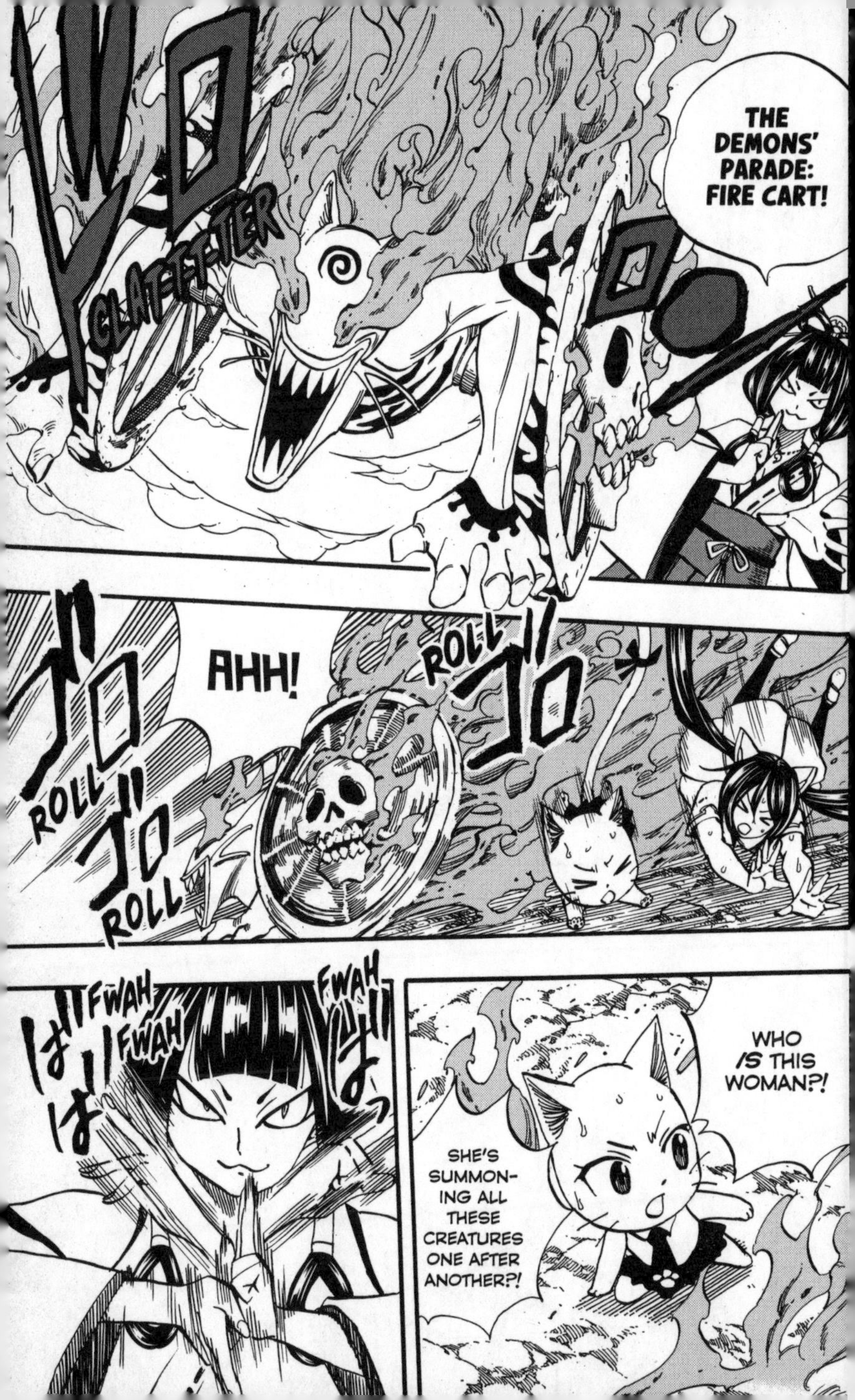
THE DEMONS' PARADE: FIRE CART!
CLATTT-TER
ROLL
AHH!
ROLL
ROLL
WHO IS THIS WOMAN?!
SHE'S SUMMONING ALL THESE CREATURES ONE AFTER ANOTHER?!
FWAH
FWAH
FWAH

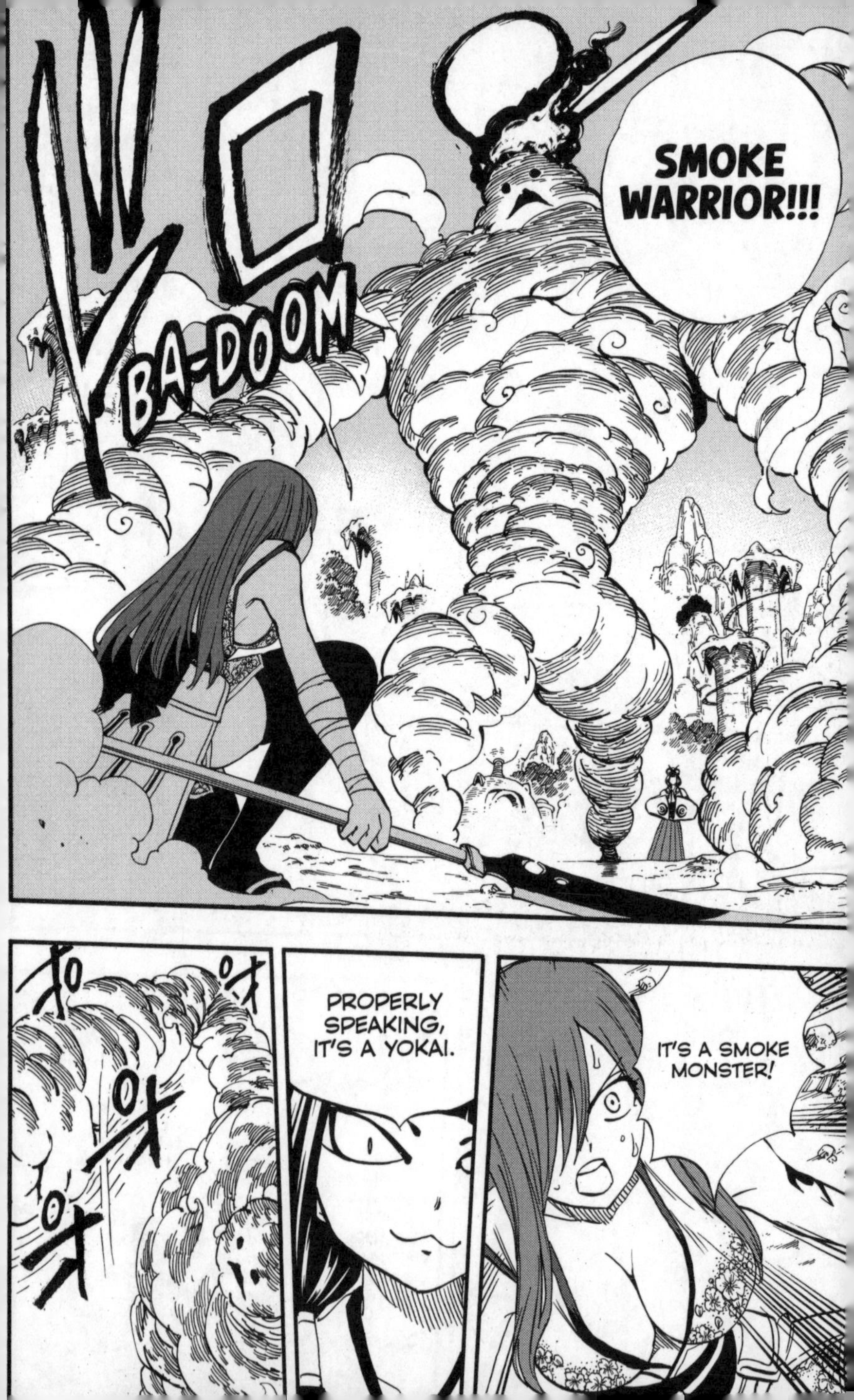
SMOKE WARRIOR!!!
BA-DOOM
IT'S A SMOKE MONSTER!
PROPERLY SPEAKING, IT'S A YOKAI.

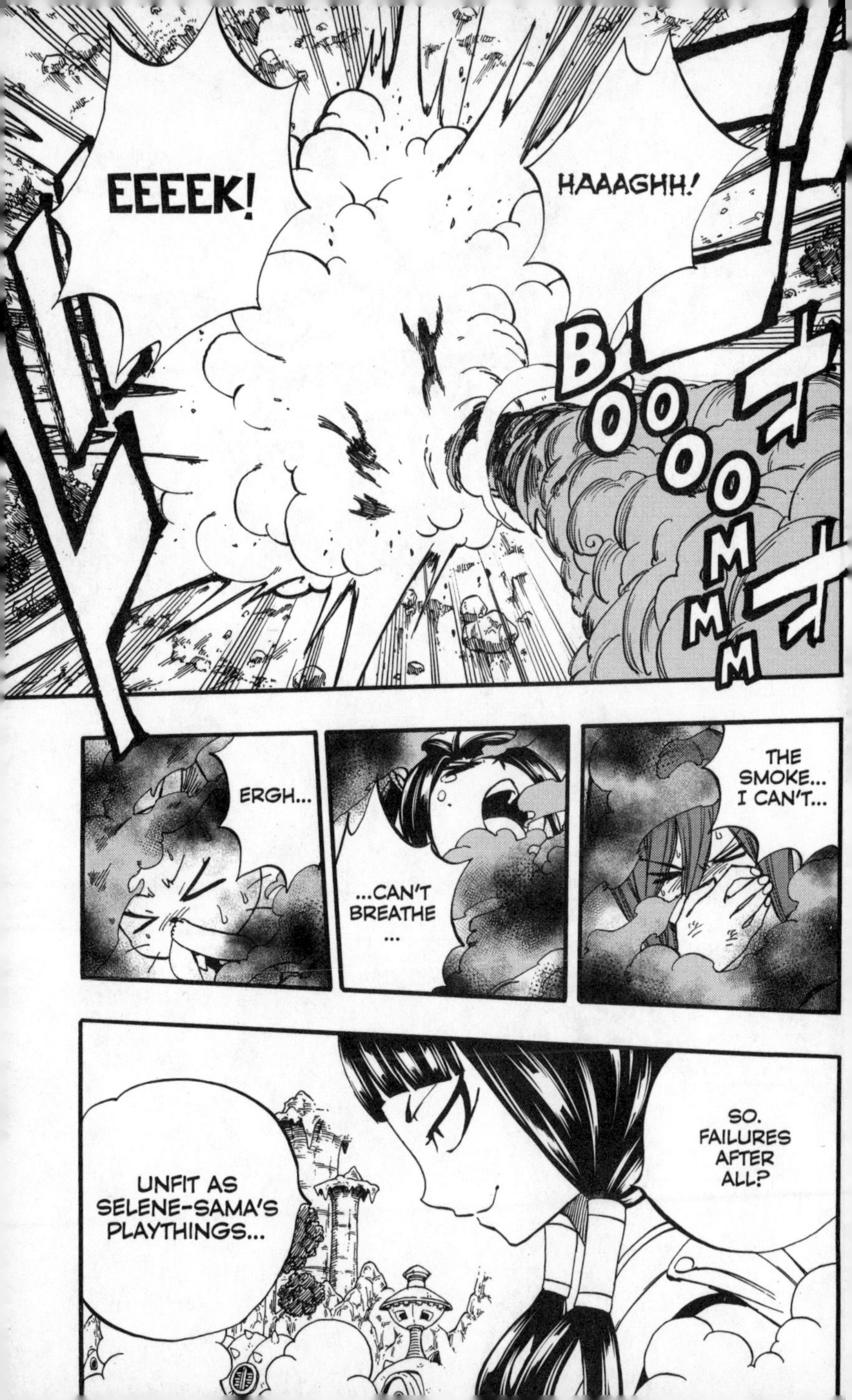
HAAAGHH!
EEEEK!
BOOOOMMM
THE SMOKE... I CAN'T...
...CAN'T BREATHE ...
ERGH...
SO. FAILURES AFTER ALL?
UNFIT AS SELENE-SAMA'S PLAYTHINGS...

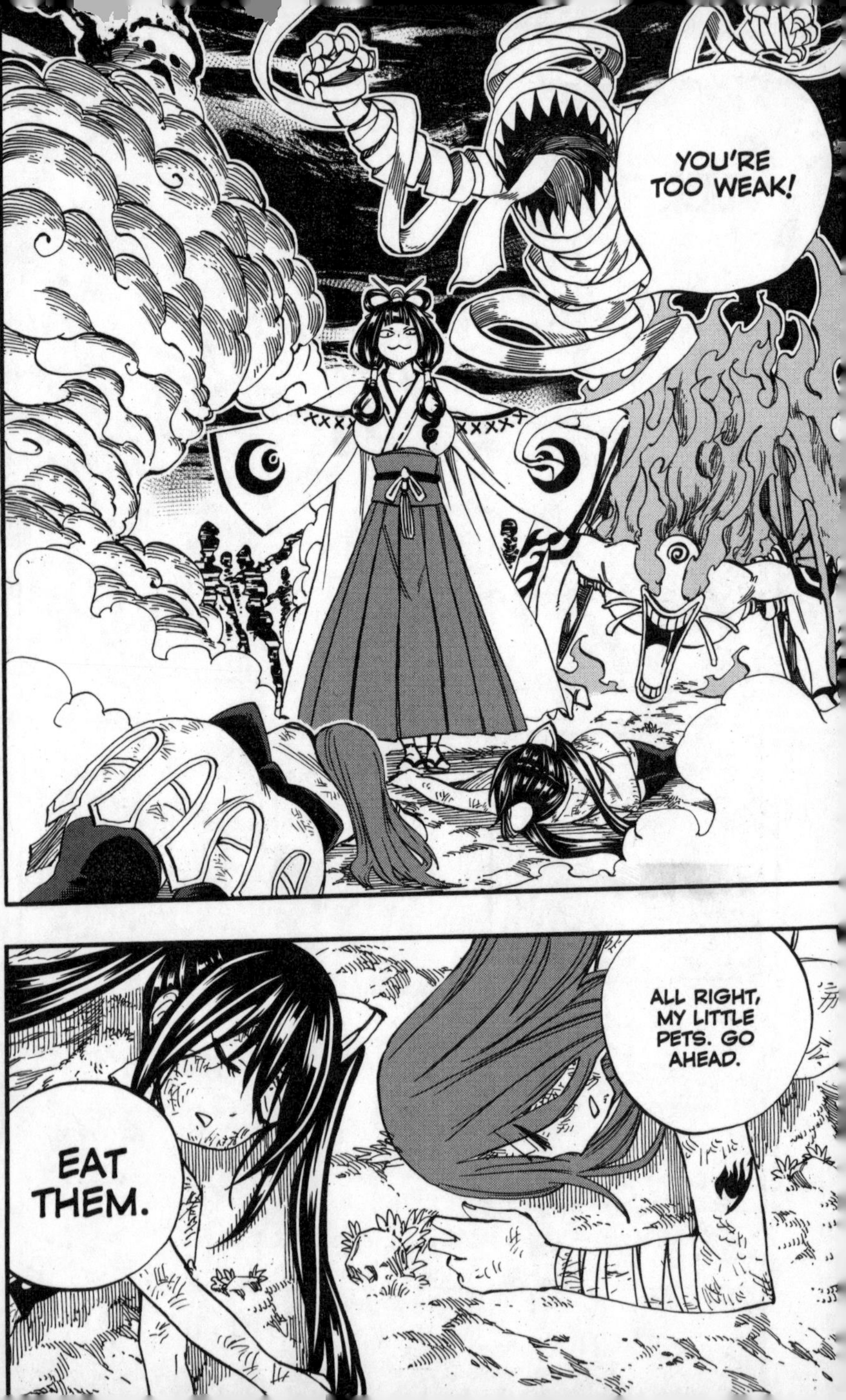
YOU'RE TOO WEAK!
ALL RIGHT, MY LITTLE PETS. GO AHEAD.
EAT THEM.

FAIRY TAIL 100 YEARS QUEST

Chapter 72: The Moonlight Divinities

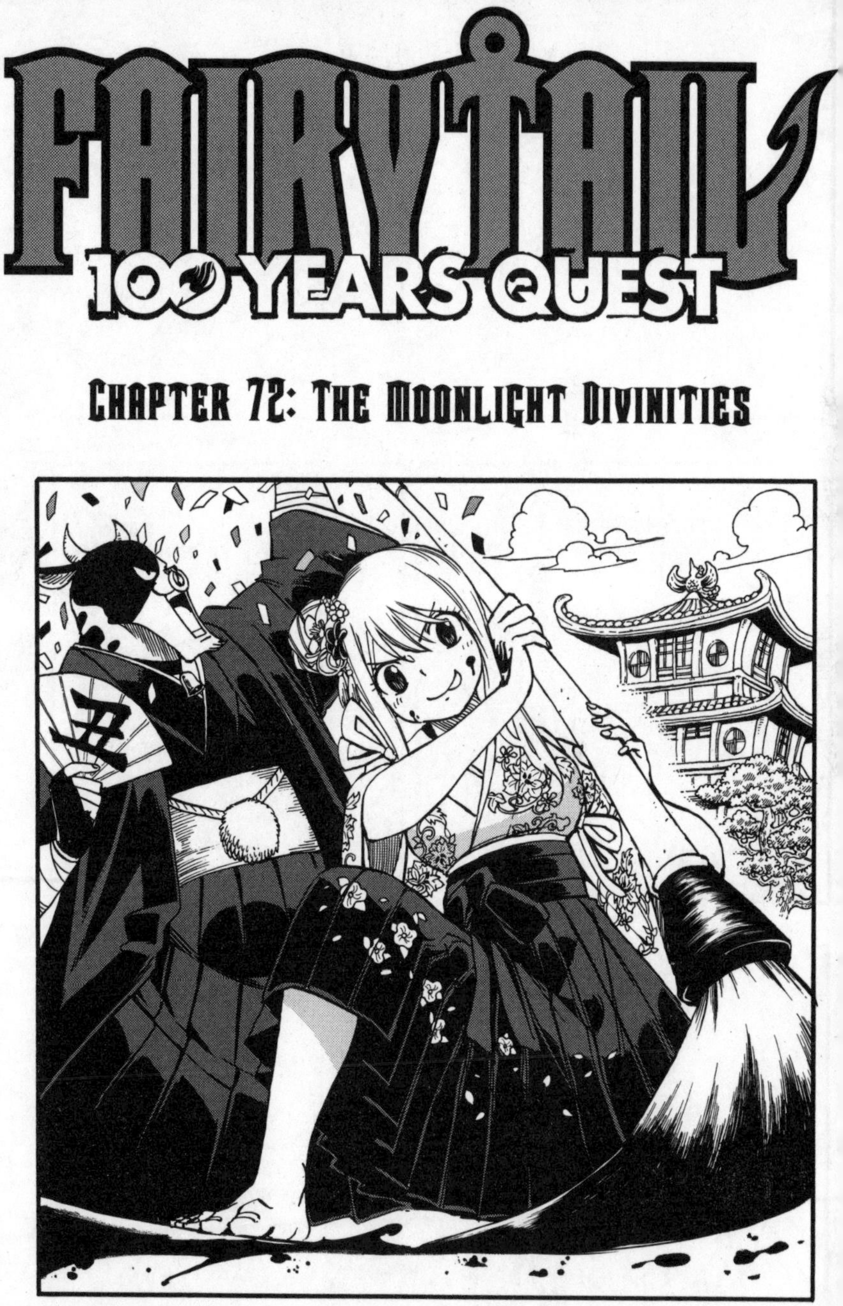

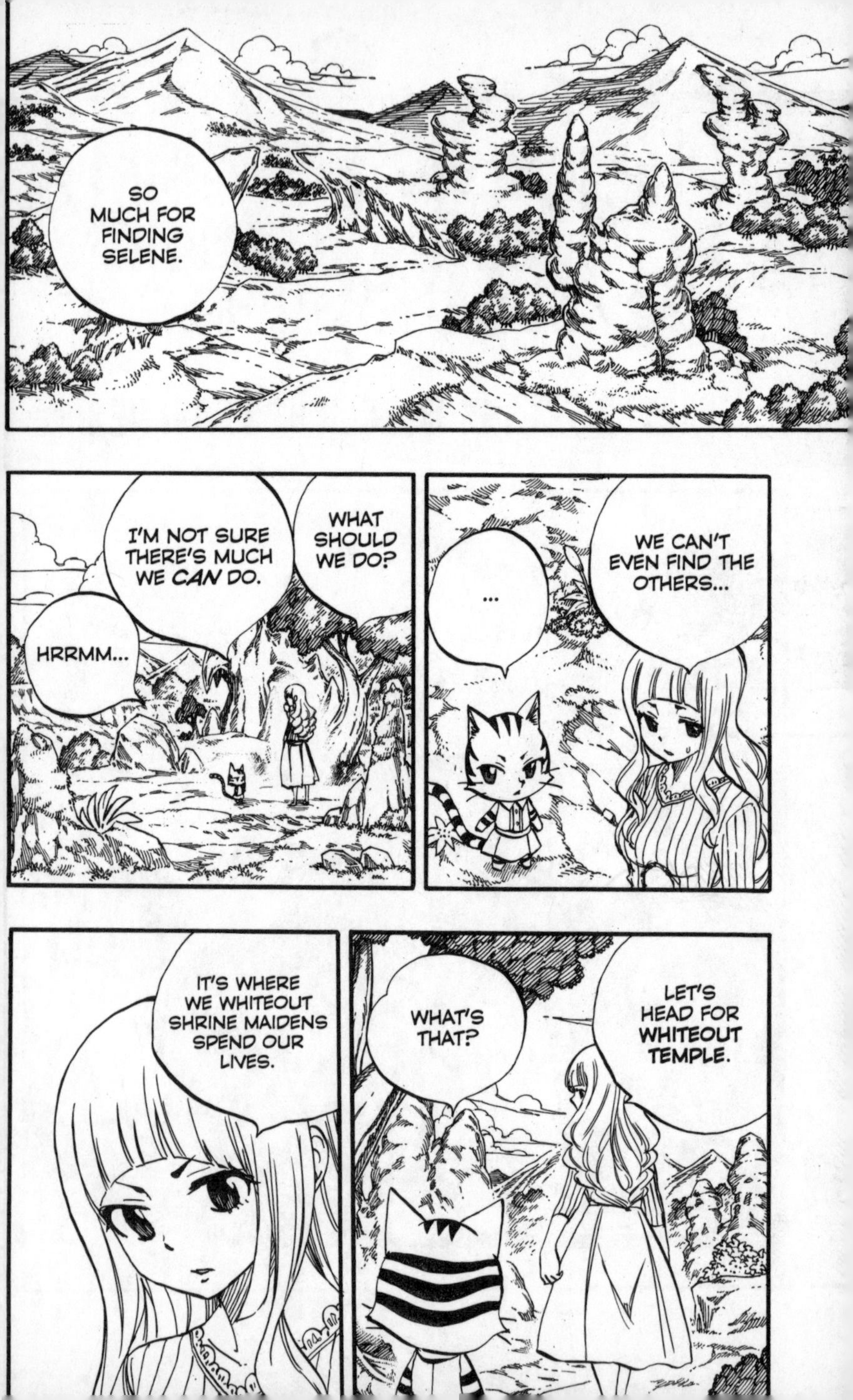
SO MUCH FOR FINDING SELENE.
WE CAN'T EVEN FIND THE OTHERS...
...
WHAT SHOULD WE DO?
I'M NOT SURE THERE'S MUCH WE *CAN* DO.
HRRMM...
LET'S HEAD FOR WHITEOUT TEMPLE.
WHAT'S THAT?
IT'S WHERE WE WHITEOUT SHRINE MAIDENS SPEND OUR LIVES.

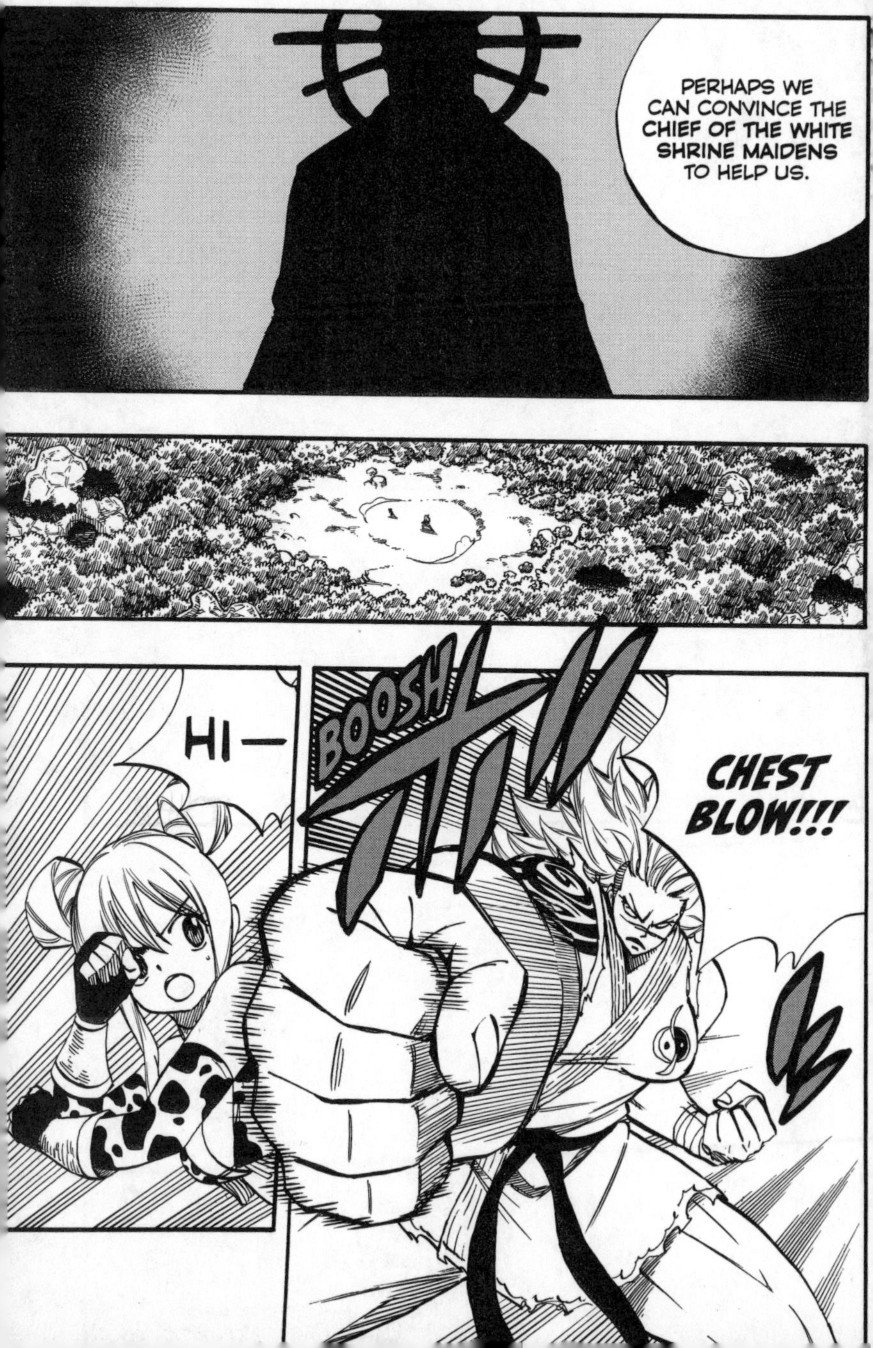
PERHAPS WE CAN CONVINCE THE CHIEF OF THE WHITE SHRINE MAIDENS TO HELP US.
CHEST BLOW!!!
BOOSH
HI—

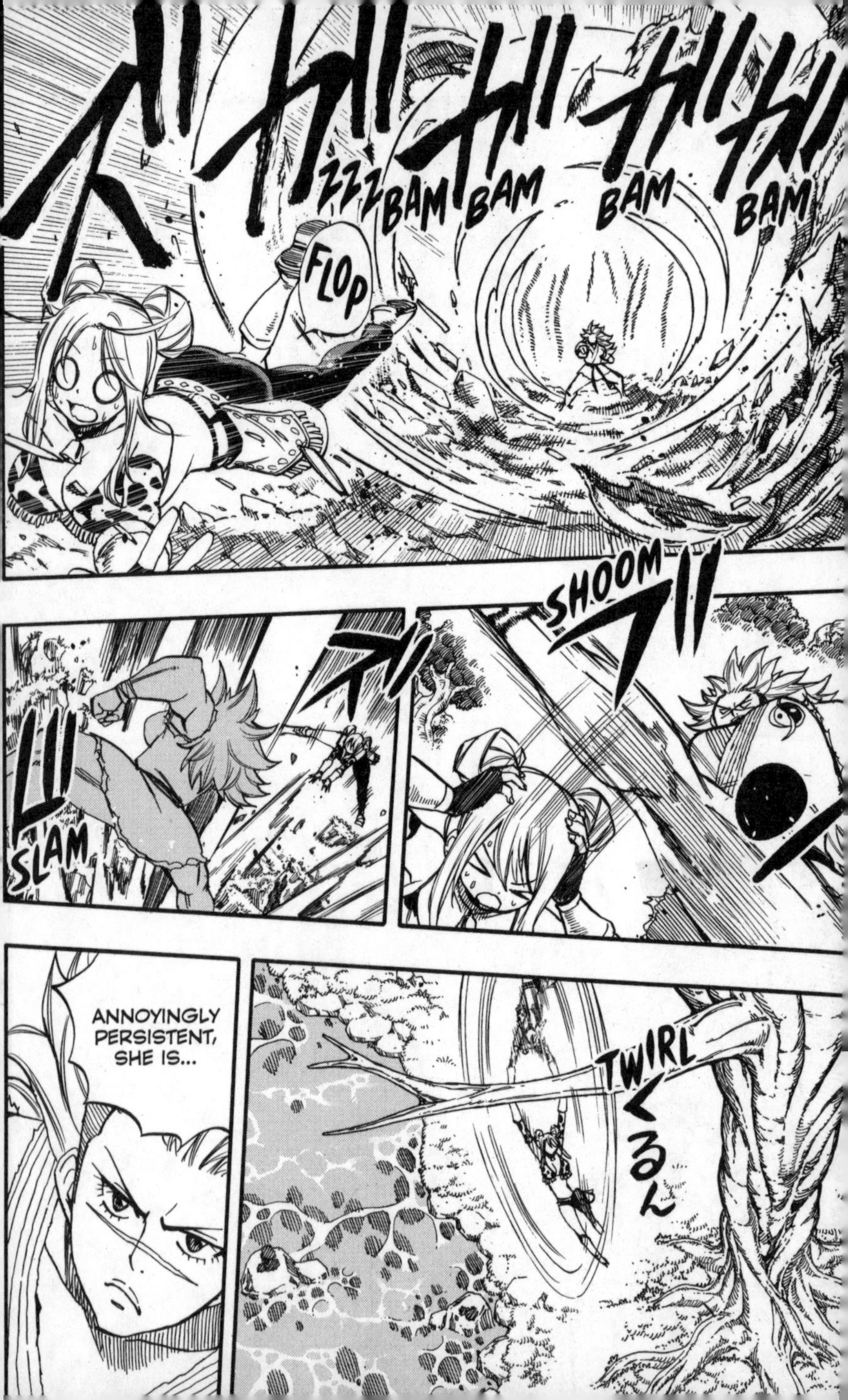
BAM BAM BAM BAM
ZZZ
FLOP
SHOOM
SLAM
TWIRL
くるん
ANNOYINGLY PERSISTENT, SHE IS...

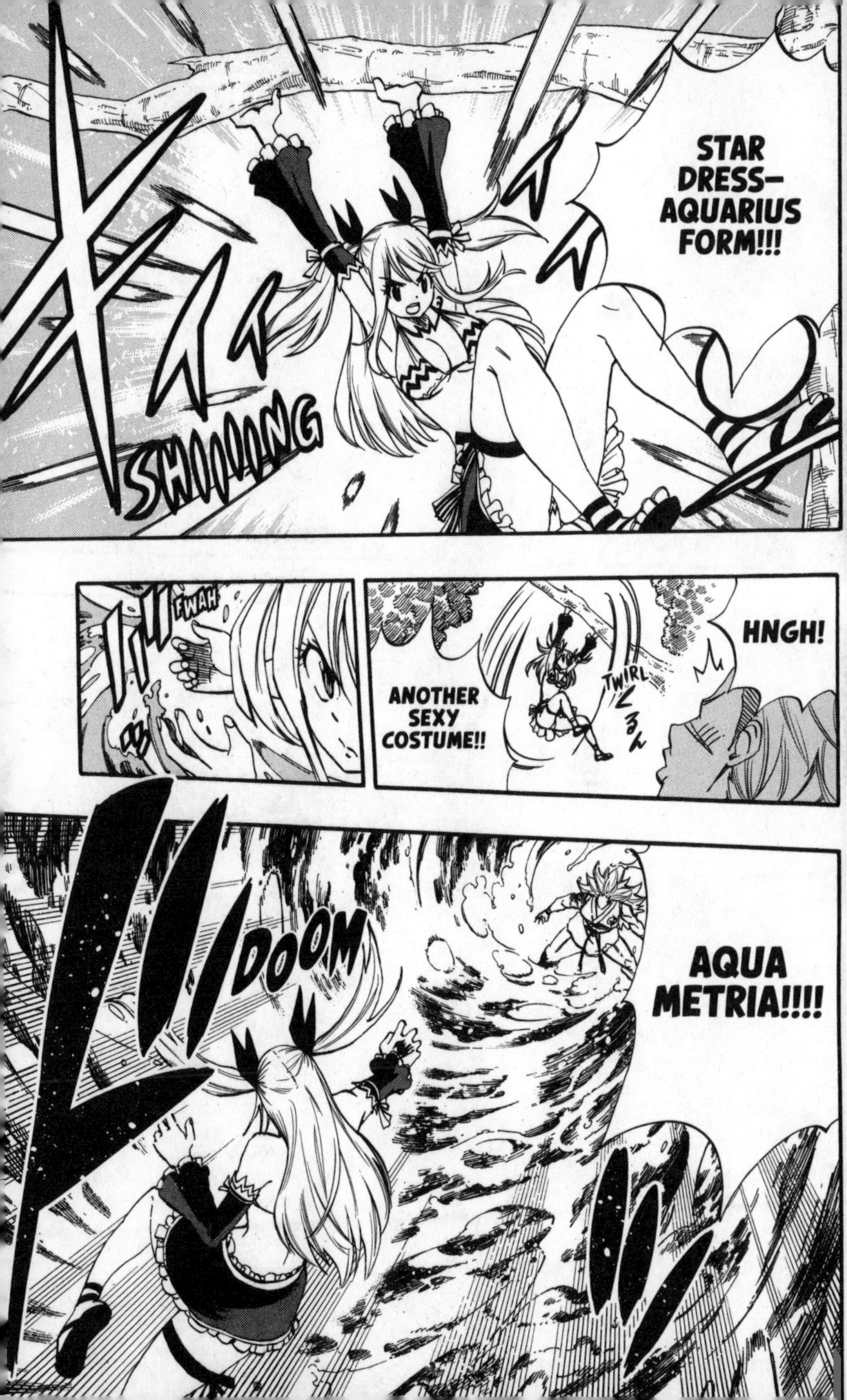
STAR DRESS- AQUARIUS FORM!!!
SHIIING
HNGH!
TWIRL
ANOTHER SEXY COSTUME!!
FWAH
AQUA METRIA!!!!
DOOM

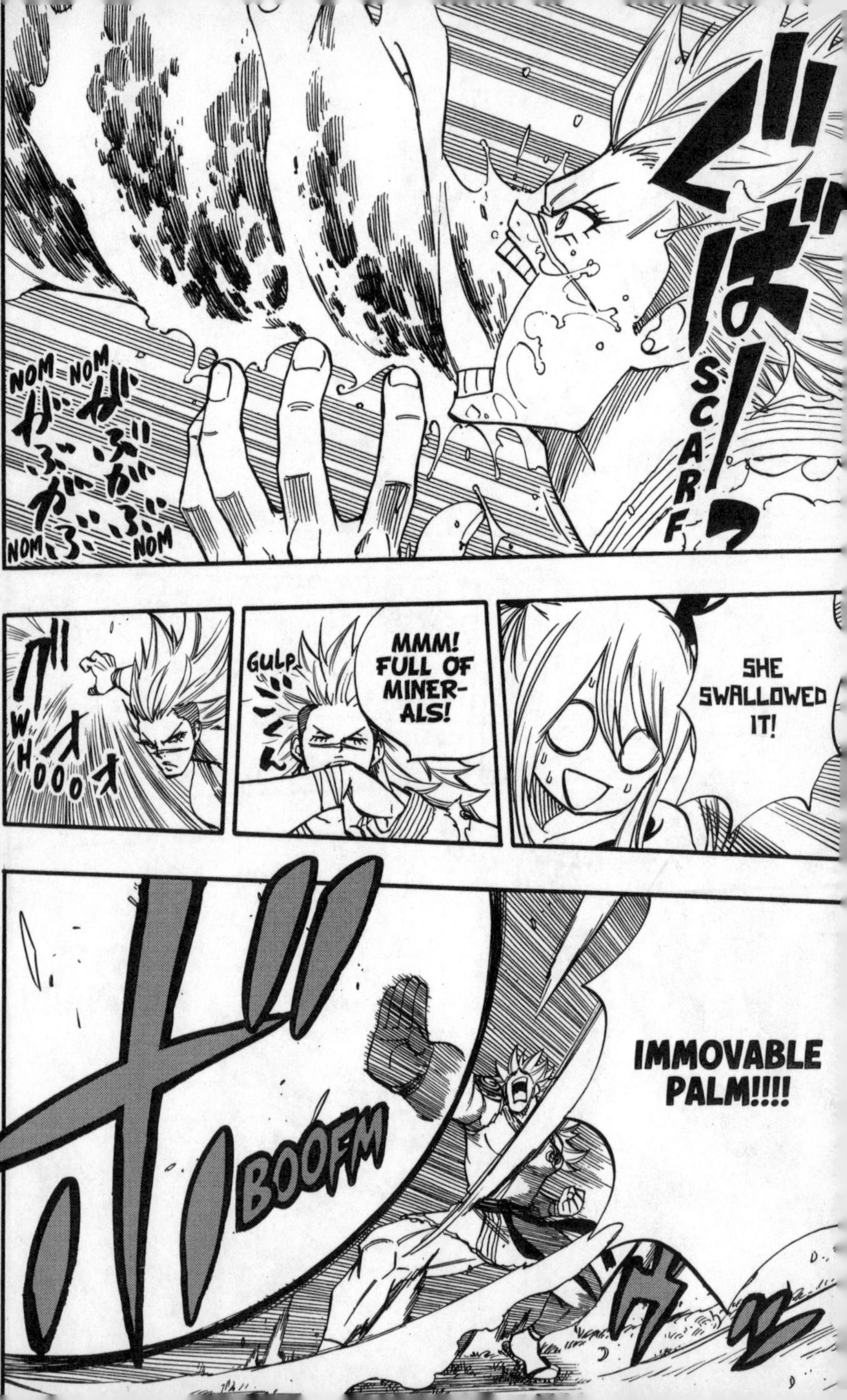
SCARF
NOM NOM
NOM NOM
SHE SWALLOWED IT!
MMM! FULL OF MINER-ALS!
GULP
ごくん
WHOOO
IMMOVABLE PALM!!!!
BOOFM

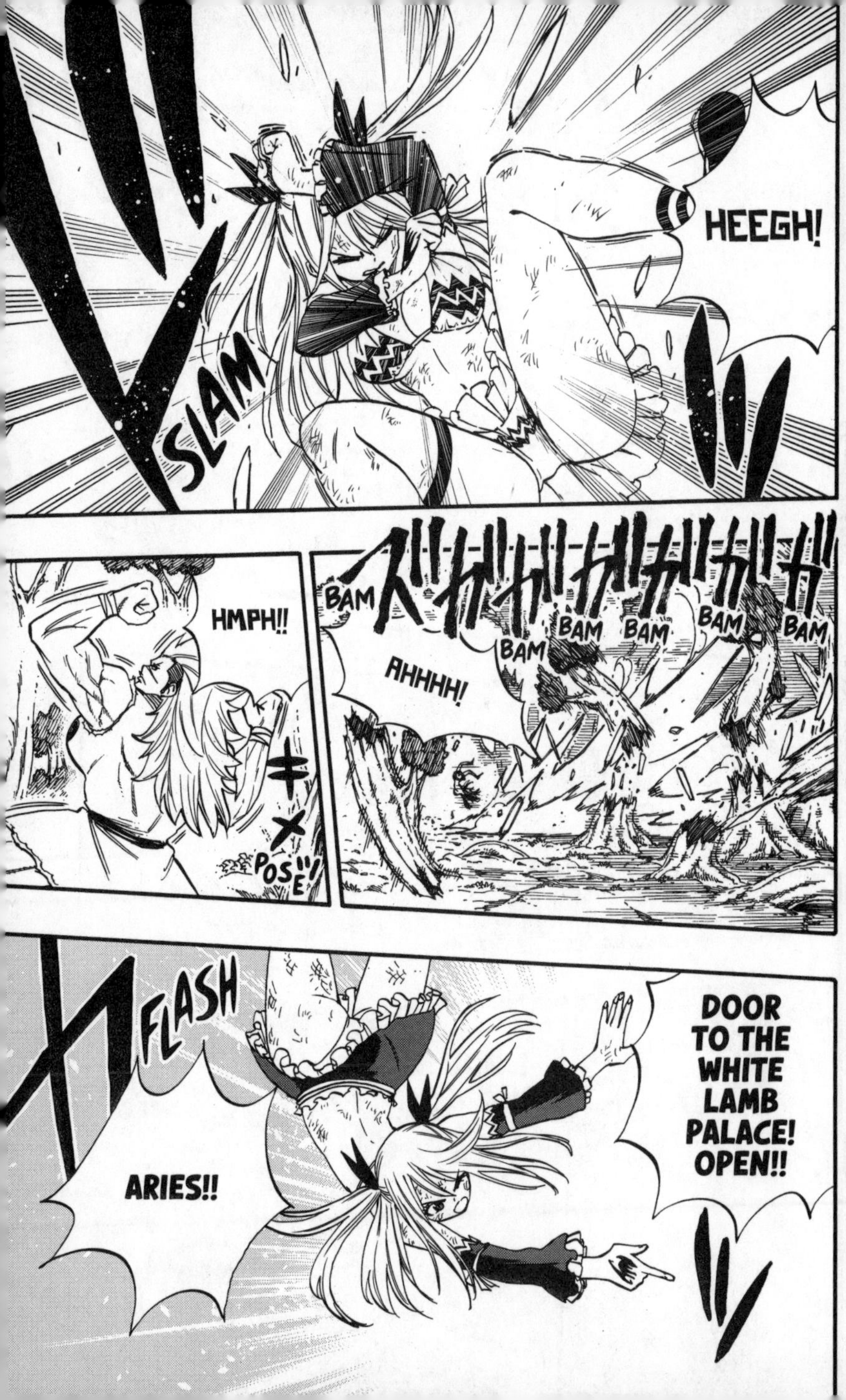

HEEGH!
SLAM
BAM
BAM
BAM
BAM
BAM
BAM
AHHHH!
HMPH!!
POSE
DOOR TO THE WHITE LAMB PALACE! OPEN!!
ARIES!!
FLASH

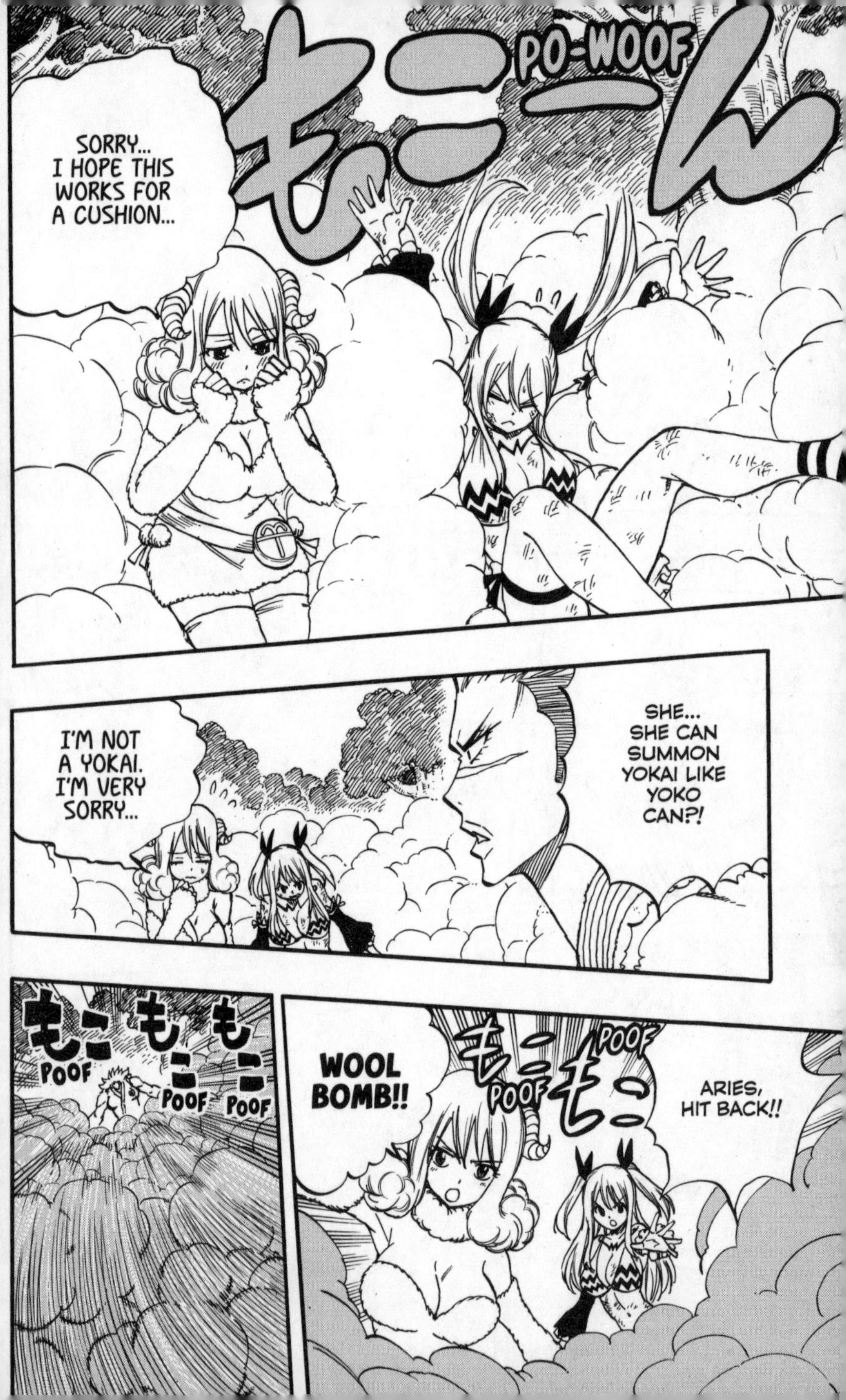
もこーん
PO-WOOF
SORRY... I HOPE THIS WORKS FOR A CUSHION...
SHE... SHE CAN SUMMON YOKAI LIKE YOKO CAN?!
I'M NOT A YOKAI. I'M VERY SORRY...
ARIES, HIT BACK!!
もこもこ
POOF POOF
WOOL BOMB!!
もこもこもこ
POOF POOF POOF

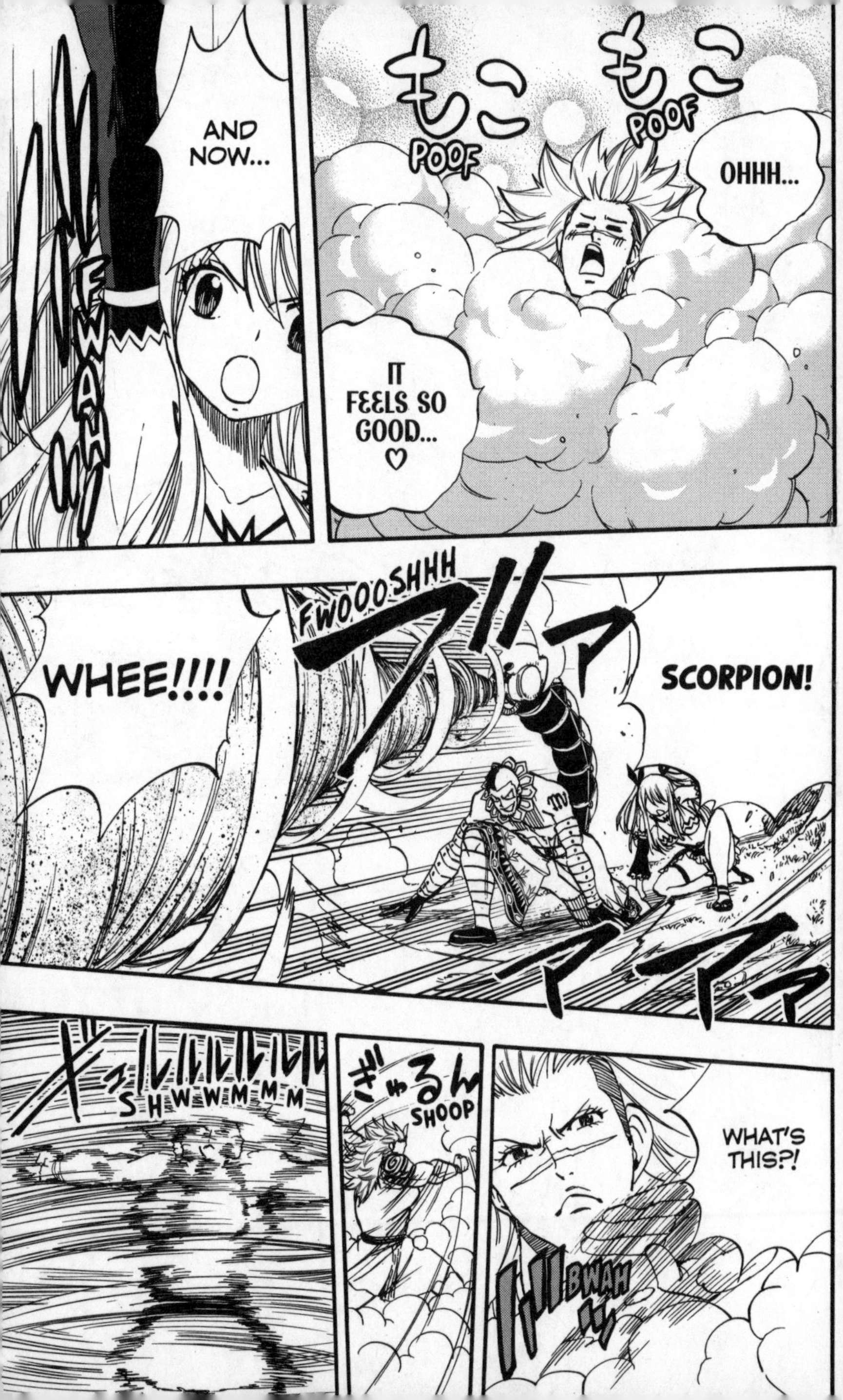

もこ もこ
POOF
POOF
OHHH...
IT FEELS SO GOOD... ♡
AND NOW...
FWAAH
SCORPION!
FWOOOSHHH
WHEE!!!!
WHAT'S THIS?!
BWAH
ぎゅるん
SHOOP
SHWWMMM

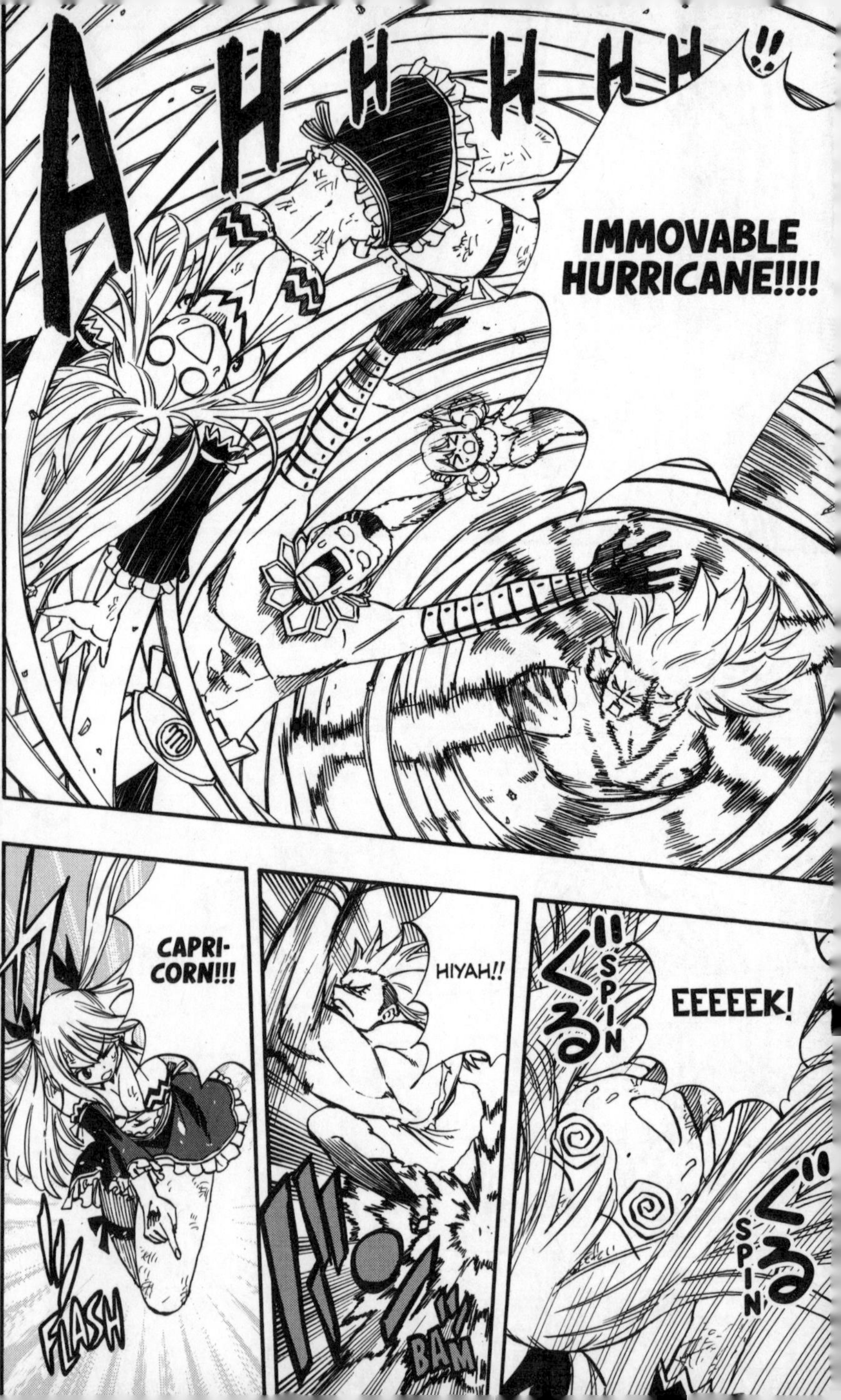
AHHHHHH!!
IMMOVABLE HURRICANE!!!!
くる SPIN
EEEEEK!
ぐる SPIN
HIYAH!!
BAM
CAPRI-CORN!!!
FLASH

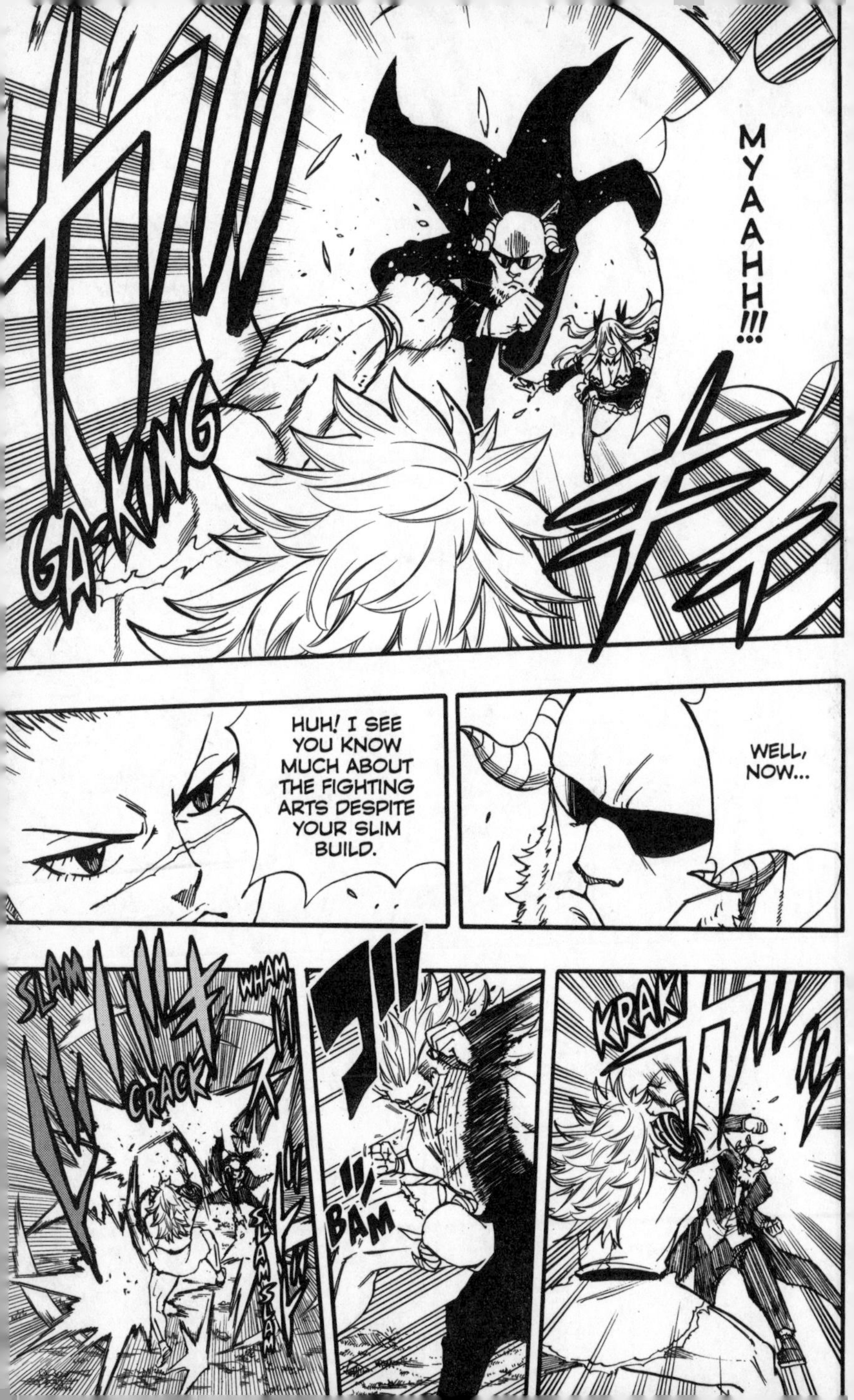
MYAAHH!!!
GA-KING
WELL, NOW...
HUH! I SEE YOU KNOW MUCH ABOUT THE FIGHTING ARTS DESPITE YOUR SLIM BUILD.
KRAK
BAM
WHAM
SLAM
CRACK
SLAM SLAM

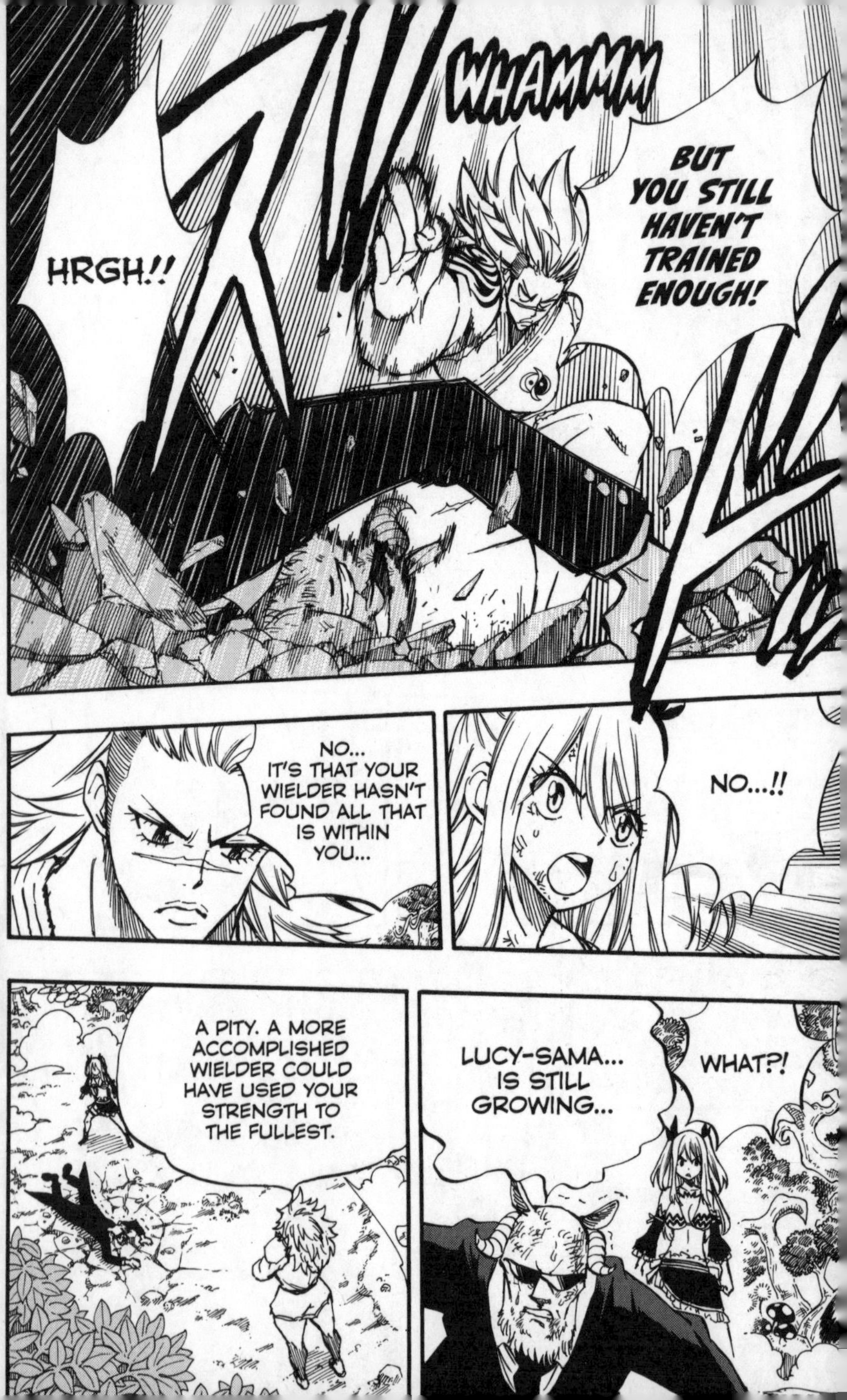
WHAMMM
BUT YOU STILL HAVEN'T TRAINED ENOUGH!
HRGH!!
NO...!!
NO... IT'S THAT YOUR WIELDER HASN'T FOUND ALL THAT IS WITHIN YOU...
WHAT?!
LUCY-SAMA... IS STILL GROWING...
A PITY. A MORE ACCOMPLISHED WIELDER COULD HAVE USED YOUR STRENGTH TO THE FULLEST.

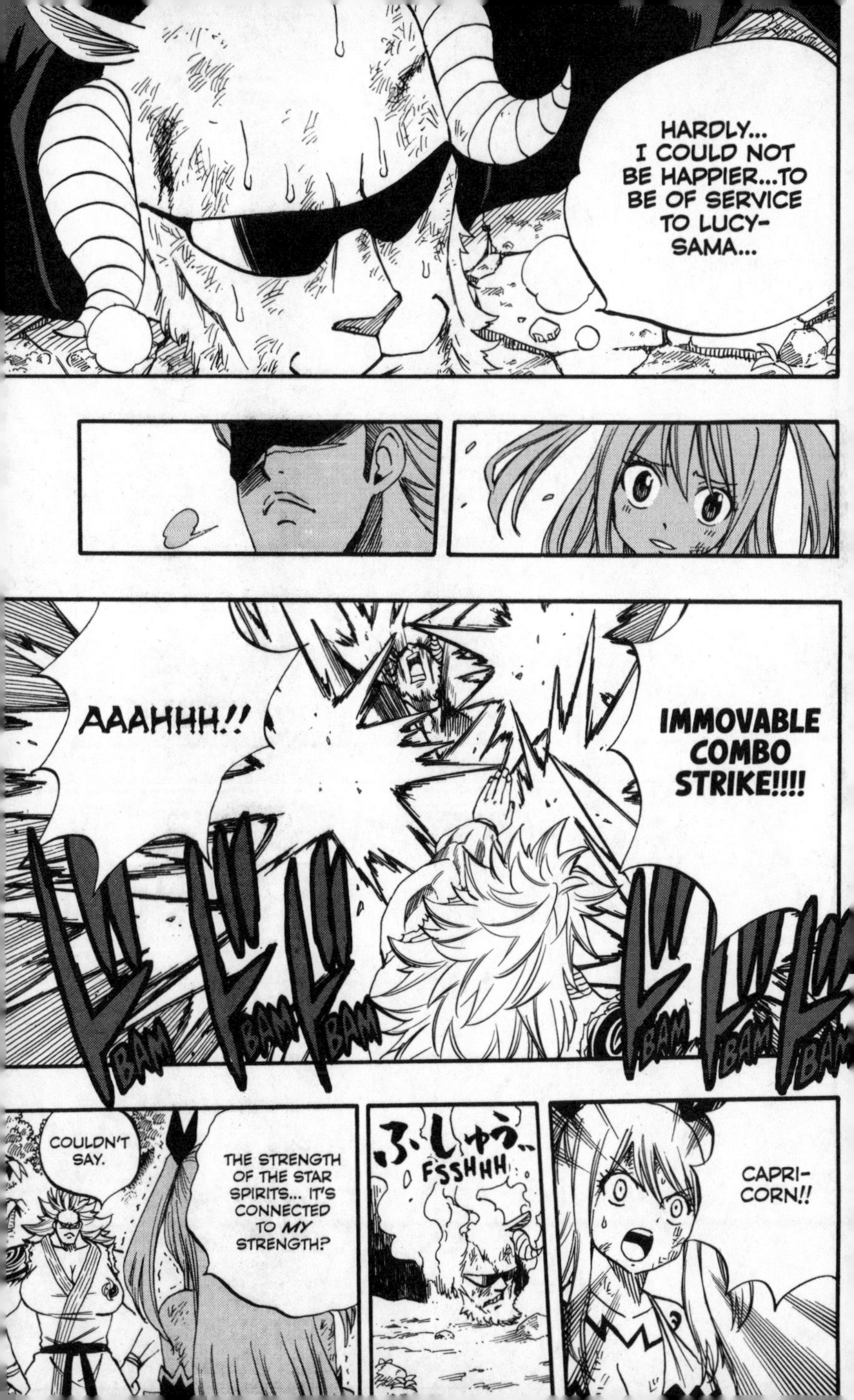
HARDLY... I COULD NOT BE HAPPIER...TO BE OF SERVICE TO LUCY-SAMA...
IMMOVABLE COMBO STRIKE!!!!
AAAHHH!!
BAM BAM BAM
BAM BAM BAM
CAPRI-CORN!!
ふしゅう...
FSSHHH
THE STRENGTH OF THE STAR SPIRITS... IT'S CONNECTED TO *MY* STRENGTH?
COULDN'T SAY.

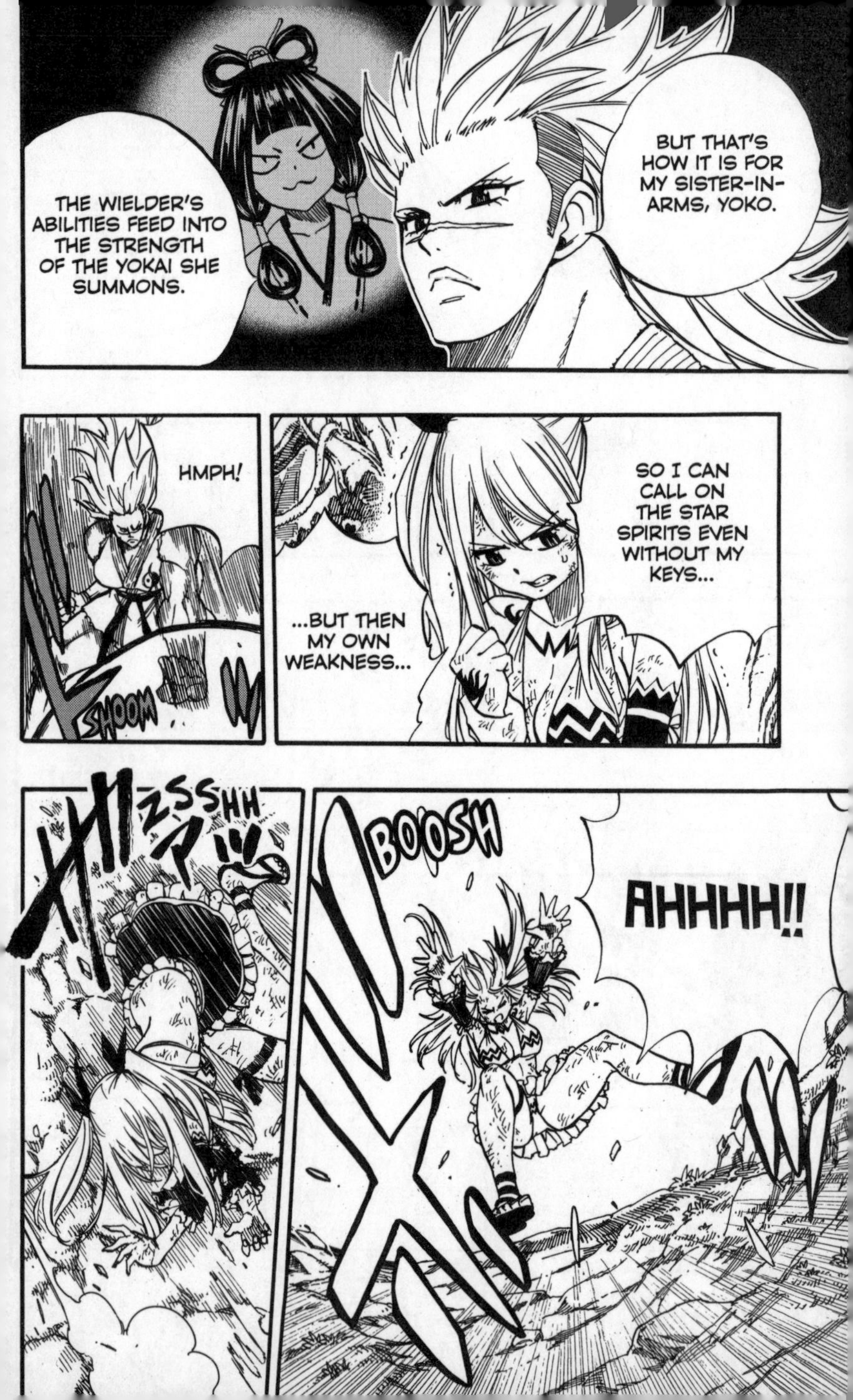
BUT THAT'S HOW IT IS FOR MY SISTER-IN-ARMS, YOKO.
THE WIELDER'S ABILITIES FEED INTO THE STRENGTH OF THE YOKAI SHE SUMMONS.
SO I CAN CALL ON THE STAR SPIRITS EVEN WITHOUT MY KEYS...
...BUT THEN MY OWN WEAKNESS...
HMPH!
SHOOM
BOOSH
AHHHH!!
ZSSHH

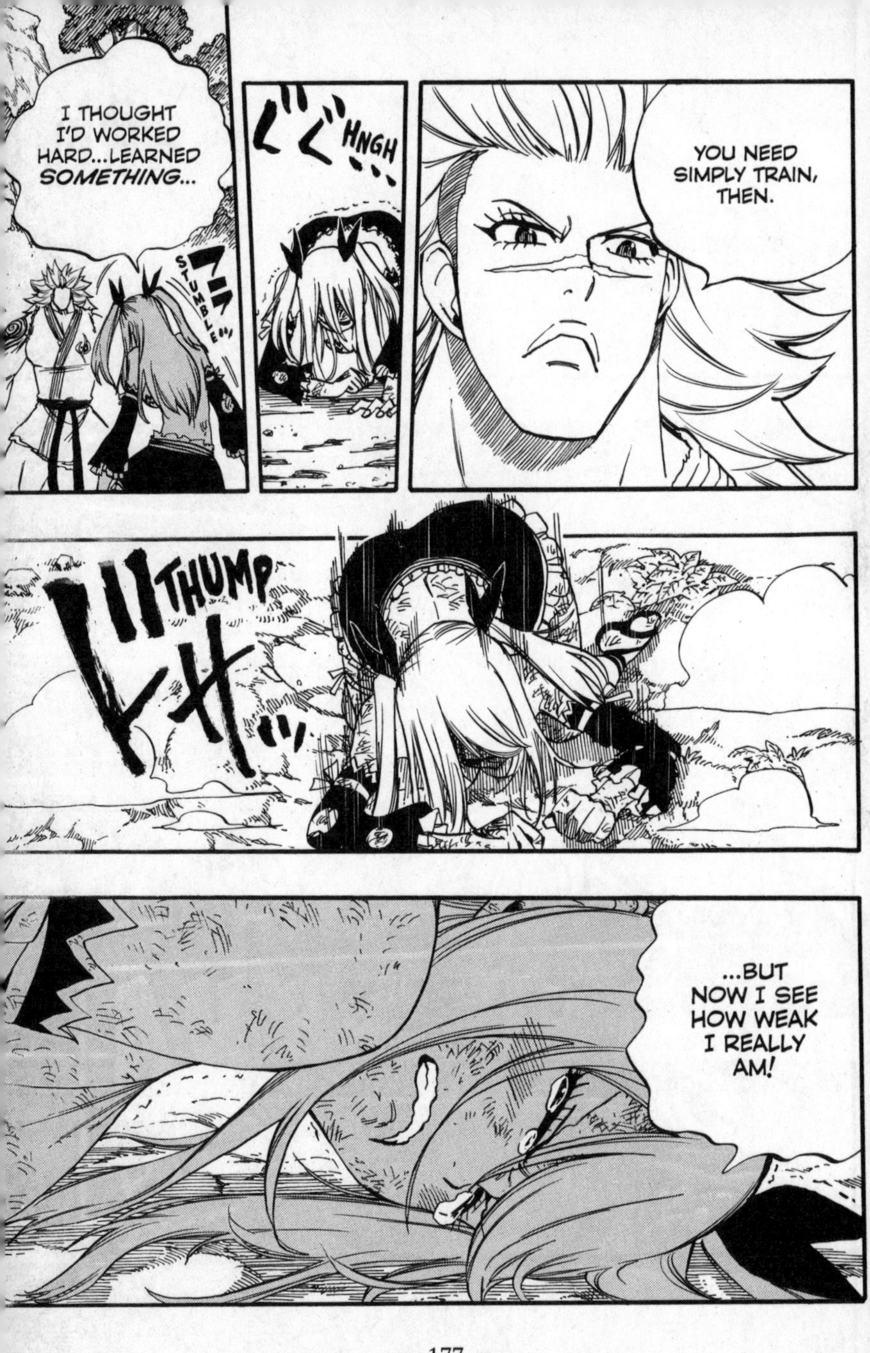
YOU NEED SIMPLY TRAIN, THEN.
ぐぐ
HNGH
I THOUGHT I'D WORKED HARD...LEARNED *SOMETHING*...
フラ
STUMBLE
ドサ
THUMP
...BUT NOW I SEE HOW WEAK I REALLY AM!

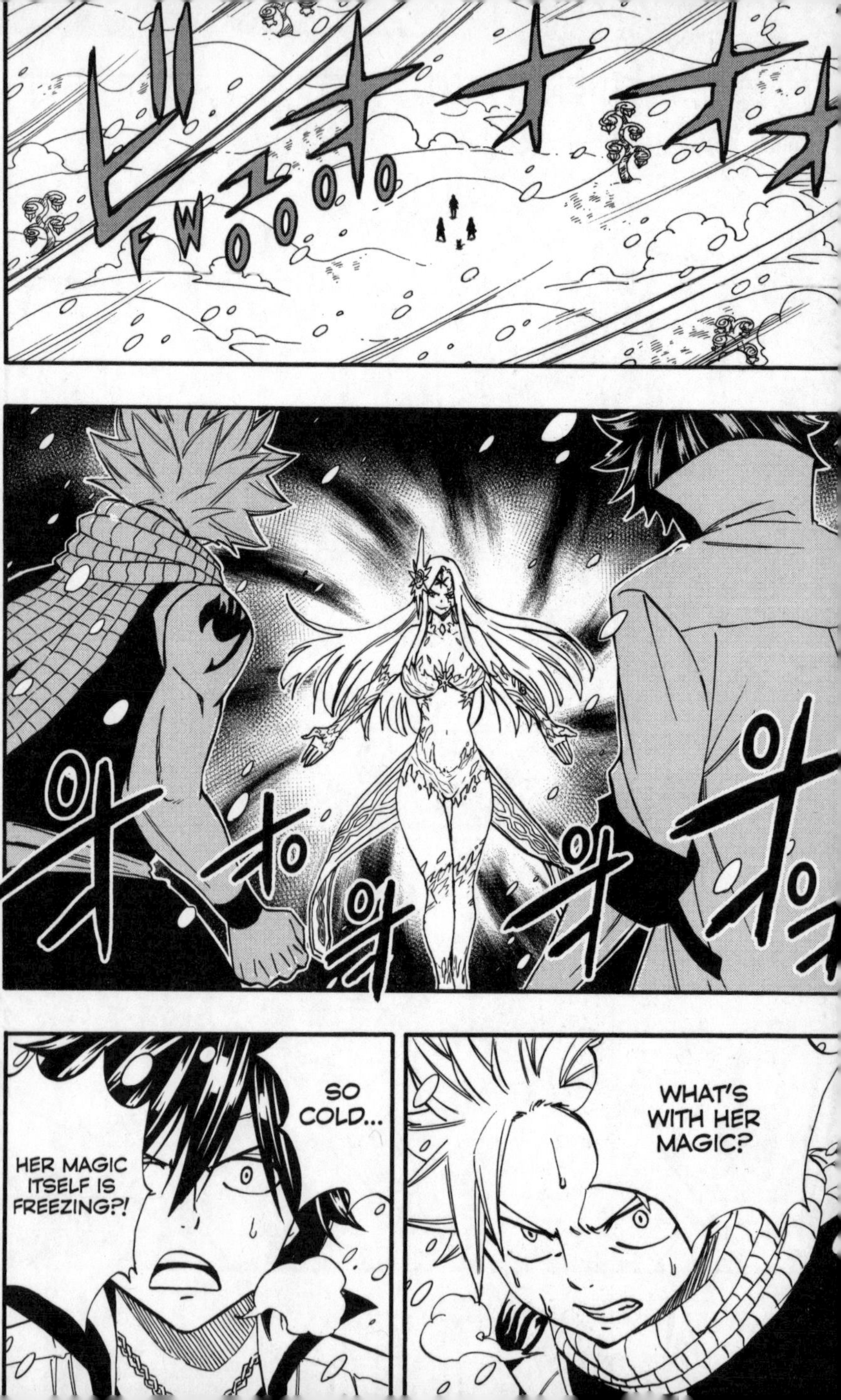
FWOOOO
WHAT'S WITH HER MAGIC?
SO COLD...
HER MAGIC ITSELF IS FREEZING?!

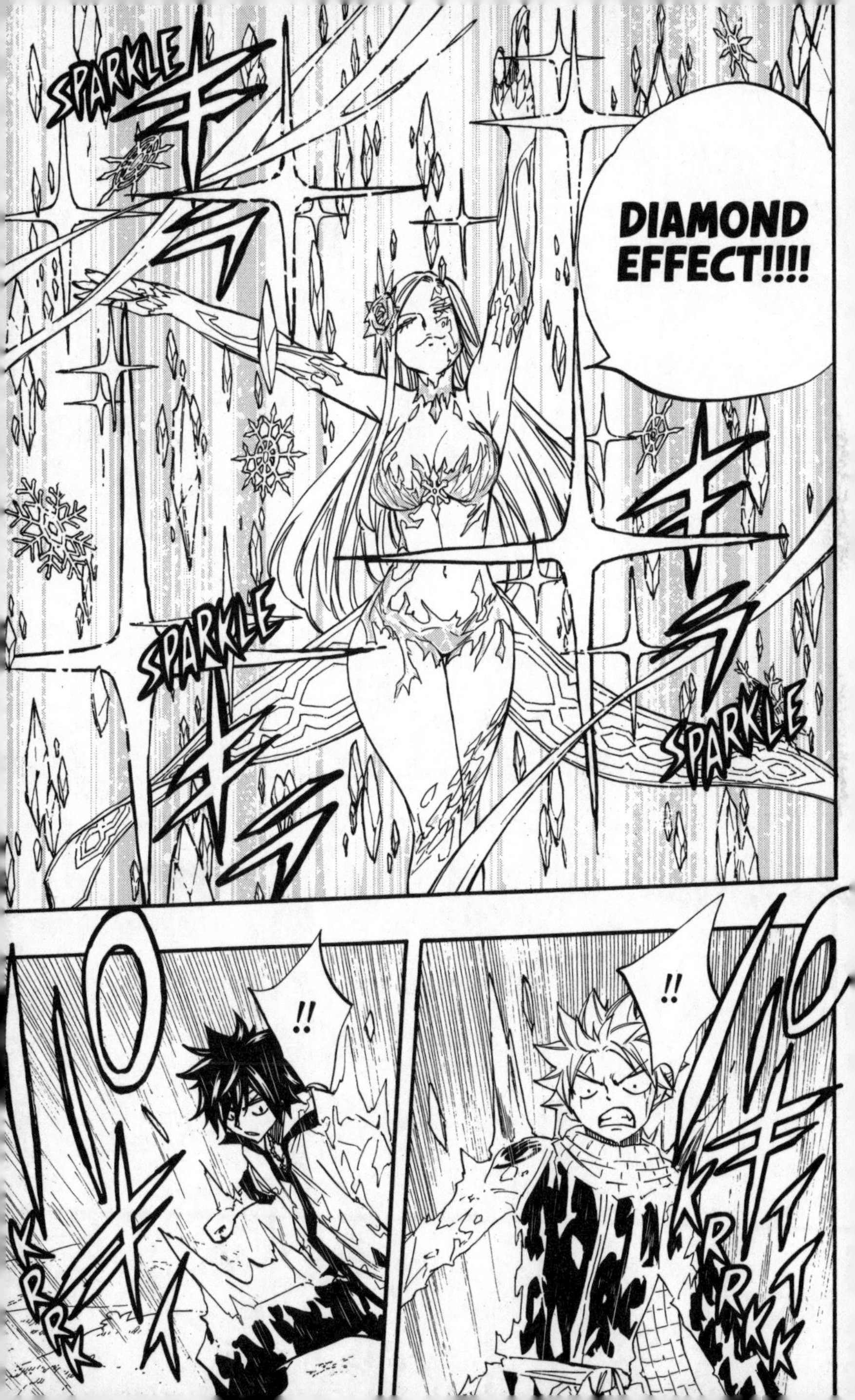
DIAMOND EFFECT!!!!
SPARKLE
SPARKLE
SPARKLE
!!
KRRRK
!!
KRRRK

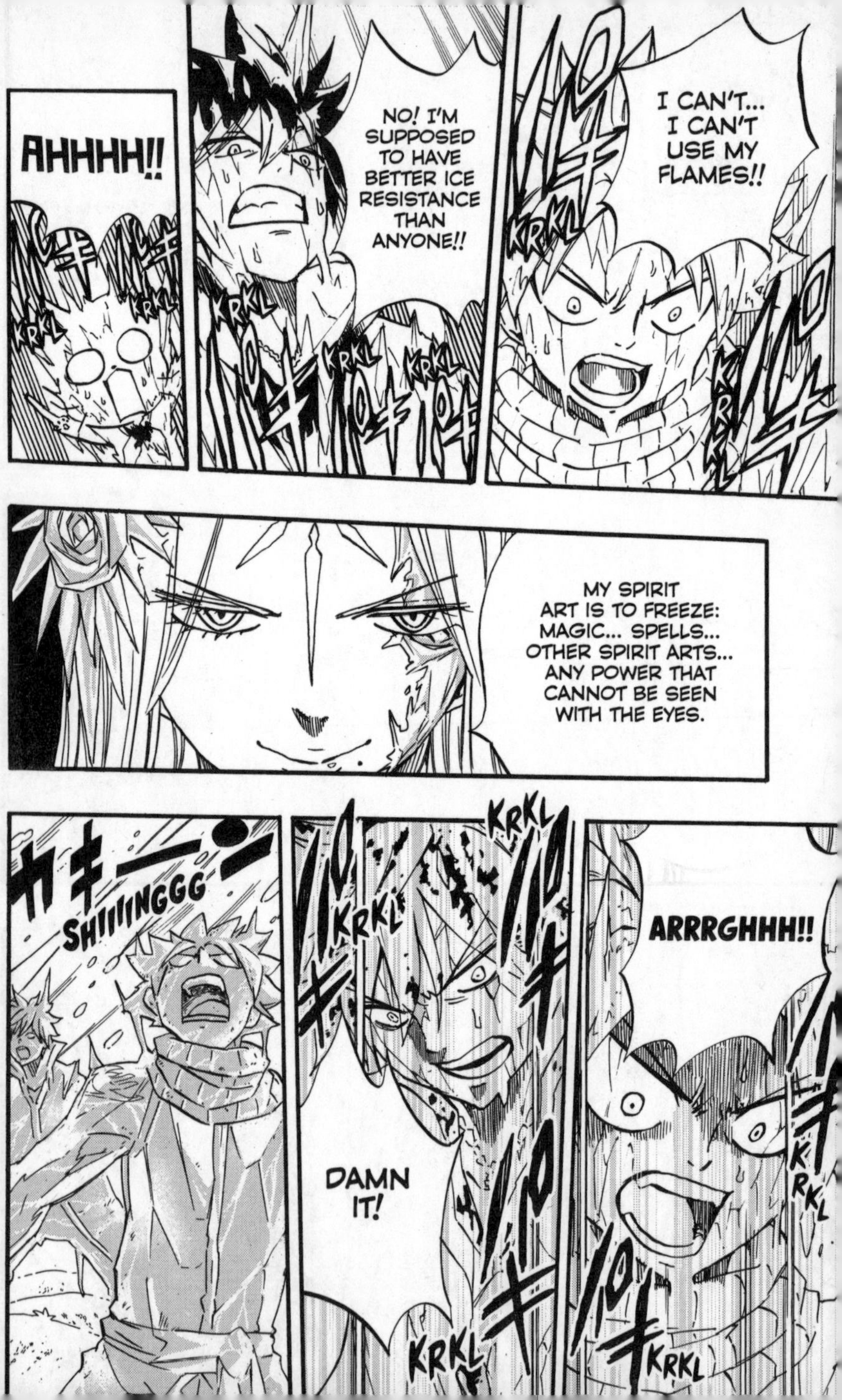
I CAN'T... I CAN'T USE MY FLAMES!!
KRKL
KRKL
NO! I'M SUPPOSED TO HAVE BETTER ICE RESISTANCE THAN ANYONE!!
KRKL
KRKL
KRKL
AHHHH!!
KRKL
KRKL
MY SPIRIT ART IS TO FREEZE: MAGIC... SPELLS... OTHER SPIRIT ARTS... ANY POWER THAT CANNOT BE SEEN WITH THE EYES.
ARRRGHHH!!
KRKL
KRKL
KRKL
KRKL
DAMN IT!
KRKL
SHIIIINGGG

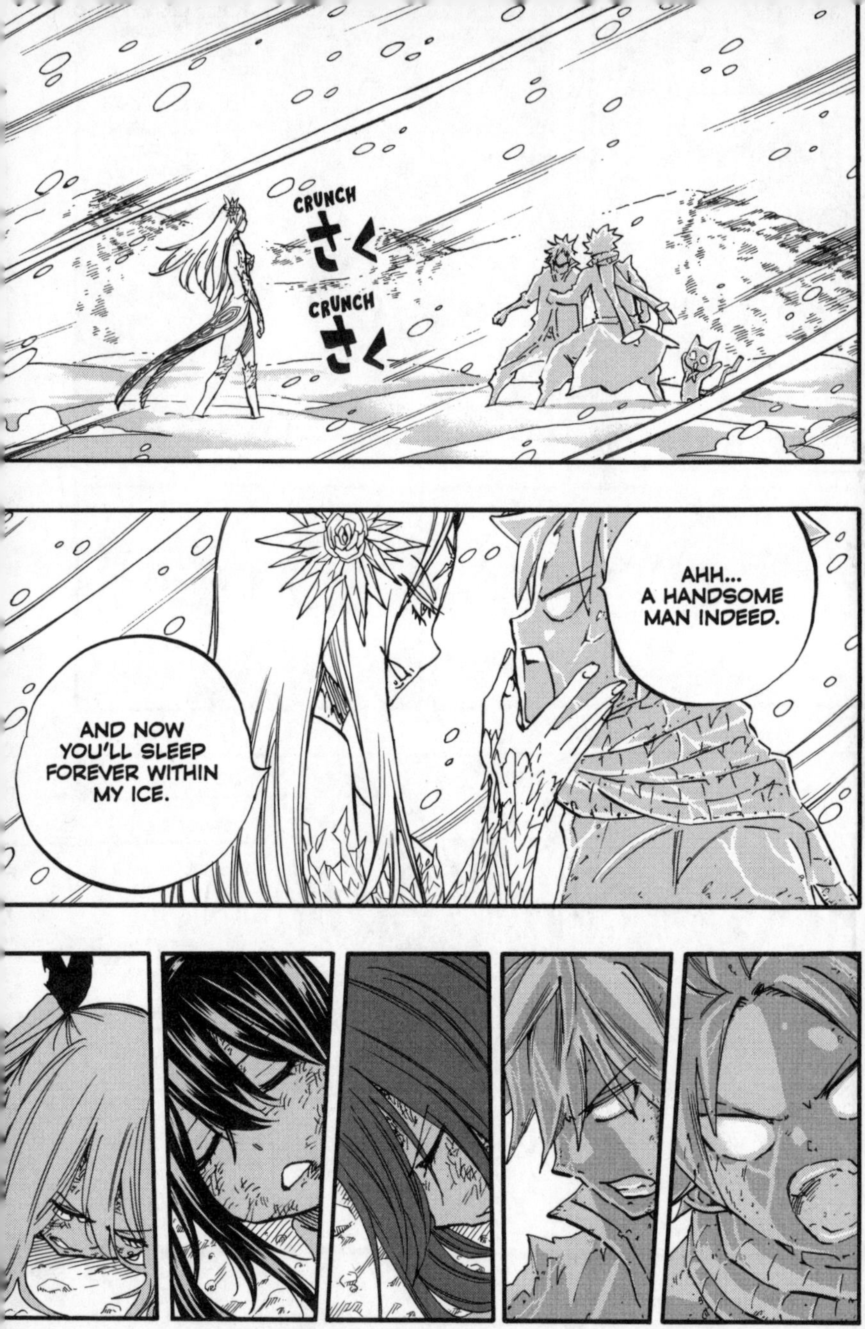
CRUNCH
さく
CRUNCH
さく
AHH... A HANDSOME MAN INDEED.
AND NOW YOU'LL SLEEP FOREVER WITHIN MY ICE.

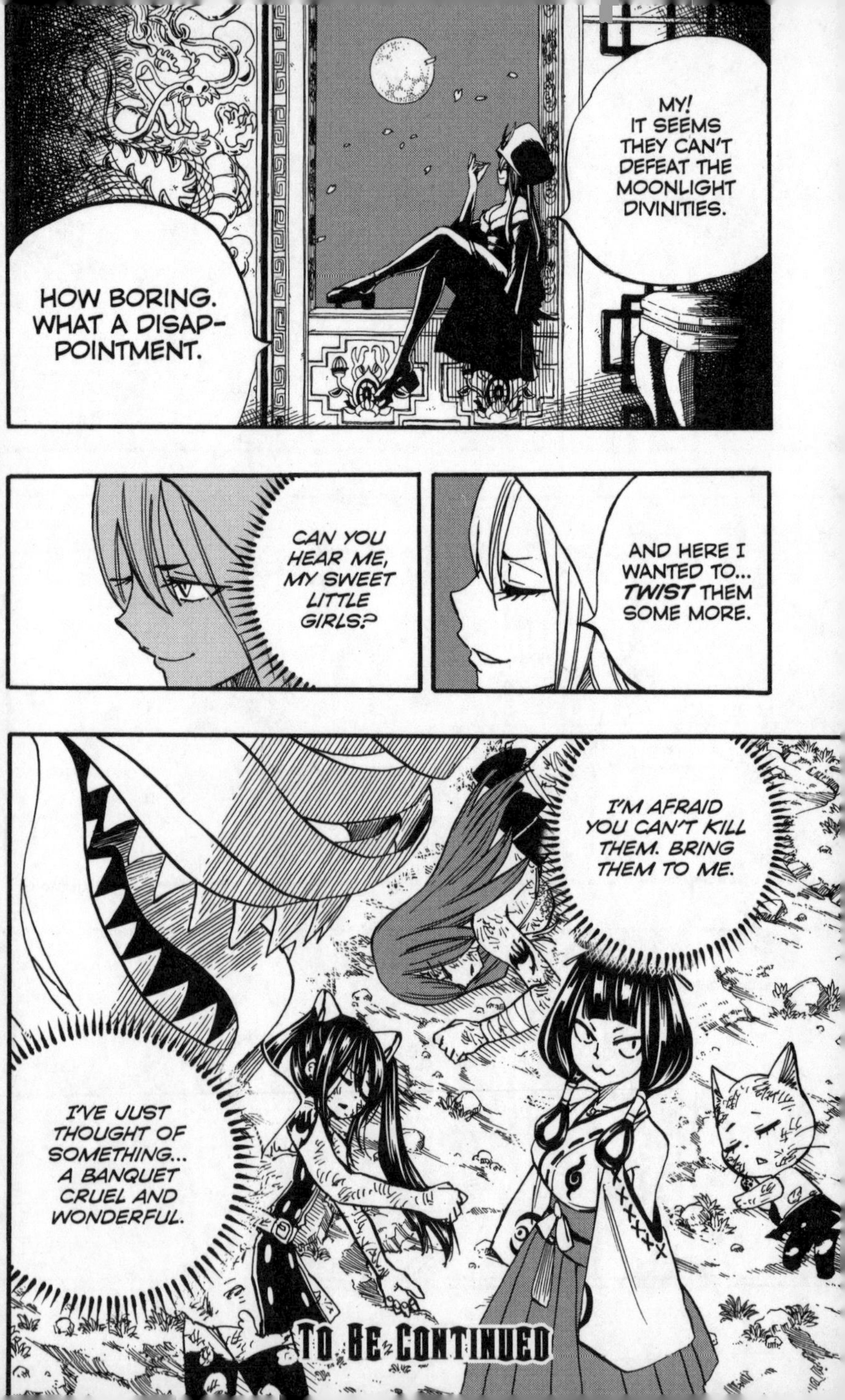
MY! IT SEEMS THEY CAN'T DEFEAT THE MOONLIGHT DIVINITIES.
HOW BORING. WHAT A DISAPPOINTMENT.
AND HERE I WANTED TO... *TWIST* THEM SOME MORE.
CAN YOU HEAR ME, MY SWEET LITTLE GIRLS?
I'M AFRAID YOU CAN'T KILL THEM. BRING THEM TO ME.
I'VE JUST THOUGHT OF SOMETHING... A BANQUET CRUEL AND WONDERFUL.
TO BE CONTINUED

BONUS MANGA FARIS FATIGUED

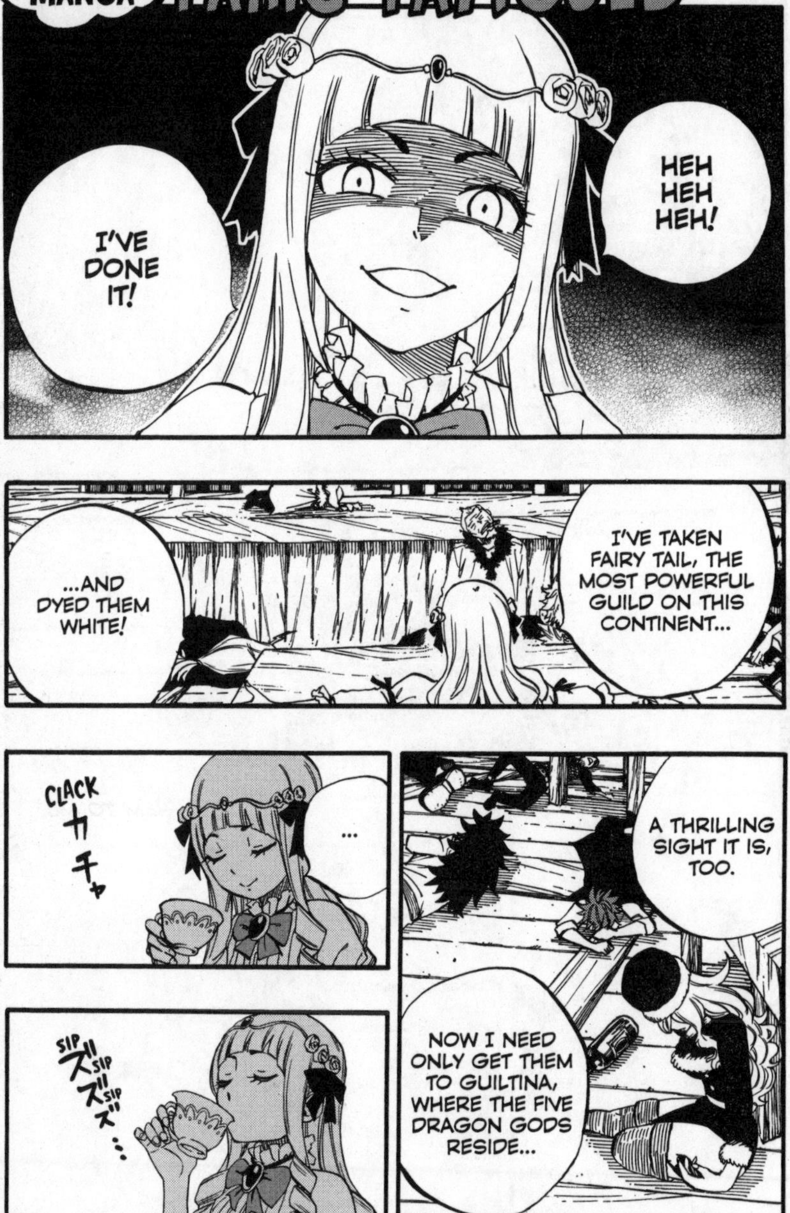
HEH HEH HEH!
I'VE DONE IT!
I'VE TAKEN FAIRY TAIL, THE MOST POWERFUL GUILD ON THIS CONTINENT...
...AND DYED THEM WHITE!
A THRILLING SIGHT IT IS, TOO.
NOW I NEED ONLY GET THEM TO GUILTINA, WHERE THE FIVE DRAGON GODS RESIDE...
...
CLACK カチャ
SIP SIP SIP ズズズ...

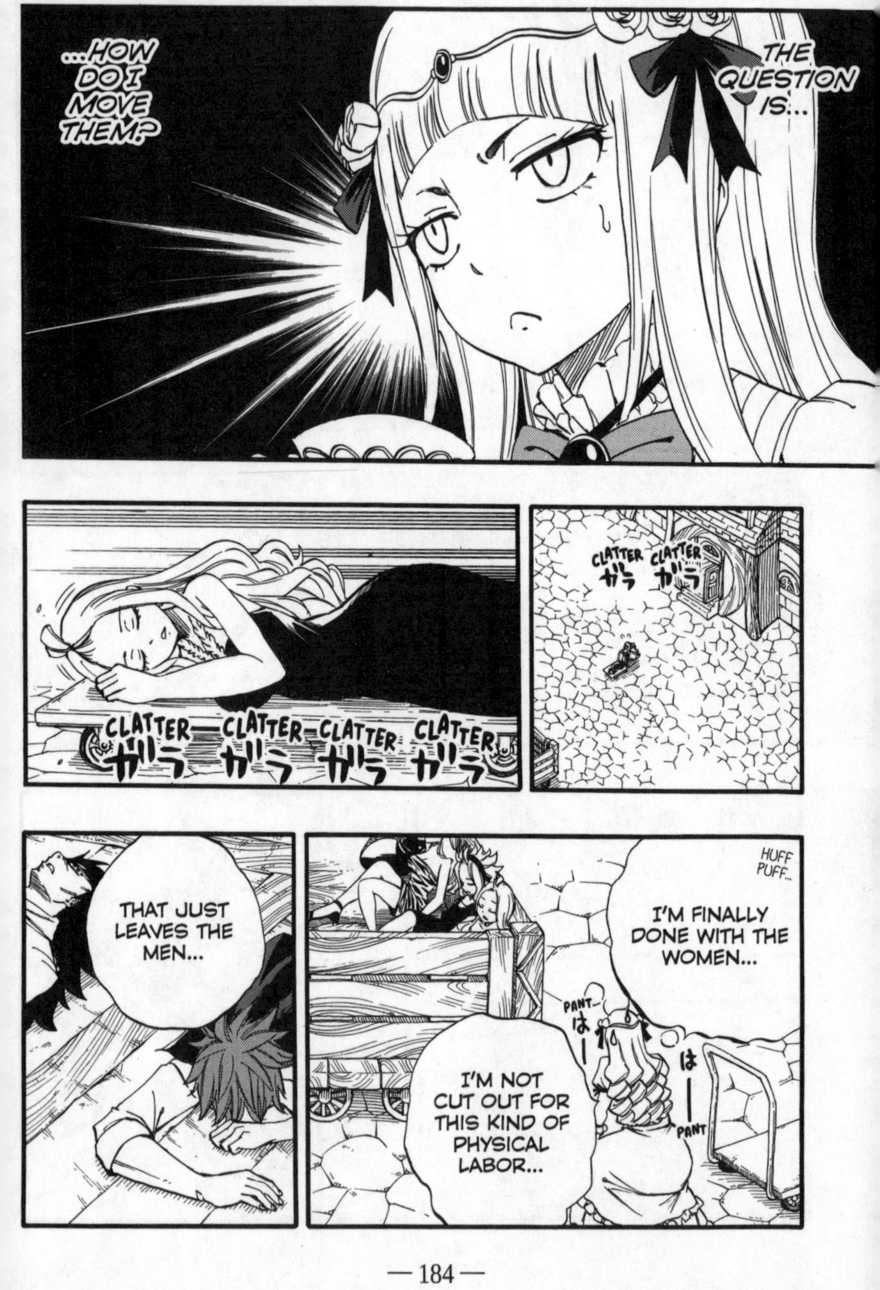
THE QUESTION IS...
...HOW DO I MOVE THEM?
CLATTER ガラ CLATTER ガラ
CLATTER ガラ CLATTER ガラ CLATTER ガラ CLATTER ガラ
HUFF PUFF...
I'M FINALLY DONE WITH THE WOMEN...
PANT はー
はー PANT
I'M NOT CUT OUT FOR THIS KIND OF PHYSICAL LABOR...
THAT JUST LEAVES THE MEN...

FAIRY TAIL 100 YEARS QUEST GUILD

(KANAGAWA PREFECTURE UMI)

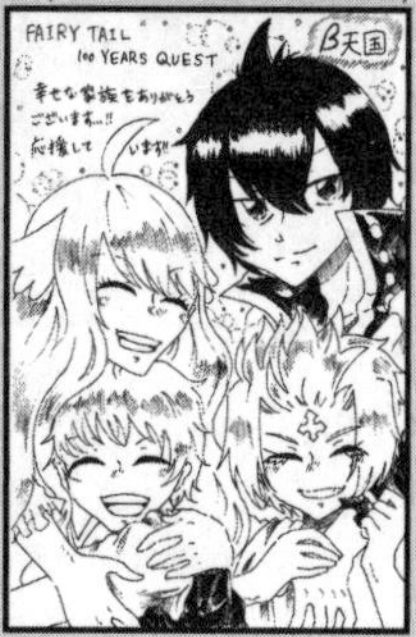
FAIRY TAIL
100 YEARS QUEST
B天国
幸せな家族をありがとうございます…!!
応援しています!!

▼ THANKS—I'M SO GLAD TO SEE THEM FINDING HAPPINESS!

(TOKYO PREFECTURE AIANE)

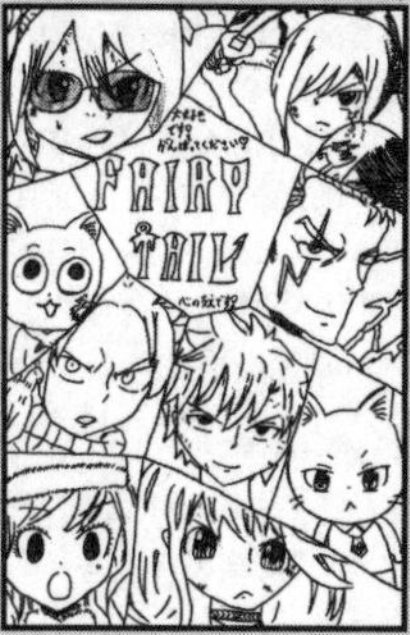
FAIRY TAIL

▲ THANKS FOR SUPPORTING ME!

(SHIZUOKA PREFECTURE RIONA YANABA)

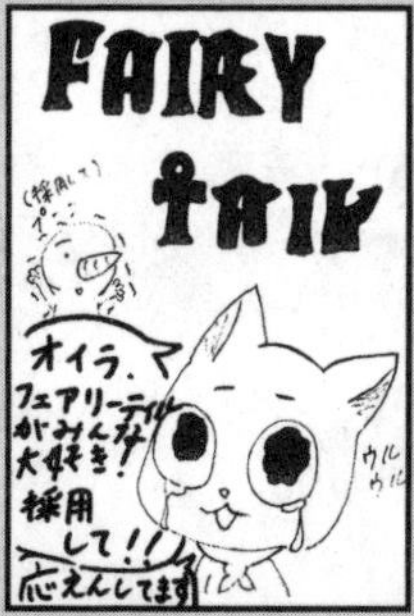
FAIRY tail
オイラ、マ
フェアリーテイルがみんな大好き!
採用して!!
応えんしてます
ウルウル

▲ SIMPLE AND CUTE—LOVE IT.

(OSAKA PREFECTURE NANA MINAMI)

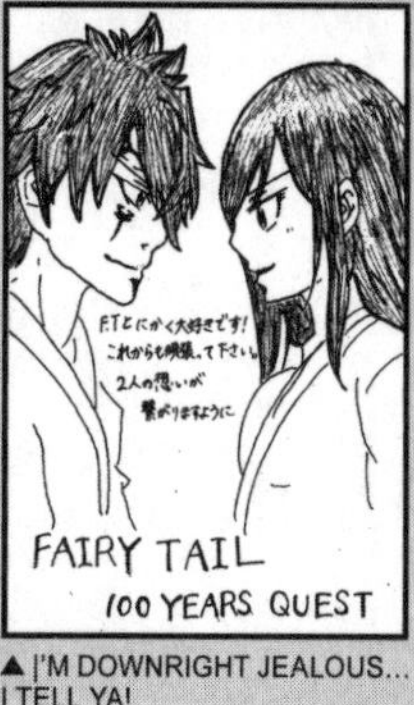
F.Tとにかく大好きです!
これからも頑張って下さい。
2人の想いが
繋がりますように
FAIRY TAIL
100 YEARS QUEST

▲ I'M DOWNRIGHT JEALOUS... I TELL YA!

▼ THAT SMILE ON HER FACE IS FANTASTIC.

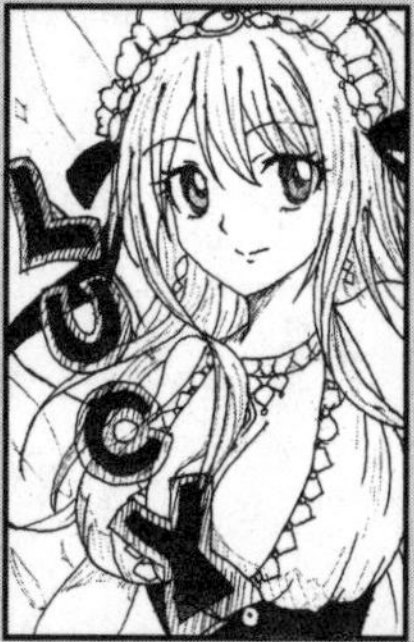
LUCY

(CHIBA PREFECTURE SOUTA SUZUKI)

FAIL CORNER

(OITA PREFECTURE IKA)

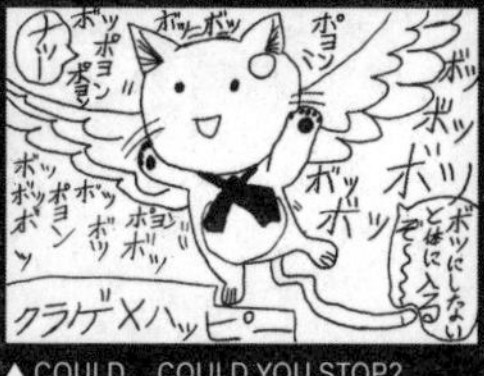
クラゲ×ハッピー

▲ COULD... COULD YOU STOP?

EDITOR'S NOTE: DRAWING SUBMISSIONS LIMITED TO JAPAN.

TRANSLATION NOTES

Down on Her Knees, page 26

The Japanese expression is dogeza, meaning prostration or to prostrate oneself, as the Mage is doing here. This is a particularly humble gesture of supplication.

Moonlight Divinities, page 122

The Japanese expression gekka bijin is usually written 月下美人 and means "a moonlight beauty," that is, a beautiful woman whose looks are only enhanced by the moonlight that shines down on her. Here, bijin is written 美神, using the character for "god" or "deity" rather than the character for "person" (the two can be homophones).

The Demons' Parade, page 134

The Japanese expression *hyakki yakou*, literally "night parade of one hundred demons," refers to processions of monsters believed to parade through the streets of the world. The group might be orderly or chaotic, and may include any of a very wide variety of *yokai*, monsters from Japanese folklore. Yoko's own face resembles traditional depictions of the fox (*kitsune*), a trickster character often mischievous and sometimes downright dangerous.

CALLED YOKO OF THE DEMONS' PARADE.

Snow, Moon, and Flowers, page 136

I AM ONE OF THE MOONLIGHT DIVINITIES, HAKUNE OF THE SNOW, MOON, AND FLOWERS.

This is a direct translation of the Japanese expression setsu-getsu-ka, which often refers to a traditional motif in art. Some artists present the theme literally, creating paintings or other works that actually depict snow, the moon, and flowers (*ka* or *hana*, "blossoms," typically refers to *sakura*, cherry blossoms, in classical contexts), while others add a twist by interpreting the theme in terms of famous figures, well-known scenes, or other related ideas. Hakune herself is a snow woman (*yuki-onna*), a figure from Japanese folklore often shown as a beautiful woman. Sometimes such figures tempt men to their deaths in blizzards, but there are also stories in which they marry human men or otherwise seek hospitality in the human world. Hakune's name is written in katakana in the original, so we can't be certain of the intended meaning, but it seems possible that it means "white sound" (白音), as in the sound of falling snow.

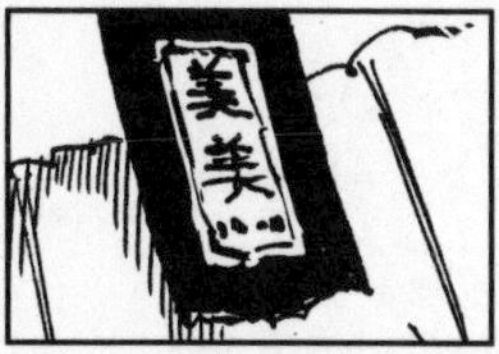
美美

Mimi, page 141

The tag on Mimi's *obi* (belt) says "Mimi," represented as the kanji for "beautiful" repeated twice. (This is the same character as the *bi* of *bijin* mentioned in the note about the Moonlight Divinities.)

Ittan-momen, page 157

This creature's name literally means "one bolt of cotton," and as can be seen on this page, it's either made of or covered in cloth. Ittan-momen are often depicted as a piece of cloth fluttering through the air.

Fire Cart, page 159

As its name implies, the Fire Cart, or *kasha,* is a carriage covered in flames.

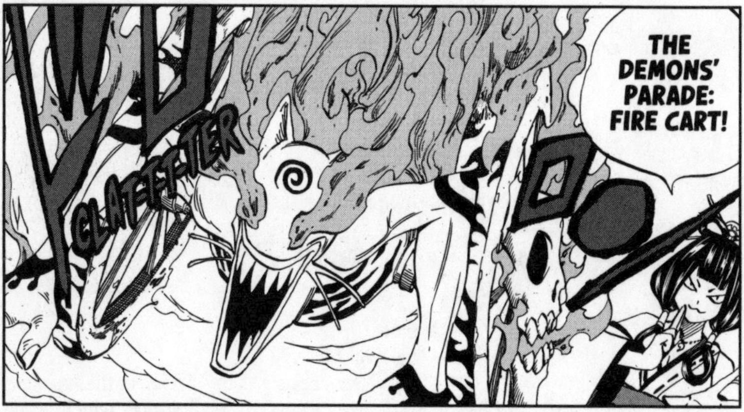
THE DEMONS' PARADE: FIRE CART!
CLATTTTTER

Smoke Warrior, page 160

Called *En'enra* in Japanese, this is a *yokai* composed of smoke and sometimes born from a fire.

Fan, page 163

The character on the fan Taurus is holding reads *ushi,* "cow," "bull," or sometimes "ox." This is the character used specifically for the zodiac animal; in everyday usage, the character 牛 (also read ushi) is more common.

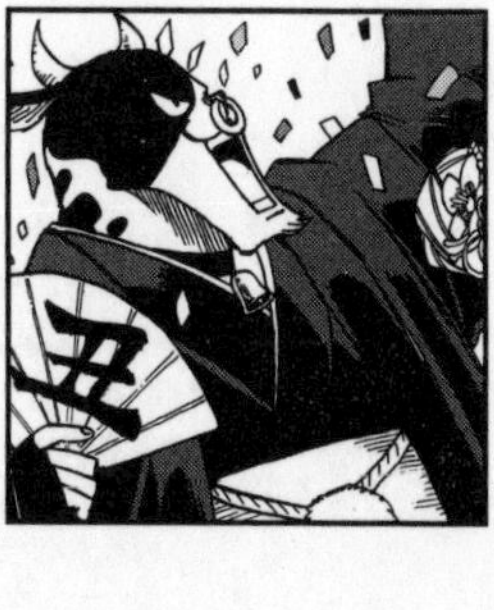
丑

A Kodansha Comics Trade Paperback Original
FAIRY TAIL: 100 Years Quest 8 copyright © 2021 Hiro Mashima/Atsuo Ueda
English translation copyright © 2021 Hiro Mashima/Atsuo Ueda

Published in the United States by Kodansha Comics, an imprint of
Kodansha USA Publishing, LLC, New York.

Publication rights for this English edition arranged through
Kodansha Ltd., Tokyo.

First published in Japan in 2021 by Kodansha Ltd., Tokyo.

ISBN 978-1-64651-233-1

Original cover design by Hisao Ogawa (Blue in Green)

Printed in the United States of America.

www.kodansha.us

1st Printing
Translation: Kevin Steinbach
Lettering: Phil Christie
Editing: David Yoo
Kodansha Comics edition cover design by Phil Balsman

Publisher: Kiichiro Sugawara

Director of publishing services: Ben Applegate
Associate director of operations: Stephen Pakula
Publishing services managing editorial: Madison Salters, Alanna Ruse
Production managers: Emi Lotto, Angela Zurlo